First World War
and Army of Occupation
War Diary
France, Belgium and Germany

51 DIVISION
Divisional Troops
Royal Scots (Lothian Regiment)
8th Battalion Pioneers
1 December 1915 - 31 March 1919

WO95/2857/1

The Naval & Military Press Ltd
www.nmarchive.com
Published in association with The National Archives

Published by

The Naval & Military Press Ltd

Unit 10 Ridgewood Industrial Park,
Uckfield, East Sussex,
TN22 5QE England
Tel: +44 (0) 1825 749494

www.naval-military-press.com

www.nmarchive.com

This diary has been reprinted in facsimile from the original. Any imperfections are inevitably reproduced and the quality may fall short of modern type and cartographic standards.

© Crown Copyright
Images reproduced by permission of The National Archives, London, England, 2015.

Contents

Document type	Place/Title	Date From	Date To
Heading	WO95/2857/1		
Heading	51st Division 1-8th Bn Royal Scots (Pioneers) Aug 1915-Mar 1919		
Heading	51st Division 1/8th Royal Scots Vol VI August 15		
Miscellaneous	1/8th Bn The Royal Scots (Pioneers)	01/08/1915	01/08/1915
Diagram etc	Diagram		
Heading	51st Division 1/8th Royal Scots Vol VII Sept 15		
Miscellaneous	1/8th Bn The Royal Scots (Pioneers)	01/09/1915	01/09/1915
Heading	51st Division 1/8th R. Scots Vol VIII Oct 15		
Miscellaneous	War Diary Of 1/8th Bn. The Royal Scots (Pioneers)	01/10/1915	01/10/1915
Heading	51st Division 1/8th Royal Scots (Pioneers) Nov Vol IX		
Miscellaneous	War Diary Of 1/8th Bn. The Royal Scots (Pioneers)	01/11/1915	01/11/1915
Heading	1/8th R. Scots Rgt Dec Vol X		
Heading	War Diary Of 1/8th Bn The Royal Scots (Pioneers) From 1st December 1915 To 31st December 1915 Volume 14		
War Diary	Bouzincourt	01/12/1915	29/12/1915
War Diary	Flesselles	30/12/1915	31/12/1915
Heading	War Diary Of 1/8th Bn. The Royal Scots (Pioneers) From 1st January 1916 To 31st January 1916 Volume XI		
War Diary	Flesselles	01/01/1916	24/01/1916
Heading	War Diary Of 1/8th Bn. The Royal Scots (Pioneers) From 1st February 1916 To 29th February 1916 Volume XII		
War Diary	Flesselles	04/02/1916	04/02/1916
War Diary	Daours	08/02/1916	12/02/1916
War Diary	Sailly-Le-Sec	18/02/1916	27/02/1916
War Diary	Daours	28/02/1916	28/02/1916
War Diary	Flesselles	29/02/1916	29/02/1916
Heading	War Diary Of 1/8th Bn. The Royal Scots (Pioneers) From 1st March 1916 To 31st March 1916 Volume XIII		
War Diary	Flesselles	01/03/1916	01/03/1916
War Diary	Autheux	06/03/1916	06/03/1916
War Diary	Honval	09/03/1916	09/03/1916
War Diary	Canettemont	09/03/1916	09/03/1916
War Diary	Louez	11/03/1916	15/03/1916
War Diary	Flesselles	03/03/1916	05/03/1916
War Diary	Louez	20/03/1916	20/03/1916
Heading	War Diary Of 1/8th Bn. The Royal Scots (Pioneers) From 1st April 1916 To 30th April 1916 Volume 14		
War Diary	Louez	00/04/1916	30/04/1916
Heading	War Diary Of 1/8th Bn The Royal Scots (Pioneers) From 1st May 1916 To 31st May 1916 Volume 19		
War Diary	Louez	00/05/1916	31/05/1916
Heading	War Diary Of 1/8th Bn The Royal Scots (Pioneers) From 1st June 1916 To 30th June 1916 Volume 16		
Miscellaneous			
Heading	51st Divisional Pioneers 1/8th Battalion The Royal Scots (Pioneers) July 1916		

Heading	War Diary Of 1/8th Bn. The Royal Scots (Pioneers) 1st To 31st July 1916 Volume 17		
War Diary	Louez	13/07/1916	31/07/1916
Heading	51st Divisional Troops 1/8th Battalion The Royal Scots (Pioneers) August 1916		
War Diary	Mametz Wood	01/08/1916	05/08/1916
War Diary	Bivouacs at D.12.d. On Albert-Amiens Rd.	06/08/1916	09/08/1916
War Diary	Pont Remy	10/08/1916	12/08/1916
War Diary	Staple	12/08/1916	14/08/1916
War Diary	Armentieres	14/08/1916	31/08/1916
Heading	War Diary Of 1/8th Bn. The Royal Scots (Pioneers) From 1st September To 30th September 1916 Volume 23		
War Diary	Armentieres	03/09/1916	25/09/1916
War Diary	Estaires	26/09/1916	30/09/1916
Miscellaneous	1/8th Bn. Royal Scots (Pioneers), Operation Orders by Lieut-Col. W. Gemmill, D.S.O., Commanding.	25/09/1916	25/09/1916
Miscellaneous	1/8th Bn. The Royal Scots (Pioneers), Orders For Entrainment For Move To Reserve Army Area. by Lieut.-Col. W. Gemmill, D.S.O., Commanding. Appendix II	29/09/1916	29/09/1916
Miscellaneous	1/8th Bn. The Royal Scots (Pioneers), Amendments to Orders For Entrainment For Move To Reserve Army Area. by Lieut.-Col. W. Gemmill, D.S.O., Commanding. Appendix III	29/09/1916	29/09/1916
Miscellaneous	Additional Instructions For Move To Reserve Army Area	30/09/1916	30/09/1916
Heading	War Diary Of 1/8th Bn The Royal Scots (Pioneers) From 1st October 1916 To 31st October 1916 Volume 20		
War Diary	Estaires	01/10/1916	01/10/1916
War Diary	Hardinval	02/10/1916	02/10/1916
War Diary	Thievres	03/10/1916	03/10/1916
War Diary	Louvencourt	04/10/1916	04/10/1916
War Diary	Courcelles & Colincamps	04/10/1916	17/10/1916
War Diary	Louvencourt	17/10/1916	17/10/1916
War Diary	In Camp Near Mailly-Maillet	18/10/1916	21/10/1916
War Diary	Mailly Wood P.18.b	22/10/1916	30/10/1916
Operation(al) Order(s)	1/8th Bn The Royal Scots (Pioneers), Operation Order No. K.4 by Lieut.-Col. W. Gemmill, D.S.O., Commanding.	01/10/1916	01/10/1916
Operation(al) Order(s)	1/8th Bn The Royal Scots (Pioneers), Operation Order No. K.5 by Lieut.-Col. W. Gemmill, D.S.O., Commanding.	02/10/1916	02/10/1916
Operation(al) Order(s)	1/8th Bn The Royal Scots (Pioneers), Operation Order No. K.6 by Lieut.-Col. W. Gemmill, D.S.O., Commanding.	04/10/1916	04/10/1916
Miscellaneous	1/8th Bn The Royal Scots (Pioneers) Warning Order	16/10/1916	16/10/1916
Miscellaneous	Amendment To Operation Orders No. K.4	17/10/1916	17/10/1916
Operation(al) Order(s)	1/8th Bn The Royal Scots (Pioneers), Operation Order No. K.7 by Lieut.-Col. W. Gemmill, D.S.O., Commanding.	17/10/1916	17/10/1916
Heading	War Diary Of 1/8th Bn The Royal Scots (Pioneers) From 1st November 1916 To 30th November 1916 Volume 25		
War Diary	Mailly Wood Camp P.18.b.10.30	01/11/1916	25/11/1916

Type	Description	Start	End
War Diary	Ovillers Huts X.13.b.4.9	27/11/1916	30/11/1916
Operation(al) Order(s)	1/8th Bn The Royal Scots (Pioneers), Operation Order No. K.8 by Lieut.-Col. W. Gemmill, D.S.O., Commanding.	12/11/1916	12/11/1916
Operation(al) Order(s)	1/8th Bn The Royal Scots (Pioneers), Operation Order No. K.9 by Lieut.-Col. W. Gemmill, D.S.O., Commanding.	25/11/1916	25/11/1916
Miscellaneous	March Table To Accompany Operation Order No. K.9		
Heading	War Diary Of 1/8th Bn. The Royal Scots (Pioneers) From 1st December 1916 To 31st December 1916 Volume 22		
War Diary	Ovillers Huts X.13.b.4.9	01/12/1916	31/12/1916
Heading	War Diary Of 1/8th Bn The Royal Scots Pioneers From 1st January 1917 To 31st January 1917 Volume No.27		
War Diary	Ovillers Huts X.13b.4.9	01/01/1917	12/01/1917
War Diary	En Route From Ovillers	12/01/1917	12/01/1917
War Diary	Sarton	12/01/1917	13/01/1917
War Diary	Sarton to Bernaville	14/01/1917	14/01/1917
War Diary	En Route Bernaville to Le Plessiel	15/01/1917	16/01/1917
War Diary	Le Plessiel	16/01/1917	30/01/1917
War Diary	Arras	31/01/1917	31/01/1917
Operation(al) Order(s)	1/8th Bn The Royal Scots (Pioneers), Operation Order No. K. 10 by Lieut.-Col. W. Gemmill, D.S.O., Commanding.	11/01/1917	11/01/1917
Miscellaneous	Instructions For Move To The New Area	11/01/1917	11/01/1917
Operation(al) Order(s)	Operation Orders No. K. 11z By Lieut Colonel W. Gemmill D.S.O. Commanding	12/01/1917	12/01/1917
Miscellaneous	Instructions For Move To Bernaville Area	13/01/1917	13/01/1917
Miscellaneous	Instructions For Move To Le Plessiel	14/01/1917	14/01/1917
Heading	War Diary Of 1/8th The Royal Scots Pioneers From 1st February 1917 To 27th February 1917 Volume 28		
War Diary	Arras	01/02/1917	28/02/1917
Heading	War Diary Of 1/8th The Royal Scots Pioneers From 1st March 1917 To 31st March 1917 Volume 29		
War Diary	Arras	01/03/1917	08/03/1917
War Diary	Maroeuil	09/03/1917	31/03/1917
Miscellaneous	Instructions For Move To Maroeuil	07/03/1917	07/03/1917
Miscellaneous	Instructions For Operation (Provisional)	24/03/1917	24/03/1917
Heading	War Diary Of 1/8th Bn The Royal Scots (Pioneers) April 1st-30th 1917 Volume 30		
Miscellaneous	Amendment To Instructions For Operation	24/03/1917	24/03/1917
War Diary	Maroeuil	01/04/1917	08/04/1917
War Diary	Ecurie	09/04/1917	11/04/1917
War Diary	St Catherine	12/04/1917	18/04/1917
War Diary	St Laurent Blangy G.18A4.0	19/04/1917	21/04/1917
War Diary	St. Laurent Blangy	22/04/1917	30/04/1917
Miscellaneous	Instructions For Operations	07/04/1917	07/04/1917
Miscellaneous	Instructions For Move To Ecurie On "Y" Night	07/04/1917	07/04/1917
Miscellaneous	Copy No.1	07/04/1917	07/04/1917
Heading	War Diary Of 1/8th The Royal Scots Pioneers From 1st May 1917 To 31st May 1917 Volume 31		
War Diary	St Laurent Blangy G18a4.0	01/05/1917	31/05/1917
Miscellaneous	Transport Arrangements For Move To Frevillers	31/05/1917	31/05/1917
Miscellaneous	Transport Arrangements For Move To Frevillers	30/05/1917	30/05/1917
Heading	War Diary Of 1/8th The Royal Scots From 1st June To 31st June 1917 Volume 32		

Type	Description	From	To
War Diary	Frevillers	01/06/1917	03/06/1917
War Diary	Frevillers to Monchy Cayeaux	04/06/1917	04/06/1917
War Diary	Monchy Cayeaux to Coyecque Area	05/06/1917	05/06/1917
War Diary	Coyecque	06/06/1917	07/06/1917
War Diary	Coyecque to Bonningues Les Ardres	07/06/1917	10/06/1917
War Diary	Bonningues Les Ardres	11/06/1917	15/06/1917
War Diary	Bonningues to Poperinghe	15/06/1917	15/06/1917
War Diary	Camp A29 C Central Near Poperinghe	16/06/1917	20/06/1917
War Diary	Camp A 29c Central	20/06/1917	30/06/1917
Operation(al) Order(s)	1/8th Bn The Royal Scots (Pioneers) Operation Order No. 1	03/06/1917	03/06/1917
Miscellaneous	Transport Arrangements For Operation Orders No.1	03/06/1917	03/06/1917
Operation(al) Order(s)	1/8th Bn The Royal Scots (Pioneers) Operation Order No. 2	04/06/1917	04/06/1917
Operation(al) Order(s)	1/8th Bn The Royal Scots (Pioneers) Operation Order No. 3	06/06/1917	06/06/1917
Miscellaneous	Transport Arrangements For Operation Order No. 3	06/06/1917	06/06/1917
Operation(al) Order(s)	1/8th Bn The Royal Scots (Pioneers) Operation Order No. 3	15/06/1917	15/06/1917
Operation(al) Order(s)	Transport Arrangements For Operation Order No. 4	15/06/1917	15/06/1917
Heading	War Diary Of 1/8th The Royal Scots Pioneers From 1st July 1917 To 31st July 1917 Volume 33		
War Diary	Camp 29 C Central	01/07/1917	13/07/1917
War Diary	Camp A28 A1.9	13/07/1917	31/07/1917
Operation(al) Order(s)	1/8th Bn The Royal Scots (Pioneers) Operation Order No. 4	23/07/1917	23/07/1917
Miscellaneous	Instructions For Work On "Z"	23/07/1917	23/07/1917
Miscellaneous	Administrative Instructions For Active Operations	23/07/1917	23/07/1917
Heading	War Diary Of 1/8th The Royal Scots From 1st August To 31st August 1917 Volume No. 34		
War Diary	Rear Camp A 28a 1.9 Forward Camp Canal Bank	01/08/1917	06/08/1917
War Diary	Rear Camp A.28.a 1.9 Forward Camp B22d 60.05	07/08/1917	10/08/1917
War Diary	A28a 1.9 B22d 60.05	11/08/1917	31/08/1917
Heading	War Diary Of 1/8th The Royal Scots From 1st September To 30th September 1917 Volume No. 35		
War Diary	A28a 19 B22d 60.05	01/09/1917	15/09/1917
War Diary	Ghent Cottages B22d 60.05	16/09/1917	27/09/1917
War Diary	Browne Camp A23 B 9.1	28/09/1917	30/09/1917
Operation(al) Order(s)	1/8th Bn The Royal Scots (Pioneers) Operation Order No. 5	19/09/1917	19/09/1917
Miscellaneous	Administrative Instructions To Operation Orders No.5	19/09/1917	19/09/1917
Operation(al) Order(s)	1/8th Bn The Royal Scots (Pioneers) Operation Order No. 6	24/09/1917	24/09/1917
Miscellaneous	Transport Arrangements For Operation Order No. 6	24/09/1917	24/09/1917
Operation(al) Order(s)	1/8th Bn The Royal Scots (Pioneers) Operation Order No. 7	28/09/1917	28/09/1917
Miscellaneous	Transport Arrangements For Operation Order No. 7		
Heading	War Diary Of 1/8th Bn. The Royal Scots From 1st October 1917 To 31st October 1917 Volume No.36		
War Diary	Proven to Bapaume	01/10/1917	05/10/1917
War Diary	Courcelles Le Comte	05/10/1917	07/10/1917
War Diary	Henin Sur Cojeul Neuville Vitasse	07/10/1917	12/10/1917
War Diary	Henin Neuville Vitasse	12/10/1917	29/10/1917
War Diary	Henin To Beaulencourt	30/10/1917	31/10/1917
Miscellaneous	Addendum No.1 To Operation Order No. 8	05/10/1917	05/10/1917

Type	Description	Start	End
Operation(al) Order(s)	1/8th Bn The Royal Scots (Pioneers) Operation Order No. 8	05/10/1917	05/10/1917
Miscellaneous	Transport Arrangements For Operation Order No. 8	05/10/1917	05/10/1917
Miscellaneous		12/10/1917	12/10/1917
Operation(al) Order(s)	1/8th Bn The Royal Scots (Pioneers) Operation Order No. 9	29/10/1917	29/10/1917
Miscellaneous	Transport Arrangements For Operation Order No. 9	30/10/1917	30/10/1917
Heading	War Diary Of 1/8th Bn The Royal Scots From 1st November 1917 To 30th November 1917 Volume No.37		
War Diary	Beaulencourt	01/11/1917	01/11/1917
War Diary	Railway Camp Lechelle	02/11/1917	14/11/1917
War Diary	HQ-Railway Camp	15/11/1917	15/11/1917
War Diary	Transport Cap Metz	16/11/1917	16/11/1917
War Diary	Bn. H.Qr Neuville	17/11/1917	20/11/1917
War Diary	H. Qrs & Coys Metz Rear H.Qr Transport Neuville	20/11/1917	27/11/1917
War Diary	H Qrs Transport At Q3 D Central Coys In Dugouts In K 27-21	27/11/1917	30/11/1917
Operation(al) Order(s)	1/8th Bn The Royal Scots (Pioneers) Operation Order No. 11	19/11/1917	19/11/1917
Miscellaneous	Instructions For Work On Z Day	19/11/1917	19/11/1917
Miscellaneous	Administrative Instructions Operation Order No. 11	19/11/1917	19/11/1917
Heading	War Diary Of 1/8 Bn. The Royal Scots 1st December 1917 To 31st December 1917 Volume No.38		
War Diary	Rear H.Qr Transport at Royaulcourt Adv H.Qr Map At K 27.21	01/12/1917	05/12/1917
War Diary	H Qrs Fremicourt Coys Near Lebecquiere	05/12/1917	09/12/1917
War Diary	H Qrs At Fremicourt	09/12/1917	31/12/1917
Operation(al) Order(s)	1/8th Bn The Royal Scots (Pioneers) Operation Order No. 10	31/12/1917	31/12/1917
Heading	War Diary Of 1/8 Bn. The Royal Scots From 1st January To 31st January 1918 Volume No.39		
War Diary	H. Qrs & Transport Fremicourt Coys At Buigny Beumetz	01/01/1918	06/01/1918
War Diary	Fremicourt Buigny & Beumetz	06/01/1918	21/01/1918
War Diary	Achiet Le Grand Ritz Camp	22/01/1918	27/01/1918
War Diary	Pioneer Camp	28/01/1918	31/01/1918
Operation(al) Order(s)	1/8th Bn The Royal Scots (Pioneers) Operation Order No. 12	19/01/1918	19/01/1918
Miscellaneous	Amendment No.1 To Operation Order No. 12	19/01/1918	19/01/1918
Miscellaneous	Transport Arrangements	20/01/1918	20/01/1918
Heading	War Diary Of 8th Bn. The Royal Scots From 1st February To 28th February 1918 Volume No.40		
War Diary	Pioneer Camp Sheet 57 C G2d.4.5	01/02/1918	08/02/1918
War Diary	Pioneer Camp	08/02/1918	12/02/1918
War Diary	HQ. Fremicourt A B C Coys Buigny D Coy Beaumetz	13/02/1918	20/02/1918
War Diary	Fremicourt	20/02/1918	28/02/1918
Miscellaneous	Transport Arrangements For Operation Order No. 13	11/02/1918	11/02/1918
Operation(al) Order(s)	1/8th Bn The Royal Scots (Pioneers) Operation Order No. 13	11/02/1918	11/02/1918
Miscellaneous	Transport Arrangements	11/02/1918	11/02/1918
Heading	51st Divisional Troops War Diary 1/8th Battalion The Royal Scots Pioneers March 1918		
Heading	War Diary Of 1/8 Bn The Royal Scots From 1st March 1918 To 31st March 1918 Volume No.41		
War Diary	HQ. Fremicourt 2 Coys Buigny 1coy Beaumetz	01/03/1918	07/03/1918

Type	Description	From	To
War Diary	Fremicourt	08/03/1918	21/03/1918
War Diary	Cambrai Front	22/03/1918	22/03/1918
War Diary	Bn. H.Q & Cambrai Front Transport 1m.W Of Grevillers	22/03/1918	23/03/1918
War Diary	N. Bancourt	24/03/1918	24/03/1918
War Diary	Bn. H.Q. & A B C' Coys at Loupart Wood	25/03/1918	27/03/1918
War Diary	Canteleux	28/03/1918	29/03/1918
War Diary	Bas Rieux	30/03/1918	31/03/1918
Miscellaneous	Casualties		
Heading	51st Divisional Troops War Diary 1/8th Battalion The Royal Scots Pioneers April 1918		
Heading	War Diary Of 1/8 Bn. The Royal Scots From 1st April 1918 To 30th April 1918 Volume No.42		
War Diary	Bas Rieux	01/04/1918	10/04/1918
War Diary	On Pacaut Front	10/04/1918	12/04/1918
War Diary	Busnes	13/04/1918	13/04/1918
War Diary	Hollanderie N. Busnes Rear HQ Transport At Fontes	13/04/1918	15/04/1918
War Diary	St Hilaire	15/04/1918	22/04/1918
War Diary	Adv. H.Q. Berguette Rear HQ Lilette A&B. Coys W Of St Venant C. Coy Matringhem	23/04/1918	27/04/1918
War Diary	Adv. H.Q Fauquelon A. C Coys. Fauquelon Rear HQ Lilette Chateau B Coy Matringhem	28/04/1918	30/04/1918
Miscellaneous	Casualties Query April 1918		
Miscellaneous	1/8th Royal Scots	24/04/1918	24/04/1918
Miscellaneous	Report On Operations	09/04/1918	09/04/1918
Heading	War Diary Of 1/8th Bn. The Royal Scots (Pioneers) From 1st May 1918 To 31st May 1918 Volume No.43		
War Diary	St. Venant	01/05/1918	31/05/1918
Miscellaneous	Casualties During May 1918		
Heading	War Diary Of 1/8th Bn. The Royal Scots (Pioneers) From 1st June 1918 To 30th June 1918 Volume No.44		
War Diary	Bray Camp	01/06/1918	30/06/1918
Miscellaneous	Casualties During June 1918		
Heading	51st (Highland) Div. Troops. 1/8th The Royal Scots (Pioneers) July 1918		
Heading	War Diary Of 1/8th Bn. The Royal Scots (Pioneers) From 1st July 1918 To 31st July 1918 Volume No.45		
War Diary	Roclincourt	01/07/1918	31/07/1918
Miscellaneous	Casualties During July 1918	01/08/1918	01/08/1918
Miscellaneous	Report On Operations Commencing	21/07/1918	21/07/1918
Heading	War Diary Of 1/8th Bn. The Royal Scots (Pioneers) From 1st August 1918 To 31st August 1918 Volume No.46		
War Diary	Nanteuil	01/08/1918	31/08/1918
Miscellaneous	Casualties During August 1918	01/09/1918	01/09/1918
Heading	War Diary Of 1/8th Bn. The Royal Scots (Pioneers) From 1st September 1918 To 30th September 1918 Volume No.47		
War Diary	Fampoux	01/09/1918	30/09/1918
Miscellaneous	Casualties During September 1918	01/10/1918	01/10/1918
Operation(al) Order(s)	51st Divisional Artillery Operation Order No. 152	27/08/1918	27/08/1918
Map	Map		
Heading	War Diary-8th Royal Scots October 1918		
Heading	War Diary Of 1/8th Bn. The Royal Scots (Pioneers) From 1st October 1918 To 31st October 1918 Volume No.48		

War Diary	Field	01/10/1918	31/10/1918
Miscellaneous	Casualties During October 1918	01/11/1918	01/11/1918
Miscellaneous	Report On Operations Commencing	06/11/1918	06/11/1918
Heading	War Diary Of 1/8th Bn The Royal Scots (Pioneers) From 1st November 1918 To 30th November 1918 Volume 49		
War Diary		01/11/1918	30/11/1918
Miscellaneous	Casualties During November 1918		
Heading	War Diary Of 1/8th Bn The Royal Scots (Pioneers) From 1st December 1918 To 31st December 1918 Volume 50		
War Diary		01/12/1918	31/12/1918
Miscellaneous	Casualties During December 1918	31/12/1918	31/12/1918
Miscellaneous	Headquarters "A" 51st (Highland) Division	01/02/1919	01/02/1919
Heading	War Diary Of 1/8th Bn. The Royal Scots (Pioneers) From 1st January 1919 To 31st January 1919 Volume No.51		
War Diary		01/01/1919	31/01/1919
Miscellaneous	Casualties During January 1919	31/01/1919	31/01/1919
Heading	War Diary Of 1/8th Bn The Royal Scots (Pioneers) From 1st February 1919 To 28th February 1919 Volume No.52		
War Diary		01/02/1919	28/02/1919
Miscellaneous	Casualties For February 1919	28/02/1919	28/02/1919
Heading	War Diary Of 1/8th Bn The Royal Scots (Pioneers) From 1st March 1919 To 31st March 1919 Volume 53		
War Diary		01/03/1919	31/03/1919
Miscellaneous	Casualties during March 1919		

WO95/7857/1

51ST DIVISION

1-8TH BN ROYAL SCOTS
(PIONEERS)
AUG 1915-MAR 1919

FROM 7 DIV 22 BDE

121/6807

57 51/5 Division
/P

1/8th Royal Scots.
Vol VI
August 15

Confidential

War Diary
1/9th Bn The Royal Scots (Pioneers)
From 1st August 1915 to 31st August 1915

5th. — Draft of 50 other Ranks received.

1st to 15th. — In Billets near CALONNE-SUR-LA-LYS. Training under Royal Engineers carried out daily, varied by company training and short route marches.

14th. — 2nd Lieut R Weir rejoined from sick leave.

16th — The Battalion moved into Billets with Headquarters and two Companies at GORRE and two companies at LE TOURET, relieving the 9th Seaforths the Pioneer Battalion of the 9th Division.

18th. — Word was received that the Battalion had been transferred to the 51st (Highland) Division as a Pioneer Battalion.

19th. — Major General Sir T Capper Bart commanding 7th Division and Brig General Lawford commanding 22nd Infantry Brigade inspected and addressed the Battalion prior to departure to join the 51st Division. The Battalion marched to FOUQUEREUIL and entrained, leaving at 1.30 p.m. and arrived at MÉRICOURT - 51st Divisional Railhead - at 10.30 p.m. Marched to billets at BOUZINCOURT.

22nd. — The Battalion having been allotted the line BOUZINCOURT - ALBERT - AVELUY work was started for the defence of these villages. B & C Companies being employed - B at ALBERT, C at AVELUY. The arrangement for work was fixed as follows - Companies leave Billets at 8 am and work is generally started by 9 o'clock at ALBERT and 9.30 at AVELUY. Lunch consisting of a haversack ration is taken from 11.30 to 12.30 and work is carried on till 3 when the companies march back, usually reaching billets at 4 pm when dinner is issued, tea being at 6 pm.

23rd - A & D Companies went out - A going to ALBERT and D to AVELUY.

24th The whole battalion went out. A & B at ALBERT, C & D at AVELUY. № 3 Platoon A Coy under 2nd Lieut R. C. Ovens started work in HÉDAUVILLE Wood, felling trees and cutting brushwood.

25th to 31st Work continued as above. A start was made with the construction of a bathhouse in the village for the use of the Battalion both for bathing purposes and washing clothes.

30th The M.G. Section under Lieut Jn. Enslie started work on communication trench running along the RUE BAPAUME, leading from ALBERT to the front trenches, deepening and draining them.

Casualties for month.
Officers - Sick 1 (2nd Lieut G. T. Thomson)
Other Ranks - Sick. 15.

Strength   Officers   31
           Other Ranks 820

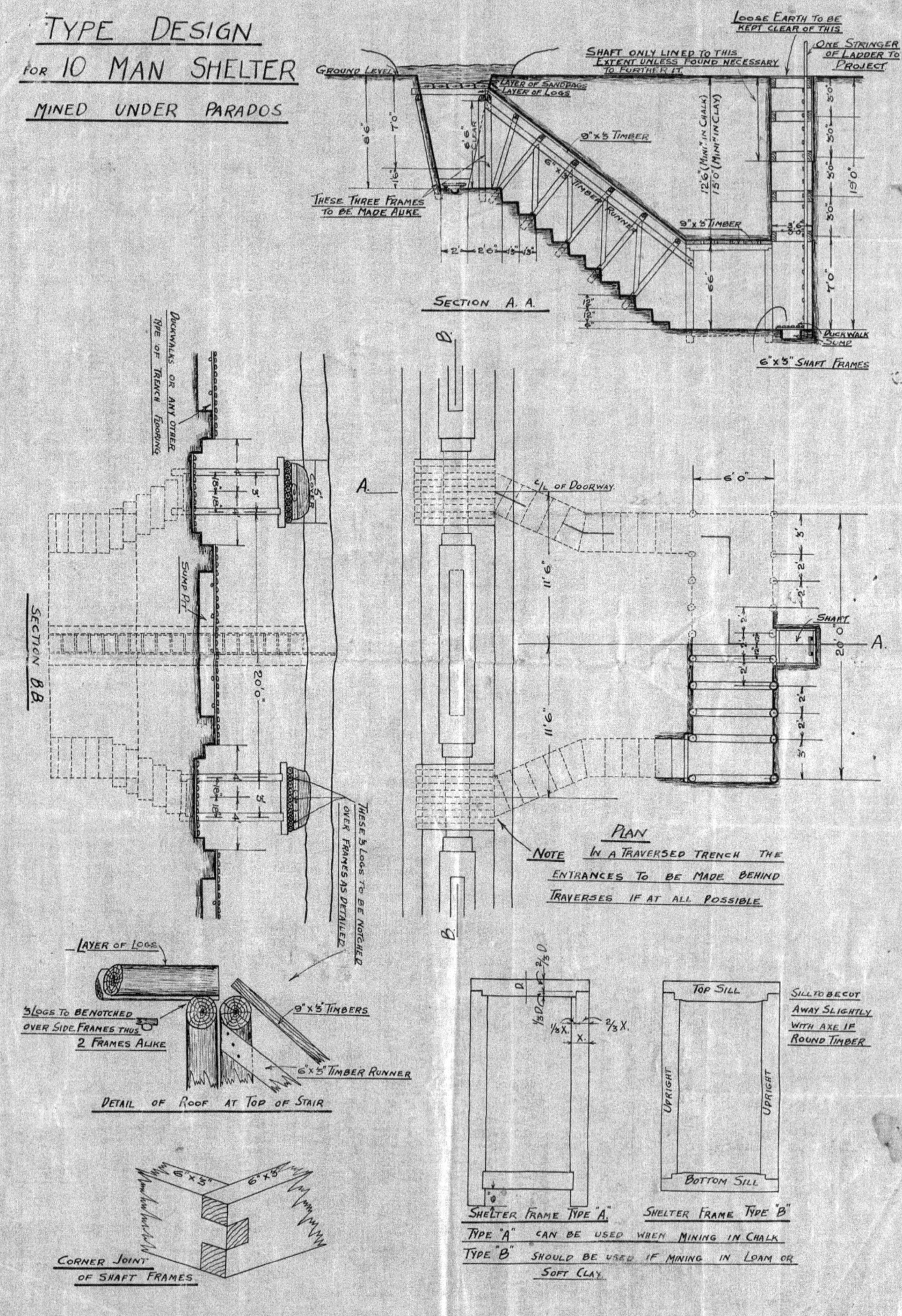

H.R.S

121/6920

51st Division

1/5th Royal Scots.
Oct VII
Sept. 15

Confidential

War Diary
of
1/9th Bn. The Royal Scots
(Pioneers)
From 1st September 1915 to 30th September 1915.

In Billets at BOUZINCOURT (SOMME).

1st to 30th — During the month the Battalion was constantly employed on working parties — working by day until 21st inst — daily except on Wednesdays, when work stopped at 12 noon at ALBERT and AVELUY.

9th — Extract from the London Gazette:-
  Capt. B. McEwen to be Major (temp) d/19-5-15
  2nd Lieut. R.A.D. Ritchie to be Lieut (temp) d/19-5-15
  2nd Lieut. R.B. Ovens — do — d/1-6-15
  2nd Lieut. R. Weir — do — d/2-6-15

12th — Lieut J.L. Kemp appointed Adjutant vice Capt. C.S. Grant Suttie. The Black Watch who relinquished the appointed.

21st to 30th — A Company less 1 platoon, B Company less 1 platoon and C. Company and 2 platoons of D Company started working by night on support trenches in rear of the front line near AUTHUILLE and beyond AVELUY — the arrangement being: Parade about 6 pm. 4 hours work — Companies generally reaching billets about 2 am. when cocoa was issued to the men. Day work was still carried on by No 3 Platoon (A Coy) in HÉDAUVILLE WOOD, No 6 Platoon (B Coy) on the dam at AVELUY and Nos 13 & 15 Platoons (D Coy) in AVELUY Village

23rd — A draft of 50 Other Ranks joined the Battalion. Captain J. Rowbotham (8th R.L.I attached) rejoined from sick leave, having been wounded in action at FESTUBERT on 16th May.

24th — While working near AUTHUILLE this night B Company sustained ten casualties, mostly very slight, owing to the bursting of four shrapnel shells over among them.

During the month a dry canteen, under supervision of the Chaplain was opened and quickly proved very popular. The Bath House was also opened for use, it being possible to bath the whole battalion in less than a fortnight. The Battalion also undertook the cleaning out of the village ponds, the Machine Gun Section being detailed for this work.

Casualties for month:-

Officers.   Other Ranks.
   Nil.   Wounded   11
                   Sick.   26

Strength:-
Officers 31   Other Ranks 812

124/7381

5 RS.

51st Division

1st Bn R. Scots.
Vol VIII
Col 15

Confidential.

WAR DIARY

of

1/8th. Bn. THE ROYAL SCOTS (Pioneers).

from 1st Octr.1915 to 31st Octr.1915.

During the whole month the Battalion was constantly engaged in work, both by day and night. The following work was carried out:-

Dugouts were constructed in the front line trench and support trench, some of these being mined and others excavated.

This proved heavy work, all the timber having to be carried up to the work by night. "C" Company was considerably hampered in their work by enemy bombs, "minenwerfer", &c., on one occasion having two men killed and three wounded.

Work was also carried on in GEMMILL TRENCH and BISSET TRENCH.

The work of repairing the bank of the river Ancre was successfully completed by a platoon of "B" Company, which then undertook the construction of "Lothian Road", leading from MARTINSART to AUTHUILLE. The Machine Gun Section were constantly employed on "Pioneer Road" between AVELUY and MARTINSART. For this work infantry working parties were supplied, varying in strength from 50 to 100 men.

5th October. 2nd Lieut. D.A.G. Pearson was admitted to the Field Ambulance, sick.

16th October. Leave again commenced for the Battalion, the allotment being one officer and seven other ranks per week.

23rd October. The allotment of the Battalion was increased to two officers and fourteen other ranks per week.

During the last ten days of the month, officers of the 16th. Bn. Royal Irish Rifles, the Pioneer Battalion of the 36th (Ulster) Division, were attached to the Battalion for purposes of training. These officers came in parties of four and were attached one to each company. They were conducted round the work in hand, and also shown the work on the defences of ALBERT and AVELUY, completed by the Battalion last month.

During the month, beds were constructed for all ranks of the Battalion, and considerable improvements carried out in the Billets. The Bath-house continued to prove highly satisfactory, and the washing of shirts &c. was got under way.

28th October. A draft of forty other ranks was received.

Casualties for the month:-

    Officers:-   Sick 1 (2nd Lieut D.A.G.Pearson).

    Other Ranks:-   Killed   2

                          Wounded   7

                          Sick   25

Strength:-   31 Officers   803 Other Ranks.

51 S/S Kwann
1ère Royal Sashi (Pionniers)
Nov!
vol IX

1771/181

6 Rs.

CONFIDENTIAL.

WAR DIARY

of

1/8th. Bn. THE ROYAL SCOTS (Pioneers)

From 1st November, 1915 to 30th November, 1915.

During the month no event of outstanding interest for the Battalion occurred. Work went on steadily, the arrangements being the same as for last month, every Wednesday being a whole holiday. "A" Company was constantly employed in CONISTON STREET and mining Machine Gun Shelters in the Front Line in F.1 Sector. "B" Company worked in the front line in F.2 Sector, "C" Company in the front line in F.1, while "D" Company was employed in the front line in the BOIS d'AVELUY, F.1 Sector and also at the KEEP in AVELUY. The Machine Gun Section and No. 6 Platoon (B.Coy.) continued the work on LOTHIAN and PIONEER ROADS, in addition repairing the MARTINSART - ENGLEBELMER Road and draining and clearing MARTINSART. Each company had their joiners working at AVELUY making "duckwalks" and trestles for the trenches.

The work being done consisted of cleaning, draining and flooring trenches, making traverses and rebuilding firesteps, parapets and parados, digging sumps, revetting with corrugated iron, expanded metal, and angle-iron pickets.

From the 22nd to the end of the month, "D" Company were billeted in AVELUY for strategical purposes, continuing their work just the same as usual.

Towards the end of the month, very wet weather set in, following on a hard spell of frost, which caused great havoc in the trenches. Part of the front line became practically untenable and it was decided to dig a new trench a short distance behind. This was dug by three platoons of "A" Company, 2 platoons of "C" Company, and wire was put up in front by one platoon of "D" Company. This new trench was given the name of MITCHELL TRENCH.

11th November.- No. 646 Sgt. FRANK STEVENSON, "A" Company, was awarded the Medaille Militaire, "for his coolness and bravery in attending the wounded and the efficient manner in which he commanded his platoon at/

at FESTUBERT on 17th-18th May, 1915, when his Officer and platoon Sergeant were casualties". The presentation was made by the Army Commander at ACHEUX on the 14th November.

During the month the Divisional Football League was got well under way, and the Battalion Team continued to uphold their reputation.

Casualties for the month:-

    Officers:-   Nil.

    Other Ranks:-   Killed   1

                                       Died of Wounds   2

                                       Wounded   12

                                       Sick   20

Strength:-   31 Officers,   770 Other Ranks.
on 30/11/15.

7 Rs.

Army Form C. 2118.

WAR DIARY
or
INTELLIGENCE SUMMARY.
(Erase heading not required.)

War Diary
of
11th Bn. the Royal Scots (Pioneers)
from 1st December 1915 to 31st December 1915.

Volume 14.

Army Form C. 2118.

WAR DIARY
or
INTELLIGENCE SUMMARY.
(Erase heading not required.)

Instructions regarding War Diaries and Intelligence Summaries are contained in F.S. Regs., Part II. and the Staff Manual respectively. Title pages will be prepared in manuscript.

Hour, Date, Place	Summary of Events and Information	Remarks and references to Appendices
1st to 20th December. BOUZINCOURT.	Work was carried on as during last month, all four companies continuing their work on Front line and Support trenches. No. 6 Platoon of "B" Company and the Machine Gun Section continued work on PIONEER and LOTHIAN Roads and also repairs to ENGLEBELMER - MARTINSART Road. The weather for the most part being very wet, conditions in the trenches were exceedingly disagreeable and the work considerably hampered. The Battalion continued to have a whole holiday every Wednesday, when football matches were played. A Theatre of Varieties having been opened for the Division at SENLIS, the companies were marched over in succession on Wednesday evenings to see the performance. The rate of leave to all ranks of the Battalion continued to be most satisfactory, 2 Officers and 32 Other Ranks leaving each week; Leave for those going to Scotland was also extended to nine days.	
21st December.	"D" Company 17th(S)Bn. Northumberland Fusiliers (N.E.R.) Pioneers, which was attached to the Battalion, left to join its own Headquarters, and "B" Company of the same unit took its place, 2Platoons/	

(73989) W4141—463. 400,000. 9/14. H.&J.Ltd. Forms/C. 2118/10.

Army Form C. 2118.

WAR DIARY
or
INTELLIGENCE SUMMARY.
(Erase heading not required.)

Instructions regarding War Diaries and Intelligence Summaries are contained in F. S. Regs., Part II. and the Staff Manual respectively. Title pages will be prepared in manuscript.

Hour, Date, Place	Summary of Events and Information	Remarks and references to Appendices
21st December.	2 Platoons being attached to "A" Company and 2 to "D" Company for instruction.	
23rd December.	"C" Company paraded at 9-0 a.m. in full marching order and marched by MILLENCOURT and HERENCOURT to BEAUCOURT, which was reached at 1-30 p.m. The Company was billeted there for one night and moved the next morning at 9-30 a.m. via VILLERS-BOCAGE to FLESSELLES, where they arrived at 1-0 p.m.	
24th December.	Billets were cleaned out.	
26th December.	No. 12 Platoon proceeded to NAOURS under Lieut. COWAN, where work was carried out quarrying stone.	
27th December.	No. 10 Platoon, under Capt. PRINGLE, went to ST. VAST to carry out wood-cutting there, the timber being used for bed making and stables.	
26th December.	Tools were withdrawn from the trenches.	
27th December.	Preparations were made for leaving the area on the following day.	
28th December.	The Battalion (less "C" Coy.) paraded at 9-15 a.m. and left BOUZINCOURT and, marching by SENLIS, WARLOY, VADENCOURT and BEAUCOURT/	

Army Form C. 2118.

WAR DIARY
or
INTELLIGENCE SUMMARY.
(Erase heading not required.)

Instructions regarding War Diaries and Intelligence Summaries are contained in F. S. Regs., Part II. and the Staff Manual respectively. Title pages will be prepared in manuscript.

Hour, Date, Place	Summary of Events and Information	Remarks and references to Appendices
28th December.	BEAUCURT, arrived at ST. GRATIEN at 1-30 p.m. where a halt was made, the Battalion being billeted in the village.	
29th December.	At 9-30 a.m. the Battalion continued the march via MOLLIENS and VILLERS-BOCAGE, to FLESSELLES, which was reached at 12-30 p.m. and went into billets there. "D" Company left the Battalion at ST.GRATIEN and proceeded to ARGOEUVES to build stables.	
30th December. FLESSELLES.	"A" and "B" Companies and the Machine Gun Section carried out company training etc. No. 11 Platoon ("C"Coy.) was attached to "A" Company for training, while No. 9 Platoon ("C"Coy.) was employed wood-cutting.	
31st December.	"A" and "B" Companies with 1 Platoon of "C" Company commenced digging a system of trenches on rising ground near FLESSELLES Station. These are intended to be used by the Infantry for Attack Practice, Bombing Practice, etc. The Machine Gun Section was employed at Ordnance assisting in work there. Casualties for the month/	

Army Form C. 2118.

WAR DIARY
or
INTELLIGENCE SUMMARY.

(Erase heading not required.)

Instructions regarding War Diaries and Intelligence Summaries are contained in F.S. Regs., Part II. and the Staff Manual respectively. Title pages will be prepared in manuscript.

Hour, Date, Place	Summary of Events and Information	Remarks and references to Appendices
	Casualties for the month:-	
	Officers:- Nil.	
	Other Ranks:- Wounded 2	
	Sick 28	
	Strength:- 31 Officers 801 Other Ranks.	
	[signature] Lieut.-Col.,	
	Comdg., 1/8th.Bn.The Royal Scots (Pioneers).	
	January, 1916.	

Army Form C. 2118.

WAR DIARY
or
INTELLIGENCE SUMMARY.
(Erase heading not required.)

Hour, Date, Place	Summary of Events and Information	Remarks and references to Appendices

Instructions regarding War Diaries and Intelligence Summaries are contained in F.S. Regs., Part II. and the Staff Manual respectively. Title pages will be prepared in manuscript.

Confidential.

War Diary.
of
1/8th. Bn. The Royal Scots (PIONEERS)

From 1st. January 1916. To 31st. January 1916.

Volume XI

Army Form C. 2118.

WAR DIARY
or
INTELLIGENCE SUMMARY.
(Erase heading not required.)

Instructions regarding War Diaries and Intelligence Summaries are contained in F.S. Regs., Part II. and the Staff Manual respectively. Title pages will be prepared in manuscript.

Hour, Date, Place	Summary of Events and Information	Remarks and references to Appendices
FLESSELLES. January.1916 9th. Janra	During January. 1916, the Headquarters were in FLESSELLES, BUT the Companies were very much scattered. The weather was cold and wet for the most part. " D " Company at ARGOEUVES, were joined by No. 11 Platoon " C " Coy.. Work in stables was continued all month. No. 12 Platoon under Lieut. Cowan. proceeded from NAOURS TO LONGPRE to work in Quarries at MONTIERES. No. 4 Platoon, under 2nd. Lieut. Constable took the place of No. 12 Platoon at NAOURS and a few days later was joined by Captain Watson and Lieut. Meek. with No. 1 Platoon. No. 2 Platoon, under 2nd . Lieut. Snow, joind Lieut. Ovens. who had been detailed from the Battalion all winter, at BERTANGLES to carry out wood-cutting. Capt. Pringle, being at St. VAAST, only " B " Coy., No. 9 Platoon, and the Machine Gun Section were left at FLESSELLES. They were employed bed-making in the village.	
13th. Jan.	While at work at ARGOEUVES an unfortunate accident befell " D " Company. On the 13th. a fall occurred in a quarry which	

(73989) W4141—463. 400,000. 9/14. H.&J.,Ltd. Forms/C. 2118/10.

Army Form C. 2118.

WAR DIARY
or
INTELLIGENCE SUMMARY.
(Erase heading not required.)

Instructions regarding War Diaries and Intelligence Summaries are contained in F. S. Regs., Part II. and the Staff Manual respectively. Title pages will be prepared in manuscript.

Hour, Date, Place	Summary of Events and Information	Remarks and references to Appendices
16th Jan.	resulted in the death of one man, and injuries to three others. On the 16th. three Officers from home joined the Battalion for a month's training in Pioneers Work:- Lieut. Bremner (who had been wounded at FESTUBERT, May 16th.) 2nd. Lieut. Burnett, and 2nd. Lieut. Sharp. A fourth Officer - 2nd. Lt. Sutherland - arrived a few days later, having been detained at the Base. During the month 1 Officer, and 2 N.C.Os. attended the Divisional Grenade School weekly. Lieuts. Ritchie and Stevenson, and 2nd.Lts. Bremner & Meek were at the course. There was a Divisional School of Instruction under Lieut.-Col. Baird, 1/8th. Argyll & Sutherland Highlanders at VILLERS-BOCAGE, which 2nd. Lieut. Constable attended for a fortnight.	
18th Jan.	On the 18th. the 1/6th. Scottish Rifles were made assistant Pioneers to the 51st. Division, and were sent to be trained by us in Pioneering. Captain Inch. was appointed instructor and commenced demonstrations in wiring at once. Then a Divisional Show Ground was laid out by Capt. Barr. R.E. and the Scottish	

WAR DIARY
or
INTELLIGENCE SUMMARY.

(Erase heading not required.)

Army Form C. 2118.

Instructions regarding War Diaries and Intelligence Summaries are contained in F.S. Regs., Part II and the Staff Manual respectively. Title pages will be prepared in manuscript.

Hour, Date, Place	Summary of Events and Information	Remarks and references to Appendices
24th Jan.	Rifles, under Capt. Inch's directions and a few picked N.C.Os. set to work to dig the trenches, revet them, make dug-outs,&c,. On January. 24th. Lieut. & Adj. J.C. Kemp left the Battalion and after being in the Q Office for a week became Staff-Captain (on probation) of the 153 rd. Inf. Bde.. Lieut. R.A.D. Ritchie became Acting Adjutant. Captain T. Stewart became G.S.O. 4 temp. to the 51st. Highland Division. On New Years Day a List of Officers mentioned in Despatches was published. The following were mentioned :- Lt. Col., Brook. (Killed). Lt. Col., Gemmill. Lieut. Martin. Lieut. Jamieson. Lieut. Ritchie. R.S.M. Thomson. P.M. McDougall. Corp. Richardson. Pte. Cairney. In a Despatch, a few days later, Lieuts. Jamieson and Martin were awarded the Military Cross, and Pipe-Major McDougall and Sgt. F. Stevenson the D.C.M.	

Army Form C. 2118.

WAR DIARY
or
INTELLIGENCE SUMMARY.
(Erase heading not required.)

Instructions regarding War Diaries and Intelligence Summaries are contained in F.S. Regs., Part II and the Staff Manual respectively. Title pages will be prepared in manuscript.

Hour, Date, Place	Summary of Events and Information	Remarks and references to Appendices
	Leave was slightly reduced during the month, but remained satis-factory - 2 Officers, and 25 Other Ranks leaving each Sunday. Before the New Year all N.C.Os. and men who had been in this country since 1st. January 1915 had been granted leave. Football was played very energetically and the Battalion Team won everyv match it played. A Cup-Tie Competition was started in which we have won in the first two rounds and are now in the semi-final. The Divisional Theatre was open and most of the Battalion took the opportunity of seeing a very good show. Casualties for the Month :- Officers :- Sick. 1. Killed 1 (accidentally) Other Ranks. :- Sick. 21 O Strength :- 34 Officers and 877 Other Ranks. Drafts received during Month:- 82 Other Ranks (from 5th.Entren.Bn.) on 21st. January. 1916. 12 Other Ranks.(from Base) 23/1/16. R.A.Drummond Pitcher Lieut., Act. Adj. 1/8th. Bn. The Royal Scots (Pioneers). for O. C.	

Army Form C. 2118

WAR DIARY
or
INTELLIGENCE SUMMARY
(Erase heading not required.)

51

9 R.S.

Confidential.

War Diary
of
11th Bn. The Royal Scots (Pioneers).
From 1st February, 1916 to 29th February, 1916.

Volume No. XII

Army Form C. 2118.

WAR DIARY
or
INTELLIGENCE SUMMARY.
(Erase heading not required.)

Instructions regarding War Diaries and Intelligence Summaries are contained in F.S. Regs., Part II. and the Staff Manual respectively. Title pages will be prepared in manuscript.

Hour, Date, Place	Summary of Events and Information	Remarks and references to Appendices
FLESSELLES.	The weather during February was thoroughly bad, rain or snow falling almost every day.	
1st February.	On the 1st of February, all outlying companies and platoons returned to FLESSELLES and companies paraded for the next few days for training.	
4th February.	Orders having been received that the Battalion would move to DAOURS, "D" Company were sent out in advance to prepare billets and make beds.	
DAOURS. 8th February.	The remainder of the Battalion left FLESSELLES at 9 a.m. and, marching by VILLERS-BOCAGE, MOLLIENS, ST. GRATIEN and QUERRIEUX, arrived at DAOURS about 2-30 p.m.	
11th February.	"C" Company moved to billets about a mile east of CORBIE for the purpose of quarrying.	
12th February.	Lieut. R.B. OVENS with his platoon started cutting timber in a wood two miles west of DAOURS. While at DAOURS the remainder of the Battalion was occupied with company training and physical exercises (7 a.m. to 7-30 a.m.)	

(73989) W4141—463. 400,000. 9/14. H.&J.,Ltd. Forms/C. 2118/10.

Army Form C. 2118.

WAR DIARY
or
INTELLIGENCE SUMMARY.
(Erase heading not required.)

Instructions regarding War Diaries and Intelligence Summaries are contained in F. S. Regs., Part II and the Staff Manual respectively. Title pages will be prepared in manuscript.

Hour, Date, Place	Summary of Events and Information	Remarks and references to Appendices
DAOURS. 12th February.	Two Companies dug trenches for bombing practice but, owing to an imminent shift, the trenches were not completed. Pioneer training was carried out and experiments in wiring. Instruction in wiring was given to the 6th Scottish Rifles by day and by night.	
SAILLY-LE-SEC. 18th February.	The Battalion moved to SAILLY-LE-SEC, marching by CORBIE. "C" Company rejoined the Battalion.	
20th February.	Two platoons under Capt.J.S.PRINGLE returned to work at the quarry one mile east of CORBIE. The remainder of the Battalion were occupied repairing the SAILLY - CHIPPILLY road which was in a very bad state. The weather was wretched and the men had to work under very disagreeable conditions.	
26th February.	A warning order was received that the Battalion would move to BRAY on 27th or 28th to be billeted in tents.	
27th February.	Above order cancelled.	
DAOURS. 28th February.	Battalion returned to DAOURS.	
FLESSELLES. 29th Feby.	Battalion marched to FLESSELLES via AMIENS, arriving at 3-15p.m	

(73989) W4141—463. 400,000. 9/14. H.&J.Ltd. Forms/C. 2118/10.

Army Form C. 2118.

WAR DIARY
or
INTELLIGENCE SUMMARY.
(Erase heading not required.)

Instructions regarding War Diaries and Intelligence Summaries are contained in F.S. Regs., Part II and the Staff Manual respectively. Title pages will be prepared in manuscript.

Hour, Date, Place	Summary of Events and Information	Remarks and references to Appendices

March, 1916.	During February leave was further reduced, 2 Officers and 22 Other Ranks obtaining leave perweek. On the 24th it was stopped altogether.
	
	 Casualties for the month:-
	   Officers:- Nil.
	   Other Ranks:- Sick 35.
	
	 Drafts Received:-
	 24th February, 16 O.Ranks from Base. 4 O.R.from 5th.Entrench.Bn.
	
	 Strength:- 34 Officers 870 Other Ranks.
	
	          D. Gemmill
	          Lieut.-Col.,
	 Comdg., 1/8th.Bn. The Royal Scots
	          (Pioneers).	

Army Form C. 2118

51

WAR DIARY
or
~~INTELLIGENCE SUMMARY~~
(Erase heading not required.)

Confidential

War Diary
of
1/8th Bn. The Royal Scots (Pioneers)
From 1st March 1916. to 31st March 1916.

Volume XIII

Army Form C. 2118

WAR DIARY
or
INTELLIGENCE SUMMARY
(Erase heading not required.)

Instructions regarding War Diaries and Intelligence Summaries are contained in F.S. Regs., Part II. and the Staff Manual respectively. Title Pages will be prepared in manuscript.

Place	Date	Hour	Summary of Events and Information	Remarks and references to Appendices
FLESSELLES	1st		The weather during March was very bad indeed. Snow lay almost continuously for the first fortnight and, although there was one week of beautiful spring weather following it, the end of the month was as disagreeable as ever. The battalion, which had arrived at FLESSELLES on the last day of February, remained there for a few days, and the companies were engaged in collecting timber and brushwood which had already been cut, and conveying it to BERTANGLES Station.	
AUTHEUX	6th		The battalion moved north to AUTHEUX, leaving FLESSELLES at 9-15 a.m. and marching via NAOURS, VALHEUREUX and CANDAS, arrived at 2-0 p.m.. Here the companies were occupied with company training for two days.	
HONVAL and CANETTEMONT	9th		The move north was continued and marching by NEUVILLETTE and REBREUVIETTE arrived at the villages of HONVAL and CANETTEMONT. The two days spent here were bitterly cold, snow lying deep all around.	
LOUEZ	11th		Paraded at 10 a.m. and, joining the 153rd Brigade at WAMIN, marched to LOUEZ via LIENCOURT, AVESNES-LE-COMTE and HABARCQ, arriving at our destination at 7-30 p.m. Billets were found in a large Sugar Factory at 9-30 p.m. when another battalion left for the trenches. This march was very long (more than 20 miles) probably the longest done	

Army Form C. 2118

WAR DIARY
or
INTELLIGENCE SUMMARY
(Erase heading not required.)

Instructions regarding War Diaries and Intelligence Summaries are contained in F.S. Regs., Part II. and the Staff Manual respectively. Title Pages will be prepared in manuscript.

Place	Date	Hour	Summary of Events and Information	Remarks and references to Appendices
LOUEZ	11th		by this battalion in France, but the men marched well, being helped by long halts made for dinners and teas.	
	13th		On the nights of 9th, 10th and 11th, the 51st (Highland) Division relieved the FRENCH in the LABYRINTH and neighbouring trenches. "A" Company, working for the 154th Brigade, commenced to improve two communication trenches to the West of the BETHUNE Road - BOYAU de GENIE and the BOYAU de LILLE.	
	14th		"B" Company started work the same as "A" Coy. in the BOYAU d'ANZIN and the BOYAU de MADAGASCAR.	
	15th		The Battalion having been billeted outside of the Divisional area, moved to new billets north of the R.SCARPE. Headquarters, "A" Company and Transport were billeted in LOUEZ, while the "B", "C" and "D" Companies and the Machine Gun Section went to MAROEUIL. The battalion were very lucky in this charge as the same evening as the move was completed the Factory was shelled. For the remainder of the month the work was carried on steadily by the battalion on various parts of the front, from communication trenches in the rear to first line work. "A" Coy. worked for the 154th Brigade, "B" Coy. for the Division generally, "C" Coy. for the 153rd Brigade and "D" Coy. for the 152nd/	

Army Form C. 2118

WAR DIARY
or
INTELLIGENCE SUMMARY

(Erase heading not required.)

Instructions regarding War Diaries and Intelligence Summaries are contained in F.S. Regs., Part II. and the Staff Manual respectively. Title Pages will be prepared in manuscript.

Place	Date	Hour	Summary of Events and Information	Remarks and references to Appendices
LOUEZ	3rd		152nd Brigade. Conditions were far from pleasant as a fresh fall of snow followed by heavy rain caused the trenches to become very wet and muddy indeed.	
FLESSELLES	3rd		On Friday the 3rd the Battalion Football Team played the semi-final of the Divisional Cup Competition against the North Irish Horse but, after a good first half, the game became a farce and we eventually won by 13 goals to one.	
	5th		On Sunday the 5th the final was played against the Divisional Cyclists in the presence of Major-General Harper. The first half again was very equal, the sides crossing over with one goal each but, as in the semi-final during the second half, our opponents fell off badly and we finished with a score of 7 goals to one, thereby winning the competition, having played nearly twenty matches without a reverse. Major-General Harper congratulated both teams on their success in the competition and presented a silver matchbox, appropriately inscribed, to each member of the Royal Scots team.	
LOUEZ	20th		On the 20th Leave was re-started but the allotment given to the battalion was greatly reduced, the numbers allowed away every week being 2 officers and	

1875 Wt. W593/826 1,000,000 4/15 J.B.C. & A. A.D.S.S./Forms/C.2118.

Army Form C. 2118

WAR DIARY
or
INTELLIGENCE SUMMARY
(Erase heading not required.)

Instructions regarding War Diaries and Intelligence Summaries are contained in F. S. Regs., Part II. and the Staff Manual respectively. Title Pages will be prepared in manuscript.

Place	Date	Hour	Summary of Events and Information	Remarks and references to Appendices
			and 8 other ranks. Leave parties now travel by BOULOGNE instead of by HAVRE.	
			Casualties for month:-	
			Officers:- Sick 1 (Lieut.J.W.Emslie).	
			Other Ranks:- Wounded 1	
			Sick 27	
			Injured 2	
			Drafts Received:-	
			Officers:- 2 (Lieut A.G.A.Jamieson 24/3/16 and Captain R.B.Kerr 31/3/16).	
			Other Ranks:- 150	
			Strength:- 36 Officers 970 Other Ranks.	
			R.MeansRitchie Lt. A/Adj for Lieut.-Col., Comdg., 1/8th. Bn. THE ROYAL SCOTS (Pioneers).	

Army Form C. 2118

WAR DIARY
or
INTELLIGENCE SUMMARY
(Erase heading not required.)

Confidential

War Diary
of
1/9th Bn. The Royal Scots (Pioneers)
From 1st April 1916. to 30th April 1916.

Volume X.14

Army Form C. 2118

WAR DIARY
or
~~INTELLIGENCE SUMMARY~~
(Erase heading not required.)

Instructions regarding War Diaries and Intelligence Summaries are contained in F. S. Regs., Part II. and the Staff Manual respectively. Title Pages will be prepared in manuscript.

Place	Date	Hour	Summary of Events and Information	Remarks and references to Appendices
LOUEZ	APRIL		During April the Battalion continued to work in the trenches. The first three weeks of the month were very wet and work was carried on under very disagreeable conditions, but the last week was very beautiful and spring like. Apart from weather altogether, the work was not at all pleasant. Dead bodies were encountered by all companies when digging new trenches or when clearing out old ones. Work was being constantly interrupted too by shelling and trench mortars, and several times the work of a week was destroyed in a very few minutes. Mines were not infrequent. One which went up, however, on the 4th April gave 2nd Lieut J.SHARP ("C" Coy.) and 2nd Lieut F.I.L.SUTHERLAND ("B"Coy.) a chance of distinguishing themselves with their Platoons. On this occasion very valuable consolidation was done in very close proximity to the enemy. Owing to the accommodation being increased in LOUEZ, by means of double-tiered beds, dugouts and the erection of a hut, "D" Company and the Lewis Gun Section were brought from MAROEUIL and billeted in the village, and latterly two Platoons of "B" Company found room after the Corps Light Railway had been formed. In MAROEUIL only "C" Company remained but, towards the end of the month, were joined by two Platoons of "B" Company. It being considered that the Transport was too far up, on 1st April it moved back to a field just north of DUISANS to a point L.8.a.10.5. This ground was in the area of the 5th Division but permission was obtained to use it. As regards the work of the companies:- "A" Company worked for the 154th Brigade on the right of the Divisional Front in L Sector. The work of improving various communication trenches - BOYAU d'ANZIN, GENIE, ROCADE and LILLE - was continued, after which the company went further forward and were engaged in digging, revetting and generally improving the BOYAU FILATIERS and other trenches. Four dugouts were mined in the rear of TRENCH BONVAL and a tunnel was driven under the road at ROCLINCOURT. "B" Company also worked for the 154th Brigade for the greater part of the month and, to enable them to be nearer to their work, they were put in dugouts near/	

Army Form C. 2118

WAR DIARY
INTELLIGENCE SUMMARY
(Erase heading not required.)

Place	Date	Hour	Summary of Events and Information	Remarks and references to Appendices
LOUEZ	APRIL		near ROCLINCOURT. The company took over the dugouts on 4th April and were not finally relieved till the 26th. Various improvements were carried out. A new trench was dug between the NOUVEAU and the ANCIEN GRAND COLLECTEUR. BOYAU CENTRAL, CHARLES and GRAND COLLECTEUR were deepened and revetted and firesteps were built in BOYAU FANTOME and other trenches. Dugouts were mined in these trenches and a Company Headquarters made. In order to rest the men and give them a chance to get a bath, 12 men came back to LOUEZ every second night for two days. On the 23rd Captain YOUNG brought two Platoons out for good, and on the 26th commenced work for the 153rd Brigade in the DOUBLEMENT TRENCH. On the 24th and 26th the two other Platoons came back and, after two days rest each, returned again to work on the 154th Brigade Front, but did not occupy the dugouts, marching from LOUEZ every day. "C" Company worked for the 153rd Brigade in N Sector and probably had the most unpleasant sector on the whole front. A new fire trench was opened out and revetted to the East of the MOULIN. Five dugouts were mined here. A continuation of the support line was dug and revetted. Seven shelters were constructed in the fire trench and one at Company Headquarters. "D" Company worked for the 152nd Brigade in M Sector. A front line trench, originally German, with traverses running towards the enemy, was converted for use, and was remetted and firestepped. A straight trench was traversed and deepened and the LABYRINTHE COMMUNICATION TRENCH was improved. Work was also done in the INTERMEDIATE LINE. In order to keep the Light Railways in the Corps Area in good working order and to obtain a permanent staff to work the trolleys, a Railway Company was formed on the 17th April, consisting of 3 officers and 120 other ranks from each Pioneer Battalion of the 17th Corps. Captain WATSON, Lieut OVENS and 2nd Lieut. CONSTABLE were the officers sent from this Battalion and the men were drawn from three companies - 90 from "A", 15 from "B" and 15 from "D". 2 officers and 40 other ranks were billeted in MAROEUIL and the remainder at MONT-ST. ELOY. A great deal of work was done in LOUEZ during the month. Dug-outs capable of holding nearly 200 men were erected, and beds were put into the/	
	27th APRIL			

Army Form C. 2118

WAR DIARY
or
INTELLIGENCE SUMMARY
(Erase heading not required.)

Place	Date	Hour	Summary of Events and Information	Remarks and references to Appendices
LOUEZ	APRIL		the billets. Ablution benches were made and a great deal of labour was expended improving the north bank of the R.SCARPE. Trenches were dug as a protection against shell fire. An old building was converted into a bath-house - the floor being cemented and a spray bath being fitted in. Systematic washing and ironing of clothes was arranged. The Battalion was lucky as regards shelling billets, LOUEZ never being fired at, and no damage being done in MAROEUIL the few times shells landed there. Captain R.B.KERR went to a Lewis Gun Course at CAMIERS and on his return on the 25th was appointed Lewis Gun Officer. He at once commenced to train the Lewis Gun Section and also a squad of ten men from "C" Company was to provide each company with a Lewis Gun detachment. LEAVE. Leave was suspended on the 12th April but recommenced on the 26th The Battalion allotment was still very poor - only 2 officers and 8 other ranks obtaining leave each week. After consultation with Company Commanders, it was decided that men who had proceeded on leave once should go again before men who had arrived in FRANCE the first time after those who had been on leave had returned. Therefore the following rule was made:- That men should proceed on leave in the order in which they reached France, either from leave or for the first time.	
	30th APRIL		On the 30th April, The "Pick and Rifle", a small chronicle of the Battalion's doings during the previous week, was produced. Notes were sent in by Company Commanders. The "Pick and Rifle", which was edited by Major M'EWEN, will be produced weekly if possible. The Divisional Grenade School was re-opened at HERMAVILLE on the 23rd April. Captain J.ROWBOTHAM was appointed Commandant. 2nd Lieut J.SHARP and 2nd Lieut H.E.R.JONES attended the course and four N.C.Os. also. The Divisional Anti-gas School, which opened in March, was continued all month and 2nd Lieut F.I.L.SUTHERLAND and Captain J.S.PRINGLE attended the course/	

Army Form C. 2118

WAR DIARY
~~INTELLIGENCE SUMMARY~~

(Erase heading not required.)

Instructions regarding War Diaries and Intelligence Summaries are contained in F. S. Regs., Part II. and the Staff Manual respectively. Title Pages will be prepared in manuscript.

Place	Date	Hour	Summary of Events and Information	Remarks and references to Appendices

LOUEZ	30th APRIL		course and seven N.C.Os. also. In case of emergency, towards the end of the month, officers were appointed to understudy the Adjutant, Transport Officer and Quartermaster, viz., 2nd Lieut G.D.WILSON, Lieut A.BLAIR and 2nd Lieut F.A.BURNET.
			
			 Casualties for the month:-
			     Officers:- Nil.
			     Other Ranks:- Wounded 4
			                                Injured 3
			                                Sick 27
			
			 Drafts Received:-
			     Officers:- 1 (Lieut A.BLAIR.)
			     Other Ranks:- 20 3rd April.
			                              30 9th April.
			
			 Strength:- 36 Officers 964 Other Ranks.	

R.A.Bramkelvin Lt. A/Aj. fr

Lieut.-Col.,
Comdg., 1/8th.Bn. The Royal Scots (Pioneers).

Army Form C. 2118

WAR DIARY
~~INTELLIGENCE SUMMARY~~
(Erase heading not required.)

Vol 15 (Pioneers)

War Diary
of
11th Bn. The Royal Scots (Pioneers)
From 1st May, 1916, to 31st May, 1916.

Volume 19

51

12 R.

Army Form C. 2118

WAR DIARY
or
INTELLIGENCE SUMMARY

(Erase heading not required.)

Instructions regarding War Diaries and Intelligence Summaries are contained in F. S. Regs., Part II. and the Staff Manual respectively. Title Pages will be prepared in manuscript.

Place	Date	Hour	Summary of Events and Information	Remarks and references to Appendices
LOUEZ	May.		During May the Battalion continued work in the line. "A" Company (less 2 Platoons still with the Light Railway Coy.) worked all month for the 154th Infantry Brigade. The greater part of the time was spent in mining deep shelters. These were constructed on either side of BOYAU "G" and in the BONNAL Trench. A dugout and observation post for the Artillery Battle Headquarters was started on the LILLE ROAD. Revetting, firestepping and building of traverses was also done between L.22 and L.23. The support line was wired. "B" Company was divided, 2 Platoons working for the 154th Infantry Brigade and 2 for the 153rd Brigade. The former were employed mining dugouts in the BONNAL, FANTOME and BIDOT TRENCHES. The latter improved the DOUBLEMENT TRENCH by building traverses and firesteps. For the last week of the month all 4 Platoons were together working in 153rd Brigade area. Here they were occupied improving the support line between MERCIER and CLAUDOT. Wiring was done in front of the support line. "C" Company worked for the 153rd Infantry Brigade. Several dugouts were constructed in the NEW DOUBLEMENT. The support line between the MERCIER and VISSEC was revetted, firestepped and duckwalked; also the support line left of ZIVY AVENUE. For a short time 1 Platoon was engaged on FORT "A", living in dugouts at ARIANE. The support line was wired. "D" Company worked for the 152nd Infantry Brigade. The INTERMEDIATE LINE from point 774 to point 403 was traversed. The LABYRINTH Communication trench was cleaned out and duckwalked. Some wiring was done in front of the support line. On the Division extending its front, the garrisons of firstly ECURIE and MAISON BLANCHE had to be supplied by the Battalion, and latterly that of NEUVILLE ST. VAST also.	
	23rd		Captain MITCHELL moved to ECURIE with 1 Platoon of "A" Company and 1 Platoon of "B" Company. 1 Platoon of "A" Company remained in reserve in LOUEZ.	
	24th.		Captain RICHARDSON, "B" Company, moved to MAISON BLANCHE with 2 Platoons. 1 Platoon remained in reserve in LOUEZ.	

Army Form C. 2118

WAR DIARY
or
INTELLIGENCE SUMMARY
(Erase heading not required)

Place	Date	Hour	Summary of Events and Information	Remarks and references to Appendices
LOUEZ.	24th.		Captain STEWART, "D" Company, moved 3 Platoons to ARIANE, leaving 1 in LOUEZ. Captain THORBURN, "C" Company, moved from MAROEUIL and occupied Billets in LOUEZ, MAROEUIL being vacated by this Battalion entirely.	
	26th.		To make way for 1 Platoon of "C" Coy. in ARIANE, "D" Coy. moved 1 Platoon to MAISON BLANCHE.	
	31st.		Platoon of "C" Coy. was withdrawn to be in reserve in LOUEZ, and the remainder moved to NEUVILLE ST. VAST. "D" Company was withdrawn from ARIANE and MAISON BLANCHE and 3 Platoons moved to NEUVILLE ST. VAST, 1 Platoon being in reserve in LOUEZ. The follwoing day (1st June) Battalion Advanced Headquarters were opened at ARIANE. The Divisional Grenade School, of which Captain ROWBOTHAM was still commandant, was open all month and the following officers attended:- 2nd Lieut.BURNET, and 2nd Lieut. COWAN. 4 N.C.Os. also attended. 2nd Lieut BAILEY and 2.N.C.Os. were at the Anti-Gas School, and Lieuts. BLAIR and STEVENSON and 2nd LieutsJONES and SNOW and 6 N.C.Os. attended a course of Physical Training and Bayonet Fighting. Leave was increased to 2 officers and 8 other ranks on the 6th May, to 2 officers and 10 other ranks on the 9th, but was reduced to 1 Bfficer and 6 other ranks on the 25th. Casualties during Month:- Officers:- Wounded 1 (2nd Lt.W.I.M.CONSTABLE 21/5/16 and at duty). Injured 1 (Capt. J.S.PRINGLE) 10/5/16). Sick 1 (Capt. W.H.INCH 18/5/16).	

Army Form C. 2118

WAR DIARY
INTELLIGENCE SUMMARY
(*Erase heading not required.*)

Summary of Events and Information

Summary of Events and Information (Contd.):-

Casualties during Month (Contd.):-

  Other Ranks:-   Killed   7

                    Died of Wounds 1

                    Wounded   12

                    Sick   23.

Reinforcements:-

  Officers:-   1 (Capt. R.M.THORBURN rejoined from home 16/5/16.)

  Other Ranks:-   11   19/5/16.
                    25   20/5/16.
                    41   24/5/16.
                    17   31/5/16.

Strength:-   37 Officers and 1011 Other Remks.

R.A.Grant Ritchie B. A/Adj for   Lieut.-Col.,

Comdg., 1/8th.Bn.The Royal Scots (Pioneers).

June, 1916.

Army Form C. 2118.

WAR DIARY
or
INTELLIGENCE SUMMARY
(Erase heading not required.)

51

16

13 R.

Confidential

War Diary
of
18th Bn. The Royal Scots. (Pioneers)
From 1st June 1916. to 30th June 1916.

Volume XX.

Army Form C. 2118.

WAR DIARY
or
INTELLIGENCE SUMMARY

(Erase heading not required.)

Instructions regarding War Diaries and Intelligence Summaries are contained in F.S. Regs., Part II. and the Staff Manual respectively. Title Pages will be prepared in manuscript.

Place	Date	Hour	Summary of Events and Information	Remarks and references to Appendices
			No operation order affecting the Battalion was issued during this month, the disposition of the Battalion being the same as at the end of May, viz:- "A" Company (2 Platoons) and 1 Platoon of "B" Company at ECURIE, "B" Company at MAISON BLANCHE, and "C" and "D" Companies at NEUVILLE ST. VAAST, with 1 Platoon per company in rest at LOUEZ and relieving every 3 days. Four Lewis Guns were at ECURIE and four at NEUVILLE ST. VAAST. Advanced Headquarters were at ARIANE. "A" Coy.(with 1 Platoon "B" Coy.) formed the garrison of ECURIE and worked in the area of the 154th Inf.Brigade. "B" Coy. formed the garrison of MAISON BLANCHE and worked in the area of the 153rd Inf.Brigade. "C" and "D" Companies formed the garrison of NEUVILLE ST. VAAST and worked in the area of the 152nd Brigade.

3 officers and 120 other ranks were still employed under the C.E. on construction and maintainance of the XVIIth Corps Light Railway.

The principal work of the Battalion was the making of deep shelters (as per attached plan) in front line system and also the repairing of trenches where damaged by shells and weather; considerable work was also done assisting the R.F.A. with shelters, observation posts and gun emplacements.

There was considerable activity on the Divisional front towards the end of the month by our Artillery and Trench Mortars to which the enemy made rather a feeble reply.

Several officers and N.C.Os. attended schools of instruction in Bombing, Physical Training and Protection against Gas.

Leave during the month was first of all reduced and then stopped altogether. | |

2449 Wt. W14957/M90 750,000 1/16 J.B.C. & A. Forms/C.2118/12.

Army Form C. 2118.

WAR DIARY
or
INTELLIGENCE SUMMARY

(Erase heading not required.)

Instructions regarding War Diaries and Intelligence Summaries are contained in F. S. Regs., Part II. and the Staff Manual respectively. Title Pages will be prepared in manuscript.

Place	Date	Hour	Summary of Events and Information	Remarks and references to Appendices
			2.	

The health of the Battalion during the month was very satisfactory; in accordance with Divisional Routine Orders, a start was made to re-innoculate all officers and men who had not been done for a year.

The Transport animals were very much improved in condition during the month, grazing having helped them considerably.

The weather was very wet and the temperature much below normal.

Honours and Rewards:-
From the London Gazette Supplement dated 3/6/16.

Captain J. ROWBOTHAM awarded the Military Cross.

4373 Sergt. Archibald T. } awarded the Military Medal.
7033 L/Cpl. Anderson J. }

1184 Sergt. McKean A. mentioned in Despatches.

Casualties during the month:-

Officers:- Injured 1 (Lieut. A. BLAIR 24/6/16);
Wounded 1 (2nd Lieut. W. T. GRAY 14/6/16).
Major B. M'EWEN transferred to Machine Gun Corps 19/6/16.
Captain D. M. STEWART transferred to Royal Flying Corps 18/6/16.
2nd Lieut. H. E. R. JONES do. do. 22/6/16.

Other Ranks:- Wounded 10
Died of Wounds 1
Sick 43

Army Form C. 2118.

WAR DIARY
or
INTELLIGENCE SUMMARY

(Erase heading not required.)

Summary of Events and Information

3.

Reinforcements:-

    Officers:-   Captain W.E.WALLACE   )
                   2nd Lieut. A.DOUGLAS.)
                      "   T.R.C.SPENCE.)
                      "   W.T.GRAY.   ) From Home 6/6/16.
                      "   S.K.GRAHAM.   )
                      "   C.C.SCOTT.   )
                      "   G.REID.   )

                Captain PRINGLE from Hospital 21/6/16.

    Other Ranks:- 28 on 21/6/16.

Strength:- 41 Officers and 1003 Other Ranks.

                                            [signature]   Lieut.-Col.,
                                        Comdg., 1/8th.Bn.The Royal Scots
                                             (Pioneers).

51st Divisional Pioneers.

1/8th BATTALION

THE ROYAL SCOTS (Pioneers)

JULY 1916

CONFIDENTIAL. Army Form C. 2118.
No. 3092A
HIGHLAND DIVISION.

Vol 75
17

WAR DIARY
or
INTELLIGENCE SUMMARY
(Erase heading not required.)

Confidential.

War Diary
of
1/8th. Bn. The Royal Scots (Pioneers).
1st. to 31st. July, 1916.

Volume 2.

Army Form C. 2118.

WAR DIARY
or
INTELLIGENCE SUMMARY

(Erase heading not required.)

Instructions regarding War Diaries and Intelligence Summaries are contained in F. S. Regs., Part II. and the Staff Manual respectively. Title Pages will be prepared in manuscript.

Place	Date	Hour	Summary of Events and Information	Remarks and references to Appendices
Lousy.	July.		For the first fortnight of the month the Companies worked as for the preceding month - the disposition being the same, except that "B" Company withdrew from MAISON BLANCHE on the 1st. The 60th. Division, which eventually relieved the 51st. Division, on the 13th., arrived ten days before this, and the 1/12th. Loyal North Lancs., Pioneers to the new Division were attached to this BATTALION for administration.	
	13th.		On the 13th. the Battalion withdrew to MAROEUIL where it was billeted for the night. Transport remained near DUISANS.	
	14th.		The Battalion marched to MONCHY BRETON, via AUBIGNY - SAVY - TINQUES and arrived at 3 p.m. That evening the men of the Battalion with XVII th. Corps Railway Coy. proceeded to BOUQUEMAISON and joined the Battalion on its arrival the following day.	
	15th.		The Battalion moved to BOUQUEMAISON by motor lorry, leaving MONCHY BRETON at 8 a.m. and travelling via ST. POL and FREVENT, arrived at 11 a.m.	
	16th.		Battalion marched to CANDAS, leaving BOUQUEMAISON at 6-50 a.m. and arriving at destination at 11-50 a.m. Route-marches of 6 - 8 miles each day were carried out.	
	17th-19th.		The 17th. and 19th. were spent in CANDAS.	
	20th.		The Battalion moved to MERICOURT by train from CANDAS, and on arrival were billeted in RIBEMONT. Transport on the night of the 19th. proceeded to FLESSELLES, and on the 20th. proceeded to MERICOURT, arriving at 3 p.m.	
	21st.		The Battalion moved to bivouacs to the north of MEAULTE, leaving RIBEMONT at 12 noon and arriving at destination at 3-0 p.m.	

Army Form C. 2118.

WAR DIARY
or
INTELLIGENCE SUMMARY

(Erase heading not required.)

Instructions regarding War Diaries and Intelligence Summaries are contained in F. S. Regs., Part II. and the Staff Manual respectively. Title Pages will be prepared in manuscript.

Place	Date	Hour	Summary of Events and Information	Remarks and references to Appendices
	July 21st.		The Battalion was attached to the 154th. Infantry Brigade for work. At 7 p.m. "A" Company left MEAULTE and proceeded to the front for work, attached to the 4th. Gordons. The remainder of the Battalion with exception of Transport left at 9 p.m., and, marching via MAMETZ village, reached MAMETZ WOOD at 2 a.m. and bivouacked.	
	22nd.		Orders were received to dig a trench from HIGH WOOD to link up with Division on left, but, owing to daylight coming on it was impossible to carry this out. Transport proceeded to a field to the west of FRICOURT. At 2 p.m. "D" Company and 2 Platoons "C" Company went forward to work, but barrage fire prevented this, and the Company returned, having suffered some casualties. During the day, the bivouacs occupied by the Battalion were again shelled and casualties were again suffered. The Battalion dug itself in during the day.	
	22nd/23rd. Night		In the evening orders were received that the 51st. Division (154th.Inf. Bde.) would attack HIGH WOOD, the assault being timed for 1-30 a.m. This Battalion was to be held in readiness for consolidation work ; "B" Coy. were to be ready to wire 2000 yards of ground, and stores were prepared for this and then carried up. Companies were to be in the following positions at 1-30 a.m. "A" Coy. S.14.a.5.8, "B"Coy. near the south end of HIGH WOOD, "C" Coy. to the left of cross roads S. 16.c.1.4, and "D"Coy. to the right of same cross roads. Headquarters were close to MARLBORO' WOOD, S.20.d.8.7. No consolidation being required all companies were withdrawn again to MAMETZ WOOD at 10 a.m.	
	23rd/24th.		From noon 22nd. to noon 23rd. the Battalion had over a hundred casualties including 5 officers wounded (2nd.Lt.T.A.MEEK, W.I.M.CONSTABLE, and A.DOUGLAS) In the afternoon Captain ROWBOTHAM went up to the front with four men and at great risk in broad daylight taped out a trench joining HIGH WOOD and WINDMILL.	

2449 Wt W14957/M90 750,000 1/16 J.B.C. & A. Forms/C.2118/12

WAR DIARY or INTELLIGENCE SUMMARY

Army Form C. 2118.

(Erase heading not required.)

Place	Date	Hour	Summary of Events and Information	Remarks and references to Appendices
	July. 31st.		4.	

CASUALTIES :-

    Officers.   Wounded. 3. { 2nd. Lieut. MEEK. T.A. 22nd.
                                                 { " CONSTABLE.W.I.M.23rd.
                                                 { " DOUGLAS. A. 22nd.

    Wounded at Duty. 2nd. Lieut. DODS. J.B. 26th.

    To Royal Flying Corps. 2nd. Lieut. COWAN.W.W. 6th.
                                          " BAILEY.D.H.7th.

    Other Ranks. Killed. 13
                 Wounded. 124
                 Do. 28 remg. at Duty.
                 Died of Wounds. 6
                 Missing. 3
                 Sick. 41

REINFORCEMENTS.

    Officers. Lieut. Hodgson.W.E. (1/6th. R.Scots.) 5:7:16.
                2nd.Lt.Gray. J.T.
                Lt.
                2nd. Baxter. C.R. }
                " Mackie. J. } 21:7:16.
                " Lowson. W. }
                " Dods. J.B. }

                Major. Todd. J.A. }
                Capt. Allison. G.E. } 24:7:16.
                2nd.Lt.Todd. W.J.W. }

Commdg. 18th Bn. The Royal Scots
(PIONEERS)
Lieut.-Col.,

Army Form C. 2118.

WAR DIARY
or
INTELLIGENCE SUMMARY

(Erase heading not required.)

Instructions regarding War Diaries and Intelligence Summaries are contained in F. S. Regs., Part II. and the Staff Manual respectively. Title Pages will be prepared in manuscript.

Place	Date	Hour	Summary of Events and Information	Remarks and references to Appendices
July.				
	24/25th.		At night "C" and "D" Companies cut this trench, "A" Company working on HIGH ALLEY.	
	25th.		Work continued as on previous night.	
	25/26th.		Bivouacs were heavily shelled from 12-30 p.m. to 6 p.m. The men were well dug in and few casualties occurred. "B" and "C" "D" Company wired new trench from HIGH WOOD westward. "B" and "C" Companies commenced new communication trench known as THISTLE ALLEY. 2nd. Lieut. J.B.DODS was wounded slightly and remained at duty.	
	26th.		On the afternoon of the 26th. the 154th. Inf.Bde was relieved by the 153rd. Inf.Bde. and 2 Companies of the Battalion (B and D) withdrew to Transport lines for a rest. During the night "A" and "C" Companies continued work on THISTLE ALLEY and HIGH ALLEY.	
	27th.		The Germans fired a great many gas shells.	
	28th.		Quiet all day, Major TODD relieved the C.O. and the M.O. also went back for a rest. "B" and "D" Companies relieved "A" and "C" Companies in the afternoon. Work was continued, "B" Company on "THISTLE ALLEY. "D" Company continued digging and wiring new trench on west of HIGH WOOD.	
	29th.		Work continued as on previous day. "B" Company completed THISTLE ALLEY with exception of 100 yards next to BLACK WATCH TRENCH which was not deep enough.	
	30th.		C.O. relieved Major Todd. Bivouacs shelled in the afternoon. The 153rd. Infantry Brigade attacked HIGH WOOD, the assault being timed at 6-10 p.m. Four Platoons were sent up for consolidation work, but were not required, except one Platoon which did some work for the 5th.Gordons.	
	31st.		Orders to dig a trench from SUTHERLAND TRENCH to new forward position of Division on left received. At considerable risk Lieut. R.B.Ovens and 2nd. Lieut. J.Sharp succeeded in taping out this trench, but little work was done owing to hostile fire.	

51st Divisional Troops

1/8th BATTALION

THE ROYAL SCOTS   (Pioneers)

AUGUST 1 9 1 6

WAR DIARY / INTELLIGENCE SUMMARY

Army Form C. 2118.

CONFIDENTIAL
No 31 (?)
18th R. Scots
HIGHLAND DIVISION
(Pioneers) 5½ Divn

Place	Date	Hour	Summary of Events and Information	Remarks and references to Appendices
MAMETZ WOOD	August 1st		A + C Coys moved night to built up with 19th Division on our left flank. Work on communication	
	2nd		the night through battle activity. B + D Coys into Sabha B Transport. A + C Coys working in HIGH ALLEY and THISTLE ALLEY - improving communications - B + D Coys	
	3rd + 4th + 5th		relieved A + C who returned to Sabha B Transport lines.	
Bivouac	6th		Entrained at above hall.	
D.12.d.			Relieved by Middlesex Pioneer Battalion of 33rd Division - Battalion moved to Bivouac at D.12.d. (ALBERT-AMIENS Rd.)
ALBERT-AMIENS Rd.	7th + 8th		Transport and two companies arriving at 3 p.m. - the two companies from MAMETZ WOOD m/- marching Bivouac till midnight - after arrival at 7 p.m.	
	9th		Battalion remained in rest bivouac. Transport moved to COULANVILLE and stayed the night then Division proceeded to an a train at MIENS and ABBEVILLE - Transport marched to Road and marched via LONGPRÉ - PICQUIGNY to PONT REMY - Battn has to entrain at EDGEHILL Station - H.Q. Coy. & M.T.S. Coy arrived Stn at 8.15 a.m. but finding no train available moved on to MERICOURT Station and entrained then at 3 p.m. Detrained at LONGPRÉ Station at 9.15 p.m. C + D Coys marched down to MERICOURT Billets at PONT REMY arriving at 5 + 7 p.m. C + D Coys marched down to MERICOURT Station. Entrained at 11 p.m. + 1 a.m. (10th) and reached PONT REMY at 11 p.m. + 1 a.m. (10th)	
PONT REMY	10th		Resting in Billets + bivouac	
	11th + 12th		Hd Qrs A.B. + C. Companies Transport (Except 1st 4 S.S. Wagon + teams) entrained at PONT REMY Station at 7.30 p.m. and arrived at STEENBECQUE at 6.30 a.m. marched to STAPLE - arriving at 11 a.m. - 100 men of A Coy under lt of PONT REMY as entraining party Major J Mayne Railway officer	98.

WAR DIARY of INTELLIGENCE SUMMARY

Army Form C. 2118.

(2.)

Place	Date	Hour	Summary of Events and Information	Remarks and references to Appendices
PONT RENY	Aug 11-12		"D" Company entrained at PONT RENY with remainder of the Transport at 1.30 a.m. (12") and arrived at STAPLE at 3 p.m. "A" Company entraining party did not reach billets at STAPLE till 11.30 p.m. The railway arrangements worked exceedingly well and all	
STAPLE	13"		R.T.O. PONT RENY congratulated the entraining party on their work. Brigadier in billets at STAPLE. Battalion Church Parade with morning. The Commanding Officer addressed the Battalion after parade and congratulated them on the work done during the time the Division was in action, and expressed his satisfaction to all ranks. Lieutenant and Adjutant J.E. KENP rejoined and took up duties of Adjutant, after having been attached No. 753 Infantry Brigade for six months, in acting Staff Captain. Battalion moved up to ARMENTIÈRES, the Division relieving the 1st NEW ZEALAND Division	
	14"		of 2nd ANZAC Corps. Transport moved off at 4 a.m. moving with 154 Inf. Bde. group. Battalion via HAZEBROUCK MERVILLE and LA GORGUE and reached Billets at 5.30 p.m. Battalion marched at 2 p.m. entraining at EBBLINGHEM Station at 4.30 p.m. arriving STEENWERCK at 6 p.m. and detrained. Marched to ARMENTIÈRES, billets being reached at 8.30 p.m. Major General Sydney Lawford C.B. Comdg 41st Division who formerly commanded the 12th Inf. Bde. which the Battalion was in, was at STEENWERCK Station to meet the Battalion and expressed the pleasure it gave him to see all ranks looking so well. The Battalion was	
ARMENTIÈRES			deeply grieved the know down this by Major General Lawford's visit. Battalion billeted in  (sheet 36 N.W.) & Transport at about 2 kilometres away	

WAR DIARY
INTELLIGENCE SUMMARY

Army Form C. 2118

Place: ARMENTIERES

Date: August

15th — C & D Companies moved ul- k no Illili - e at the Station - L Platoon at MENTIERES and D at HOUPLINES - A Coys remaining at Headquarters in the Factory. Companies employed their spare time and levelling bath and formed stores - making the empty magazine behd Rte Transport lines.

16th — Companies employed improving billets and building shellproof cover - A Coy worked improving trenches & Right Brigade Sector - 2 Platoons by night - and 2 Platoon or 17th. Capt W.H. Ireland rejoined from Hospital and 2nd Lieut. P.W. Brown joined the Battalion from Home.

17th — "B" Company under Major J. TAIT took on the work of running a saw mill at the town - also provise offers. B. Coy then became the Headquarters Coy Any - and is responsible for supplying timber and all stores to the other Companies. A party of "B" Company were also engaged in making concrete blocks. Orders were received that the Battalion was to be responsible for the maintain and improvement of all Communication trenches in the Divisional front. A. C. & D Companies being detailed for this work. "B" Coy into HQ Coy by thus making batteries in addition to running the Timber yard, Cement works, R.E. dumps etc. This will be full scale. Lined m

22nd — Lt. Nº 1796 Pte. A. Ballachine attached the Military Medal (15/8/16)

23rd — Orders received award Military Medal (15/8/16) Andrew small Ossest Military Medal (15/8/16) and Nº 7033 LCorpl. W. Maxwell awarded the Military Cross (21/5/16). Orders received that the Battalion would leave the Machine Gunners up MENTIEDES Defences from 6 to 26 "- mile. These defences are allotted to four stations one to each Company - they consist chiefly of replacements of Headqtr, Field Gun and Machine Guns with a few trenches. All are very well wired. Then are 6 memorial of the Battalion in can of alarm o

29th — Welk continues as afore. The R.O.C II Army presented medal decoration to Lieut Maxwell and the N.C.O's of the Battalion at a Parade held near BAILLEUL — the Commanding Officer + Adjutant were present at the parade.

WAR DIARY

INTELLIGENCE SUMMARY

Army Form C. 2118

(4)

Place	Date	Hour	Summary of Events and Information	Remarks and references to Appendices
ARMENTIERES	29th-30th		Reconnoitering heavy rain and high winds prevail very trying for the men working in Communication trenches.	
	30th		Draft of 26 other ranks joined the Battalion.	
	31st		Captain John M. Morgan R.A.M.C. - Medical Officer 11th Battalion awarded the Military Cross.	
			Casualties - during month of August.	
			Officers - Wounded (shell shock) Captain J. Richardson	
			" " " 2/Lieut. J.K. Graham	
			Sick - Capt. & Adjt. Kerr	
			" G. Alison	
			R.m.Run Cpls - Lieut. A.P.A. Jameson	
			O.R. - Killed 4 - Wounded 20 (1 died)	
			wounded at duty 7 - Sick 39 -	
			Reinforcements - Officers -	
			7/8/16 - 2/Lieutenants - J.K. Graham -	
			W.O.S. McKendall - D.M. McKays - S. Davidson - W.J. Plennall -	
			16/8/16 - Capt. W.H. Ent (rejoined).	
			21/8/16 - Lieut. P.P. Alison (")	
			Total Strength at 31/8/16 - (including attached).	
			Officers 48.	
			O.R. 848	

Wm of Hunt
Adjutant.
1/11th Bn = The Royal Scots.
(Pioneers)

31/8/16.

Army Form C. 2118

CONFIDENTIAL
No. 21/A
HIGHLAND DIVISION.

WAR DIARY
or
INTELLIGENCE SUMMARY
(Erase heading not required.)

Confidential

War Diary
M.R.H. Royal Horse Artillery
from 1st September to 30th September 1916.

Volume 23

16 R.S.

Army Form C. 2118

WAR DIARY
or
INTELLIGENCE SUMMARY
(Erase heading not required.)

Place	Date	Hour	Summary of Events and Information	Remarks and references to Appendices
ARMENTIERES	3rd September		"A" Company moved out of ARMENTIERES and was billeted at A.18.a.50.80. (Sheet 36 N.W.) Their billet was the section of hutments for the Reserve Brigade. Before starting the Rosiery, the Platoons were employed digging trenches at L of the Divisional & Brigade School and the remainder of the Coy. fitting up huts H.Q. of the Symmetric and Brigade Schools.	
	4th		25 men of "A" Company returned to Battalion Headquarters and were attached to "B" Company + the employed in joining and fitting up for billeting purposes timber etc. for the hutments. Owing to the Battalion being so scattered it was decided for the time being not to keep up a bath room of our own but to make use of the excellent Divisional Bath Rooms at PONT DE NIEPPE. The Battalion allotment — was 3 - 5 p.m. on Mondays & Tuesdays — the capacity of the Bath Rooms being 200 — 250 men per hour —	
	10th		2/Lieuts A. D. JONES joined the Battalion. A larger list of reinforced.	
			the Base. One Platoon of C+D Coys was detailed to work exclusively on the railways & their respective sectors of the front. Their Platoons were placed under the supervision of the Field Companies R.E.	
	15th		24 Other ranks joined the Battalion as reinforcements from the Base —	
	19		20 Other ranks joined the Battalion as reinforcements from the Base on reinforcements — 2 Platoons of "A" Company came back to Battalion Headquarters to work with "B" Company in the pkps to the form — the remaining two continuing work under the Divisional Schools —	

WAR DIARY or INTELLIGENCE SUMMARY

Army Form C. 2118

Place	Date	Hour	Summary of Events and Information	Remarks and references to Appendices
ARMENTIÈRES	19 September		A harassing order has received that the Division might be relieved in a week's time. All work on communication trenches was stopped and C & D Companies started work on the front line reforming damages etc. The two platoons of "A" Coy are also told on to their work, one platoon being attacked to each of "C" & "D" Coys.	
	20		Preliminary operation orders for the relief of the Division received — Arrangements made in the Battalion for the relieving of Company and trench stores.	
	22		"D" Coy. was relieved by the "C" Coy. "A" Coy. 3rd Australian Pioneer Battalion — and moved from HOUPLINES Établ. near Battalion Headquarters.	
	23		Bnd has received that the Division would probably entrain at FLETRE on the 30th September — and have a period of training before doing anything else. Training Scheme received.	
	24		"C" Coy. was relieved by "C" Coy. 18th Bn. Northumberland Fusiliers (Pioneers). Bn remained in their present billets. Orders were received that the Battalion would move to the ESTAIRES area under its orders Nº IS 154 Infantry Brigade on the morning of 25th. — Operation orders issued at 2.30 a.m. in morning of 25th. Bn & D Coy. Hd. Qrs moved to GDG 9 a.m. C & G Transport & A.G. Transport to en route. Operation Order attached. Battalion moved to Billet G. 1 pm. Hd. Qrs moved to Battalion Bivvy Billets 2 1/2 miles from ESTAIRES on the main ESTAIRES - NEUF BERQUIN Road. The Battalion bivvy in fields along the road.	APP. I.
ESTAIRES	26 & 27		Infantry training carried out. Officers NCO & men inoculated under Major Jas Keith.	
	27		Draft of 11 Ors, and 1 officer joined the Battalion from the Base.	

WAR DIARY / INTELLIGENCE SUMMARY

Army Form C. 2118

Place	Date	Hour	Summary of Events and Information	Remarks and references to Appendices
ESTAIRES	28th			
	29th			
	30th		Orders received that the Battalion would entrain at MERVILLE on 30th inst. for CANDAS. Training continued.	
			B.C.'s Bn. at 6 a.m. for MERVILLE; Major Tait-King, Division of Entraining Officer and at C. finding a fatigue party of 2 Offrs. & 100 men for entraining duty. 6 men killed at MERVILLE C. finding A.G. Bn. at 8 p.m. for BAILLEUL West Station with 2 S.S. Wagons & Machine gun. (30/1). The remainder of Battalion ran to entrain at 6 a.m. Entrained at 3 a.m. (1 Coy). H.Qrs. travel to MERVILLE. Operation orders + amendments etc. attached.	APP. II APP. III APP. IV
			Reinforcements - Officers - Capt. Mrs. Muir (rejoined) OTR 33 - 10 2/Lt. A.D. Jordan 24 - 15 2/Lt. P.A. Burnett (rejoined) 19 - 19 11 - 24 6 - 30 93	
			Casualties - Officers - 2/Lt. P.A. Burnett (sick). Major U.C. Hodgson (") Capt. Mrs. Kerr (R.M. Gun Offr.) Lieut. J.S. Stevenson (sick).	
			OTR Wounded 3 Sick 33 36	
			Strength at 30/9/16 = 48 Officers = 913 OTR.	

30/9/16
Adjutant
1/8 B - Black Watch (Regular)

SECRET.   Copy No. 16

APPENDIX I

1/8th Bn. THE ROYAL SCOTS (Pioneers),

OPERATION ORDERS
by Lieut.-Col. W. GEMMILL, D.S.O., Commanding.

25th September, 1916.

1. The Battalion will move to-day to the ESTAIRES Area in accordance with the following arrangements.

2. For the Battalion, less "A" and "C" Companies, Reveille will be at 6-30 a.m. Breakfast 7-30 a.m. Battalion parade ready to move off at Battalion Headquarters at 9 a.m. in the following order:-

   Cyclists
   Signallers
   "B" Company
   "D" Company
   Stretcher Bearers
   Details
   Transport.

3. "C" Company will parade at Company billets and will join the column at Railway Crossing on ERQUINGHEM - ARMENTIERES Road at 9-30 a.m., falling in in rear of "D" Company.

4. "A" Company will move off from present billeting area in time to reach BAC St. MAUR by 10-30 a.m., where it will fall in in rear of "C" Company. Route - via CROIX du BAC, Bac St. MAUR. The head of the column to halt just short of the main ARMENTIERES - SAILLY Road.

5. The Transport Officer will arrange transport as under:-
(a) 2 baggage wagons and mess cart will report at Battalion Headquarters at 8 a.m. along with horses for "B" and "D" Company tool wagons and cookers; one water cart and medical cart. This transport is allotted as under:-
   1 baggage wagon for "B" and "D" Companies' Officers' kits.
   1 baggage wagon for Headquarters, Orderly Room and
      Signalling stores.
The 2 limbered G.S. Wagons presently at Battalion Headquarters are allotted as under:-
   1 limber for Quartermaster.
   1 limber for Lewis Gun magazines from "B" and "D" Companies.
The mess cart is for Headquarters, "B" and "D" Companies' mess boxes.
   Above will be loaded by 8-45 a.m. and ready to move off.

(b) Horses for "C" Company 2 tool wagons and cooker will report at "C" Company billet at 8 a.m. and also 2 limbered G.S. Wagons. These will take officers' kits, company baggage and Lewis Gun magazines.

(c) Horses for "A" Company tool wagons and cooker and also 2 limbered G.S. Wagons to report at "A" Company Headquarters not later than 8 a.m. The limbers to be used as in para (b).

(d) The remainder of the transport, including 1 limber allotted to Transport Officer and 1 for S.A.A., will join the Battalion in ERQUINGHEM Village at 10 a.m. and will march in rear of the column. Vehicles allotted to "A" and "C" Companies will march in rear and take their proper places in the column on joining up.
   Officers chargers will be sent to their various billets in accordance with above.

6. BRAKESMEN./

2.

6. BRAKESMEN. Companies will detail 1 man to march in rear of each wagon in which their company kit, etc., is loaded. Officers' servants will march with their companies, details at Battalion Headquarters being attached to "B" Company.

7. BLANKETS. (a) "A" Company blankets must be carried on the tool wagons.

(b) A motor lorry will be at Battalion Headquarters at 1-30 p.m. to take blankets to new area. "B" and "D" Companies and all details will have blankets stacked outside the Q.M.Stores before moving off, rolled in bundles of 10 and labelled. Os.C."B" and "D" Companies will each detail 2 men (unable to march) to load the blankets and accompany the blankets. After loading at Battalion Headquarters, the lorry will proceed to "C" Company and pick up blankets there. O.C."C" Company will arrange to have these stacked and leave 2 men in charge.

8. Lewis Gun Handcarts will be "brigaded" and march in rear of column and in fron of transport under the Battalion Lewis Gun Sergeant. Every effort will be made to ensure that these do not break down and there is no hitch.

9. Billeting party as under will report to the Staff Captain, 154th Infantry Brigade at the Town Major's Office in ESTAIRES at 9 a.m. :-

Quartermaster, Lieut R.Weir, Q.M.Staff except R.Q.M.S.
Party will be mounted on bicycles provided by the Sergeant i/c Cyclists. One cyclist with bicycle must, however, accompany the column. The remainder will march on foot.

10. Particular attention will be paid to march discipline.

11. Acknowledge.

Lieut.,
Issued at 2.30 a.m.   Adjt.,1/8th Bn.The Royal Scots
(Pioneers).

Copy No.   1 - Adjutant for Commanding Officer.
            2 - Headquarters.
            3 - "A" Company.
            4 - "B" Company.
            5 - "C" Company.
            6 - "D" Company.
            7 - Quartermaster.
            8 - Transport Officer.
            9 - Medical Officer for Stretcher Bearers.
           10 - Signals.
           11 - Cyclists.
           12 - Regtl. Sergeant-Major.
           13 - Divisional Gas Officer.
           14 - 154th Infantry Brigade.
           15 - 1/2nd Highland Field Co., R.E.
           16 - File.

APPENDIX II

S E C R E T. Copy No. 14.

1/8th Bn. THE ROYAL SCOTS (Pioneers),
ORDERS FOR ENTRAINMENT FOR MOVE TO RESERVE ARMY AREA
by Lieut.-Col. W.GEMMILL, D.S.O., Commanding.

NOTE. At midnight on the night of 30th Sept/1st Oct. the time changes back to Greenwich time, i.e., an extra hour has to be put in at midnight. All times given below are in accordance with present time, i.e., some will require alteration.

1. (a) "A" Company entrains at BAILLEUL West Station in train No. 18, due to depart at 3-28 a.m. on 1st October. Company will move off at 8 p.m. on 30th September. The following transport will accompany the Company:-
    Company Commander's horse, Company cooker, 2 tool wagons and "C" Company No. 1 tool wagon.
    On these will be carried, in addition to their usual load, rations for consumption on 1st October, Officers' kits and Company baggage.
   (b) A motor lorry will be at Battalion Headquarters at 8 p.m. on 30th September to take blankets and greatcoats of "A" Company to the Station. O.C."A"Company will arrange to have these stacked and labelled, and a party of 1 N.C.O. and 3 men detailed to accompany the lorry and unload it at the Station
   (c) Company detrains at DOULLENS South Station and should report to R.T.O. Billets have been arranged at DOULLENS for the day. Company will move on in the evening and rejoin the Battalion at its billets, location of which is not yet known.
   (d) Any telegraphic reports necessary during the journey will be sent to the Division c/o A.D.R.T.2. and repeated to Division c/o A.D.R.T.3.
   (e) O.C."A"Company is in command of the train.
   (f) Lewis Gun handcarts will accompany the company, magazines being loaded in limbers.

2. (a) Major J.TAIT is entraining officer at MERVILLE, representing the Division.
    2 Officers and 100 men of "B" Company will be told off as entraining party.
   (b) "B" Company will parade at 6-30 a.m. on 30th September and march to MERVILLE Station, where Major Tait and entraining party will report to R.T.O. at 7-45 a.m., remainder of the Company going into billets near the Station. Breakfast before moving off. Company cooker will accompany the Company with rations for dinner and tea on 30th Sept., also Company Commander's horse. Cooker horses and the charger will return to the Transport lines at once.
   (c) Rations for 1st October, blankets, and Officers' kits will be sent down on the 30th Sept. Blankets and kits to be left at Company Headquarters with 2 men as guard.
   (d) Divisional Gas Officer and staff will accompany "B" Company.
   (e) Lewis Gun handcarts will move with Company, magazines being loaded on limbers.

3. The Battalion, less "A" and "B" Companies and Transport, will parade at 6 a.m. on the 1st October and march to MERVILLE Station. Detailed orders will be issued later.

4. (a) The Transport will move off from the present lines at 4 a.m. on 1st October to MERVILLE Station. Horses of Headquarters Officers and Os.C. "C" and "D" Companies will be left and will accompany the column.
   (b) Lieut Graham will accompany the Transport and assist the Transport Officer.
   (c)/

2.

(c) All wagons must be loaded up and back in the lines by 3-30 a.m.
(d) Transport is allotted as under:-

 2 limbers for Quartermaster for stores, Pioneers' and Shoe
  makers' kit.
 2 limbers for Lewis Gun magazines (already loaded).
 1 limber for Transport Officer.
 1 limber for Orderly Room baggage.
 1 limber for Signals and Armourer Sergeant's kit.
 1 limber surplus - meantime.
Mess cart to take mess boxes of Hdqrs., "B" and "D" Coys.
Medical cart to be loaded up at Medical Officer's Inspection
 Room.
 The baggage wagons will travel to the Station empty. Supply
wagons accompany the Transport.
 O.C. "B" Company will arrange to guide horses for his cooker
when the transport arrives at the Station.

5. A motor lorry will be at Battalion Headquarters at 5-30 a.m.
on 1st October for blankets of "C" and "D" Companies and details.
These will be labelled and stacked outside Company Headquarters.
Details blankets at the road junction near Headquarters' Mess.
Companies will arrange to load these. This lorry will also take
Officers' kits from "C" and "D" Companies and Bn. Headquarters.
These, along with "B" Company kits, must all be reloaded into
the baggage wagons at the Station, "C" and "D" Companies being
allotted one baggage wagon, Hdqrs. and "B" Company the other.

6. The Battalion travels by train No. 22 due to leave MERVILLE
at 8-05 a.m. and to arrive at CANDAS at 13-20 p.m.

7. Acknowledge.

                  Lieut.,
29th September, 1916. Adjt., 1/8th Bn. The Royal Scots
Issued at 6.30 p.m.   (Pioneers).

Copy No. 1 Adjutant for Commanding Officer.
   2 Headquarters.
   3 O.C. "A" Company.
   4 O.C. "B" Company.
   5 O.C. "C" Company.
   6 O.C. "D" Company.
   7 Medical Officer.
   8 Transport Officer.
   9 Quartermaster.
  10 Divisional Gas Officer.
  11 Signals.
  12 Regtl. Sergt.-Major.
  13 Entraining Officer.
  14 File.

APPENDIX III

SECRET.   Copy No. 14

1/8th Bn. THE ROYAL SCOTS (Pioneers).

AMENDMENTS TOMORROWS FOR EMBARKMENT FOR MOVE TO RESERVE ARMY AREA.

by Lieut.-Col. W.GEMMILL, D.S.O., Commanding.

---

1. The following amendments will be made to Operation Orders dated 29th September, 1916.

2. In para 1 sub-para (c) delete all except the first sentence.

3. The whole Battalion on detrainment will move to a staging area South of DOULLENS and will march the following day to a billeting area which will be notified later.

4. Acknowledge

29th September, 1916.
Issued at 10 p.m.

                                          Lieut.,
Adjt., 1/8th Bn.The Royal Scots
                          (Pioneers).

Copy No. 1 Adjutant for Commanding Officer.
      2 Headquarters.
      3 O.C."A"Company.
      4 O.C."B"Company.
      5 O.C."C"Company.
      6 O.C."D"Company.

Copy No. 7 Medical Officer.
      8 Transport Officer.
      9 Quartermaster.
     10 Divisional Gas Officer.
Copy No. 14 File.
     11 Signals.
     12 Regtl.Sergt.-Major
     13 Entraining

SECRET.   Copy No.

APPENDIX IV

1/8th Bn. THE ROYAL SCOTS (Pioneers),

ADDITIONAL INSTRUCTIONS FOR MOVE TO RESERVE ARMY AREA

by Lieut.-Col. W.GEMMILL, D.S.O., Commanding.

NOTE.- All times given below are in accordance with the present time which, for the sake of simplicity, will be adhered to until after the departure of the train.

----

1. The Battalion, less "A" and "B" Companies and the Transport, will parade ready to move off at 5-45 a.m. to-morrow as under, Reveille being at 4-15 a.m. and Breakfast at 4-45 a.m.:-

   Cyclists
   Signallers
   "C" Company
   "D" Company
   Stretcher Bearers
   Lewis Gun handcarts of "C" and "D" Companies, brigaded under Cpl Lowe, "D" Company.
   Details.

   Head of the column to be at the Orderly Room, facing east. Dress - full marching order with steel helmets.

2. DIXIES. The Quartermaster will arrange to leave 8 dixies for breakfast for each of "C" and "D" Companies and a proportion for details. These will be cleaned after the meal is over and carried to the Station, where they will be loaded on the cookers.

3. The Transport Officer will have Officers' chargers at their billets in accordance with the above.

4. O.C."B"Company will arrange to have a party in readiness at MERVILLE Station to unload blankets and Officers' kits from the motor lorry which should arrive at the Station about 6-30 a.m. Kits will be reloaded as per para. 5 of Operation Order dated 29th inst. Blankets will be placed on tool and other wagons as may be most suitable.

5. O.C."B"Company will arrange to have his entire Company paraded at the Station at 7 a.m.

6. The Battalion billets on arrival in New area are provisionally fixed at HARDINVAL. O.C."A"Company will march there direct from DOULLENS South.

7. Refilling Point on 1st October will be on the main road between BEAUVAL and DOULLENS.

8. Acknowledge.

                                              [signature]
                                              Lieut.,
30th September, 1916.
Issued at 4 p.m.   Adjt., 1/8th Bn. The Royal Scots
                                              (Pioneers).

Copy No. 1 Adjt. for Command-   Copy No. 7 Medical Officer.
            ing Officer.   8 Transport Officer.
        2 Headquarters.   9 Quartermaster.
        3 O.C."A"Company.   10 Signals.
        4 O.C."B"Company.   11 Regtl.Sergt.-Major.
        5 O.C."C"Company.   12 File.
        6 O.C."D"Company.

Army Form C. 2118.

CONFIDENTIAL
No. 2/A

HIGHLAND DIVISION.

WAR DIARY
or
INTELLIGENCE SUMMARY.
(Erase heading not required)

Vol 20

Confidential

War Diary
1st Highland Royal Engineers (Reserve)
From 1st October 1916 to 31st October 1916

Volume 20

Army Form C. 2118.

WAR DIARY
INTELLIGENCE SUMMARY

Army Form C. 2118

Place	Date	Hour	Summary of Events and Information	Remarks and references to Appendices
	OCTOBER			
ESTAIRES	1st		Battalion (less "A" Company (which had moved to BAILLEUL) left ESTAIRES at 6 a.m. travelled to MERVILLE - Entrained (less 'A' Coy) at 1.30 p.m. - marched to HARDINVAL, which A.G. had already reached coming from DOULLENS Station.	
HARDINVAL	2nd		Battalion left at 10 a.m. and marched to THIÈVRES - (Operation Order attached.) The march APP. I. was carried out in very hot weather.	APP. I.
THIÈVRES	3rd		Battalion left at 10 a.m. and marched to LOUVENCOURT which was reached about 11.30 a.m. - The weather made the march again trying (O.O. attached)	APP. II.
LOUVENCOURT	4th		Battalion left at 1 p.m. and marched to billets at COURCELLES - an Ain & COLINCAMPS (O.O. attached) - At the last moment orders were received that on arrival at COURCELLES billets at LOUVENCOURT and 'B' Company were left. A arrival at COURCELLES 'A' Company and that there was only accommodation for one Company at COLINCAMPS - 'A' Company had the Battalion Hd. Qrs., C & D Companies (Transport) being at COURCELLES - 2/Heads - 7000 + 22 men of 'A' Co. left for Divisional Hd. Qrs. to hold existing Railhead (BUS-les-ARTOIS). The following Officers were detached for special duty.	APP. III.
COURCELLES & COLINCAMPS			Capt. C.E. ALISON to conducting A/ Town Major of COURCELLES. Capt. J. YOUNG " " " " LOUVENCOURT. Lieut. R.N. THORBURN " " " " BUS-les-ARTOIS. " " " " " I/C. Stores & Transport.	

WAR DIARY / INTELLIGENCE SUMMARY

Army Form C. 2118 (2)

Place	Date	Hour	Summary of Events and Information	Remarks and references to Appendices
COURCELLES & COLINCAMPS	October 4th		Lieut. S. REID was detailed for special work at Divisional HQrs. & Co. carry out a reconnaissance of the Divisional Drilling area. That night 110 men of C.G. were sent to [undertake] a thorough [sorting] at COLINCAMPS. Sidney 7. at the train did not arrive.	
	5th		Half a Communication trench [started] in trench = 150 men of C.G. on REVEL Trench, 150 men of D.G. on SONIS Trench. 50 men of A.G. on PASTEUR Trench. The remainder of B.G. were employed in increasing the accommodation in COLINCAMPS with a view to having D.G. billeted there.	
	6th		Half a Communication trench continued — this amounted to repairing & improving already existing trenches. A wall-trench of the billets at COURCELLES having been much [damaged]. C.G. were employed in making doub-tier beds in billets in order to accommodate men when billets had been allotted. Later men received to send 24 skilled miners to be attached to the 174 Tunnelling Company R.E. at BEAUSSART. C Company found this party.	
	7th		A.C. continued work on REVEL, SONIS, PASTEUR & JENA Communication trenches. D Company employed at night making dumps near the front-line at RED SAP. D Company moved to COLINCAMPS — only Battalion Headquarters & grenades etc. C.G. at COLINCAMPS, the transport hour & Q.M. Stores having moved back to BUS-les-ARTOIS.	WCC

WAR DIARY or INTELLIGENCE SUMMARY

Army Form C. 2118.

(3)

Place	Date	Hour	Summary of Events and Information	Remarks and references to Appendices
COURCELLES & COLINCAMPS	8		A, C & D Companies men all employed by night - burying cables - A & D in NAIRNE Street & TRIANGLE Trench, C in HONE Avenue. 'B' Company still at LOUVENCOURT	
	9		Being engaged in attack practice along with the Infantry.	
	10		'D' Company started work repairing dugouts for R.A.M.C. Remainder of A, D, C, and A.T.C. Coys. started to lay a 60 cm. railway to the front from COLINCAMPS. The remaining half of battalion on G, R.E. and the Battalion only responsible for the forward part of the line.	
	12		Lieut. & Quartermaster J. CLARK left the Battalion for duty as Quartermaster at 4th Army HAVRE—meets authority from G.H.Q.	
	13 / 14 / 15		Endeavouring find a railway. Dugouts started & further road at COURCELLES. On the 14th the R.A.M.C. dugouts continued by D Coy, more dugouts made by D Coy & front line. 15th Captain W.A.R.M.N. BEALE appointed Officer Commanding. Remaining left to train Brigades & Division. 2/c Division & Ord. Line Transport.	
	16		Warning order received that the Division must be prepared to stand now to the 31st Division at that when and more front to take in the line in front of BEAUMONT HAMEL - M.T. Wagon all loaded up. (Off) Warning now attached.	
	17		All not unexpected pending orders to move to rest area.	APP. IV

WAR DIARY

INTELLIGENCE SUMMARY
(Erase heading not required)

Army Form C. 2118.

(4.)

Instructions regarding War Diaries and Intelligence Summaries are contained in F. S. Regs., Part II. and the Staff Manual respectively. Title pages will be prepared in manuscript.

Place	Date OCTOBER	Hour	Summary of Events and Information	Remarks and references to Appendices
COURCELLES COLINCAMPS & LOUVENCOURT	17th		Orders received to move to new area about MAILLY-MAILLET. It was decided to move the Battalion independently. Operation orders for the move attached.	APP. V.
In camp near MAILLY-MAILLET	18th		Battalion arrived in new Billets (huts + tents) in Wood South West of MAILLY-MAILLET (ref P.18.b. 10.30). Phil - 57 D - 1/40,000 - P.18-d - 20.50 - Battalion Hd. Qrs. moved to P.18.b. 10.30.	
	19th		"C". Coy. started work on Battle Hd. Qrs. dugouts in front of WHITE CITY - Remainder of Battalion engaged cleaning up camp which was turned into a programme move & General work from early morning - 1 Platoon "A" Coy. made field OVENS & 2nd Lieut JONES proceeded to AUCHONVILLERS & went to reconnoitre trench tramways - 1 Platoon "A" Coy under 2nd Lieut TODD moved direct from Bus-les-Artois to LEALVILLERS (Bns. Hd. Qrs.) for hutting work.	
	20th		About 6 a.m. Enemy shelled Hd. Qrs. Hutton Camp with high velocity shells and casualties were killed 2 Wren died 21 other ranks - Ingleterre Comforts sent - Cards tonight of Battalion moved into then Hutt huts - B.G. employed on burying 2nd AVENUE - "D" Coy burying & Avenue & improving MIDDLE St. - 2 Platoon "A" Coy Engrs collecting & digging in KNIGHTSBRIDGE & UXBRIDGE Road - Continued work on dugouts - A & C Coys sent back 2 Lieuts S.A.A. returns to front line - 2nd Lieut BAXTER took over command of "D" Coy & Lieut Coy transferred from	
	21st		Sherwood Park to FORCEVILLE - Draft of 1 O.R. joined the Battalion from Base.	

2353 Wt. W25441/1454 700,000 5/15 D. D. & L. A.D.S.S./Forms/C. 2118.

Army Form C. 2118.

WAR DIARY
INTELLIGENCE SUMMARY.
(Erase heading not required.)

(5.)

Place	Date	Hour	Summary of Events and Information	Remarks and references to Appendices
MALLY WOOD O.18.B	October 22-23 24-25		Work continued improving trenches, making dugouts, laying railways etc. Word received that the Divine Operations would not start before 26th. The 1st & 2nd day was definitely fixed as the 28th Oct. Operation orders & instructions for attack received. Battalion to be relieved two nights later not up to knock except two platoons who are to move forward in rear of 153 Inf. Bde. Consolidate return to Oppiere - well humoured and camps rendered very disagreeable by constant rain following on two days' frost.	
	26th		Z day postponed till 30th Oct. Well carried on as usual.	
	28th		2 day postponed till 1st Nov. - Lieutenant Franck - Major J. Tait granted one month's Special leave to Scotland - 2nd Lieut. Q.P.O.R. joined the Battalion from the Base.	
	30th		2 day postponed till 5th Nov. - Work carried on on dugouts etc - "B" Coy was made responsible for the upkeep and improvement of BROADWAY Trench and the ESSEX STREET.	

Casualties during Month.

Officers:
2/Lieut. J. M. Graham - to CALAIS on Draft Conducting Officers.
2m. Lt. Lieut. Clark - KHAIRE - for duty.

O.R.
Killed 2
Wounded 21
Wounded (at duty) 8.
Sick 60
Injured 3 (1 died of wounds)

Reinforcements.
Officers Nil -
O.R - 9 - 22/10/16
" 9 - 29/10/16

Strength at 31/10/16
6 Officers 44
O.R. 856

Allenby Lieut.
Captain 1/5 B. The Royal Scots (Marries).

APPENDIX I

SECRET.   Copy No. 14

1/8th Bn. THE ROYAL SCOTS (Pioneers),

OPERATION ORDER No. R.4.

by Lieut.-Col. W.GEMMILL, D.S.O., Commanding.

1st October, 1918.

1.   The Battalion and Divisional Salvage Company will move to-morrow into the Vth Corps area, and will be billeted in THIEVRES.

2.   The Battalion will parade ready to move off at 10 a.m. in the following order:-

            Band
            Cyclists
            Signals
            "D" Company
            "C" Company
            "B" Company
            "A" Company
            Stretcher Bearers
            Divisional Salvage Company
            Lewis Gun handcarts, brigaded under Sgt.
                    Souness.
            Transport.
Head of the column to be at the Orderly Room, facing north.
All details will march with their Companies.

3.   Transport is allotted as under:-

            1 baggage wagon for "A" and "B" Companies.
            1 baggage wagon for "C" and "D" Companies.
            These to take Company mess boxes as well as Officers' kits.
            2 limbers for Lewis Gun magazines (already loaded).
            2 limbers for Quartermaster for stores, Pioneers' &
                    Shoemakers' kit.
            1 limber for Transport Officer.
            1 limber for Headquarters
            1 limber for Orderly Room
            1 limber for Signals and Armourer Sergeant's kit.
            Mess cart for Battalion Headquarters.

   These wagons will report at billets, etc., at 9 a.m. and must be completely loaded by 9-30 a.m.
   Brakesmen will be detailed by companies, etc., as usual.
   Transport Officer will have Officers' horses at their billets in accordance with the above.

4.   Billeting party have proceeded to the new area to-night. The R.Q.M.S. and two of the Quartermaster's staff will cycle on ahead of the column to-morrow to assist the billeting party, bicycles being provided by the Sergeant i/c Cyclists.

5.   No horses are to be stabled on unfinished horse standings.

6.   Refilling Point will be at VAUCHELLES LES AUTHIE on the afternoon of the 2nd October.

7.   Blankets will be rolled in bundles of 10, and labelled and stacked at Company Headquarters, those of all details being dumped at the Orderly Room. Further instructions later.
   Blankets were badly rolled to-day - more attention must be paid to this in future.

8.   Acknowledge.

Issued at   4   p.m.   Adjt., 1/8th Bn.The Royal Scots
Copy No/   (Pioneers).

SECRET.   Copy No. 15

APPENDIX II

1/8th Bn. THE ROYAL SCOTS (Pioneers),

OPERATION ORDER No. K.5,

by LIEUT.-COL. W. GEMMILL, D.S.O., Commanding.

2nd October, 1916.

1. The Battalion and the Divisional Salvage Company will move to-morrow to billets at LOUVENCOURT, the route being through VAUCHELLES LES AUTHIE, as under.

2. The Battalion and the Divisional Salvage Company will parade ready to move off at 10 a.m. in the following order:-

        Band
        Cyclists
        Signals
        "A" Company
        "B" Company
        "C" Company
        "D" Company
        Stretcher Bearers
        Divisional Salvage Company
        Lewis Gun handcarts brigaded.
        Transport.

The head of the column to be on the bridge near the Orderly Room, facing south.

All details will march with their Companies.

Markers from the four companies, Stretcher Bearers and Divisional Salvage Company will report to the Regimental Sergeant-Major on the bridge at 9-40 a.m. Companies, etc., will fall in on their markers.

3. The allotment of transport for the move will be the same as for to-day (vide O.O. No. K.4 dated 1st Oct.1916.).

These wagons will report at billets, etc., at 9 a.m. and must be completed loaded by 9-30 a.m. They will then return and be formed up near the Church.

Brakesmen will be detailed as usual.

Officers' horses to be at their billets in accordance with the above.

The Transport Officer will arrange to have the route reconnoitred early to-morrow morning and will report to the Orderly Room by 9-30 a.m. at the latest if he considers the hills on the route as laid down in para. 1 too steep for the Transport.

4. The Quartermaster's staff will report to Lieut R.Weir at the Town Major's Office at LOUVENCOURT at 9-30 a.m. to-morrow to assist in billeting. Bicycles for this purpose will be provided by the Sergeant i/c Cyclists.

5. Blankets of all companies and Divisional Salvage Company will be rolled in bundles of 10, labelled and stacked outside their Company Headquarters, those of details being stacked outside the Medical Officers' Inspection Room, by 8 a.m.

2 men per Company and Divisional Salvage Company will be detailed as loading party and guard.

Blankets will be moved by motor lorry as under:-
Blankets of "A", "B" and "C" Companies will be loaded on the lorry at Company Headquarters at 8 a.m. Company guards detailed will accompany the lorry which will proceed to LOUVENCOURT and dump the blankets. The lorry will then return here and take on the second journey blankets from "D" Company, all details and Divisional Salvage Company, and, in addition, the Salvage Company Stores.

2.

8. Acknowledge.

(signature)

Lieut.,
Issued at 1030 p.m.   Adjt., 1/8th Bn. The Royal Scots
(Pioneers).

Copy No. 1 Adjutant for Commanding Officer.
         2 Headquarters.
         3 O.C. "A" Company.
         4 O.C. "B" Company.
         5 O.C. "C" Company.
         6 O.C. "D" Company.
         7 Medical Officer.
         8 Transport Officer.
         9 Quartermaster.
        10 Signals.
        11 Regtl.-Sergt.-Major.
        12 Cyclists.
        13 Divisional Gas Officer.
        14 Divisional Salvage Company.
        15 File.

SECRET.   Copy No. 16

APPENDIX III

1/8th Bn. THE ROYAL SCOTS (Pioneers),

OPERATION ORDER No. M.6.

by Lieut.-Col. W.GEMMILL, D.S.O., Commanding.

                                                  4th October, 1916.

1.   The Battalion and the Divisional Salvage Company will move to-day, 4th instant, to billets at COURCELLES AU BOIS and COLINCAMPS, Headquarters, "B" and "C" Companies and Divisional Salvage Company being billeted at COURCELLES, "A" and "D" Companies at COLINCAMPS - the route being via HENENCOURT.

2.   (a) The Battalion will parade as under ready to move off at 1-15 p.m. to-day 4th inst. - Cyclists, Signals, "A", "D", "B" and "C" Companies, details, Salvage Company and Transport.

    (b) Markers will report to the Regimental Sergeant-Major at 12-45 p.m. at the N.E.F.Canteen near the Church and will be formed up on the BUS Road just clear of the village. Companies will fall in on their markers not before 1 p.m. A cyclist will be posted at the Canteen to direct Companies to their markers.

    (c) The Transport Officer will arrange to have his Transport in position before the Battalion forms up.

    (d) Lewis Gun handcarts will march in rear of their Companies.

    (e) The Medical Officer will detail a section of stretcher bearers to accompany each Company.

3.   (a) Transport is allotted as under:-

        * 1 baggage wagon for "A" and "D" Companies.
        * 1 baggage wagon for "B" and "C"   "
          1 limber for Transport Officer.
          2 limbers for Quartermaster, Pioneers' and Shoemakers' kit.
          1 limber for Orderly Room.
          1 limber for Signals and Armourer Sergeant's kit.
        * 1 limber for Headquarters.
          2 limbers for Lewis Gun magazines (already loaded).
        * Mess cart for Headquarters.

    (b) The above will all be loaded and return to the Transport lines by 12 noon. Those marked * will be loaded by 12-30 p.m. and join the Transport on the road.

4.   The N.C.O. i/c Lewis Gunners must arrange a redistribution of Lewis Gun magazines on the 2 limbers if necessary, i.e., those of "A" and "D" Companies on one, "B" and "C" Companies on the other.

5.   Blankets will be rolled in bundles of 10, labelled and stacked at Company Headquarters by 12 noon.
      G.S.wagons to move these have been allotted as under:-

        1st wagon - "A" and "D" Company blankets.
        2nd   "   - "B" and "C" Coys. Headquarters & details blankets.
        3rd   "   - Salvage Company blankets and stores.

    These will all report at 12 noon. After loading up, they will join Transport on the BUS Road, falling in in rear of the baggage wagons.

6.   On arrival at COURCELLES, "A" and "D" Companies will continue their march to COLINCAMPS, their affiliated Transport accompanying them. Captain T.S.Mitchell will be in command of the half Battalion.

7./

2.

7. Transport lines are provisionally fixed at BUS LES ARTOIS. Companies will keep cookers and tool wagons at their billets, if the situation permits, but horses will return to the Transport lines.

8. Refilling Point for 4th instant will be at 10-30 a.m. on the LOUVENCOURT – BUS LES ARTOIS Road.

9. Acknowledge.

Issued at 10 a.m.

Lieut.,
Adjt., 1/8th Bn. The Royal Scots
(Pioneers).

Copy No. 1 Adjutant for Commanding Officer.
2 Headquarters.
3 O.C. "A" Company.
4 O.C. "B" Company.
5 O.C. "C" Company.
6 O.C. "D" Company.
7 Medical Officer.
8 Transport Officer.
9 Quartermaster.
10 Regtl. Sergeant-Major.
11 Signals.
12 Cyclists.
13 N.C.O. i/c Lewis Gunners.
14 Divisional Gas Officer.
15 Divisional Salvage Company.
16 File.

APPENDIX IV

SECRET.   Copy No. 14

1/8th Bn. THE ROYAL SCOTS (Pioneers),

WARNING ORDER.

16th October, 1916.

1. Orders have been received that the Battalion will be ready to hand over on short notice to the 31st Division.

2. The Transport Officer will send the following immediately after dinner:-
    (a) "A" and "D" Company tool wagons to COLINCAMPS. These will be loaded up this afternoon and returned to the Transport lines.
    (b) "C" Company tool wagons to Company Headquarters. These will be left there and horses will return to Transport lines.
    (c) 1 limber to COLINCAMPS to load up "A" and "D" Company Lewis Gun magazines.
        The limber presently loaded with "B" Company Lewis Gun magazines will be sent to "C" Company Headquarters, where it will take on "C" Company magazines.
        Both of these will return to the Transport lines.

3. O.C. "B" Company will have his tool wagons loaded up at once.

4. The Quartermaster will arrange to cut down his stores as far as possible.

5. Acknowledge.

                                            Lieut.,
Issued at 12.30 p.m.   Adjt.,1/8th Bn.The Royal Scots
                                            (Pioneers).

Copy No. 1 - Adjutant for C.O.
          2 - O.C. "A" Company.
          3 - O.C. "B" Company.
          4 - O.C. "C" Company.
          5 - O.C. "D" Company.
          6 - Headquarters.
          7 - Medical Officer.
          8 - Transport Officer.
          9 - Quartermaster.
         10 - Reserve of Officers.
         11 - Signals.
         12 - N.C.O. i/c Lewis Gunners.
         13 - Regtl. Sergeant-Major.
       ✓ 14 - File.

S E C R E T.   Copy No. 16

                1/8th. Bn. THE ROYAL SCOTS (Pioneers).
            AMENDMENT TO OPERATION ORDERS No. K.V.
            ─────────────────────────────────────

                                                17th October, 1916.

        In para. 2 (a) add "1 Aeroplane wagon for Officers' kits,
etc."

                                        [signature]
                                                    Lieut.,
Issued at 9 p.m.   Adjt..1/8th Bn.The Royal Scots
                                                        (Pioneers).
Copies to all recipients of Operation Orders.

2.

OPERATION ORDER No. K-4.

Copy No. 1 Adjutant for Commanding Officer.
          2 Headquarters.
          3 O.C. "A" Company.
          4 O.C. "B" Company.
          5 O.C. "C" Company.
          6 O.C. "D" Company.
          7 Medical Officer.
          8 Transport Officer.
          9 Quartermaster.
         10 Signals.
         11 Regtl. Sergt.-Major.
         12 Divisional Gas Officer.
         13 Divisional Salvage Company.
         14 File.

APPENDIX V

SECRET.   Copy No. 16

1/8th Bn. THE ROYAL SCOTS (Pioneers).

OPERATION ORDER No. R.7.

by Lieut.-Col. W.GEMMILL, D.S.O., Commanding.

17th October, 1918.

Ref: Sheet 57.d. 1/40,000.

1. The Battalion and the Divisional Salvage Company will move to-morrow, 18th instant, from present area to billets in Wood P.18.d., marching independently.

2. (a) Battalion Headquarters, "C" Company, Details billeted in COURCELLES, and Divisional Salvage Company will parade at 9-45 a.m. and march via BERTRANCOURT and BUS.

   (b) "A" and "B" Companies will march from COLINCAMPS by platoons at 5 minutes intervals, the leading platoon to move off at 9-45 a.m. - route via Cross Roads P.8.b./7.c. - MAILLY-MAILLET. O.C. "A" Company will be in command.

   (c) "D" Company will move off from LOUVENCOURT at 10 a.m. - route via ACHEUX - FORCEVILLE.

   (d) Transport (less vehicles accompanying above columns), party of 1 Officer and 24 other ranks of "A" Company and Reserve of Officers, will leave BUS LES ARTOIS in time to be at the Cross Roads in BERTRANCOURT at 10-30 a.m., where they will fall in in rear of the column marching from COURCELLES.

3. The Transport Officer will send vehicles and horses as under:-
   (a) To be at COLINCAMPS by 8-30 a.m. -
       Horses for "A" and "B" Company cookers, 1 water cart and chargers for Os.C. "A" and "B" Companies.
   (b) To be at COURCELLES by 8 a.m. -
       One Baggage Wagon (for kits of "C" Company and H'dqrs. Officers).
       Mess Cart.
       Horses for "C" Company cooker and tool wagons, medical cart and O.C. "C" Company's charger.
       The 2 limbers already at COURCELLES are allotted to:-
           (i) Orderly Room, and Shoemakers and Tailors kit.
           (ii) Signals and Pioneer Sergeant's stores.
       Horses for these and water cart are already at COURCELLES.
   (c) To be at LOUVENCOURT by 9-30 a.m. -
       1 limber to take Officers' kits, etc.
   (d) At BUS LES ARTOIS.-
       1 limber for Quartermaster for stores.
       1 limber for Reserve of Officers' & Armourer Sergeant's kit.
       1 limber for Transport Officer.
       2 limbers with Lewis Gun magazines, already loaded.

4. Transport from COLINCAMPS will be loaded up and returned to COURCELLES by 9-30 a.m. and join Headquarters column there.

5. If blankets cannot be packed on transport, they must be carried on the men, mackintosh capes being loaded on wagons.

6. Companies will detail the necessary brakesmen, and Lieut Todd's party providing brakesmen for transport moving from BUS as the Transport Officer may require.

7. Strict attention will be paid to march discipline.

8. Officers Commanding Companies Officer i/c Reserve of Officers and the Transport Officer will hand over tents and shelters in situ and obtain receipts from Town Majors, receipts to be forwarded to the Orderly Room on arrival.

9. Details of Cyclists, Signals and Stretcher Bearers will march

with the Companies to which they are at present attached.

10. Acknowledge.

[signature]

Lieut.,

Issued at 7.45 p.m.　　　Adjt., 1/8th Bn. The Royal Scots
　　　　　　　　　　　　　　　　　　　　　(Pioneers).

Copy No. 1 - Adjutant for C.O.
        2 - Headquarters.
        3 - O.C., "A" Company.
        4 - O.C., "B" Company.
        5 - O.C., "C" Company.
        6 - O.C., "D" Company.
        7 - Medical Officer
        8 - Transport Officer.
        9 - Quartermaster.
      10 - Regtl. Sergeant-Major.
      11 - Signals.
      12 - Cyclists.
      13 - N.C.O. i/c Lewis Gunners.
      14 - Divisional Salvage Company.
      15 - Reserve of Officers.
      16 - File.

Army Form C. 2118.

WAR DIARY
or
INTELLIGENCE SUMMARY
(Erase heading not required.)

P/51

Vol 21

18 R&f

Place	Date	Hour	Summary of Events and Information	Remarks and references to Appendices

Reproduced

War Diary
of
11th Bn. The Royal Scots (Lothian)
From 1st November 1916 to 30th November 1916

Volume 25

Army Form C. 2118.

WAR DIARY
INTELLIGENCE SUMMARY.
(Erase heading not required.)

Place	Date	Hour	Summary of Events and Information	Remarks and references to Appendices
MALLEY WOOD Camp. P.18.6.10.30	NOVEMBER 1st 2nd 3rd		Work on Road at the time included:- A.Coy - Making R.A.M.C. Dressing Station at UXBRIDGE Road, Soup Kitchen in SUNKEN ROAD, dumps in NORTH ALLEY - N° 3 Platoon still on railway - N° 1 Platoon Building Latt-house & Canteen ; B.Coy. clearing BROADWAY and ESSEX STREET - C.Coy. clearing FETHARD STREET and BROOK STREET :- D.Coy. enlarging DEATH-TRAP dugout & making second entrance and STAIRWAY & clearing SEAFORTH TRENCH. - Z' day was postponed to November 7th -	
	4th		Captain W.H. INCH 1/4th the Battalion on appointment 8th 2nd in command of 1/4th SEAFORTH HIGHLANDERS, 154 Inf Bde. -	
	5th		The Wild Battalion was notified the day Word received that Z' day might be November 9th -	
	9th		Word received that Z day would be November 13th :- Wild Battalion employed digging new Communication trench from junction of 2nd AVENUE and 88th Trench to Post-end of BEVINGTON STREET. Trench was 5 feet deep, 2 feet wide at the foot and had a slope of 4/1 and a wide berm on either side. - Draft of 10 O.R. joined Battalion from Base on 7th inst. -	
	10-11th		Battalion employed clearing front line - Owing to muddy front line becoming quite impassable, having in most parts to liquid mud. All that was required was, to clear him sufficiently to enable men to pass right-along it - and to stay in it for about 2 hours (1/2 night) and then leave the trench and the parapet for the we-work. - Draft of 7 O.R. joined the Battalion from the Base. -	

2353 Wt. W3544/1454 700,000 5/15 D. D. & L. A.D.S.S./Forms/C. 2118.

WAR DIARY
INTELLIGENCE SUMMARY

Army Form C. 2118.

Place	Date	Hour	Summary of Events and Information	Remarks and references to Appendices
MAILLY Wood Camp. P.18.c.10.30	NOVEMBER	11th	Corporal J.S. Stahl 'B' Coy granted a commission direct into the Battalion and posted to 'A' Coy.	
		12th	Zero hour fixed for 5.45 a.m. on 13th. Battalion kept until night 13th except following parties:- A Coy. - 10 Officers & 45 O.R. to work at Tunnels A.B.& C. after they knocked down at Zero transit with Burman hut. B Coy. - 10 Officers & 45 men to accompany attack & carry up ammunition, bombs and consolidate final Objective. 2 First Battle and 4 Carrying Parties - 'C' Coy. One Platoon to work on Sap S- small communication trench to Summer line - O.C. Coy's Platoon - Sap R - also making C.T. between C.T. Luman & Sap R - All above parties moved up on night of 12/13. 6 Lt. Porter to fire Zero hour. - (Operation Orders attached) Above parties returned at various times this day and night. - 2/Lieut. W. Lawson i/c Carrying Party at Sap S wounded; 2/Lieut. G.D. Wilson i/c Carrying Party at Sap R wounded. 2 Officers for money C.T. & left Sap R & Sap S failed and Platoon had to start digging C.T. but neither were completed. B Coy. parties had worked until night when they went up to consolidate Green Line. 2nd Lieut. BEAUMONT HAMEL. An Platoon 17th Coy. 2nd Lt. Upham MAILLY - AUCHONVILLERS Road with 11 Field Coys. 2 Platoon Y.C. Coy employed day with A.G. permanent railway platoon (Lieut Owens) after clearing ESSEX STREET trench towards BEAUMONT HAMEL. Two Platoons 17th D.G. worked up at night to	App. I.
	Night 13/14th			

Army Form C. 2118.

WAR DIARY
INTELLIGENCE SUMMARY.
(Erase heading not required)

(3.)

Place	Date	Hour	Summary of Events and Information	Remarks and references to Appendices
MAILLY WOOD Camp P.18.c.10.30.	NOVEMBER night 13/14		Continue the communication trench from Sap R to the German front line — This has furnished the trench dug to the CRATER and to the front German line in the Platoon of 'D' Coy. went up to continue the communication trench at Sap S which had been started by 'C' Coy Platoon. This has not however completed this night —	
	14		Two Platoons of 'B' Coy went up to finish the communication trench at Sap S and succeeded in digging it through to the front German trench. C. Coy. sent up two platoons to assist in consolidation of YELLOW line (Serre Objective) under 2/Lt Field G. R.E. 2/Lieut. J.B. DODS who has built this party been wounded — 'D' Coy. sent one Platoon to lend up wiring and has the talk formed from AUCHONVILLERS halt a view to extending the to German front trench railway by night. For this task 'D' Coy sent up two platoons at night to work along its permanent railway platoon. Two Platoons of 'B' Coy. were sent to work with 1/1 Field Coy. R.E. repairing the AUCHONVILLERS - BEAUMONT Road. Filling shell holes — an underpass etc. Two Platoons of 'A' Coy. + the Platoon of 'C' Coy. all under Capt. T.B. MITCHELL were placed at disposal of 152 Inf. Bde. and were ordered of O.B.C. 152 Bde went up to consolidate MUNICH Trench. On arrival at it's position, it was found that the enemy were still holding this trench. Capt. MITCHELL therefore decided to dig a new trench about 200 yards west of MUNICH Trench, extending from	

WAR DIARY

INTELLIGENCE SUMMARY

Army Form C. 2118.

Place	Date	Hour	Summary of Events and Information	Remarks and references to Appendices
HAWLEY WOOD Camp P.18.C.8.10.30.	NOVEMBER	from	LEAVE AVENUE on the EAST and to cover the divisional front. However, this was nearly completed when Capt. MITCHELL received word that this should not be used as a jumping-off place by the attacking troops the following morning. Instead of cutting a firestep therefore 2 cut steps up were the parapet all along the trench which actually ran from Q.6.C.20.40 to Q.6.C.45.85. He also cut a communication trench back to join LEAVE AVENUE from the WEST.	
		15th	A party of "A" Coy. west of to carry on repair to BEAUMONT Road. "B" Coy. to the eastward end of R.E. Plank Road. Permanent railway platoon was employed all day furthering R.E. Stores up the Railway from AUCHONVILLERS to Railhead which was formed about 70 yards from Post Sierra front line at about Q.10.b.70.50.	
		Night 15/16	The wild of "C" Coy. along with one platoon of "A" (replacing party which was employed as above) continued preparing tracks and laying roadway towards BEAUMONT HAMEL. They met a number of shell holes etc but was especially shelled and disposed. A platoon of "A" Coy. went out to work on BEAUMONT Road. "B" + "D" Coys. were placed at the disposal of O.C. 154 Inf. Bde. who had taken over the line from 152 + 153 Bdes. to be employed under his orders. There was that "D" Coy. was to extend to trench dug by Arty. the previous night (called NEW MUNICH trench) due NORTH to join up with the 2nd Division on the left.	

Army Form C. 2118.

WAR DIARY
INTELLIGENCE SUMMARY. (5)

Place	Date	Hour	Summary of Events and Information	Remarks and references to Appendices
MAILLY WOOD Camp. P.16.B.10.30	NOVEMBER Night 15/16		B.G. moved to cut saps from NEW MUNICH Trench to MUNICH Trench. If the task was found to be held by us. This did not prove to be the case, and in the afternoon of Brigadier having returned, little work was done - Hostile Shelling was not heavy.	
	16th		Lieut. TODD's Platoon ('A' Co.) which had hitherto being working under the D.O.R.E. building half-hour shelters, has now left-up from FORCEVILLE and sent out to carry on the work of clearing the BEAUMONT Road with the 1/1 Fld. Co. R.E. -	
	Night 16/17		9 O.R. of H.E.R. JONES and 2/Lieut. J.C. TAYLOR joined the Battalion 14th inst. and have posted to D & C Co's respectively. Draft of 13 other ranks joined from I.T. Base - 3 platoons of 'D' Co. under Lieut. R. WEIR moved up after dinner to dugouts in SEAFORTH TRENCH where they were to remain over night - they were under the 154 Inf. Bde. for work. Owing to the failure of the attack on MUNICH Trench, no work was possible - Lieut. WEIR was killed by a shell striking the dugout in which he was sheltering in BEAUMONT HAMEL during hostile barrage -	
	17th		2 platoons of 'A' Co. were employed repairing BEAUMONT Road - 2 platoons of 'C' Co on railway which ran extended almost up to the SUNKEN ROAD at Q.11.a.70.30. - Lieut. TODD's Platoon moved up from FORCEVILLE and accomodated in dugouts in Wood - employed on BEAUMONT Road. 3 platoon of 'D' Co. returned from dugouts in SEAFORTH TRENCH to Wood -	

WAR DIARY of INTELLIGENCE SUMMARY

Army Form C. 2118.

Place	Date	Hour	Summary of Events and Information	Remarks and references to Appendices
MAILLY WOOD Camp. P.19.P.10.30	NOVEMBER 17th		Word received that on relief the Division would be allotted to the CAMPLES area and that the Battalion would be employed erecting accommodation for schools, training billets etc.	(6)
	night 17/18th		1 platoon of "B" G. went up to assist field ovens with railway which was completed this night as far as the SUNKEN ROAD at Q.11.P.70.30. in BEAUMONT-HAMEL. Remainder of "B" G. (3 platoons) and 2 platoons of "A" G. worked under 1/1 field G. R.E. on BEAUMONT Road. It was found impossible to move Lieut. WEIR'S body to a cemetery - he was accordingly left where he was buried - Q.11.A.70.75 - L'BEAUMONT-HAMEL. A cross was erected and the grave railed in. Draft of 3 O.R. joined from the Base.	
	18th night 18/19th		By the Battalion was ordered to erect 1/2 D.E. of contributing a Strong Point - at the NORTH-EASTERN end of BEAUMONT-HAMEL about Q.5.a.80.80 - Two Platoons "C" were detailed for digging the hole and two platoons of "C" and "D" for wiring it. The platoons left Camp at 11 p.m. - A chief casualty of this platoon of "O.C." was not met with at 2 a.m. to complete the digging and consolidating of the actual hole. Owing to the darkness the night and the ground now ill had was considerably hampered and was not finished. The platoon of "A" G. went out to carry on hill on the BEAUMONT Road with the 1/1 2nd G.R.E. "B" G. went up in the afternoon to complete wiring of new strong point - stores for which had been previously carried	

WAR DIARY / INTELLIGENCE SUMMARY

(7)

Army Form C. 2118.

Place	Date	Hour	Summary of Events and Information	Remarks and references to Appendices
MAILLY WOOD Camp P.18.e.10.30	NOVEMBER			
	19th		H.Q. Runt Orm' platoon from AUCHONVILLERS. 'B' Co. completed moving, but did not get half Kamp till 1 a.m. – An platoon of 'A' Coy. went out at midnight. Continued digging and improving the new strong Point – Working list 2/2 Field Co. R.E.	
	night 19/20			
	20th		2 Platoons of 'A' Co. continued work on BEAUMONT Road.	
	night 20/21		2 Platoons of 'D' Co. went out to inform HARPER Strong Point (O.S.a.80.50) – 'C' Co. sent other parties. Co. men each went 2 platoons BURNET to man all the strong points in the defences of BEAUMONT–HAMEL — viz. BURN WORK, CAMPBELL WORK, HAMILTON WORK, all working & carrying with Return with R.E. Field Companies. Learn respond to Battalion at Mailly Keep. Rather low. – viz. – 1 officer + 3 O.R. to Ludendorf + 2 O.R. to Saturdays.	
	21st		2 Platoons of 'A' to BEAUMONT Road. – Orders received that on relief the ½party of the Division would be transferred to the II Corps. – Pioneer Battalion to move fore line to forward quarters. Orders received that a Goufin ready tower at station where. 'D' Co. formed Lieut. W.B. WALLACE Posted to D.S. in 2nd. & Command I.C.	
	22nd		D. G. moved at 10.0 a.m. to Divisional Headquarters at VINA HILL near AVELUY – W.24.b.2.5 (Sheet 57D 1/40000.), taking with them then tool waggon and cookers. They will in report to the Divisional Headquarters for orders accommodation. – They were not allotted at	

WAR DIARY
INTELLIGENCE SUMMARY

Army Form C. 2118.

(8.)

Place	Date	Hour	Summary of Events and Information	Remarks and references to Appendices
MAILLY WOOD CAMP R.18.8.10.30	NOVEMBER 22nd		New Headquarters of 4th Canadian Division was entered by the Bn. Bn. G. returned from Battalion Hdqrs. at AUCHONVILLERS Station & Division at Div. & MAILLY-MAILLET. O vas of relief, but stopped & found am - 72 Total casualties in the Battalion since commencement of operations on 13th NOV (to 21st) are :- Officers - 1 Killed : 3 Wounded - Total 4 Other ranks - 1 Killed : 35 Wounded : 12 Wounded (at duty) - Total 48 Total casualties : all ranks - 52.	
	23rd		Andre received letter to confirm would move on 23rd to new area the billets at USNA HILL. W.24.b.95 (on AVELUY - LA BOISELLE Road) "B" G. aboard J.D. G. Lieut. OVENS' Platoon headed on Trench Tramway to "/3 Borden Field Cy RE (7th Division) and moved back from AUCHONVILLERS to MAILLY Wood - Lieut. C.H. SHAW returned to the Battalion from work under C.R.E. - 2 Lieut. F.A. BURNET said no 5153 of Bde. Hdrs Am. to instruct the Battalion of that Brigade is artificial coverings.	
	24th		B Coy any moved at 10 a.m. to USNA HILL to await O.C.G. left with them - Lt Colonel Gemmell left in there route learnt England. Major Gold assumed command of the Battalion. Andre received that the Battalion would move more from	

WAR DIARY
INTELLIGENCE SUMMARY.

Army Form C. 2118.

Place	Date	Hour	Summary of Events and Information	Remarks and references to Appendices
MAILLY WOOD Camp R.16.c. F.10.30	NOVEMBER 24th		Area on 27th Nov., Hd. Qrs. and 3 Coys A.T. at OUILLERS Huts, 1 Coy at OUILLERS POST Huts. Transports at CROMWELL Huts (W.18.a.5.7) and Quartermasters Stores at AVELUY.	
	25th		Operation Order for move issued (Copy attached) - Hd. Qrs, B,C+D Coys, to go to OUILLERS Huts, "A" Coy to OUILLERS Post Huts.	APP. II.
OUILLERS HUTS X.13.c. F.4.9.	27th		Battalion moved to new area Bn. could not get into huts till 5 p.m. - Brigadier of Battalion a/k the move - Hd Qrs + 3 Coys (A.B+C) at OUILLERS HUTS (X.13.c.F.4.9) - D.Coy remaining at USNA HILL. All other Billets are NISSEN Crinder Huts and are extremely comfortable.	
	28th		Lt. OVENS reconnoitered Twist Railway. Lt. MAXWELL surveyed Roads in forward area - Capt. MORGAN R.A.M.C. (M.D.) went on leave - Capt. McDOUGALL (9 N.M.N.J. Field Amb.) has run duties of M.O. - B.Coy. worked by night - cleaning & draining Road from R.35.d.4.5 to Bde. Hd. Qrs. at Rag Cutting.	
	29th		1 Platoon of A.Coy. camouflaged Huts at X.8.d. - Remainder of A.Coy. repairing tank roadway to Bde. Hd. Qrs. (K.29 central). B.Coy. as march; C.Coy carried up supply of memay material for work on front line.	
	30th		During night 29-30/11 C.Coy started wiring of Front Line, working parties left at night. Unit for A+B Coys. as usual - Fatigue parties of 100 men each have supplied to amm'n. work on roads and to carry up wire etc. Lieut R.B. OVENS awarded the Military Cross.	

Army Form C. 2118.

WAR DIARY
INTELLIGENCE SUMMARY.
(Erase heading not required.)

(10.)

Place	Date	Hour	Summary of Events and Information	Remarks and references to Appendices
OVILLERS HUTS. X.113.b.4.9	NOVEMBER 30th		No. 8629 Sergt. A. JOHNSTONE – the D.C.M. – Ltr. for gallantry and good service on 13th November 1916 + subsequent days. – Casualties during Month. After: Killed – Lieut. R. WEIR. Wounded – 2/Lieut. U. LOWSON (since died of wounds). 2/Lieut. E.O. WILSON. 2/Lieut. J.B. DODS. O.R. – 2/Lieut. W.T. SRAY. To Hospital – 2/Lieut. C.C. SCOTT. O.R. Killed 2; Died of wounds 1; Wounded 38; Wounded (gas) 1; Wounded (shell shock) 1; Wounded (at duty) 15; To hospital – sick 63; To Hospital – injured 1. Officers. 4. 3. Other ranks. 798. Strength at 12 noon 30/11/16	
			Reinforcements. 1st – 5 O.R. 3rd – 2 " 7th – 10 " 10th – 7 " 15th – 8 " 18th – 3 " 35 "	

Richard Trent
Adjutant, 1/6th Seaforth (Pioneers)

S E C R E T.   APPENDIX I.   Copy No. 11

1/8th Bn. THE ROYAL SCOTS (Pioneers),

OPERATION ORDER No. K.8,

by Lieut.-Col. W. GEMMILL, D.S.O., Commanding.

12th November, 1916.

1. Parties from "A", "B", "C" and "D" Companies will parade to-night in accordance with instructions issued to Officers concerned for work in connection with to-morrow's offensive Operations.

2. The Medical Officer will detail stretcher bearers as under:-

   4 Stretcher Bearers to parade with "B" Company at 2.15 a.m. on 13th instant.
   2 Stretcher Bearers to parade with "D" Company at 12 midnight to-night.

3. Battalion Headquarters and the remainder of the Battalion will remain in present quarters.

4. All men detailed for work to-night as per paras. 1 and 2 above will go to bed after tea and remain there until time for parade.

5. The following special rations have been issued:-

   Rum - chewing gum - chocolate - special breakfast ration for to-morrow.

6. Specially detailed runners for each Company will wear the letter "R" (already issued) on the left sleeve above the elbow. This will enable these men to use any trench in any direction they may require without being held up by the Trench Traffic Control Posts.

7. From 12 noon to-day until 4 a.m. on 13th inst., a GAS ALERT will be considered to be on. All troops within 1,500 yards of the line will wear their box respirators accordingly.

8. Officers i/c parties will report at the Orderly Room immediately before moving off and also on return from work.

9. With reference to to-morrow's Operations, the Commanding Officer wishes to say that he knows Officers and men will remember that they belong to a Battalion which has a great reputation to keep up and that they will one and all do their best to carry out the duties allotted to them.

10. Acknowledge.

                                                        Lieut.,
Issued at 3.45 p.m.   Adjt., 1/8th Bn. The Royal Scots
                                              (Pioneers).

Copy No. 1 - Adjutant for C.O.   Copy No. 7. - Medical Officer.
        2 - Major Todd   8 - Transport Officer.
        3 - O.C., "A" Company.   9 - Quartermaster.
        4 - O.C., "B" Company.   10 - Sergeant-Major.
        5 - O.C., "C" Company.   11 - War Diary.
        6 - O.C., "D" Company.   12 - File.

SECRET.　　　　　　　　APPENDIX II.　　　　　　　　Copy No. 78.

1/8th Bn. THE ROYAL SCOTS (Pioneers).

OPERATION ORDER No. X.9.

by Major J.A.TODD, Commanding.

25th November, 1918.

Reference Maps:-
57c.S.E.) 1/20,000.
57d.S.E.)

1. The Battalion will move into new billets in the II Corps Area on 27th November in accordance with the attached March Table.

2. The allotment of transport for "A" and "C" Companies and details is as under:-

   1 "B" Coy. tool wagon to each of "A" and "C" Coys. for blankets
   1 Baggage wagon for kits of "A" and "C" Company officers.
   1 Baggage wagon for Headquarters officers' kits and blankets of all details.
   1 Limbered wagon for Battalion Headquarters.
   1 Limbered wagon for Orderly Room and Signals.
   1 Limbered wagon for Shoemakers', Tailors' & Pioneers' kits.
   1 Limbered wagon for Transport Officer.
   2 Limbered wagons for Quartermaster.
   2 Limbered wagons for Lewis Gun Magazines (already loaded).

3. The Transport Officer will arrange to have these wagons, together with horses for cookers, watercart, medical cart, and chargers at the Camp in suitable time in accordance with the attached March Table.

4. O.C. "D" Company will arrange that his 2 tool wagons are used to move all tools and blankets of "B" and "D" Companies to new billets.

5. The watercart presently at Battalion Headquarters will accompany "A" Company and remain at OVILLERS POST Huts on completion of the move.

6. On completion of the move, Company tool wagons, cookers, watercarts and medical cart will remain with Companies. Remainder of transport will return to Transport Lines at CROMWELL HUTS - W.18.a.5.7.

7. The Quartermaster's Stores, Battalion Post Office, etc., will be in AVELUY.

8. O.C. "A" Company will arrange to go round the Camp with the Camp Commandant on the morning of the 27th and obtain from him a duplicate "clean" receipt - that the Camp is left clean and tidy. One copy will be forwarded to the Orderly Room, the other being handed to the Camp Commandant.

9. The Transport Officer will go forward on 26th inst. and secure Transport Lines and billets at CROMWELL HUTS - also Q.M. Stores at AVELUY from the Town Major there.

10. O.C. "D" Company will arrange to obtain billets for Headquarters and 3 Companies at OVILLERS Huts, and for 1 Company at OVILLERS Post Huts, from the Town Major of OVILLERS, and will have guides at the entrances to these Camps to guide Companies to their lines.

11./

MARCH TABLE TO ACCOMPANY OPERATION ORDER NO. K.9.

Date	No.	Company, &c.	From.	To.	Time of starting.	Route.	Remarks.
November 27th	1.	Bn. Headquarters "C" Company Details	MAILLY WOOD CAMP	OVILLERS HUTS.	9-30 a.m.	Via MAILLY-MAILLET, BOUZINCOURT, AVELUY.	To march under orders of O.C. "C" Company.
"	2.	"A" Company	MAILLY WOOD CAMP	OVILLERS POST N.1	10-30 a.m.	As above.	Under O.C. "A" Company
"	3.	"B" Company "D" Company	USNA HILL	OVILLERS HUTS.	10 a.m.		To move under orders of O.C. "B" Company.
"	4.	Bn. Transport (less transport with Companies).	FORCEVILLE	CROMWELL HUTS (N.15.a.5.7.)			To move under orders of transport officer.
"	5.	Quartermaster's Stores, etc.	FORCEVILLE	AVELUY.			

2.

11. Refilling Point will be at W.16.d. - Time 9 a.m.

12. Acknowledge.

[signature]
Lieut.,

Issued at 4 p.m.   Adjt., 1/8th Bn. THE ROYAL SCOTS
(Pioneers).

Copy No. 1 - Adjutant for C.O.   Copy No. 9 - Quartermaster.
       2 - O.C. "A" Company.   10 - Signals.
       3 - O.C. "B" Company.   11 - Cyclists.
       4 - O.C. "C" Company.   12 - Regtl. Sergt.-Major.
       5 - O.C. "D" Company   13 - 51st (H.) Division.
       6 - Headquarters.   14 - Camp Commandant,
       7 - Medical Officer.   MAILLY WOOD.
       8 - Transport Officer.   ✓ 15 - War Diary.
                                        16 - File.

Army Form C. 2118.

WAR DIARY
or
INTELLIGENCE SUMMARY.

CONFIDENTIAL.
No 21(?)
HIGHLAND DIVISION.

Vol 22

19 RS

Confidential.

War Diary
of
1/8th Bn. The Royal Scots (Pioneers).
From 1st December, 1916 to 31st December, 1916

Volume 26

CONFIDENTIAL. Army Form C. 2118.

Nº 21 (A) (1)

HIGHLAND DIVISION.

WAR DIARY

~~INTELLIGENCE SUMMARY.~~

(Erase heading not required.)

Place	Date	Hour	Summary of Events and Information	Remarks and references to Appendices
OVILLERS HUTS. X.13.b.4.9.	DECEMBER 1st		Work on Road: A.Coy. - 3 platoons on fatal midway up to R.29 Central; 1 platoon Camouflaging WOLFE Huts - B.Coy. - repairing the road OBAPAUME Road from POZIERES Sentroads and Nr POZIERES - COURCELETTE Road (R.35 & R.29). C.Coy. training the front-line - D.Coy. at Divisional Headquarters (USNA HILL) emptying into tr. —	
	2nd		This was a whole Holiday for the Battalion and all men were bathed.	
	3rd			
	4th		D.Coy. (less 2 platoons) moved from USNA HILL to OVILLERS Huts - 24 men sent to attached to 260th Bde. R.F.A. to make dugouts. Arrangements made for 2 platoons of D.Coy. under relief. H.E.R.JONES to carry on burying of front-line - A.Coy. & B.Coy. to find parties to fall material up daily to Ammunition dump at COURCELETTE from where Infantry carrying parties take it up to the line -	
	5th		Staff Capt. 9 Gen. joined Battalion -	
	6th		Lieut. & Adjutant J.C. KEMP appointed Staff Captain 9th 153 Infantry Brigade - 2/Lt A.O. JONES appointed Acting Adjutant.	
	7th		2nd Lieut. F.I.S. Sutchel and returned to the Battalion from being home on leave last night. Nº 15 Platoon DCoy. moved from USNA HILL to OVILLERS Huts today. The working party under 2nd Lieut. H.E.R.JONES while working in the front-line in front of COURCELETTE Captured a prisoner, there was a considerable amount of artillery activity but no suffered no casualties.	E.J.

2353 Wt. W2344/1451 700,000 5/15 D. D. & L. A.D.S.S./Forms/C. 2118.

WAR DIARY
or
INTELLIGENCE SUMMARY.

Army Form C. 2118.

Place	Date	Hour	Summary of Events and Information	Remarks and references to Appendices
QUILLERS HUTS X.13.6.4.9.	December 8th			
	9th		The Work of the Battalion was carried on as usual. Major Tait rejoined the Battn: from leave. Lt: Q.M. R.D. Whyman came up with Major Tait. 15th rove his station with this Battn.	
	10th		Work was carried on as usual. Revd: R. Howie Reynolds from leave. 6 O.R. rejoined from the Base. There was a Celebration for the Battn: Batt: & Revd: Reynolds was held in the Central Church at 10.30 A.M. There was Holy Bath & men bathed.	
	11th		A large draft of 300 O.R. joined the Battn: from the Base dept. They were all drawn from 2nd/4th Bns: of Royal Scots 1st 2nd 27th 2/4th & 2/9th; & took to a very good class of men. It was arranged with Bde: to hold a Course of Instruction & Wiring to the Infantry Units in the Bde: 2nd/9th HLI, R Nore, 2Lt: Rutherland, 2nd Lt: J.T. Gray & 2Lt: W.T. Gray Company. Unit to the Bde: Nore 2 Lt: HER Nore 2Lt: Rutherland 2nd Lt: J.T. Gray & 2Lt: W.T. Gray Infantry Unit to the Bde: 29th HE.R Nore 2Lt: Rutherland 2nd Lt: J.T. Gray & 2Lt: W.T. Gray Company will be Instructors. A large working party, drawn from all 4 Companies, while returning from work came under heavy enemy shell fire at R.34. c.7.4. Shut-5Y0 S.E. & suffered Casualties 1st. 1 killed & Wounded.	
	12th		Unit from 153 & 154 Brigade went through a course of Instruction in Wiring today. Pte: McLean of C Coy: who was killed yesterday was buried at our Line Cemetery at 2 P.M.	
	13th		The Trench Railway & Carried forward to R.29 b.5.6. D Coy are employed making Shelter in Sunken Rd R.27 c 7.9. Shelter for 25 men are complete.	

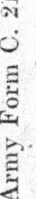

WAR DIARY or INTELLIGENCE SUMMARY

Army Form C. 2118.

(3)

Place	Date	Hour	Summary of Events and Information	Remarks and references to Appendices
OVILLERS HUTS X.13.6.4.9.	DECEMBER 14th		Received intimation to carry Trench Railway to E. MIRAUMONT Rd. A & C Coys are employed on Pys. B Coy Road (COURCELETTE) D Coy in Shelters	
	15th		A Coy's Kitchen is being made in Sunken Rd R.29.c.7.9. & nearing completion, a few men of C Coy are employed on same.	
	16th		Capt Morgan M.O. of this Bn. proceed from leave today. Work on COURCELETTE Rd also handed over today to a Cavalry Pioneer Bn.	
	17th		B Coy: Started shelters for troops in EMIRAUMONT Rd. 2nd Lt. J.T. Gray is reconnoitring thoroughly dugouts in our right & left section of our for the division. Arrangement have been made with the 157 Bde to start a course of training in Wiring under 2nd Lt HERIOT on Monday. A Dugout has been started in COURCELETTE Rd to be used as an advanced dressing Station. B Coy have 12 men & 3 N.C.O's employed on the from the Adj. Capt Mitchell takes over the duties of A.E. 512th Divisional Railway Coy today, providing & supplying as hitherto for forward dumps. A Coy is detailed to maintain Tramway.	
	18th		A draft of 6 O.R arrived from Base today, all men in this draft are rejoining from hospital. D Coy. started clearing, draining & putting in order 10th Divl. Communication Trench.	
	19th		Capt Watson & 2Lt W.J.W. Todd rejoined the batt. today from leave.	

Army Form C. 2118.

WAR DIARY
or
INTELLIGENCE SUMMARY. (A)
(Erase heading not required.)

Instructions regarding War Diaries and Intelligence Summaries are contained in F. S. Regs., Part II. and the Staff Manual respectively. Title pages will be prepared in manuscript.

Place	Date	Hour	Summary of Events and Information	Remarks and references to Appendices
OVILLERS HUTS X.13.b.6.9	DECEMBER 20th		Lt Colonel Gemmill DSO returned from leave today. On the evening of the 19th & again the evening of the 17th with a Hy? Velocity gun. Fortunately there were no casualties or damage although some of the shells landed quite close.	
	21st		Capt Pringle rejoined the battalion from leave today.	
	22nd		A draft of 8 men joined the Bn. from the base.	
	23rd		Today arrangement were made for "C" Coy to work along with the 174th Tunnelling Coy on dugouts in W. MIRAUMONT RD, first shift starts tomorrow. 2Lt H.E.R Jones awarded the Military Cross.	
	24th		This was a holiday for the Bn. although several small parties engaged on urgent work had to be sent out. Bn Church Parade was held in the Sea Tins Church Tent at 9.45 AM but the men had to be dispersed owing to enemy shelling the Camp. RC Service was held to one of the huts at 10.30 AM & C of E Service in the Same Hut at 11.30 AM. About half of the men was billeted during the Course of the day. As arranged "C" Coy started its first shift at 4 PM on Dugouts in W. MIRAUMONT RD.	
	25th		Companies paraded for work as usual. The men got an extra ration of Plum Pudding with their dinner but it has been decided to postpone the usual Xmas dinner of the Bn. until	[signature]

WAR DIARY or INTELLIGENCE SUMMARY. (3)

Place	Date	Hour	Summary of Events and Information	Remarks and references to Appendices
OUILLERS HUTS X.13.b.4.9	DECEMBER			
	25th Contd		The Division is back in rest-billets which how we expect about the 12th of January	
	26th		The Bn. has been instructed by Div. to supervise the work on the COURCELETTE Rd. which is being done by the Cavalry Pioneers. B Coy have sent 3 men to work on a dugout in KINORA TRENCH for Machine Gunners.	
	27th		Intimation received from Division HQrs that the Div. will be relieved by the 2nd Div. on the 12th & 13th of Jany.	
	28th		The work of the Bn. carried on as usual.	
	29th		Capt. McRae & Lt. Brennan returned from leave today.	
	30th		Intimation received from Div. that the relief will start on the 12th from the Div. was moved by stages to the Bruigny St Maelou Area (BUIGNY ST MAELOU) via MARIEUX, BERNAVILLE, YVRENCH & BRAILLY, to all few days march. This was a holiday for the Battalion with the exception of a few parties at work. A draft of 4 O.R. reported from the base today.	

WAR DIARY or INTELLIGENCE SUMMARY

Army Form C. 2118.

Place	Date	Hour	Summary of Events and Information	Remarks and references to Appendices
DIVISIONAL HUTS	December 31st		Casualties during Month	

Officers:- 2nd Lieut. Ck. Snow (to Eng. 17.12.16) ⎫ To Hosp.
   "   J.A. Burnet   ⎬ Sick.
   "   G. Ria   ⎪
   "   A. Davidson   ⎭
   "   C.C. Scott

O. Ranks :-   To Hosp Sick 92
      Killed in Action 1 (Sgt. McLean); Wounded 12;
      Died of Wounds 3; Wounded - at duty 9.

Officers:- 2nd Lieut. C.C. Scott (from Hosp)

Strength:- 40 Officers + 1040 (other Ranks)

Reinforcements:- OR   5   on 1.12.16
          9   3.12.16
          6   8.12.16
       306   11.12.16
          6   18.12.16
          3   22.12.16
          3   24.12.16
          4   31.12.16
        346

A. Jones. 2nd Lieut,
Act. Adj. 1/8th Bn. The Royal Scots
(PIONEERS)

Army Form C. 2118.

CONFIDENTIAL
No 21(A)
HIGHLAND DIVISION.

WAR DIARY
or
INTELLIGENCE SUMMARY.
(Erase heading not required.)

Vol 23

Confidential

War Diary
of
1/5th Bn. the Royal Perth Grouse

From 1st January 1917 to 30 January 1914

Volume No 27.

Army Form C. 2118.

CONFIDENTIAL.
No. 217(?)
HIGHLAND DIVISION.

WAR DIARY
INTELLIGENCE SUMMARY. (1)
(Erase heading not required.)

Instructions regarding War Diaries and Intelligence Summaries are contained in F. S. Regs., Part II. and the Staff Manual respectively. Title pages will be prepared in manuscript.

Place	Date	Hour	Summary of Events and Information	Remarks and references to Appendices
OVILLERS HUTS X.13.b.4.9	JANUARY 1919	12	Work on hand:— A Coy: Divisional Tramways from Poziers Dump to 'C' Dump at R.34 c.T.6. The Tramway from Poziers Dump X.9.6 Central to Centre Way R.34 d.23 was & running order when the Company took over, being a heavy section, harrow gauge track on which a Petrol Tractor was used for haulage. From Centre Way to 'C' Dump the line was relaid by A Coy with a lighter section harrow gauge rail. Dumps were formed at R.29 central & R.24 c.5.3 & the line completed & & running order to 'C' Dump on 25th December. Over this latter section the Centre Way to 'C' Dump the trollies are hand pushed. This branch line for Artillery Battery was also laid, one being completed the other almost so. The laying of this line entailed a considerable amount of difficult work as the ground over which it was laid traversed had nothing new or less than a succession of shell holes full to the lip with water. The had filling in & about 300 yds to length of the completion has proved very troublesome as a means of getting material relieved of all work forward to a front which cannot be got to by horse or motor transport. It is calculated that 25 tons of forward every day.	[signature]

WAR DIARY or INTELLIGENCE SUMMARY. (2)

Army Form C. 2118.

Place	Date	Hour	Summary of Events and Information	Remarks and references to Appendices
OUVILLERS HUTS X.13.d.4.9.	JANUARY 1917 1st Cont'd		Work on hand. B Coy: are employed on shelters for the troops in support & making & repair of roads. Shelters In all 16 shelters have been erected & completed 12 eleven in sunken road R.29 central & five in W. MIRAUMONT R.24.c.6.4. These shelters are sound roofed & are built in emplacements cut in the bank full sunken road to what they lie parallel. Each shelter accommodates twelve men. Roads. This Company has also put in repair the road running from X.5.a.3.y towards COURCELETTE. This road was very much broken up by shell fire & this is to be repaired almost daily on this account. It is now however in good order as far as FOUR TREE CORNER, from which point a log road is being made towards COURCELETTE. C Coy: were at first employed wiring our front line but on account of the great difficulty experienced in getting wiring material forward this work was stopped until better arrangements could be made. C Coy were then attached to A Coy: for a time on railway work but are now working with the 174th Tunnelling Coy RE in Dugout & W.MIRAUMONT Rd, & this work is going on satisfactorily. D Coy: for about 10 days on our front. Company &2 1st part of the Coy were employed erecting huts separately putting in order Divisional Headquarters. & the rest, with the exception	C.J.

Army Form C. 2118.

WAR DIARY
or
INTELLIGENCE SUMMARY. (3)
(Erase heading not required.)

Place	Date	Hour	Summary of Events and Information	Remarks and references to Appendices
OUILLERS HUTS X.13.6.4.9.	JANUARY 1917			
	1st Contd		exception of a few men & an H.Q. Coy't at D.H.Qrs. as a maintenance party, the Coy. were employed on the Shelters at B.H.Qs for a few days, but were taken from that work to put on to cut return 104 STREET Communication Trench from Br: Hqrs forward to the front line. The work was carried on under considerable difficulty, finally given up by order of the Division. Then Coy. b was employed erecting shelters to the support line. A working party drawn from the Coy. under Lt. HERSTONE & 2/Lt J.T. GRAY endeavoured to widen TOP/90 June of No Mans Land. Minor works being done by detailed parties as follows.

1 SM & 44 O.R. training dugout for 253 Tr & 260 Tr R.F.A
3 O.R. training M.G. Coys dug out to Hessian Trench
19 O.R. "   R.A.M.C. dugout at COURCELETTE Rd
24 O.R. of men working at R.E. Nashville.
Lt R.A.P. Ritchie & Lt R.B. Owens returned from leave today. The weather still continues very unsettled, rain almost every day with little sunshine in front. | |
| | 2nd | | | [signature] |
| | 3rd | | Work continued as usual. | |

Army Form C. 2118.

WAR DIARY
or
INTELLIGENCE SUMMARY. (H)
(Erase heading not required.)

Instructions regarding War Diaries and Intelligence Summaries are contained in F. S. Regs., Part II. and the Staff Manual respectively. Title pages will be prepared in manuscript.

Place	Date	Hour	Summary of Events and Information	Remarks and references to Appendices
OUILLERS HUTS. X.13.b.49.	January 1917.	4ᵗʰ	Received intimation from Division that representatives from the Pioneer Bn. of the 2nd Division were to visit our Bivouac with the view of meeting them prior to their Bn. relieving our Bn. Information with regard to the front line, when taken over from us probably about the 12/13ᵗʰ of the month. B Coy. is again standing a working party tonight to wire the front line.	
		5ᵗʰ	Four Officers of the De.L.I. Pioneers from the 2nd Division arrived here today when shown over the work to hand as far as it was possible during daylight. They were given an opportunity of discussing with our Coy. Commanders all work on hand, the arrangements of our working parties. The C.R.E. offered also credits our Transport Lorries & Grenades stores. The weather has improved though hard frost at night. Am. Ammunition during the day.	
		6ᵗʰ	A letter of the hour hand to hand treat bullets have come in from Division. Then is no alteration to the tour from the situation already received. The Bn. will travel on the morning of the 12ᵗʰ inst. to an exchange of Bouzincourt by 10·30 AM ready to be billeted to the MARIEUX area for night of 12/13ᵗʰ. A train is available for all extra stores that this will relieve transport considerably.	A.A.

2353 Wt. W2344/1454 700,000 5/15 D. D. & L. A.D.S.S./Forms/C. 2118.

WAR DIARY
INTELLIGENCE SUMMARY (5)

Army Form C. 2118.

Place	Date	Hour	Summary of Events and Information	Remarks and references to Appendices
OUILLERS HUTS X.13.b.4.9	JANUARY 1917			
	7th		First half during day our aeroplanes changing "b" string were driving enemy flights with Gen. Sir Paul of the D.C.L.I. arrived today to understudy them agreeable with the [struck through] Burning of kept reform full light Railway Tramway Ens with a view of taking over Capt. Mitchell took 10% Railway when the Regiment rest. All men were given a Holiday today except a few sent working parties with carrier in reserve. Most of the men used baths that I placed change of underclothing.	
	8th		The following officers joined the Bn. today from the 4th Res. Bn. at home. Capt. A.B. Falconer 2nd Lt A. Mackay, G.R. Fenwick, G. Burns, Two Couplers, A. Munro. Rumour of the moon. Have received intimation from Bn. that an Artillery bombardment of the enemy lines will commence 9 AM tomorrow, will continue for Hr 10:11:12. The bombardment to range toward the Copse or on left.	
	9th		2nd Lt Sharp returned from leave today. The weather is very unsettled. Rain + sleet Gen. will take remedies. All work except will Tramway Rly & shelters on account of heavy bombardment. Two parties have been known regarding the new road in the 12th Bn: The Bn. + b band will visit Parlyle below Bys on bell roads at Bonquement. by Mr Ralrage Bn. next Evader by Bn. Band	A.J.

Army Form C. 2118.

WAR DIARY
or
INTELLIGENCE SUMMARY. (c)

(Erase heading not required.)

Instructions regarding War Diaries and Intelligence Summaries are contained in F. S. Regs., Part II. and the Staff Manual respectively. Title pages will be prepared in manuscript.

Place	Date	Hour	Summary of Events and Information	Remarks and references to Appendices
OVILLERS HUTS. X.13.d.9.	JANUARY 1917			
		10th	Lt Wallace rejoined the Bn. to-day from leave. All men on detached works rejoined the Bn. to-day. Pay Commander, Transport Officer & the Q.master met the C.O. in the orderly room & discussed matters regarding the move back to the rest area.	
		11th	The Bn. was employed during the day preparing for the move tomorrow.	Operation Order for move from Officers & Le Plessier attached. Appendix C9.
		12th	The Bn. paraded at 8 A.M. for the first stage of the march back to rest billets. Transport in the following order at 8.15, Cyclists Advance Gd, band & Coy followed by B. C. & D Coys. Transport bringing up the rear. The Coys marched with a distance of 20 yds between Coys. Coy Cookers bringing up the rear of each Coy. Coys. via road T.2.C1.HER.T.6m was used. A.halt at SARTON when the Bn. was a½ hour for the night. After 1/2 stage march The march was via BOUZENCOURT, FORCEVILLE, ACHEUX & MARIEUX to SARTON a distance of 18 miles over very bad road. Coys cut up with traffic. A halt of an hour was made just outside FORCEVILLE & the men had a hot dinner. At BOUZENCOURT the Div. Railway Coy formed the Bn. to a few men further on the Bn. Band joined in left half in motor lorries & march forward with us cheering the rest of the Journey. 6 Battalions after Dinner served Chocolate. Came over hot & the men kept going day as they marched.	

Army Form C. 2118.

WAR DIARY
or
INTELLIGENCE SUMMARY. (7)
(Erase heading not required.)

Instructions regarding War Diaries and Intelligence Summaries are contained in F. S. Regs., Part II. and the Staff Manual respectively. Title pages will be prepared in manuscript.

Place	Date	Hour	Summary of Events and Information	Remarks and references to Appendices
EN ROUTE FROM QUILLERS to SARTON	12th		Evening then walking up Steep. The head of the column reached SARTON at 3.40 P.M. 2 hours afterwards all the men were in billets & the arrival from Gympanich had ground about billets for the Transport but tea was arranged without much delay. Lt. C.O. expressed himself satisfied with the men marching on, & men getting not showing the march	
SARTON	13th		The Bn. Billet to the 13th at Sarton. Orders were received clearing the stay that the Bn. would march on to next stage of the march at 7AM on the 14th being there of it. Roads at Sarton at 7.30 AM.	
			Finishing BERNAVILLE. The Drum Band played in the village during the afternoon.	
SARTON TO BERNAVILLE	14th		The Bn. paraded at 7 AM moving off at 7.15 in the following order Pipe Band, B.C. Subord. D./Adjt & H. Pl. with 200 yards distance between Corps. There had been a slight fall of snow during the night & it was Cloudy when the Bn. started but cleared up soon after we started. The march was a morning of about 16. Pl. Road surface being good the marching was most easy. There are Pl. 12.? If fast the day was an ideal one for marching. The head halts were made 10 - 18 minutes in every hour with an hour halt between Haichual & Fienfreul for dinner. The Bn. Reached BERNAVILLE at 2 P.M. the billeting party under Major TATHAM & 2 Lt MACKAY having gone ahead to arrange. The men again marched well and any sign of falling out. The road was via the outskirts of DOULLENS, HEM, HARDIVILLE, FIENVILLERS to BERNAVILLE a distance of 14 miles	ag

2353 Wt. W2544/1454 700,000 5/15 D. D. & L. A.D.S.S./Forms/C. 2118.

WAR DIARY
or
INTELLIGENCE SUMMARY.

Army Form C. 2118.

(Erase heading not required.)

Place	Date	Hour	Summary of Events and Information	Remarks and references to Appendices
EN ROUTE BERNAVILLE TO LE PLESSIEL	15th		As day the last stage of the journey was done on Cluch'in, being LE PLESSIEL that the Bn is to billet during training. Orders were received that the Bn had to leave by the Starting Point 15 Bernaville's arrt of M of BERNETS billets by 8.20 A.M. The Bn moved off in the following order C.O.A.B followed by the Valeago Coy transport. The O.P was covered by the Bn itself. The day was splendid for marching, prob. rather got the first mile not such easy to harden the transport. The road taken was thro BERNETS, CANDONVILLE, St RIQUIER, MILLENCOURT to LE PLESSIEL. A distance of 16 miles. An hour halt for dinner was made before entering St RIQUIER & the Bn reached its destination at 3 P.M. The men marching well not a falling out on arriving we found we were the only unit billeted in the place. that we were occupying the billets vacated by the 8th Royal Sussex Reg. However a few of the men billets had beds in them but there were a considerable amount of work to be done before the billets were made really comfortable. The Div: Band were billeted for the night. his but gone to BUNGY St MACLON Environs.	
	16th		The Bn. was employed fitting cloth. equipment shovels & improving billets. C party of 2 2OR under 2 Sr Shaw left here to-day for PORT LE GRAND to work for CRA. It is not yet known what work they are to be employed on. The Co met Coy Comdrs to-morrow matter regarding	A.S.

WAR DIARY
or
INTELLIGENCE (SUMMARY). (9)

Army Form C. 2118.

Place	Date	Hour	Summary of Events and Information	Remarks and references to Appendices
LE PLESSIEL	16th Cont'd		The training of the Bn. which has 7 improvement tablets. Arrangements were also made for the time stores awaiting C. Roy. Bay. & Wet Canteen was also started.	
	17th		Bn. employed on improvement of billets.	
	18th		The R.E. dump at LE PLESSIEL has been taken over by us. 2nd Lieut Evans being in chief every day. The Church Chaplain all troops in the DRUCAT Area. C.R.E. has arranged that on supervise the erection of NISSEN HUTS in this area occupied by the 153 Inf. Bde. Huts are to be built at DRUCAT, NEUILLY L' HOPITAL, MILLENCOURT & CAOURS. 2nd Lieut Wallace is in charge of the work. The infantry supply working parties. The weather is very hot & thus is a good deal of sickness about.	
	19th		A party of 1 NCO & 12 men were sent today to Bde H.Qrs. to inspect & keep clean areas under Br. Rech. Work & billets is being gone on with. All men not employed on the were cleared to small guards wherever a suitable piece of ground could be formed. The training programme for this Bn. is to certain next that it is impossible to set it ask the afternoon the Bn. had a short route march to Abbeville a distance of 3½ miles & were entertained to a Cinema by Capt from explosion by the Y.M.C.A. Hen. The Bn arrived back at 8 P.M. after a most enjoyable outing.	

Army Form C. 2118.

WAR DIARY
or
INTELLIGENCE SUMMARY. (10)
(Erase heading not required.)

Place	Date	Hour	Summary of Events and Information	Remarks and references to Appendices
LE PLESSIEL	20/12		38 O.R. joined the Bn. to-day from the base all except 6 Privates were N&/S men, some Returning from hospital at base & 24 from the Res: Bn. at home. A training List has been made out for the coming week training & Coys. The training for the 1st week is mainly Close order, close rifle exercises, Physical training. During the afternoon from 1.30 to 2.30 Musketry. Rousing games. On Wednesday & Saturday afternoons there is football & cross country running. Route march on Thursday & Saturday.	
	21/12		The Bn. Church parade was held in the open at 9.30 am. The R.C. going to the Church at DRUCAT. During the afternoon football matches were played. B Coy beating A & D Coy beating C. Bn: Sports are being got up & representatives from each Pl attending a meeting organising same.	
	22/12		The Bn. Carried regular training to-day, the hours being from 9 AM to 12 noon & from 1.30 PM to 2.30. Capt Young & 2/Lt Baylis returned from leave to-day. Every seven feet he let in with the ground is so hard & takes for Ball to move. 2/Lt J.J. Gray returned from leave to-day. A Coy Xmas dinner was held tonight starting at 6 PM to nothing up at 10 PM. The arrangements were splendid & the dinner themselves was greatly enjoyed. B Coys. dinner came off tonight. Twas a success	[signature]
	23/12			

2353 Wt. W3544/1454 700,000 5/15 D.D. & L. A.D.S.S./Forms/C. 2118.

Place	Date	Hour	Summary of Events and Information	Remarks and references to Appendices
LE PLESSIEL	24th		The Bn. Games as per programme during the forenoon & went for another route march in the afternoon when the Y.M.C.A. again gave a Concert & Cinema show for the Bn. Coy dinners came off at night.	
	25th		The first ethic hold a thaw would be welcome by everyone. The rest of the Corps Chinmen were here tonight namely D Coy & the French & the Indians & were French engraved evening. The detachment under 2nd/Lieut Seymour rejoined the Bn. today from PORT LA GRAND.	
	26th		Two platoons under Capt H Young & 2nd/Lieut Allison left here today to work at PORT LE GRAND for the CRA but reasons all their instructions from the CRE. It is understood they will be employed building hone standings for the Artillery which remain behind when the Bn. moves.	
	27th		The final ethic hitch v it is batting astle	
	28th		Word has been received today that the Bn. along with the 1/1st & 1/2nd Field Engrs R.E. will both Champetown & Gladipem to move at short notice & that we head for an Unadmim to take in the ARRAS Area. The party working at PORT LE GRAND will be withdrawn tomorrow & move will be on the 30th? Bn. Bn. Football League played the 1st v 3rd Septr Boys. T.M. Battery in the 2nd round & beat them	AQ

WAR DIARY or INTELLIGENCE SUMMARY

Place	Date	Hour	Summary of Events and Information	Remarks and references to Appendices
LE PLESSIEL	29th		All detailed parties having today. Instructions from Division; The Bn & its Transport will leave by two routes to ARRAS where they will be under the 6th Corps. Transport will move separately, taking two days for the journey, their destination being LATTRE ST QUENTINE, at the end of the first nights march they will halt at BONNIERES reaching their destination next day. The rest of the Bn will take will be AUXI LE CHATEAU FREVENT, NABAREG, to ARRAS.	
	30th		Transport moved off at 9.30am. Bn's 30 buses arrived to convey the Bn. & D Coy had been left behind until men transport was available. The Bn. less D Coy left LE PLESSIEL at 12 noon & reached ARRAS at 7 PM that evening. The journey was without incident but the estl was indicisive, personally the men had their Gerham Greatcoat Flankeis with them. Billets for the night were arranged for in the Wharf Bn being put into the prison where they were fairly comfortable. most of the men being in beds. D Coy arrived during the night having been delayed until 5.30 PM at LE PLESSIEL waiting for buses. Early the morning instructions were received that we were to work under the XVII Corps. A & C Coys on to ANZIN to work from there for the 9th Division B, C Coy on trench on roads near ARRAS under the C.E. & will be billeted in ARRAS with Bn. HQrs:	
ARRAS	31st			A.J.

WAR DIARY
or
INTELLIGENCE SUMMARY.
(Erase heading not required.)

Army Form C. 2118.

Place	Date	Hour	Summary of Events and Information	Remarks and references to Appendices
			Casualties during month:-	
			Officers.	
			(Sick)	
			Lieut. R.A.D. Ritchie	
			Lieut. J. Brenner	
			2nd Lt. Brighton	
			2nd Lt. N. McYork	
			Chaplain R Howie	
			Other Ranks:-	
			Draft to from Base 672	
			Non patient 44	
			Reinforcements receiving month:-	
			Officers:-	
			Capt. Falconer O.B.	
			2/Lieut. Mackay, A.	
			Lumsch, V.R.	
			Bruton, G. Jones 8.1.19	
			Campbell Lw.	
			Munro. A.	
			Calder. R.	
			Moncur. Jm.	
			Smith. Q.R. Joined 21.1.19.	
			Lieut Roscoe M.O. from Horn. 1911-19.	
			2/Lieut Brinet F.R. " 16.1.19	
			Strength 28.12 noon 31.1.19	
			= 48 Officers + 1090 O.Ranks	
			A.J. 1/8 Bn The Royal Scots	
			(signed)	

S E C R E T.   Copy No. 1

1/8th. Bn. THE ROYAL SCOTS (Pioneers).

OPERATION ORDER No. K.10.

By Lieut.-Colonel W. GEMMILL, D.S.O., Commanding.

11th. January, 1917.

1. The Battalion, Divisional Salvage Company, and the Divisional Band will move to SARTON on 12th. instant, via BOUZINCOURT and ACHEUX.

2. a. The Battalion, less 1 officer and 35 Other Ranks from "A" Coy., will move in the following order with 200 yards distance between each Company - the first Company to move off at 8-15 a.m.:-

   Band.
   Signallers.
   Cyclists.
   "A" Company.

   followed by "B", "C", and "D" Companies and Stretcher Bearers.
   b. The Divisional Salvage Company will join the Battalion at BOUZINCOURT at 9-30 a.m., and will march 200 yards in rear of "D" Company.
   c. The Divisional Band will join the Battalion as per instructions already sent to the Officer in Charge.
   d. The Transport Officer will arrange to have all Transport forward as arranged. All wagons must be loaded and ready to move off at 7-45 a.m.

3. Strict attention will be paid to march discipline, and in connection with this, Officers Commanding Companies will bear in mind that there is a large number of newly-joined men in their Companies who will require careful watching.
   When marching at ease N.C.Os. and men will carry their rifles slung on one shoulder.
   An officer will march in rear of each Company.
   No man will fall out on the line of march without written authority from an officer to do so. This authority should state the man's name and number, date and time of falling out, and also the destination of the Battalion on that date. A duplicate will be kept, and sent to the Orderly Room on completion of the march.
   The Regimental Police will move in rear of the Column and bring on any stragglers.

4. Bonnets will be worn. Steel helmets will be carried outside the pack, being secured by the pack braces. Leather jerkins and emergency rations will be carried inside the pack, and the waterproof sheets under-neath the pack flap. Box Respirators will be worn on top of the pack.

5. Refilling Points will be as under :-
   On 12th.Jan. - On HEADAUVILLE - WARLOY road (V.4.a) 7-30 a.m.
       13th.Jan. - Do. Do.
       14th.Jan. - ½ mile east of BEAUQUESNES on BEAUQUESNES-RAINCHEVAL road. at 8-0 a.m.
       15th.Jan. - ½ mile, south-east of BERNAVILLE on FIENVILLERS -BERNAVILLE road at 8-0 a.m.
   The party of 1 Officer and 35 Other Ranks will be rationed by the 2nd. Division on 14th. inst.

6. On the morning of the 14th. inst. the Officer of "A" Coy. left behind will report to the A.A.& Q.M.G., 2nd. Division at USNA HILL for orders.

7. Separate instructions are being issued regarding the detail of the move.

/ Continued.

Continued.

8. Acknowledge.

Issued at 4 p.m.

                                                       A. Jones 2nd. Lieut.,

                                       Adjt., 1/8th. Bn. The Royal Scots (Pioneers)

Copy No. 1 - Adjutant for Commanding Officer.
         2 - Headquarters
         3 - "A" Company.
         4 - "B" Company.
         5 - "C" Company.
         6 - "D" Company.
         7 - Quartermaster.
         8 - Transport Officer.
         9 - Medical Officer for Stretcher Bearers.
      10 - Signals.
      11 - Cyclists.
      12 - Reg. Sergeant-Major.
      13 - Div. Salvage Co.
      14 - Div. Band.
      15 - File.

1/8th. Bn. THE ROYAL SCOTS (Pioneers).

INSTRUCTIONS FOR MOVE TO THE NEW AREA.

By Lieut.-Colonel W. GEMMILL, D.S.O., Commanding.

11th. January, 1917.

1. Loading of TRANSPORT.

All blankets, great-coats, and water-proof capes will be rolled and ready for loading before breakfast at 6-30 a.m.
All wagons must be ready to move at 7-45 a.m.
"D" Company will detail 1 officer and 8 men to load the lorries.
All Companies will carry their blankets and water-proof capes to the lorries.

2. ALLOTMENT OF TRANSPORT.

Transport will be allotted as under :-
(a). Blankets and Water-proof Capes,

2 lorries are allotted for the blankets of Coys. and Details.
1 lorry for water-proof capes of Coys. and Details.
Blankets will be rolled in bundles of 10, labelled and securely tied with wire.

(b). Great-coats,

1 G.S. Wagon is allotted to each Company for Great-coats.
These great-coats must be rolled in bundles of 5, labelled and securely tied with wire.

(c). Company Tools.
2 G.S. Wagons) are allotted to each Company for tools, and
4 Pack Animals) Officers' Baggage. (If there is any spare room on third lorry, it may used for Officers' Baggage).

(d). Details,

1 G.S. Limber is allotted to Transport.
1   do.   Headquarters.
1   do.   Orderly Room and Signals.
1   do.   Shoemakers, Tailors, & Pioneer Sergt.
2   do.   Quartermaster and Armourer Sergt.
1   do.   for Lewis Guns.
1 Mess Cart is allotted to Headquarters.

3. BRAKESMAN.

Companies and Details will detail one brakesman for each vehicle.

4. UNLOADING PARTIES.

The Medical Officer will submit to the Orderly Room the names of 8 men to accompany the lorries. These men will be in charge of the Pioneer Sergeant who will be responsible that the blankets &c. are unloaded on arrival at SARTON. This party will carry a haversack ration.

5. Billets.

Sergeant Main and 4 cyclists will proceed direct to SARTON - leaving Battalion Headquarters at 8-0 a.m. They will report to Major Todd at the Town Major's Office in SARTON.

6. COOKERS. &c.

One cooker will march in rear of each Company.
The two water-carts will march at the head of the Transport.

A. Jones 2/Lieut.,
Act. Adjt., 1/8th. Bn. The Royal Scots (Pioneers).

Issued to holders of O.O. No. K.10.

SECRET.   Copy No. 2

1/8th. Bn. THE ROYAL SCOTS (Pioneers).

OPERATION ORDERS. No. K 11z

By Lieut.-Colonel W. GEMMILL, D.S.O., Commanding.

12th. January, 1917

1. The Battalion, Divisional Salvage Coy., and the Divisional Band will move to-morrow to BERNAVILLE via HEM, FIENVILLERS - "B" company proceeding to VACQUERIE.

2. The column will parade at 7-0 a.m. to-morrow and will move off in the following order, with 200 yards distance between Companies :-

   Cyclists.
   Signals.
   Pipe Band.
   "B" Company.
   "C" Company.
   Divl. Band.
   "D" Company.
   "A" Company.
   Salvage Coy., and Stretcher Bearers.

3. Company Cookers will march in rear of their Companies.

4. March discipline and rests will be as detailed in Operation Order No. K 10, of 12th. instant.

5. Refilling Point on 14th. instant, will be ¼ mile east of BEAUQUESNES, on the BEAUQUESNES - RAINCHEVAL road.

                                                        2nd. Lieut,
Issued at 4 p.m.   Adjt., 1/8th. Bn. THE ROYAL SCOTS (Pioneers)

    Copy No. 1 - Adjutant for Commanding Officer.
            2   - Headquarters.
            3   - "A" Company.
            4   - "B" Company.
            5   - "C" Company.
            6   - "D" Company.
            7   - Quartermaster.
            8   - Transport Officer.
            9   - Medical Officer for Stretcher Bearers.
           10   - Signals.
           11   - Cyclists.
           12   - Regimental Sergt.-Major.
           13   - Divl. Salvage Coy.
           14   - Divl. Band.
           15   - File.

No 2

1/8th. Bn. THE ROYAL SCOTS (Pioneers).

INSTRUCTIONS FOR MOVE TO BERNAVILLE AREA.

By Lieut.-Colonel W.Gemmill, D.S.O., Commanding.

13th. January, 1917.

1. **LOADING OD TRANSPORT.**

    All blankets and water-proof capes will be rolled and deposited at the Q.M.Stores by 6-0 a.m.
    All Coys. &c. will carry their blankets &c. to the Q.M.Stores.

2. **ALLOTMENT OF TRANSPORT.**

    a. Lorries. 1st. lorry - "Blankets of "B" and "A" Coys. ("B" Coy. must be loaded first.)
    2nd. lorry - "Blankets of "C" and "D" Companies.
    3rd. lorry - "Water-proof capes of all Coys. and Details. also blankets of details.

    (b). The allotment of the other Transport will be the same as for the 12th.
    (c). The mess-cart will be at the Orderly Room at 6-30 a.m.

3. **BRAKESMEN.**

    As for 12th. instant.

4. **LOADING AND UNLOADING PARTIES.**

    A party under Sergeant Alexander has been detailed to load and proceed with the lorries to destination, where they will unload and stack the blankets. This party will parade at the Q.M.Stores at 6-45 a.m.

5. **BILLETING.**

    Sergeant Main's party will leave Battalion Headquarters at 7-15 a.m.

A.Jones 2nd.Lieut.

Adjt., 1/8th. Bn. THE ROYAL SCOTS (Pioneers).

Issued with Operation
Order No. K 11.

1/8th. Bn. THE ROYAL SCOTS (Pioneers).   Copy No.

INSTRUCTIONS FOR MOVE TO LE PLESSIEL.

By Lieut-Colonel W. GEMMILL, D.S.O., Commanding.

14th. January, 1917.

1. The Battalion, Divisional Band, and the Divisional Salvage Coy., will move to-morrow to LE PLESSIEL via St. RIQUIER and MILLENCOURT.

2. The column, less "B" Company will parade in column of route, ready to move off at 7-30 a.m. in the following order :-

    Cyclists.
    Signals.
    Pipe Band.
    "C" Company.
    "D" Company.
    Divl. Band.
    "A" Company.
    "B" Company.
    Salvage Coy.
    Stretcher Bearers.

3. The Battalion will march with 200 yards distance between Coys.

4. "B" Company will parade ready to move off, and proceed to BERNAVILLE, where they will join the Battalion.

5. March discipline will be strictly maintained.

6. Refilling Point to-morrow will be ¼ mile S.E. of BERNAVILLE on FIENVILLERS - BERNAVILLE road at 8-0 a.m.

7. LOADING OF BLANKETS.

    Blankets will be rolled and labelled as before.
    1st. Lorry;- will be at VACQUERIE at 5-45 a.m. for "B" Coy. Blankets, and will return to BERNAVILLE ready to receive "A" Coy. blankets at 6-15 a.m.
    2nd. Lorry will be in a central position for "C" and "D" Companies billets at 6-0 a.m. "C" Coy. will finish loading before 6-15 a.m., "D" Coy. before 6-30 a.m.
    3rd. Lorry will be at Q.M. Stores at 6-a.m. and will be loaded with waterproof capes of all the Coys. and Details, and also the blankets and greatcoats of Details.
    Companies and Details will load their own blankets.

8. The Mess Cart will be at Billet No. A 51 (opposite "B" Street) at 7-0 a.m.

9. UNLOADING PARTY.

    A party under Sergt. Alexander, will be detailed to proceed with the motor lorries. This party will parade at 6-50 a.m. at the Q.M. Store

10. BILLETING.

    Sergt. Main's party will leave Battalion Headquarters at 7- a.m.

                                                    2nd. Lieut.,
                                Adjt., 1/8th. Bn. The Royal Scots (Pioneers

Issued at 7 p.m.
as detailed in O.O.K 11.

Army Form C. 2118.

WAR DIARY
or
INTELLIGENCE SUMMARY.

(Erase heading not required.)

Vol 24

21 RS.

Confidential.

War Diary
of
1st The Royal Scots Greys
From 1st February 1917 to 27th February 1917.

VOLUME 28.

WAR DIARY
or
INTELLIGENCE SUMMARY.

Army Form C. 2118.

Place	Date	Hour	Summary of Events and Information	Remarks and references to Appendices
ARRAS.	1st Feby, 1917		A & C Coys. moved to ANZIN East. HqTrs will be billeted there. Transport Cons forward to LOUEZ today & are billeted there. The QM stores are also billeted in LOUEZ. The HQrs & B & D Coys moved into new billets today north of the billets being at the Rue de la Prefectures in new place.	
	2nd		B & D Coys started work today making a new forced map Ref. Sheet 57B NW 3 G 5 d 6.1 to G 16 central. The Road at present is only a track & the work consists of grading, metalling & draining Road. Owing to the severe frost the men are chiefly engaged on attacking broken frozen houses nearly to use as metal.	
	3rd		A Coy & eng. Corps clearing up & levelling up the bottom of FIGHTIERS Trench communicating at LILLE RD & working toward Tunnel at ROCLINCOURT AVENUE.	
	4th		C Coy are cleaning out ROCLINCOURT AVENUE. Today completed their work yesterday. Today the 31st Div. Operation Order for the move was received & we expect the Division to arrive in this area about the 11/12/17.	
	5/6/7/ 8th		Coys are still employed on the same work. Frost still holds. Instructions received today is that the 51st Div. will take over a circle of the XVII Corps front. Front ie. HqTrs G 4/12/17 ie the new front line between MAISON de la COTE RD (exclusive) & LUCE RD (inclusive) 1500 yds	

Army Form C. 2118.

WAR DIARY
or
INTELLIGENCE SUMMARY.
(Erase heading not required.)

Place	Date	Hour	Summary of Events and Information	Remarks and references to Appendices
ARRAS.	8th Sept.		152nd Coy: Bn. will take over the line on 11/12th. A & C Coys will come under the 51st Div on night of 9/10th. B & D Coys will continue work under the XVII Corps.	
		9ᵃ	Fost. & Lts. told. Home leave to stopped under further orders.	
		10ᵃ	Major Todd returned from leave today.	
		11ᵃ/12ᵃ	Capt. Abson took over command of C Coy: & Coy.	
		13ᵃ	First shell holes but shoot some signs of thaw.	
		14ᵃ	A Coy: are employed as follows: Cleaning & Repairing ANZIN & GOYLE Trenches, Repairing Trench between BLANCHARD's entrance to tunnel at FERME DE CAUE, Repairing Trench between MARINE Trench & NOEL AVENUE. A successful raid was carried out today by the Bn. on our left. 30 prisoners were taken & much damage done to enemy's emplacements.	
		15ᵃ	The Baton J.4 & Daylight to attached to C Coy for work.	
		16ᵃ	A Working Party of 6 Platoon no. 572 from 152nd Inf.y Bde. is attached for work on Communication Trenches & to work on the orders of Capt Mitchell. The weather thaw & Cgr. of having what about the work of B. Coy on roads to the canal & mine made. NCO & Young Blackwood & Knoll Jones the Bn. today & was posted to A Coy	

WAR DIARY or INTELLIGENCE SUMMARY.

(Erase heading not required.)

Army Form C. 2118.

Place	Date	Hour	Summary of Events and Information	Remarks and references to Appendices
ARRAS				

WAR DIARY or INTELLIGENCE SUMMARY

Casualties during February:-

O.R.
Killed:- nil
Wounded:- 2
To Hosp.(Sick) 62   64

Officers:- Yo Hosp.(sick)
   2/Lieut. R. CALDER   3.2.19
   Lieut. J. BRENNER   18.2.19

O.RANKS:-
14.2.19 — 6
16.2.19 — 9
18.2.19 — 12
21.2.19 — 11
25.2.19 — 3
            21

Reinforcements:-
Officers:-
2/Lieut. YOUNG. W.G. }
       BLACKWOOD W.T. } 16.2.19
       HOWIE. A. (from 6/7th Cam Scot.)
       MacDONALD, J.H.S. 21.2.19
Chaplain Middleton. H.S. 21.2.19
Lieut. BREMNER. T. 3.2.19
      DAVIDSON. S. 26.2.19
2/Lieut. BRUNTON. G. 14.2.19

Strength at 28.2.19 = 51   6ff   O.R.
                           1018

Strength at 28.2.19 = 51 Offs. 1018 O.R.

Alex Lyell
Adj. 1/8th Bn The Royal Scots (Pioneers)

Army Form C. 2118.

WAR DIARY
or
INTELLIGENCE SUMMARY.
(Erase heading not required.)

Vol 25

22 RS

Confidential.

War Diary.
of
1/5th The Royal Scots Pioneers.

From 1st March 1917 to 31st March 1917

Volume 29.

WAR DIARY or INTELLIGENCE SUMMARY

Army Form C. 2118.

Place: ARRAS.

Date	Hour	Summary of Events and Information	Remarks
1st March 1917		The Bays are employed as follows: A Sqn. cleaning Horse Lines & Bivouacs in the front line. B Sqn. making new road between St Catherine & Maroeuil Range. C Sqn. & Reconnaissance Kiosk & front line. D Sqn. widening road from Maroeuil Range to St Aubin. The weather continues mild & dry.	
2nd		The enemy artillery has been very active today shelling the trench system behind our front line. Unfortunately a working party of A Sqn were caught in the shell fire & suffered casualties. One being killed & 2 wounded. Are Blues Pte Clement & Mackean. Instructions have been received from the O.R.E. 3rd Cav. Div. to the effect that no officer is to serve part of his time from the Regt. & to be put in charge of Me. Lft. by the L.M. Gun Squadron & the Brigade to replace the dummy machine guns of the Brigade to be crushed at LOVAE Cavalry stop. The Stewart & Markham are ordered to 3rd &c.	
3rd		The 3rd B. today from the 7th Div. Bn the 47th Res. Bn at home were posted to B Sqn.	
4th		Today our Transport were inspected by F.M. Haig Lord C. the Calls (These having been out & in the Arr.) Today a shell landed near D Sqn billet wounding on our Cpl Armory E. of the McKenzie & Brandon. Returned from leave today.	
5th		The 6th Dragoon Gds Regt. made a long successful raid into the enemys lines today.	

WAR DIARY
or
INTELLIGENCE SUMMARY. (2)

(Erase heading not required.)

Army Form C. 2118.

Place	Date	Hour	Summary of Events and Information	Remarks and references to Appendices
ARRAS	5th March		Battn today capturing 1 Officer & 20 O.R. enemy also a machine gun. The Actg a great amount of damage to the trenches & obtained breech blocks, numbers of the enemy. The enemy (Bavarian) put up a good fight. There were 6 Lt. & 1 and standing.	
	6th		Received orders from Bde. Bn. today that the 2 Coy. billeted in Arras where the H.Q. of the Bn. would move to MARŒUIL in the evening of the 5th inst. & were to billeted there. Then 2 Coys. from the Citadel Bn. moved to MARŒUIL with the two remaining B & D Coys. would on the march to the S. D. Coy. Person Pl. Lt. and Pl. Sgt. Bar for work on the 5.2. No enemy shells ARRAS during their forming up 10:30 to 11:30 & while same to & Bly Officers were too knocked. It unfortunately the mess Cook Pte Murray was killed & Pl. Boyd was knocked about but my duty Pte. 4 m of the gunners were hurt. Sgt. Murray was buried at 6:30PM at LOUEZ cemetery.	
	7th		Instruction for the new Bn. front today a copy of which is attached.	
	8th		Trench work continued by A and C Companies. Tanks under construction by B and D Companies hostility practical funeral. Sun Ravated sun & Partions of 1st. Div. (West YORKS) bis C Cold wet stone steel. B and D Companies moved to MARŒUIL for the instructions attached.	

WAR DIARY
or
INTELLIGENCE SUMMARY.
(Erase heading not required.)

Army Form C. 2118.

Place	Date	Hour	Summary of Events and Information	Remarks and references to Appendices
MAROEUIL	9th March		Work in trenches continued by A and C Companies, B and D being employed in improvement of billets. Weather cold with some snow. Nos 1st & 3rd Platoons returned to join C.C.S. having been taken ill in the morning.	
	10th		C.S.M. died at 4 a.m. this morning in No. 1 C.C.S. from Cerebral Haemorrhage. His duties taken over by R.Q.M.S. Bitz. Weather milder.	
	11th		Nos 1st and 3rd M., R.D. Whyman have remained in Cemetery, AUBIGNY. Capt. Bos MATHERS & C.O. Officials, 1/Lt Finn, Lt T. and 2nd O/R moved to AGNIERES to meet under instructions of Fifth Army Engineers (Relieving Lucas & J.) 2/Lt. Backie and 11 O/R remain at MAROEUIL for transport work. 2/Lt Anfield & 2/Lt Aus.f.Co. Weather much milder but some snowstorms.	
	12th		B & D Companies carried out a reconnaissance of lines to be reoccupied. Weather mild but overcast. Some snow. R.S.M. Thomas took a staff of 9 men cooked from the BASE. Work in trenches continued by A and C Companies. B Coy. working on Marie & ROCLINCOURT–THELUS ROAD, D Coy started a dug-out at junction of FIRST AVENUE and THURSDAY AVENUE for R.A.M.C. AID POST.	
	13th		Weather mild but dull. Took no above being carried on.	
	14th		Weather overcast – some rain. Work much hindered by trench sides falling in and	

Army Form C. 2118.

WAR DIARY
or
INTELLIGENCE SUMMARY.
(Erase heading not required.)

(4)

Instructions regarding War Diaries and Intelligence Summaries are contained in F. S. Regs., Part II. and the Staff Manual respectively. Title pages will be prepared in manuscript.

Place	Date	Hour	Summary of Events and Information	Remarks and references to Appendices
Appdiceux	14th March	Capt	Regiment marched on the road which "B" Coy is repairing 3rd K. Y.L.I. Seels returned from short leave. D.R.O. No. 729 intimates the khaki battle dress is D.S.O. of this unit headdress promoted the following station decoration:— Order of St Maurice and St Lazarus — Cavalier.	
	15th "		weather cold but bright — a rain, M.B. Cuny is transferred from Authil.	
	16th "		weather bright — some haze. 2/L. Crawford returns from field ambulance 2/Lt. Davidson goes to Tramway HQrs. to control and direct Divisional Trench Railways. Tramway Headquarters completed by "A" Coy also weather dry and mild. "A" Coy (assisted by working parties — 14 kaisors of Infantry) are clearing GENIE and AIZIN communication trenches and Tunnel under LILLE ROAD.	
	17th "		THURSDAY AVENUE.	
	18th "		weather dry and bright. 2/Lt Blackwood to feel out 4 Communications. Seven killed at B and D Coy's Church Quarters. B Coy: still working on road CHEMIN CREUX to FISH AVENUE, clearing a trench alongside the road.	
	19th "		weather dull — heavy rain in evening and though the night. Company

WAR DIARY
or
INTELLIGENCE SUMMARY. (5)

Army Form C. 2118.

Place	Date	Hour	Summary of Events and Information	Remarks and references to Appendices
MAROEUIL	Contd. 19th	March	C Company clearing and repairing the following communication trenches:— ECURIE AVENUE, FISH TRENCH, THURSDAY AVENUE, SOLE AVENUE, FLAPPERS, RIPPART. D Company have completed a shaft & dug out (AID POST, POEUXCOURT) and have erected an O.P. New tunnel in FISH AVENUE.	
	20th	March	Weather cold – some rain. Work on various C.T.'s continued. Stopped Chamber (AID POST) commenced.	
	21st	"	Weather dry and mild – trenches very muddy. Snow during night. An O.P. finished in TRENCH 40.	
	22nd	"	Weather still cold with some sleet and strong wind. Another O.P. finished near FISH TUNNEL. Another O.P. started in COLLECTEUR. Engt. Short cut trench continues. Clearing of C.T.'s continued. Enemy	
	23rd	"	Cables laid in various trenches, tracks (alternative to C.T.'s) between and trench bridges strengthened. STEM BRIDGE put in by 'B' Coy. on POEUXCOURT–THELUS Road.	
	24th	"	Hard frost during night, bright sun during day. The C.O. left for short leave (official)	
	25th	"	The Adjt. returned from leave to-day. O.P. logs, transport officer & guards met the C.O. myn Total (?) encampment	

WAR DIARY
or
INTELLIGENCE SUMMARY. (6.)

(Erase heading not required.)

Army Form C. 2118.

Place	Date	Hour	Summary of Events and Information	Remarks and references to Appendices
MAROEUIL	25th March		The following orders just received from Div: Instruction as far as they affect the Bde are as follows. The Bde Hqrs will be at 107 & 108 Field Cos RE on the stations adjacent to Events. Heavy Covering & an Escort than Hqrs then Pioneer Batts on y: right. The next rank would be ..[?].. taken by the CRE. CCoy: are to cut a Communication Trench from the mouth of Pin Tunnel to the German front line. They will be called to do the work probably at nightfall on 28th. B.Coy. have to open & clear Trench from PORTIN COURT to the direction of THÉLUS through the German lines. A Tench also in Connection. They are to harten it but it is expected the main trench. They will be called upon to start the probably in 2 nights. A & D Coys are to be in Reserve. The Reserve of Officers, ..?.. men, transport, are to be at BRAY.	
	26th "		1 Coy of 7/225 Trawler ground the Bde Bottop, eleven of them have been with the Bn before A.T. Campbell left the Bn for the Brier Battery Chyton Henderson & ...?... took charge of power at MAROEUIL & the Nursery & al ANZIN & the afternoon.	
	29th "		The weather is very unsettled & quite frosty this last ..?.. We have been intructed by Div: to take over from the 1st Fd Coy 152 Infy Bgde the Air Defence of Dumfus in Ridge. An Defence area Lt J. Brennan will be heavy gun to some Lewis guns stationed here Gunner Station over the Area near Trenier Capelle & Agy.	

2353 Wt. W2544/1454 700,000 5/15 D. D. & L. A.D.S.S./Forms/C. 2118.

WAR DIARY
or
INTELLIGENCE SUMMARY.

(Erase heading not required.)

Army Form C. 2118.

Place	Date	Hour	Summary of Events and Information	Remarks and references to Appendices
MAROEUIL	29th March		Lieut Lewis Jones & teams left today. Lieuts Lt. J. Ransome is arranged. The Coys are employed as follows:- A Coy & 6 platoon of C Coy being attached	
			1 Platoon cleaning & widening Wednesday Avenue.	
			½ " in RAMP Shaft. LILLE RD	
			½ " O'Kelly & ROADE.	
			6 Platoon Lufn. cleaning & widening GENIE TRENCH	
			B Coy.	
			Repairing ROCLINCOURT Rd between FISH AV. & COLLECTEUR	
			C Coy:	
			Cleaning & ECURIE & MADAGASCAR Avenue	
			Repairing FANTOME damaged by shell fire.	
			CHEMIN CREUX repair also damaged by shell fire.	
			FRIDAY AVENUE cleaning & repairing near firebays.	
			D Coy:	
			AID POST DUGOUT nearly completed. Chambers 65ft & 8ft with two stairways.	
			Making O.P. in front line trenches.	

Army Form C. 2118.

WAR DIARY
or
INTELLIGENCE SUMMARY.
(Erase heading not required.)

Instructions regarding War Diaries and Intelligence Summaries are contained in F. S. Regs., Part II. and the Staff Manual respectively. Title pages will be prepared in manuscript.

Place	Date	Hour	Summary of Events and Information	Remarks and references to Appendices
MARDEUIL	30.9	Much	Weather very cold frost with high wind.	
		3/30	The enemy shelled MARDEUIL intermittently during the day they fired a man of B.Coy receiving a slight wound on the arm.	

A. Smith Lt Colt
9th R Rest
Pioneers

WAR DIARY
or
INTELLIGENCE SUMMARY

Army Form C.2118.

Casualties during month of March 1919:-

Officers

To Hospital Sick :- A/Lieut Dear Wyman R.O.
10-3-19 :- Died at 42 C.C.S. Aubigny 10-3-19.
2/Lt Sunderland L.E.L. 27/3/19
T/Lt Blackmore W.E. 18/3/19
Capt W. — 16/3/19
Confined to Base August 27/3/19
Metayer Dm 10/3/19

Other Ranks :- To Hospital Sick :- 44
Wounded :- 11
Killed in Action :- 3
Died of Wounds :- 1
Wounded at duty :- 6

Died :- OR
12 (5-3-19)
10 (11-3-19)
14 15-3-19
22 26-3-19

Reinforcements :-
From 4 R.S. R/Scots from dates:-
2/Lt Grant (3-3-19) 2/Lt Calder R.
Clark W (31/3/19)
Scott W. 18-3-19 M. Lockie 19
Brown J. 26-3-19

Strength at 12noon 3 = 52 Off + 1056 OR
from 31-3-19

A. Jones Lieut.
Acting 1st Bn Y Royal (?)

S E C R E T.   Copy No.: 12

1/8th. Bn. THE ROYAL SCOTS (Pioneers).
INSTRUCTIONS FOR MOVE TO MAROEUIL.

By Lieut.-Colonel W.GEMMILL, D.S.O., Commanding.

Reference Map 51c.   7th. March, 1917.

1. Headquarters, "B" and "D" Companies and details of this Battalion billeted in ARRAS will move to MAROEUIL on the 8th. instant, in accordance with the following arrangements.

2. "B" and "D" Companies will cease work on the roads at 12 noon on the 8th. inst., and will return to billets.

3. "B" and "D" Companies, less 1 platoon from each Company, which will remain to load Transport will parade at their Company Billets at 5-55 p.m., ready to move by platoons at 100 yards distance at 6-0 p.m. in the following order :-

        "B" Company.
        "D" Company.

Details, Orderly Room Staff, Signals &c. will load their own limbers and will move with transport.

4. The route will be by the main ARRAS - St.POL road - cross roads K.10-c-3-0, LOUEZ and MAROEUIL.

5. Blankets will be neatly and firmly rolled in bundles of 10, and securely tied and labelled.   All blankets will be dumped at a convenient place near each Company H.Q., ready for loading by 5-30 p.m.   The blankets of details will be placed on the transport allotted to them.

6. The Transport Officer will arrange for Transport to be at Company billets, Headquarters, &c. as early in the evening as possible. Transport will be allotted as under :-

    Limbered G.S.Wagons :-

      1 - Headquarters.
      1 - Orderly Room & Signals.
      1 - Sanitary Squad, Armourer-Sergt., Lewis Guns.
      1 - "B" and "D" Coys. Officers' Mess Boxes.

    G.S.Wagons etc.

      2 - "B" Coy. Tools and Officers' Kits.
      1 - Blankets.
      2 - "D" Coy. Tools & Officers' Kits.
      1 - Blankets.
      1 - Canteen & O.Room Tables.
    Mess Cart - Headquarters.
    Medical Cart - Medical Equipment & Stretcher Bearers Blankets.
    Horses for "B" and "D" Company cookers.

7- BRAKESMEN.

The officers in charge of each Coy. loading party will detail one man to accompany each vehicle to their Coys.

8- ADVANCE PARTY. /   COntinued :-

2.

8- ADVANCE PARTY.

Captain Young will proceed to MAROEUIL and will report to the Town Major at 12 noon to-morrow in order to arrange billets. A small advance party, consisting of the following, will proceed to MAROEUIL after dinner, and will report to Captain Young at the Town Major's Office at 2-30 p.m. :-

    1 C.Q.M.S. from each of "B" and "D" Coys.
    1 Man from each platoon,"B" and "D" Coys.
    1 Man from Orderly Room Staff.
    1   "   Signals.
    1   "   Stretcher Bearers.
    1 Servant from each of H.Q., "B" and "D" Officers Messes.

The advance party will parade at the Orderly Room at 1-15 p.m. in full marching order under C.Q.M.S.Welsh, and will proceed to MAROEUIL, via ST.CATHERINE, ANZIN and LOUEZ.

9
~~10~~ - GUIDES.

Guides will be detailed by Captain Young to be at the entrance to MAROEUIL at 7 p.m. for the purpose of guiding the Companies &c. to their billets.

Issued at   7 p.m.   Lieut.,
                                       Adjt., 1/8th. Bn. THE ROYAL SCOTS (Pioneers

      Copy No. 1 - Adjutant for Commanding Officer.
               2 - Headquarters.
               3 - "B" Company.
               4 - "D" Company.
               5 - Quartermaster.
               6 - Transport Officer.
               7 - Medical Officer for Stretcher Bearers.
               8 - Signals.
               9 - Cyclists.
            10 - Regtl. Sergeant-Major.
            11 - Lewis Gun Sergeant.
   ✓   12 - War Diary.
            13 - File.

SECRET

1/8th. Bn. THE ROYAL SCOTS (Pioneers).

INSTRUCTIONS FOR OPERATIONS (Provisional).

By Major JAMES A. TODD, Commanding.

24th. March, 1917.

1. MOVE.

On "Y" day the Battalion will move to ECURIE.
Men will carry the following articles of kit :-
- 1 Blanket.
- Water-proof Sheet.
- Leather Jerkin.
- Spare Sox.

Packs will be dumped at the Quarter-master's Stores, those of each platoon to be kept together, and separate from those of other units. Packs should be marked on the part that goes next the man's back with indelible pencil. Os. C. Coys. at ANZIN will arrange for Transport to bring packs to Q.M.Store in Maroeuil.

2. DUMPS.

(1) For R.E. Material.

Divisional Dump - A.28.d.3.8.
Brigade Dumps. (A.29.a.5.0
(A.28.b.65.80

(2) Rations.

Divl. Ration Dump - A.28.d.3.8. (ROCLINCOURT ROAD)

3. RATIONS.

This Unit will draw rations for Z + 1 day from Divl. Ration Dump. Rations for consumption on Z + 2 and Z + 3 will be drawn as required from Dump. Hot tea will be issued in Thermos Boxes. These will be drawn and filled by units.
Rum will be issued at Divisional Dump.

4. SURPLUS KITS.

All private kits must be packed separately from Government property and will be stored separately.
Private Forrester "D" Company will be detailed to proceed in charge of Surplus Kit.

5. KITS.

Officers will wear the same uniform and equipment as the men.

6. DISTINGUISHING MARKS.

The following distinguishing marks will be worn :-
- Runners - Red Band.
- Signallers - Blue Band.

These will be drawn by Companies from the Orderly Room.

7. OFFICERS.

Five officers per Company will go to ECURIE. The remainder will go into one billet in MAROEUIL.

8. N.C.Os.

The Armourer-Sergeant and Sergt-Cook will remain in MAROEUIL. Each C.Q.M.S. will go with his Company to ECURIE. The senior Q.Q.M.S. will be acting R.Q.M.S. and will draw rations for Z + 1 day on "Y" night. (or as soon thereafter as possible).

9. TRANSPORT AND Q.M./

OVER

9. TRANSPORT AND Q.M.

The 1st. Line Transport and the Q.M. Stores will be camped in the neighbourhood of MAROEUIL. A Signal Office will be established at the Transport Lines.

10. REFILLING POINT.

Refilling Point for all units not in Trench Area will be between FREVIN CAPELLE and ACQ.

11. MOBILE VET. SECTION.

The Mobile Vetinerary Section will be at MINGOVAL. An advanced collecting post and Dressing Station will be established at L.11.a.5.7.

12. SOUP KITCHEN.

The Div. Soup Kitchen has been established at A.28.c.3.3.

13. WOUNDED.

Walking wounded will go to the Collecting Station at ANZIN.

James A. Todd, Major,
Commdg. 1/8th. Bn. THE ROYAL SCOTS (Pioneers).

Issued at 4:30 p.m.
24th. March, 1917.

```
Copy No. 1 -  Adjutant for Commanding Officer.
        2 -  O.C. "A" Company.
        3 -  O.C. "B" Company.
        4 -  O.C. "C" Company.
        5 -  O.C. "D" Company.
        6 -  Transport Officer.
        7 -  Quartermaster.
        8 -  Regtl. Sergeant-Major.
        9 -  Medical Officer.
       10 -  War Diary.
       11 -  File.
```

Vol 26

Confidential

War Diary
of
1/8th. Bn. The Royal Scots (Pioneers)

April 1st — 30th, 1918.

Volume 30

Copy No. _____

S E C R E T.

AMENDMENT to INSTRUCTIONS FOR OPERATIONS.

The following addition will be made to para.3

RATIONS :-

Each man will carry on him his complete ration for consumption on "Z" day in addition to the Iron Ration.
The following Camp Kettles will be carried :-

        Per Company - 8
        H.Q. Details- 2

Acknowledge.

                JAMES A. TODD,   Major,

       Commanding 1/8th. Bn. The Royal Scots (Pioneers).

24th. March, 1917.

WAR DIARY or INTELLIGENCE SUMMARY

Army Form C. 2118.

(Erase heading not required.)

Place	Date	Hour	Summary of Events and Information	Remarks and references to Appendices
MIRBEUIL	1st April		The weather today was brighter but got stormy again towards night. The enemy again shelled Marceuil during Daunelie and gap troops transport passing through. One He suffered to casualties.	
	2nd "		Eight battles left today for a short spell. Comd [?] of Mancorp at Chamber. Lately silent. Left for todays trip to Enghien.	
	3rd "		No officers to Rouen with 2 Marceul Boy Rod. O.O. Op return to the Rush to Marceul. The enemy shell Marceul during day. Our Howitzers my from Epernay retaliate. Our heavy bombardment to go today by the Artillery at Reims. We went to Marceul & were shelled out of the town which the team taking shelter in a quite wood & feeding Cattle. We settled in a bay and stream the troops termed back to billets about 4 p.m.	
	4th "		Ordinaire served today Flat 2 day aid 1/2 lb 92 Rest 4lb 4oz shell at Epernay at midnight. 12 night. Embedding a continuing any heavy all about our Camp front the convoy from Lanis active also but have bombardment a very busy task to company to man.	
	5th "		The weather is still unsettled. Showers throughout.	
	6th "		Rain all afternoon. The Earth Trench. On any Sunday to some pleas the trenches are flooded. Lines Carp. The Transportation lies shifted today to near Brays. The Day half hour slower Operation, Gaz. Fac., Cpl. McRae to St. Duntone Stamford during Operation	E.S.

Army Form C. 2118.

WAR DIARY
or
INTELLIGENCE SUMMARY. (2)

(Erase heading not required.)

Place	Date	Hour	Summary of Events and Information	Remarks and references to Appendices
MAROEUIL	7th April		Instructions for Operations were issued to Coys. Today also Instructions to March Table for move to ECURIE. Officers Tead are attached. Lt Colonel Gemmill DSO Commanding the Bn. returned from leave & will go with the Bn. to ECURIE tonight. Major J.A. Todd will be with the Reserve.	
	8th		7 Officers at BRAY. The weather has improved today. Being the first fine Spring day for 17 days old the Bn. moved to ECURIE from billets in ANZIN & MAROEUIL as per MARCH TABLE attached. Lt Col. the Bn. to but all Ranks as under Cover of am start.	
ECURIE	9th		Coy Commanders reported all trenches & new billets by 2 am this morning. Zero as in statel below at the hour of ZERO. B, C & D Coys are to deploy in Hyd et ECURIE with "A" supported 6 platoons from East of these Coys who are in shelters in RICHOF TRENCH to use Rifle & Grenade fire.	
	ZERO 5:30 AM.		At the hour our Artillery opened a tremendous bombardment of the Hun trenches. At ZERO + 34 minutes our Infantry went over. From first we heard the attack went well. Though the officer in charge of the Bn. was tracked Field from our position at ECURIE although kept Commanding a good cross to the left we held so very little of the fighting as the enemy was very badly crowded from...	
	8:45 AM		Major Ralston commanding the 9th Reported Ed in the action Set on time a By commander to the Bn. called to 6 H.Q. for a Rest. Still on his way to the Runny Shells having been screwed though	

Army Form C. 2118.

WAR DIARY
or
INTELLIGENCE SUMMARY. (3)
(Erase heading not required.)

Instructions regarding War Diaries and Intelligence Summaries are contained in F. S. Regs., Part II. and the Staff Manual respectively. Title pages will be prepared in manuscript.

Place	Date	Hour	Summary of Events and Information	Remarks and references to Appendices
FAURIE	9th April	9.45 AM	Order. Through the aim to the attack on the Hun front line eyelets. There has been reported that everything was going well at the time that we had gained our front objective.	
		1 P.M.	C.Coy. have gone out to dut a communication Trench from Hun Tunnel across No Mans Land to the Hun front line. B.Coy. have dand out one platoon to make an ARTILLERY ROAD from our front line across NO MANS LAND & over the Hun Trenches & the platoon finds it quite enough to look the remainder of B.Coy. was getting Road material from OYB that one Coy of 12th Bn. has been working. C. OTRANTE POINT at B.13.a.6.2 D.Coy. has been detailed for this work, & 2 & 3 & 7 T.F.Coy has been to consolidate Ri found & most of the strong point. On the by the staff of our A.C. 4/2 Field Coy. R.E. have also to make strong point on the by the staff of our	
		2 P.M.	Word has just come in that the B.Coy platoon on arriving at Hun work was heavily shelled & suffered casualties 2nd Lt NOTT was severely wounded, Sgt MAULE killed & the other rank wounded. Work had to be stopped until such as the enemy opportunity.	
		6.30 P.M.	B. & D.Coys moved off from billets to work on Road & Strong front.	
		7.30 P.M.	Capt ALLEN O.C. C Coy has returned & reports the work completed without casualties.	
		8 P.M.	The C.O. & the R.S.M. have gone out to see how the work is getting on.	
		9.30 P.M.	A heavy fall of snow storm has started & the night is very dark until the sure trumpets on men at work.	

Army Form C. 2118.

WAR DIARY
or
INTELLIGENCE SUMMARY.
(Erase heading not required.)

Instructions regarding War Diaries and Intelligence Summaries are contained in F.S. Regs., Part II. and the Staff Manual respectively. Title pages will be prepared in manuscript.

Place	Date	Hour	Summary of Events and Information	Remarks and references to Appendices
ECURIE	9th April	10.45 p.m.	The C.O. along with Majors Tait & C. B. Coy have returned. Work seems to be progressing well but the ground through the shell area is very much cut up & it will take the C. Coy most of the night to clean & bank through for our Artillery. The Artillery are coming up fast to positions due in ROCLINCOURT & just from right. Heard forward of that.	
	10th	1.45 a.m.	Capt. Walton & 2nd Lt. Gray both of D. Coy have returned & report that the Wiring Party is under O.C. Campbell but that they had great difficulty in getting to Coy & the place owing to the extreme darkness & the heavy showers.	
		3.30 a.m.	Major Tait, Coy reported work finished. The Artillery good & over the 3rd Hun line & our guns are going through. This is very satisfactory.	
		4.20 a.m.	2nd Lt. H. E. R. Jones & 2nd Lt. Young of D. Coy have returned with the Coy & report that the Wiring Point at B13 d.6.2 & Campbell.	
		9.30 a.m.	New platoon of C. Coy have gone out to carry on the road started by B. Coy realizing forward on the following line from A24c1.35. to A24a.2.45. following track of old broad gauge railway at A24a.2.45. from there the front on overland track was prepared & taped to Maison de la Côte.	
		11 a.m.	C. Coy have gone out to clean a track along the C.J.R. Railway from A24 d. 2.45. to T2 Command House. B. Coy sheets out two men of salvage Buried & the work.	

WAR DIARY or INTELLIGENCE SUMMARY.

Army Form C. 2118.

(Erase heading not required.)

Place	Date	Hour	Summary of Events and Information	Remarks and references to Appendices
EURIE	10th April		A & C Coys reported late & the evening that work was comp[lete]. Heavy strain of snow in the afternoon driven down in from Bois that are on the Redoubt. The 17th Battalion are to take over our present billets & we move on the afternoon the 11th near St Pol Trench. The Knight & St Bethune were plans of the last Redoubt renewed rates at East Church was heard by & a great casualty of the troops coming before dark. We had to put the men into Cellars. I told for Co. the Cpl. Some troops have been arranged & every one was pretty comfortable. The trench received about 8.30 P.M. to all to end.	
	11th		The weather has improved & the Bn. were seen busy of taking packs. Taking back parts through the lines. To day we came under the O.C. XVII Corps for work & start tomorrow on the BAILLEUL road. What is in very bad state. Tomorrow our 1st & the Hon. part two Offs will Bn. to be employed on the road. Lt. Pearce, Lt. Philips joined the Bn. from home today.	
	12th		The weather is bright & sunny. Corps of General is keeping up well. The Transport arrived today from BRAY & the position just above two. The Padre & Officers men arrived today from NAVY No the Bn. is all together again. The whole Bn. was out working on the BAILLEU road today. The work is most urgent as the men have been there on the work.	
	13th			
	14th		Work as for yesterday. The weather is dry & hot also.	

WAR DIARY or INTELLIGENCE SUMMARY.

Army Form C. 2118.

Place	Date	Hour	Summary of Events and Information	Remarks and references to Appendices
St CATHERINE	15th April		Bn. worked on preparations. The weather has turned very cold.	
	16th "		Exhibition reviewed to slight extent by Brigade in old German front line N. LAURENT BLANGY village G.18.A.4.0. & to our underground in G.16. C.R.E. 4th Division Works Committee inspected.	
	17/4		Bn. moved to new billets in BLANGY VILLAGE where the new front line is. Transport & Horse lines & Quartermasters & new billet very limited in space to first further accommodation Bn. arr. Officers Reconnitred at HQr during the afternoon & returned the Bn. to ___ our new assembly front running from H.3.A.7.5. to H.10.A.9.35. The whole Bn. Co's tied for the work at 9P.M. D Coy etc. holding front at the POINT DU JOUR road before it reached the railway embankment. 0 Cst. Young, Wallace & Suggs wounded. Lt. Wallace & Lt. D. Morgan were killed. Place OP Priest & Bn wounded. B Coy was moving on Neuf & moving to the shelling & Casualties lost. Front with the guides & we failed to get to the ___, & the night & exceeding & dark & it is expected the front was behind a considerable amount of work to finish it before daylight.	
	18 "		C, B & C Coys reported about 5 A.M. the morning. About 700 yards & lined a day & finished the have & further 400 yards. Complete. Capt. Knight, D. Coy an estate of the work & Watson, L.D. Morgan & the 3 ___ killed last night were carried to the MILITARY CEMETRY ARRAS the evening. During the day further accommodation was found for the men. Stay as far as possible.	

Army Form C. 2118.

WAR DIARY
or
INTELLIGENCE SUMMARY.
(Erase heading not required.)

Place	Date	Hour	Summary of Events and Information	Remarks and references to Appendices
St LAURENT BLANGY G.18.A.4.0.	19th April		C/y. Completed their part of the Road but D Coy still have a few yards to do they found it difficult to break through the three wire which had to still practically to kind. A small party will be used to finish this tonight. A Coy. & working to-day on a side Road from the Point de Jour Road at H.18.Y.3. then went into work by new B.Hd. The Road in order of the work was completed before evening. The J.A. Coy Officer was wounded by a shell Close to Lieut. Owen at Lieut. Morris. new J the wounded were severe. B Coy were working on H. Road from St LAURENT BLANGY to the sunken road on the Point de Jour Road	
		10.05	B Coy. Report Shyford Road Completed. B Coy are on the Navan road on yesterday. A Coy on Reversing the far slope of the Road running from H.9.A.5.9. to H.9.d.5.8. whils along the work 2nd Lieut. Shaw was killed & his man wounded. The enemy were shelling that part very heavily all day. We Received orders to-day to first St LAWN given at point. H.14.a.2.8, H.15.c.6.3, H.15.c.9.1, & H.22.A.5.6. with the Object of trying to prevent Hun aircraft from flying Two over Artillery batteries situated in that area. 5 L.T. Lewis	
		21.15	To-day he gave Coin orders relative of the O.E. 17th Corps A Coy, a employed on Lyte Railway work near the main Road Gauge Railway when of gruen the East end of Blanky. B. Co. D. Cys on clearing up Road in 9 mon BLANGY 2nd Lieut Shaw was buried this evening in ARRAS CEMETRY of the 9th Div. fork over the Road from the 4 L Bn.	

WAR DIARY or INTELLIGENCE SUMMARY

Army Form C. 2118.

Place	Date	Hour	Summary of Events and Information	Remarks and references to Appendices
ST LAURENT BLANGY	22nd April		The Coys are employed as per yesterday. The weather is much improved. Thanks of the Cdes. The Bn is now quite comfortably installed, further accommodation having been got & certain dugouts vacated for shelter made to std kinder. The 517th Bn. are to attack tomorrow & A & D Coys are to be attached at 5.16. as Consolidation work.	
	23rd April		B & C Coys are working on tracks for OE as per yesterday. C & D Coys crossed out near CPE 517 down MR" at 6 P.M. awaiting orders for work. These two Coys were later on attached to Brigades 267 & 253 Resp. 2 A Coy & 1 D Coy & 156" Coys 1 Bde. A Coy were sent out to cut a tunnel from I.19.c.6.1 to I.19 c.4.3. which was done & the tunnel proved of valid service when the Huns counter attacked aug. a.m. morning of the 24th. The G.O.C. 51st Div Bde & a Comp. Commandy 6.17th & 2nd R.B. come & the Coy for the excellent work they had done. D Coy were not detailed for any defence work as the situation on the left flank was not very clear.	
	24th		The what RE is again working near OE XVII Corps on roads the weather is still good.	
	25th		All Coys are employed on clearing & repairing the track through ST LAURENT BLANGY village. roads & tramways. They are also making plans for RE Dumps & Camp grounds for troops along this road.	
	26th		Eit men were batted today in the 300" Div baths in ST NICHOLAS & received clean clothing & underclothing. The weather has been hot in June, the sun being very warm during the afternoon.	

Army Form C. 2118.

WAR DIARY
or
INTELLIGENCE SUMMARY.

(Erase heading not required.)

Place	Date	Hour	Summary of Events and Information	Remarks and references to Appendices
ST LAURENT BLANGY	27th April	Work as on before.		
	28"	The following Officers joined the Bn. from home. Cpln. W.A. Flemming 2nd Lt. D.G. Phillips, F.O. Marsh, J. Rees, J.B. Roberts, R.N. Wallace + G.F.B. Anderson.		
	29"/30"	Lt. R.M. Flint joined the Bn. today from home.		

Signed [illegible]
Lt Col
1/5 Royal West Surreys

WAR DIARY
INTELLIGENCE SUMMARY

Army Form C. 2118.

Casualties:-

Lieut. Wallace, W.E. } Killed in action 19-4-19.
2/Lieut. Morrison, Jas. } Killed in action 20/4/17.
2/Lieut. Snow, L.V. Killed in Action 20/4/17.
2/Lieut. Scott, C.C. Wounded 9.4.19
2/Lieut. Munro, A. " 19.4.19.
2/Lieut. Srail, D. " 19.4.19
Lieut. Orrock, K.C.   " 19.4.19 (at duty)
Capt. Mitchell, B.S. C.O.D. Cameron Alexandria 24/4/19.
2/Lieut. Dimmick, G.R. to I.E. School 3/4/17 Rej. 13/4/19.

Reinforcements:-

Captain Fleming, H.A. }
2/Lieut. Mar, J.A. }
Bailey, D.H. } Joined Battalion 28/4/19.
Ross, A. }
Dodds, J.B. }
Wallace, R.M. }
Anderson, A.F.B. }

2/Lieut. McNeil, R. - 30.4.19.
" Blackwood, W.J. - from hosp. 28/4/19.
Lieut. Rae, Ruskie, Jas. - from home 12/4/19.
2/Lieut. Sutherland, J.A. - from hosp. 8/4/19.
Capt. Pringle, J. - from 3rd Army Schl. 29.4.19.

Strength:- Officers 53 ; Other Ranks 1040 (30th Alice, 1919)

Other Ranks:-

Killed " 5
Wounded " 17
Died of W. " 1
Wounded " 7(at duty)
To Hosp (sick) " 51

Reinforcements:- 2 R/gos - 5(OR) 1/4/19
                 12 R.Scots - 4(OR) 4/4/19
                 11 R.Scots - 2(OR) 6/4/19
                 Drafts - 32 O.R. - 13.4.19.

[signature] Lieut.
Adj. 1/8 Bn. The Royal Scots
(Agency)

SECRET.

Copy No.____

1/8th. Bn. THE ROYAL SCOTS (Pioneers).

INSTRUCTIONS FOR OPERATIONS.

By Major JAMES A. TODD, Commanding.

7th. April, 1917.

1. MOVE.

   On Y/Z night the Battalion will move to ECURIE. The March Table has been issued separately.

2. DRESS.

   a. Men will wear full equipment, less packs.
   b. Men will carry 50 rounds ammunition.
   c. Water-bottles will be filled before leaving present billets.
   d. Men will carry the following :-

   > 1 Blanket.
   > 1 Waterproof Sheet.
   > 1 Leather Jerkin. (to be worn).
   > 1 pair extra Socks.

   e. The blanket, being carried, will be rolled in the waterproof sheet, and will be attached beneath the haversack by means of the pack-supporting straps.

3. PACKS, BLANKETS, and OFFICERS' VALISES.

   Packs and blankets will be dumped at the Q.M.Stores by 6 p.m. on "Y" day. Packs will be marked on part that goes next the man's back with indelible pencil, giving :- Reg.No., Rank, Name, and also the number of the platoon.
   Blankets will be rolled in bundles of ten, securely tied and labelled.
   The Transport Officer will arrange transport for the above articles as follows :-

   > 1 G.S. Wagon, for packs & officers' valises of "A" Coy,) less Res.
   > 1 G.S. Wagon,   do   do   "C" coy.) offrs..
   > 1 G.S. Wagon for blankets of both Coys.

   The above transport will report at ANZIN at 9-0 p.m. on "Y" day. "B" and "D" Coys. will carry packs, blankets, and valises direct to the Q.M.Stores.

4. COMPANY TOOL WAGONS.

   Company tool wagons will be sent to Company Headquarters at 9-0 a.m. on "Y" day to remove any Company tools not required at ECURIE. S.A.A. in bulk with Coys. can be put on these wagons.

5. THE Transport Officer will arrange to remove Coy.Cookers at 5-0p.m. on "Y" day.

6. RATIONS.

   a. Rations for "Z" day, also special breakfast ration, will be carried by the men, and will be issued by C.Q.M.Sgts. by 7p.m. on "Y" day.
   b. Rations for "Z ↓ 1 day have been dumped at ECURIE, and will be issued to Coys. on "Z" day.
   c. Rations for "Z ↓ 2" day will be sent upn on "Z ↓ 1" day if the situation permits, otherwise they will be drawn from the Advanced Divl. Dump.
   d. The following camp-kettles will be carried;-
      > per Company - 8
      > H.Q.Details. - 2
   e. C.Q.M.S. Welsh will act as RQMS with Bn. in ECURIE.

7. TOOLS /

Continued :-

2.

7. TOOLS.
Tools will be carried to ECURIE. Os. C. Coys. will arrange what proportion will be taken of each.

8. TIME.
Watches will be synchronized at 6 p.m. on "Y" day, and at midnight on "Y/Z" day. "C" Company will detail an officer to go to MARAGASTAR at these hours to check watches with a Staff Officer of the Division. This officer will report at BN.H.Q. on its arrival at ECURIE, and give correct time to the Adjt.

9. OFFICERS.
Five officers per Company will go to ECURIE.

10. RESERVE OF OFFICERS and N.C.Os. to be billeted in BRAY.
Captain Young will arrange the billeting of this party with the Town Major of BRAY.
Captain Young will received a Nominal Roll of this party from the Battalion Orderly Room at 6-30 p.m. on "X" day.
He will also arrange with the Transport Officer for transport to bring valises of reserve officers to BRAY on "Y" day.

11. Transport Lines will be near BRAY at F.20.a.3.7.

12. The Quartermaster's Stores will remain in MAROEUIL.

13. DISTINGUISHING MARKS.

The following will be worn :-

        Runners   -   Red Band.
        Signallers -   Blue Band.

14. Refilling point.
Refilling point for all units not in the trench area will be between PREVIN CAPELLE and ACQ.

15. MOBILE VET. SECTION.
The M.V.S. will be at MINGOVAL and an advanced collecting post and dressing station will be established at L.11.a.5.7.

16. MEDICAL.
The Transport Officer will detail the Medical Cart to report at 10 a.m. on "Y" day at BN. Dressing Station in MAROEUIL.

17. WORK.
No work will be done after midnight X/Y night unless otherwise ordered.

18. PROVISIONAL INSTRUCTIONS FOR OPERATIONS ARE CANCELLED.

19. ACKNOWLEDGE.

R. Jones. Lieut.,
Adjt., 1/8th. Bn. THE ROYAL SCOTS (Pioneers).

Issued at 10-30 a.m.
Copies to all holders of PROVISIONAL ORDERS.

S E C R E T.   Copy. No. 1

INSTRUCTIONS FOR MOVE TO ECURIE ON "Y" NIGHT.

1. "B" and "D" Companies will move to ECURIE on Y/Z night as shown in attached Table.

    Major Tait will be in charge of "B" and "D" Companies during the move and will arrange with O.C., 400th. (H) Field Company R.E. regarding the Move.

2. "A" and "C" Companies will move to ECURIE on Y/Z night as shown in attached table.

    Captain Alison will be in charge of "A" and "C" Companies during the move, and will arrange with 401st. (Highland) Field Company R.E. regarding the move.

3. BILLETS IN ECURIE.

    a. The 4th. Seaforth Highlanders are to be clear of our billets in ECURIE by 8-30 p.m. on "Y" night.

    b. Officers Commanding Companies will detail an offi officer to act as billeting officer for the Company on "Y" night.

    This officer will make himself acquainted with the billets allotted to his Company before "X" night. All information regarding this can be obtained from Lieut. R.S. Ovens, O.C. "A" Company.

    c. An advance party to take over billets and to act as guides to Companies on arrival, will proceed to ECURIE at 6-p.m. on "Y" day and will consist of :-

        1 Billeting Officer.)
        1 Coy. Q.M.S.   ) per Company.
        6 Men.   )

                                        A. Jones
                                                    Lieut.,
                    Adjt., 1/8th. Bn. THE ROYAL SCOTS (Pioneers).
Issued at 10-30 a.m.
    7th. April, 1917.

Copy No. 1 - Adjutant for Commanding Officer.
     "   2 - O.C. "A" Company.
     "   3 - O.C. "B" Company.
     "   4 - O.C. "C" Company.
     "   5 - O.C. "D" Company.
     "   6 - File.

Appx. No. 1

Unit	From	To.	Route	Remarks.
2 Sections 404th (Highland) Field Coy. R.E. and 1 Section 404th (Highland) Field Coy. R.E.	Maroeuil	Ecurie	A.	To join Route "A" immediately South of Cemetery Maroeuil. Not to reach Chateau Brunehaut before 12 midnight and to be clear of it by 12.15 am. To march in rear of 9/R. Black Watch.
2 companies 1/8th Royal Scots.	"	"	A.	To march in rear of 404th H. Coy. R.E. To be clear of Chateau Brunehaut by 1 am.

7th April, 1917.

[signature] Lieut:
Adj. 1/8th Bn. The Royal Scots (Pioneers).

Unit	From	To	Route	Remarks
3 Sections 401st Field Coy. R.E.	Auxin	Ecurie	Auxin-Ecurie Road	To march from Auxin at 12-30 a.m.
2 Companies 1/8th Royal Scots.	"	"	"	To march in rear of 401st F.Coy.R.E. and to be clear of Auxin before 1 a.m.

7th April 1919.

Lyons
Lieut..
Adjt. 1/8th Bn. The Royal Scots (Pioneers).

CONFIDENTIAL
N° 21(A)
HIGHLAND
DIVISION.

Army Form C. 2118.

WAR DIARY
or
INTELLIGENCE SUMMARY.
(Erase heading not required.)

10 Nyn 3/6/17

Vol 27

Confidential

WAR DIARY
OF
7/8th Bn. Royal West. Surrey

From
1st May 1917 to 30th May 1917

VOLUME 31

24.RS.

WAR DIARY or INTELLIGENCE SUMMARY.

(Erase heading not required.)

Army Form C. 2118.

Place	Date	Hour	Summary of Events and Information	Remarks and references to Appendices
ST LAURENT BLANGY G.18.d.4.0	May 1917			
	1st		The Coys are still employed under O.C. of XVII Corps on Roads Running through ST LAURENT BLANGY & on to ATHIES. N°2 Road on E. of Place buried yesterday & others entailing considerable clearing. The surface of the Roads however suffers whilst ever the others is closed up. We are still having of bursts weather.	
	2nd		2th Pattn of C.B. Coy was slightly wounded today still working on the Road near ATHIES also one of our O.R.Coy was wounded.	
	3rd 4th 5th 6th		The work continues the same & the Roads are now every good except through L'Evangu L'Empoure. The Weather continues good, very hot. Showing the Clay.	
	7th 8th		Mme O.R. Powers this both O.R. Coy. Approved the Pn. to Clay for Hospital, type O.R. of transd the Pn. from Depot the Nasty Injury, also there are some sick but in will the Bn. before.	
	8th		Many sick cases, the end part of today but fair Prairie Scenery.	
	9th		2/B. C.R.C. Sacone Approved the Bn. from England today the Poles to be Coy.	
	10th		Coys are stile employed in the Aleming Roads in the area. Matters & ground project.	
	11th		Received orders that the Syst. & Division will take over the Line from the 3rd Bu & the 12/4/13 wet. The steps to be taken over by from Brit Sport rod to CAMEL TRENCH N.W. Pn. I'm common orders the orders of the O.R.E. 5'th Dev. on Work at 8 am on 14 & inst.	

Army Form C. 2118.

WAR DIARY
or
INTELLIGENCE SUMMARY
(Erase heading not required.)

Instructions regarding War Diaries and Intelligence Summaries are contained in F.S. Regs., Part II. and the Staff Manual respectively. Title pages will be prepared in manuscript.

Place	Date	Hour	Summary of Events and Information	Remarks and references to Appendices
ST LAURENT BLANGY G.18.a.4.0	12th MAY		Handed over road in ResBn to day to the West York Pioneers of 9th Division. When Bn. was told our place in Corps Coys from cavalry of 13th Bde.	
	13.2		Three Lewis gun teams under 2/Lt Pilcher took over from the 4th Bn. Essex & the Lewis Guns of the Artists Battalion & the Hampden Ava. Batt. Group of R.B. Bn. are Holy the Sector of Area Commandant & Blangy Ord. Bn. Cp. was called on by O.R.E. Coupling the Enemy is to forward to report to G.O.C. 13th Bde Bd. for work in forward O.T. A.Coy. was sent down by A.T. Rd. H.Q.'s holds Posn. till the Line Post Cart of Evitué as the Situation of horsemen fish clear &	
	14.2		Three Coys of detected to work in galleries "H Coy in Colon Trent from T.13.d.7. East to GAVRELLE Roue Road Clearing & clearing the trench. Bd.C.Coy. worked forward from T.13.d.7.5. in a new O.T. Running to Line Trench T.20 a.2.9.	
	15.2		Wet was the warm as yesterday. D.Coy taking the place of B.Coy. The weather returning fine	
	16.2		Work forward of T.13.d.7.6. & T.20 a.2.9. Line completed length. C.Coy worked on forward part of Colon improving firer trench. A.Coy relieving from work came through a heavy barrage in return reported an new & live been moving. A great part has been lent out.	
	17.2		The Coys did not go out. trench trafty as situation on our front was uncertain. The Enemy attacks	

WAR DIARY or INTELLIGENCE SUMMARY.

(Erase heading not required.)

Army Form C. 2118.

Place	Date	Hour	Summary of Events and Information	Remarks and references to Appendices
ST LAURENT BLANGY G.15.a.4.0.	17th MAY		 Enemy attacked on our front & hung up attack through on our Right flank but was immediately driven back. Enemy a number of prisoners in our hands. The attack on our Right was easily held up. The enemy suffered heavy casualties. The Captain & R.C. Mudochs Left to Relay & take over from "D" Coy & to R.Q.M. Chapman 7th & 4th Coy, The Rev. Pere Poe was our R.C. Chaplain Relief today. Capt Perry & L/Cpl Keft. duty to take over command of the Bn Bombers & attached to the Bde. General Coy, He Officers went from the Bn duty to the Hampshire attached to the 133 Inf Bde. Other Officers were 2nd Lt J. Brenner, 2nd Lt Young & 2nd Lt Mervis to the 7th Blacks Watch. 2nd Clinard, 2nd Neale Coy & 2nd Lt Brown to 7th Gordon Highlanders.	
	18th "		The Coy succeeded. Enemy Trench. The evening saw their Right epithon joining East of Rois & Row Trench with a Traversed Trench. 2 Platoon making a O.T from CORONA SUPPORT & Junction of COLOMBO & CORONA. "B" Coy Cleaning up COLON & CORONA trenches. Coy working on new O.T from COLON & to ROW. 30 Journey and at T.19.b.5.5 & Z.30.a.2.5.	
	19th "		2nd Lt Dowdon T & Coy proceeded on 10 days special Leave. 2nd Lieut Jannon with 7th Hampshires on air Defence Suffered Casualties today. A shell burst in the entrance of a dugout at Tom "C" & 3 Pickles Mackenby 3 Men were hitting killing them all. The men bodies were brought Back to the Cemetery.	

A.D.S.S./Forms/C. 2118.

Army Form C. 2118.

WAR DIARY
or
INTELLIGENCE SUMMARY.
(Erase heading not required.)

Instructions regarding War Diaries and Intelligence Summaries are contained in F. S. Regs., Part II. and the Staff Manual respectively. Title pages will be prepared in manuscript.

Place	Date	Hour	Summary of Events and Information	Remarks and references to Appendices
ST LAURENT BLANGY G.17.c.4.0.	MAY 19		Contd. Work for today as follows:- 2 Coy clearing up trenches, CRONA SUPPORT. 3 Coy cutting new trench from CROOK to CROW 2 on & road at point T.13.d.3.3. 4 Coy continued C.T. from CORONA to COLOMBO.	
	20th		1st Essex & Hants relieved yesterday on front in 116 Bndal. Sector. Relieve 2/6 Essex & Hants in Rt. Sub Sector tonight. Work for today. 3 Coy view & (probably) 4 Coy on Crone Support, 1 Coy use same as yesterday. 2 Coy working parties used as hourly called for. 2 Coy rel'd had to withdraw about 7am.	
	21st		Work today as follows:- 3 Coy cut a Communication Boy. but a comm. trench from Railway at T.13.6.75.30 to CORONA at T.14.c.10.75. 1 Coy made new branched trench from Railway at T.13.6.70.45. 2 Coy continued a C.T. & bridge, &c. Formed teams of Electric Lamps here ready? enabled to do all the finishing at the spot on Area. The enemy of any movement in The Vicinity. & had 6 erd at top & 5' deep.	
	22nd		Coy worked today as follows:- New front T.13.6.70.45 clearing entrance & trench at the front & cutting new trench trench to about T.13.6.7.F. 1 Coy deepening Comt from CROW West & CROW East. 2 Coy found it impossible to work on new trench 16 from CRONA to COLOMBO on account of very heavy shelling, had to withdraw.	A.J.

2333 Wt. W2344/1454 700,000 5/15 D. D. & L. A.D.S.S./Forms/C. 2118.

WAR DIARY
or
INTELLIGENCE SUMMARY.

Army Form C. 2118.

Place	Date	Hour	Summary of Events and Information	Remarks and references to Appendices
ITLAURENT BEARLY GISA 4.9	May 22nd		Cold. Whole Battery started from Camp B.Bey now 7a Batt moves by getting on a badge which crosses a ditch near to the River Marsh. Tried out the Oxen. All yokes & trace harness of oxen yoked. On account of the sickness & inefficiency of 7a Col. Bee has acting as equipment WO. Emmerelin this led little sense of army generally. Capt WE Thorburn joined the Bn. today from England. Major 7.77.12. left today on 15 days of sick leave.	S.J.
		13.4	Went as follows: A.Bey. Stephenson (CAMEL) from Gamsie Pt West. B.Bey from as A.Bey. Bey again ordered to work on it. From where to cliffs. still along as the Border. saw Major & Capt Cyfrs & another front Gunner boarded ALIWFYSTS had Start-Ackron to pay. Capt Cyfrs team of the way to Liftled & to modelled. after noon left 1 to 13 days leave. Camel stay gone the you. field hq. Bn Battery of leave from and Camels	
		14.9	Work as follows. A.Bey. on Patrol. Bey or Cofl. D.Bey, 7 Gun Grow- in parties to work on the road field tilletown & Cofl. of Bn they worked	
		23.00	Work as fellows. B.Bey on CAMEL Bey on D.Bey, 1st over Bey, 97 Gun Grow to Atonia & Mongeal, late of Todnight. Last the whole Battery had Vecoly Residuction right. to fund this Ponce. 21 Bucky—the Cyfrs was bornd on Bey at A Rehelen	
		24.	Work to Move A.Bey Stephens Compny. (Ceylon). B.Bey, Stephens Compny. (CAMEL Cafts W2 Thorburn in forlin 6 D.Bey, the writer the colonel pretl.	

Army Form C. 2118.

WAR DIARY
or
INTELLIGENCE SUMMARY. (G)
(Erase heading not required.)

Instructions regarding War Diaries and Intelligence Summaries are contained in F. S. Regs. Part II. and the Staff Manual respectively. Title pages will be prepared in manuscript.

Place	Date	Hour	Summary of Events and Information	Remarks and references to Appendices
ST LAURENT BLANGY G.15.a.40.	29/4 May		Work was as follows:- B Coy Cutting new O.T. to Front Line from C.3.B.9 at I.7.d.30. C Coy working a O.T. from C.3.B.4.4 to C.3.B.0.0. D Coy making shelter in CRUMP Recess trench. Men from the Bn. also improving the main exit thence B1. Also making base & supports for the Regimental Transport Dpo & roof reinforcement & shelters etc for the men.	
	30th		Work was as follows:- A Coy completed O.T. from C.3.B.a to Front Line Coy worked on O.T. C.3.B.9.9 to Front. C.3.B.0.0. B Coy. Wells & Crumps. The weather still continues very fine. Work as per yesterday.	
	1st		to work on Comm. trench up the line. All ranks were employed chipping & getting things for the move. An Advance part of O in an Office from 12. St Enfield Highlanders Pioneers to take over. Division arrived today then 12 taken over an billet. Various matters re taking over shewn favourable also are A defense etc. We billet him as we expected all the men being shelled to the old Hun trenches. Took 5 civilian The Spring lithium and God officer took for the men were issued today. = 44	
	2nd		A transport left for PROVINCES at 7am. The morning marches the Battalion at 1.37 pm. Arrive. was received that the Bn. along with the two's Field Bys R.E. 2 ths Field Coy ambs. 134 machine gun Coy + the 11 N.B.J. Gideon. Coy were meet the Bn. Convoy at the arrows D Pot Rd at 2.00PM at 2.50 pm.	

2353. Wt. W2544/1454 700,000 5/15 D. D. & L. A.D.S.S./Forms/C. 2118.

Army Form C. 2118.

WAR DIARY
or
INTELLIGENCE SUMMARY

(Erase heading not required.)

Instructions regarding War Diaries and Intelligence Summaries are contained in F. S. Regs., Part II. and the Staff Manual respectively. Title pages will be prepared in manuscript.

Place	Date	Hour	Summary of Events and Information	Remarks and references to Appendices
ST LAURENT BLANGY G.15.a.4.0.	3rd Batln		Enemy barrage on L head Black Tommies D.T.P. The Bn left there behind at 12.30 pm & marched to the Rendezvous at War St Pt Road, being formed there by the other two platoons. There was a considerable delay using to the Guides in charge of two Convoys losing direction, supposed registration 40 yards the front at which it was expected the enemy barrage of 1st S.4.7 pm Reached PREVILLE at 7.00 pm The Bn was not have 6 guides with Capt Richardson 4 Lt. but for a difficult & dangerous relief. The battalion was found to be bright Capt Ramsay, Capt Richardson & 2nd Lieut Baker, Evans, Child & Mackenzie... ad the when found the Bn on arrival L1 - 77 OR. 9th June was Capt Ramsay - Capt Richardson & 2nd Lieut Baker, Evans, Child & Mackenzie.	RA Jones Lt Col / 7th Royal Welch Fusiliers

WAR DIARY
or
INTELLIGENCE SUMMARY.

Army Form C. 2118.

Casualties for Month:-

Officers:-
Killed - 2nd Lt. Bailey DH
Wounded - 2/Lt Colair R.
Do Sick - 2/Lt. McDonald JMS
" Dods JB
Chaplain W. Middleton to HQ 38th Army

Other Ranks:-
Killed 5
Wounded 28
Wounded at duty 6
Gassed 3
Do Gas Shell 46
Acc. Drowned 1

Other Ranks:- 14
44
58

Reinforcements:-
2nd Lieut J. Suit from Hosp. 8.5.19
" A. Munro from hosp. 10.5.19
" C.H. Snow " "
Chaplain A.J. Pirie u/s from home 19.5.19
Capt. W.E. Sherburn from Bn - to Bn. 19.5.19
Capt. Ballantyne EM from home 22/5/19
" Richardson J.
" Wilson GM
2/Lt. White A. Joined 31.5.19
" Colair JS
" Mackenzie N

Strength on 31st May 1919 = 52 Officers
983 O. Ranks

2/6/19

Lloyd Lieut.
Adj. 1/6th Royal Scots (Pnrs)

No. 10.

1/8th. Bn. THE ROYAL SCOTS (Pioneers).

TRANSPORT ARRANGEMENTS FOR MOVE TO FREVILLERS 31st. May, 1917.

By Lieut.-Colonel W. GEMMILL, D.S.O., Commanding.

30th. May, 1917.

1. The Battalion, less Transport will move to FREVILLERS on 31st. May by Bus. Transport will move by road.
   There are no restrictions as to roads West of ARRAS.
   The following Extract from A.I.No. 29 to Div. Order No. 156 is re-published :-

   Para.7. "Strict attention will be paid to march discipline of Transport. All dismounted personnel accompanying Transport will be properly dressed."

   No unauthorised person will ride on wagons without a pass signed by an officer.
   A distance of 100 yards will be kept between the Transport of Units.

2- DISTRIBUTION OF TRANSPORT.

   (A) The following Transport will report at Battalion at 4-0 p.m. to-day :-

   1 G.S.Wagon per Company for tools and part of Officers' and Sergeants Mess Boxes.
   "D" Coy. wagon will take Pioneer Sergeant's Outfit,
   "C" Company Wagon will take Shoemakers' Tools.
   "B" Company wagon will take Tailors' Tools.
   1 Medical Cart.
   These wagons will return to Transport Lines when loaded.
   Companies will detail one brakesman to accompany each wagon.
   The Medical Officer will detail 1 brakesman for Medical Cart.

   (B) The following Transport will report at Battalion to-night at 6-0 p.m.. Horses will return to Transport Lines.

   1 Baggage Wagon for "A" and "B" Coys. Officers' Kits.
   1   do   "C" and "D" Coys. Officers' Kits.
   1 Limber for Headquarters Officers' Kits
   1   "   for Orderly Room and Signals.
   1 Mess Cart for Headquarters.

   These wagons, also cookers and water-carts, will be loaded by 7-0 a.m. on 31st. instant,. "A" and "D" Company will detail brakesmen for the Baggage Wagons. The Adjutant will detail brakesmen for the   Headquarters limber and Orderly Room limber.
   Horses for 2 baggage wagons, H.Q.Limber, O.Room Limber, Cookers and Water Carts and Mess Cart will be at Battalion Headquarters at 7-0 a.m.

   (C) Transport will thus be distributed as follows :-
                                ("D" Coy. & Pioneer Sergt's Tools.
   8 G.S.Wagons for Coys. ("C" Coy. & Shoemakers' Tools.
                                ("B" Coy. & Tailors' Tools.
   1 Limber for Lewis Guns.
   1   "   for S.A.A.
                                          / 1 Limber for Transport.

SECRET.   Copy No. 11

1/8th. Bn. THE ROYAL SCOTS (Pioneers).

INSTRUCTIONS FOR MOVE TO FREVILLERS, 31st. MAY. 1917.

By Lieut.-COLONEL W. GEMMILL, D.S.O., Commanding.

30th. May, 1917.

Reference Map, ARRAS Edition 7 A.

1. The Battalion (less Transport) and the Divisional Salvage Company will move to FREVILLERS on 31st. May, 1917 by bus.
   The Transport arrangements have been issued separately.

2. Reveille on 31st. May   - 5-30 a.m.
   Breakfast   "   - 6-0 a.m.
   Dinner   "   - 11-0 a.m.

3. Baggage wagons   )
   Cookers.   )
   Water-carts.   )
   Orderly Room   ) will be loaded and ready to move
     & Signals Limber.   )   off by 7 a.m.
   H.Q. Limber & Mess Cart)

4. DRESS.

   Dress will be full marching order.   Blankets will be rolled in water-proof sheets and worn on the top of the packs.

5. PARADE.

   The Battalion will parade ready to march at 12-30 p.m.,- "A" Company leading, followed by "B", "C" and "D" Companies at 200 yards distance.   The head of "A" Company will parade at cross-roads G.18.a.4.1,- the remainder of the Battalion on road running North through the camp from that point.

6. DETAILS.

   All details except cyclists will parade with their Companies. Cyclists will parade at 8 a.m. and proceed to FREVILLERS by road under Sergt. Main who will report to Captain Richardson on arrival there.
   Personnel at present at Transport Lines who are proceeding by bus will proceed under the Pipe-Major and be at point G.20.a.9-8 on the ARRAS - St.POL Road at 1-30 p.m.   They will parade along with the Battalion on arrival there.

7. ACKNOWLEDGE.

                                                    Lieut.,
Issued at 7 p.m.
                             Adjt., 1/8th. Bn. THE ROYAL SCOTS (Pioneers).

Copy No. 1 - Adj. for C.O.   Copy No. 7 - Quartermaster.
         2 - O.C. "A" Company.   8 - Medical Officer.
         3 - O.C. "B" Company.   9 - R.S.M.(for all details
         4 - O.C. "C" Company.   10 - O.C., 31st.Sal.Co.
         5 - O.C. "D" Company.   ✓ 11 - War Diary.
         6 - Transport Officer.   12 - File.

Continued :-

    1 Limber for Transport.
    1   "   for Headquarters.
    1   "   for Orderly Room and Signals.
    2 Limbers for Quartermaster.
    2 Baggage Wagons for Officers' Kits.

    If there is more S.A.A. than can be put on one Limber the balance will be distributed on the 4 G.S.Wagons already loaded in Transport Lines.
    The Armourer' Sergeant's Tools will go on Transport or Quartermaster's limbers which ever has the lightest load.

No 3. *Please acknowledge.*

                                                              Jones. Lieut.,

Issued at   Adjt., 1/8th. Bn. The Royal Scots (Pioneers).
12-30 p.m.

    Copy No. 1 - Adjutant for Commanding Officer.
            2 - O.C."A" Company.
            3 - O.C."B" Company.
            4 - O.C."C" Company.
            5 - O.C."D" Company.
            6 - Transport Officer.
            7 - Quartermaster. (for Armourer Sergt.)
            8.- Medical Officer.
            9 - Regtl. Sergt.Major (For all details.)
          10 - War Diary.
          11 - File.

Army Form C. 2118.

WAR DIARY
or
INTELLIGENCE SUMMARY.

CONFIDENTIAL
No. 2/A
HIGHLAND DIVISION.

Vol 28

95 R.S.

WAR DIARY
of
1/9TH THE ROYAL SCOTS.
FROM
1st June to 31st June 1917

VOLUME 32

Army Form C. 2118.

WAR DIARY
or
INTELLIGENCE SUMMARY.
(Erase heading not required.)

Instructions regarding War Diaries and Intelligence Summaries are contained in F.S. Regs., Part II. and the Staff Manual respectively. Title pages will be prepared in manuscript.

Place	Date	Hour	Summary of Events and Information	Remarks and references to Appendices
FREVILLERS	June 1st		9th Bn. have settled down to their new billets. Ret. Inspection respective of Clothing & Boot turns held during the day. The weather is very heavy.	
	2nd		9th Bn. Paraded for Chu. on the Chief Gas Shell Lecture at training & musketry during the forenoon. Coll. Gr. Baseball Matches. Coy p.layers clearing the afternoon & in the Coy Lines. Training held during the evening.	
	3rd		Bn. Church Parade was held 8-45am. Followed by a Route March.	
FREVILLERS to MONCHY CAYEAUX	4th		9th Bn. Marched from FREVILLERS to MONCHY - CAYNEUX to-day via MONCHY BRETON - OCTREVILLE - ST. POL. Operation Order for move attached. Our destination was reached about 8 P.M. The Bn. marched off Moodily & split the last half at a more fatiguing out. A halt of 1½ hour duration was made near ST. POL for dinners which was found to be most useful.	
			Bathing was the lot of the Coys & all Ranks Enjoyed.	
MONCHY CAYEAUX to COYECQUE AREA	5th		9th Bn. Marched from MONCHY CAYEAUX to PRESSOUX AREA to-day via NUVIN - CREPY - VERCHIN - MATRINGHEM - REBINGHEM - RECLINGHEM. Operation Order for the move attached. Coll. D.S.H. area for dinner near MATRINGHEM, & Reclelen & was reached at 5.10 P.M. Our last Van Again very heavy for pack. Pack on the march but only Just the full out. Relief was very good & excellent bathing was to be got to the Rivers the men thoroughly enjoyed it.	

Army Form C. 2118.

WAR DIARY
or
INTELLIGENCE SUMMARY. (2)
(Erase heading not required.)

Instructions regarding War Diaries and Intelligence Summaries are contained in F.S. Regs., Part II. and the Staff Manual respectively. Title pages will be prepared in manuscript.

Place	Date	Hour	Summary of Events and Information	Remarks and references to Appendices
COYECQUE	June 6th		Othr Ranks had leave for today. The Old Revd Baptist Chaplain The former & former was held at the fields surrounding the Gun Signals. Sports were held from 5 PM to 6.15 PM. There were attended to by both Officers & men.	
COYECQUE TO BONNINGUES	7th		The Bn moves today by bus from COYECQUE to BONNINGUES. Transport went by Road. Operation Orders for the move are attached. The journey was the Sp Order & previous day. About 9 AM. Escorts arrived at Bns Dinner was served in a field by 5Th All men were billeted comfortably. We understand that we are to remain here for about a fortnight.	
BONNINGUES LES ARDRES	8th		Musical Parade this TA Rifles Reported the Bn from Orders today.	
	9th	12.15 PM	Bath & Shower Reported to R. Exeley & 2nd Mining of mens toilets from the 2/5 Bn R. Park. Appearance today at 10 am to squadron training, latter mainly forming to form the 2 PR to 3.30 PM. Op parades for Platoon company nec attention to turn paid to musketry. On been made out that war be allowed to conduct all attention to be paid to musketry relating to the ranges which we expect to have allotted to us for large.	
	10th		Sunday. R.C. Church parade at 9.30 am followed by a Wall march in the Forest. beautiful weather	

Army Form C. 2118.

WAR DIARY
or
INTELLIGENCE SUMMARY. (3)
(Erase heading not required.)

Instructions regarding War Diaries and Intelligence Summaries are contained in F. S. Regs., Part II. and the Staff Manual respectively. Title pages will be prepared in manuscript.

Place	Date	Hour	Summary of Events and Information	Remarks and references to Appendices
BONNINGUES LES ARDRES.	June	11.15	Adjut. & 2nd R. learnt the Bn. today. Training continued as per Programme hitto now received today, that an may be shipped out the Bn. from shortly.	
		A.M.	The O.C. Coy today [gave] the forward area doth to O.R.E. 7th Bn. So exchange being arranged. Coy were [warned] to arrange billets for the Bn. if it is not known what part of the line we are going to.	
	4.1		Training as per Programme continued. Received 24 horse harness & also numerous stores from the Details.	
	14.7		The Bn. Sports were held this afternoon. Every event supported. The men thoroughly enjoyed the afternoon & although a very hot wind, the Sport was held to a [?] owing to the expected arrival had to be [?] today.	
	16.9		Lecture in the Square today was received at 9.30 a.m. Capt. G.B. [Gooden] leaves for the men [march] off. Ben. ? part of Transport (A, [?], mules, [warheads] & [?]) marched by Om. & [?]	
BONNINGUES to POPERINGHE			to AUDRUICQ where entrainer was reached. The Bn. entrained at 1pm. & reached POPERINGHE at 5.30 pm. From there they detrained & marched to comp. 700 Camp so about 2.7 miles A.2 9 & centred [?] among them at 7.30 P.M. Billeting [?] had gone ahead in the [?] were fitted up & work. The remainder of the Transport went & came holding the night on the way. The weather was fine throughout the day that rain improbable.	

2353. Wt. W2541/1454. 700,000. 5/15. D.D. & L. A.D.S.S./Forms/C. 2118.

WAR DIARY or INTELLIGENCE SUMMARY.

(Erase heading not required.)

Army Form C. 2118.

Place	Date	Hour	Summary of Events and Information	Remarks and references to Appendices
Camp N° 6 and/at near PROVINS	June 18th		All hands being today improving camp. Other Coys went to work. Bn H.Q.rs of the Bn. & Coys were to of the line & are here having transport animals Brig.nr about 7 p.m.	
	17th		A & B Coys went up the line the enemy into billets in Canal Bank at N.10.2.N.W. (28 western) A Coy. did work in JAFFA TRENCH & B Coy. in STIRLING LANE widening the jumping off parallels. There was 0 TRENCHES.	
	18th		Coys working daily D has billets in CANAL BANK near 2nd B. Coys then took up the missing accommodation, the huts being on the Canal Bank. The CO & two sections & a Farm up the front with the Bn.	
	19th		4th Coy. with the line are employed as follows: A Coy. in JAFFE TRENCH widening stepping & Reatray from A. E. X LINE, B Coy. in STIRLING LANE widening stepping highly & lower of E.X LINE. Dug heads as also heavy land along thin for TRENCH. C Coy. is employed making shelters in Canal Bank. Major Tait Holt. Rev. left today for leave to England.	
	20th		C Coy O.R.ng & tvls. has been found in addition for the work being carried from are the Coys. 2nd H. Keeve has charge of this platoon for clearing & ten were used here started new transportation: the Regn. for clearing the photos & hill the cans of	

Army Form C. 2118.

WAR DIARY
or
INTELLIGENCE SUMMARY.
(Erase heading not required.)

Place	Date	Hour	Summary of Events and Information	Remarks and references to Appendices
Camp A.29 c Central	10th Oct 1916		Yesterday out the first method of sinking of the most suitable site. I was for this part of the line. Steam is at present a great resource of water both in the ground & in air.	
	22nd		Work for A Boot Coys is a before first process being made.	
	23rd		The weather has broken down at last, being very gloomy. During the night a considerable shower. Nothing during the day. 2nd Lieut. Ward relieved for four days.	
	24th		Major Feilden the sick along Canal Bank and tried to see the Dressing Stn. He failed in complete billings not & not up to the time. The weather of the Sgt. was considered at all today, but my Sgt Lt. D Coy returns & Coy this evening. Pte J. Brown was wounded early this morning. Stab out at work with B Coy on firing line at 8 feet having the ground to to ophie in Stephens distances. Ten men were been hours today, for my enquires, Pte Barnes was found in a dangerous state	
	25th		Unit is in before office. Weather if rather unsettled and there have been several heavy storms during the bout 30 hours.	
	26th		Ploy has finished their whole B Coy & Boot Coy on 27th 17 & 5th of HQ HUTS. Tenants of the Salvery. Returning of Bord dance. The other two layers working the Sgt.	
	27th		A Coy returned. B Coy this morning. C Coy unit completed their Hutting of Huts	

Army Form C. 2118.

WAR DIARY
or
INTELLIGENCE SUMMARY.
(Erase heading not required.)

Instructions regarding War Diaries and Intelligence Summaries are contained in F. S. Regs., Part II. and the Staff Manual respectively. Title pages will be prepared in manuscript.

Place	Date	Hour	Summary of Events and Information	Remarks and references to Appendices
Camp N° 29 Cabaret Rouge		5 am	Offr on duty along the same Shee Tunnel Tramway system from Maroux Camp siding to front line a distance of 500 yards. Other than work progressing, 2nd relief 29th I.T. Coy of Stoy Coy on Tramways	
		2 pm	Party out on observing	
		6.15	Sentry men out cleaning tramway track in the Tunnels	
			No casualties. Weather dense, rather colder than yesterday.	

[signature]
O.C. 1st Coy R.E.
Pioneers

Army Form C. 2118.

WAR DIARY
or
INTELLIGENCE SUMMARY

(Erase heading not required.)

Place	Date	Hour	Summary of Events and Information	Remarks and references to Appendices
Casualties during 1st & 30th of June 1917 —				

Officers: Lieut J Brewer M.C. D. wounds 24.6.17

2/Lieut Gimp J.J. Wounded — 29.6.1917
2/Lieut. Mercer R. To Hospital — 30.6.17

Other Ranks:
Complete 5
Died of W. 1
Wounded —
Wounded (many?)
Sick (15-29) 25
                35

Reinforcements: NCOs arrived of Chestnut Sqdn 3.6.17 — 1.6.17 — 10
                 Oct 90 "April 8.6.17 12.6.17 — 20
                                              21.6.17 — 12
                                              30.6.17 — 37
                                                       79

Strength on 30th June 1917 = 55 off + 1077 OR

A.Sons Lieut
Adjt for Royal Scots (Lothians)

2449 Wt. W14957/M90 750,000 1/16 J.B.C. & A. Forms/C.2118/12.

SECRET.   Copy No. 1.

1/8th. Bn. THE ROYAL SCOTS (Pioneers).

OPERATION ORDER No. 1

By Lieut.-Colonel W. GEMMILL, D.S.SO, Commanding.

Reference Map LENS 11.   3rd June 1917

DETAIL FOR TO-MORROW :-

    Reveille 5-0 a.m.   Breakfast 6-0 a.m.
    Dinner on the march.   Tea on arrival.

1. The Battalion and the Divl. Salvage Company will move by route march to MONCHY-CAYEAU, via MONCHY BRETON - OSTREVILLE - St.POL, and will parade ready to move at 8-0 a.m. at the cross-roads at the West end of the village in the following order :-

    Band.
    "D" Company.
    "C" Company.
    "B" Company.
    "A" Company.
    Salvage Coy.

2. DRESS.

    Steel helmets will be worn.

3. BILLETING PARTY.

    Captain Richardson and cyclists detailed by Adjutant will move off at 8-0 a.m.

4. TRANSPORT.

    Arrangements for Transport are being issued separately.

5.   ACKNOWLEDGE.

Issued at
   5-30 p.m.   _____ Lieut.,

    Adjt., 1/8th. Bn. THE ROYAL SCOTS (Pioneers).

✓ Copy
  No. 1 - Adjutant for Commanding Officer.
     2 - O.C. "A" Company.   No. 8 - MEDical Officer.
     3 - O.C. "B" Company.   9 - R.S.M. (for all details)
     4 - O.C. "C" Company.   10 - O.C., 51st.Div. SalvageCo.
     5 - O.C. "D" Company.   11 - War Diary.
     6 - Transport Officer.   12 - File.
     7 - Quartermaster.

Copy No. 18

1/8th. Bn. THE ROYAL SCOTS (Pioneers).

TRANSPORT ARRANGEMENTS FOR OPERATION ORDERS No. 1,

By Lieut.-Colonel W. GEMMILL, D.S.O., Commanding.

3rd. June, 1917

1. Transport is allotted as follows :-

   "A" Coy. - 2 G.S.Wagons.
   "B" Coy. - 2 do.
   "C" Coy. - 2 do.
   "D" Coy. - 2 do.

   All Company Officers' Kits will be carried on the above wagons, and brakesmen detailed by Companies.

2. 1 Baggage Wagon for blankets of "A" & "B" Coys.
   1 do. do. "C" & "D" Coys.
   "A" and "B" Coy.'s blankets will be loaded at the Church, and "C" and "D" Coys.' at the Cross Roads.
   O.C. "A" Company will detail a loading party of 4 men and an officer to superintend the loading of "A" and "B" Coy.wagon, and O.C. "C" Coy. will detail a similar party for "C" and "D" Coy. Wagon.
   O.C. "A" and "C" Companies will also detail a brakesman for each of these wagons.
   Wagons will be at loading points at 6-45 a.m. and loaded by 7-15 a.m.
   Blankets will be firmly rolled, tied in bundles of ten and labelled.

3. Great-coats will be taken by motor-lorry, and will be rolled in bundles of 5. O.C. Coys. will each detail an officer to superintend the rolling of great-coats. No articles are to be allowed in great-coat pockets or sleeves. Any man found disobeying this order will carry his great-coat in his pack.
   Great-Coats will be dumped by Companies near the cross roads by 6-45 a.m.
   The Medical Officer will detail 8 men for loading great-coats. Four men will go with the first lorry. Sergt. Alexander and 4 men will remain behind to load the remaining great-coats when the lorry returns. O.C. "D" Company will detail an officer to superintend the loading of great-coats on the first journey. The R.Q.M.S. will accompany the lorry on its first journey.

4. LIMBERS.

   (a) 2 limbers for S.A.A.
   (b) 1 " Lewis Guns.
   (c) 1 " H.Q., & Band Kits.
   (d) 1 " O.Room, Signals, & Arm.Sgt.
   (e) 1 " T.O., Pioneers, Shoemakers & Tailors
   (f) 1 " Quarter-master.

   Brakesmen for the above will be detailed as follows :-
   (a) By Transport Officer.
   (b) " Sgt. Souness.
   (c) " Medical Officer.
   (d) " R.S.M.
   (e) " Transport Officer.
   (f) " Quartermaster.
   b Medical Cart - Medical Officer.

   / All wagons to be

- 2 -

5. All wagons will be loaded by 7-30 a.m. and ready to move by 8-0 a.m.

6. Brakes-men may be allowed to put their packs on the wagons they are attending, if in possession of a chit from the Medical officer to the effect that they are unfit to carry them.

7. Travelling Kitchens will march in rear of their Companies.

Issued at
   6-15 p.m.

                                           Lieut.,
        Adjt., 1/8th. Bn. THE ROYAL SCOTS (Pioneers).

Copy No. 1 - Adjt. for C.O.   Copy No. 10 - Regtl. Sergt.Major.
        2 - O.C."A" Company.   11 - N.C.O. i/c L.Guns.
        3 - O.C."B" Company.   12 -   "   Cyclists.
        4 - O.C."C" Company.   13 -   "   Signals.
        5 - O.C."D" Company.   14 - Pioneer Sergt.
        6 - O.C.Div.Salvage Co.   15 - Armourer Sergt.
        7 - Medical Officer.   16 - Pipe-Major.
        8 - Transport Officer.   17 - War Diary.
        9 - Quartermaster.   18 - File.

1/8th. Bn. THE ROYAL SCOTS (Pioneers).

OPERATION ORDER No. 2,

By. Lieut.-Colonel W. GEMMILL, D.S.O., Commanding.

4th. June, 1917.

Reference Maps Lens 11
and Hazebrouck 5 A.

1.   The Battalion and the Divisional Salvage Company will move by route march to the COYECQUE Area via ANVIN, - CREPPY - VERCHIN - - MATRINGHEM - REOLINGHEM.

2.   Reveille 5-30 a.m.   Breakfast 6-0 a.m.
     Dinner on the march.   Tea on arrival.

3.   Companies will parade ready to move off at 7-0 a.m. in the following order :-

          Cyclists.
          Band.
          "A" Coy.
          "D" Company.
          "C" Company.
          "B" Company.

4. DRESS.

     Tam o' Shanters will be worn. Steel helmets will be carried in the straps of the pack.

5. TRANSPORT.

     Wagons will be loaded by 6-30 a.m. under arrangements as for to-day.

6. MOTOR LORRY.

     The motor lorry will leave on its first journey at 6-45 a.m. Loading and unloading parties will be detailed by the Medical Officer.

7. ACKNOWLEDGE.

Issued at 7-0 p.m.

                                              Lieut.,
                    Adjt., 1/8th. Bn. THE ROYAL SCOTS (Pioneers).

Copy No. 1 - Adjt. for C.O.   Copy No. 10 - Regtl. Sergt. Major.
         2 - O.C. "A" Company.   11 - N.C.O. i/c L.Guns.
         3 - O.C. "B" Company.   12 -   "   Cyclists.
         4 - O.C. "C" Company.   13 -   "   Signals.
         5 - O.C. "D" Company.   14 - Pioneer Sergt.
         6 - O.C. "Div. Salvage Co.   15 - Armourer Sergt.
         7 - Medical Officer.   16 - Pipe Major.
         8 - Transport Officer.   17 - War Diary.
         9 - Quartermaster.   18 - File.

SECRET.   Copy. No. 11

1/8th. Bn. The Royal Scots (Pioneers).

Operation Order No.3

By Lieut.-Colonel W. GEMMILL, D.S.O., Commanding.

6th. June, 1917.

Reference Map, HAZEBROUCK, 5 A.
    Scale 1 : 100,000

    Reveille 5-0 a.m.   Breakfast 5-45 a.m.

1. The Battalion and the Divisional Salvage Company (less Transport will move by Bus to BONNINGUES-LES-ARDRES on 7th. June.

    The Battalion in full marching order with blanket and water-proof sheet rolled on top of the pack will parade at 6-30 a.m. at cross-roads at second "L" of LE WAMEL, - "D" and "C" Companies on main road, "A" and "B" Companies on road between the river and the main road.

3. All details (except cyclists who will march with Transport) will join their Companies.

4. Transport arrangements for the move are issued separately

5. Acknowledge.

Issued at 5-30 p.m.   Lieut.,
                    Adjt., 1/8th. Bn. The Royal Scots (Pioneers).

Copy. No. 1 - Adjt. for C.O.
          2 - O.C. "A" Company.
          3 - O.C. "B" Company.
          4 - O.C. "C" Company.
          5 - O.C. "D" Company.
          6 - Transport Officer.
          7 - Quartermaster.
        b8 - Medical Officer.
          9 - R.S.M. (For all details).
        10 - O.C. 51st. Salvage. Co.
        11 - War Diary.
        12 - File.

1/8th. Bn. THE ROYAL SCOTS (Pioneers).

TRANSPORT ARRANGEMENTS FOR OPERATION ORDER No. 3.

By Lt. Colonel W. GEMMILL, D.S.O., Commanding.

6th. June, 1917.

1. The Battalion and the Divisional Salvage Company will move to BONNINGUES-LES-ARDRES on 7th. May by Bus. Transport and cyclists will move by road.

2. The following vehicles will be at Bn. Headquarters at 7-0 p.m. to-night :-

          Medical Cart.
          Orderly Room G.S.Limber.
8 G.S.Limber will report at Q.M.Stores at 7-0 p.m. to-night.

3. COOKERS AND water-carts will go to Transport Lines at 7-30 p.m. to-night.

4. The following Transport will report at 9-0 p.m. this evening as under :-
    1 G.S.Wagon to "A" & "B" Companies' H.Q. for Officers' Kits
    1   do.   "C" & "D" do.   do. & Heavy Mess Boxes.
    1 G.S.Limber for H.Qrs.   do.   do.   do.

Officers will only retain such kit as is necessary for the night, i.e. one blanket each, washing and shaving gear. The bulk will go on the baggage wagons to-night.

5. A motor-lorry will report at the Church, COYECQUE, at 7-0 a.m. to-morrow morning. R.Q.M.S. White will meet the lorry there, and will guide it round the billets collecting the following :-
    "A","B") Officers' Kits (other than mentioned in para.4)
    "C" & "D") Light Mess Boxes.

Companies will each leave one servant to look after same.
    H.Qrs. Officers' Kits and Mess Boxes.
    Camp Kettles of "A" & "B" Coys. from "A" Coy. H.Qrs.
       do.   "C" & "D" Coys. from "D" Coy. H.Qrs.

"B" Company will send their Camp Kettles to "A" Coy. Cooks immediately after breakfast to-morrow morning. "C" Company will send their camp kettles to "D" Company cooks immediately after breakfast to-morrow morning.

The following personnel will proceed with Motor Lorry.

        R.Q.M.S. White,
        4 Coy. Servants.
        1 H.Qrs. Servant.
        2 Coy. Cooks.

6. The Transport Officer will make his own arrangements regarding time of move and routes to be taken, and will notify Sergeant Main when to report for the move.

                                    Lieut.,
            Adjt., 1/8th. Bn. The Royal Scots (Pioneers).

Issued at 6-0 p.m.

    Copies to all recipients of O.O. No. 3.

S E C R E T.   Copy No. 12

1/8th. Bn. THE ROYAL SCOTS (Pioneers).

OPERATION ORDER No. 3

By Major JAMES A. TODD, Commanding.

Reference Map, HAZEBROUCK 5a.   15th. June, 1917.

1. The Battalion will move to-day at 8-30 a.m. to camp A.29.c. central by road to AUDRUICQ and from thence by rail.

2. The following Transport will accompany the Battalion, leaving here at 8-0 a.m. :-

        Coy. Tool Wagons.
        "   Cookers.
        Water-carts.

3. The remainder of the Transport will move by road to HERZEELE leaving here at 8-0 a.m., and will report to O.C., 18th. Corps Cavalry there. They will continue the march to camp, A.30-8, central on 16th. instant. There are no restrictions as to route.
    This section of the Transport will be under the orders of the Transport Officer.

4.   Reveille 5-0 a.m.   Breakfast 5-30 a.m.
    Dinner, at Audruicq, 11-30 a.m. Tea on arrival.
    Companies will parade at the positions to be pointed out to Company Commanders ready to move off at 8-30 a.m. in the following order :-

        Cyclists.
        Band.
        "A" Company.
        "B" Company.
        "C" Company.
        "D" Company.

5. Dress will be Fighting Kit, with steel helmets slung in the straps of the haversack.

6. Mens' packs with blankets rolled inside on top and held in position by pack straps will be dumped near the Q.M.Stores by Coys. by 7-30 a.m. One officer and 2 men per Coy. will be detailed to act as loading party, and will proceed with motor lorries to AUDRUICQ where they will unload, and await arrival of the Battalion.
    The third motor lorry will carry packs and blankets of all details also Headquarters valises.

7. Two platoons of "A" Coy. will proceed with Transport to AUDRUICQ at 8-0 a.m. to act as a loading-party for entraining.

8. Acknowledge.

                                                          Lieut.,

Issued at 4-30 a.m.   Adjt., 1/8th. Bn. The Royal Scots (Pioneers).

Copy. No. 12

1/8th. Bn. The Royal Scots (Pioneers).

TRANSPORT ARRANGEMENTS FOR OPERATION ORDER No. 4.

By Major JAMES A. TODD, Commanding.

15th. June, 1917.

Reference Map, HAZEBROUCK
5a.

1. a. Transport, moving by road, is allotted as follows :-

    1 G.S.Limber for S.A.A.
    1   do.   Lewis Guns.
    1   do.   Quartermaster.
    1   do.   O.Room, Signals, & Arm.S.Sergt.
    1   do.   T.O, Pioneers, Shoemakers & Tailor
    1 Medical Cart for Medical Stores.
    1 Baggage Wagon for Canteen Stores. & heavy mess boxes.
    1 Mess Cart.

    The above vehicles will be sent to positions notified to Transport Officer by 6-0 a.m. for loading.

    Brakesmen for the above will be detailed by the T.O.

    The Transport Officer will make his own arrangements re route to be taken by this section.

2. Transport moving with Battalion :-

    Tool wagons and cookers etc. will be loaded ready to move by 7-0 a.m.   Tool wagons will carry officers' valises and light mess boxes.

3. Acknowledge.

                                        Lieut.,

        Adjt., 1/8th. Bn. The Royal Scots (Pioneers).

Issued at 4-30 p.m.

Army Form C. 2118.

No 29

CONFIDENTIAL.
No 21 (A)
(HIGHLAND) DIVISION.

WAR DIARY
or
INTELLIGENCE SUMMARY.
(Erase heading not required.)

26 R.

Confidential

WAR DIARY
OF
1/8.TH THE ROYAL SCOTS PIONEERS
FROM
1st July 1917 to 31st July 1917

VOLUME 33

Army Form C. 2118.

WAR DIARY
or
INTELLIGENCE SUMMARY. ①
(Erase heading not required.)

Instructions regarding War Diaries and Intelligence Summaries are contained in F. S. Regs., Part II. and the Staff Manual respectively. Title pages will be prepared in manuscript.

Place	Date	Hour	Summary of Events and Information	Remarks and references to Appendices
Camp 27 C CENTRAL	July 1st		Coys are working in reliefs as follows A.B. & D Coys relieve one another in Coy out 3 days Coy in H.Q., two Coys together in Reliefs are 10 days in the line & 5 days out. Coys in H.Q. Reliefs subdiv. platoon 5 days & line 2, 4 days out. The work is divided as follows. Reference schemes, resembling the Railway Tracks, TORTRES, STERLING, HELIFAX & BOAR. A track from the WILLOWS to HEADINGLY is being made & lined around Bde. Hdqrs. laying light Railway track from the MIREWOO Dumps near BRIDGE 6 to AUSTERLITZ. A Railway Squad under Lt. H.S. Dawdon is superintending the Divisional Tramway from MERIWOO Dump forward to the WILLOW edge is the Branch to LANCASHIRE FARM. The Railway takes forward all the Ration returns & Engrs. in the line. 2nd 3 Coy relieved B Coy today. Capt. McPherson & Capt. Walsh went on leave to England today. Lt. W. Wilson of C Coy was slightly wounded today at CANAL BANK. The plans have gone to O.O.S. 3rd The enemy are shelling out O Trenches very heavily retiring & lot of damage to them. The relief maintenance party is all the trenches. 4th The weather on the whole is good doing some of part fine wed. have showers.	

2353 Wt. W2544/1454 700,000 5/15 D. D. & L. A.D.S.S./Forms/C. 2118.

Army Form C. 2118.

WAR DIARY
or
INTELLIGENCE SUMMARY.

(Erase heading not required.)

Instructions regarding War Diaries and Intelligence Summaries are contained in F.S. Regs., Part II. and the Staff Manual respectively. Title pages will be prepared in manuscript.

Place	Date	Hour	Summary of Events and Information	Remarks and references to Appendices
CAMP 29c CENTRAL	July 5th		During the last few days the enemy have been shelling the Canal Bank very heavily. Today from 7am till 9am the shelling was particularly heavy. About 8am the enemy had a direct hit on HQrs dugout with a 5".9 shell. Major F.G. Todd, Capt. Morgan M.O. & Sgt Parkinson were in the dugout at the time but fortunately escaped without a scratch although the centre section of the Dugout was knocked right to bits. 12 H.E.F. shells on the floor. Major Todd returned from leave today. 6th the C.O. relieved Major Todd on Canal Bank. Stay returned to Coy today. 7th Work is as before. The weather continues fine although thunder storms threaten. The shelling of the Canal Bank continues. 8th 9th The H.Qrs mess had a direct hit on it today, it is where picture of tea was but now it went in the can shelter although it penetrated the Roof the Regt were on the dugout at the time but escaped without injury. We have put in another to thing the head Cover over dugout, a bursting layer of old tyres been broken but again the Bn has been very busy supplying and carrying fatigues daily. Casualties: Lt. Rev John Chaplain of the Bn. sick to base today. 10th Capt. Morgan M.O. went on leave today.	

2353 Wt.W2544/1454 700,000 5/15 D.D.&L. A.D.S.S./Forms/C.2118.

WAR DIARY
INTELLIGENCE SUMMARY

Army Form. C. 2118.

Place	Date	Hour	Summary of Events and Information	Remarks and references to Appendices
Camp, 29 C CENTRAL	July 11th		For the last few days the enemy has been shelling the vicinity of our camp at 29 C Central but none of the shells came very close. Early this morning however two or three shells dropped into the camp wounding two men slightly. Again at 10 a.m. the camp was shelled & two men R.A.M.C. were wounded, one by a piece of shell casing. The R.A.P. has been sent to hospital. Later slightly wounded but not dangerous so arrangements were made to shift camp to another site. School was also taken in the day. R.A. H.Q. is now at C. 29 a 1.9. A bathing party consisting of 2 Coy Coy Transport men & H.Q. details while on the way to YPERINGHE for baths were shelled when they got just outside the town. Dr Clarke Lander, Reg. Med. Officer of the party wounding 16 of them. Some were severely wounded & were at expected to recover. Enemy shelling to the back area & tramway very heavy.	
	12th		A Coy under Capt Mitchell have been detailed from the Bn. & sent under A.D. & R. 55th Division clearing the enemy trenches & an attack from Ebay to 17th 17th horseshoe & Junction for inclusion in a bayonet light tramway. C Coy & remainder just arr arr 175 R R 1/20 there ranging from there. There J 7th been wounded in the 113 had YPERINGHE chest today & taken	
	13th		Three platoons had of B Coy are now to Canal Bank & have today taken & left away 4 stays. The YPERINGHE trench are now to Jons Ispour but take a considerable amount of prophylaxis. – HALIFAX	

WAR DIARY or INTELLIGENCE SUMMARY

Army Form C. 2118.

Place	Date	Hour	Summary of Events and Information	Remarks and references to Appendices
CAMP A 28 A.1.9	July 13th		**STIRLING, BOAR, WILLOWS DITCH & HEDDINGLY. JOFFRE LANE** was still like a Bog. Ordered amount of work to put in poles & to bury heavy storage every day ordered to which it is easily flooded, & the discharge is proving a difficult problem	
	14th		Lt. R.B. Owen went on leave today. His wounds in the field & from bites heavy, turn the stones are very frequent.	
	13th		Received instructions from CRE today to form an Individual Camp at B.28.d.2.5. Yds Bn. will now be distributed as follows. 1 Coy at Road Bank, 1 coy at Individual Camp, 1 coy plus detail at Rew Camp. B Coy & attached to 173rd Tunnelling Coy. laying light Railways.	
	16th		C Coy went to Individual Camp today. Capt. W.A. Fleming in Command. B Coy to Rew Camp. Lt. R. Maxwell in Command. 2 Lt. Wealth to 170th & at same Coy. Lt. A.D. Blackburn has been attached to the CRE Office for work on Tramways, R.E. Dumps.	
	17th		Major W.S. Sherburn has left totals own Camp Commandant Division at M.T. Camps.	
	18th		2 Lt. Knapp Coy on today's train. In charge of eleven OR's joined the Bn. today.	
	19th		All the men have been with the Bn. before.	

Army Form C. 2118.

WAR DIARY
or
INTELLIGENCE SUMMARY. (3)
(Erase heading not required.)

Instructions regarding War Diaries and Intelligence Summaries are contained in F.S. Regs., Part II. and the Staff Manual respectively. Title pages will be prepared in manuscript.

Place	Date	Hour	Summary of Events and Information	Remarks and references to Appendices
Camp D A282.1.9.	July 20th		Capt. H.E. Ballantyne left today to take up duties of XVIII Corps Salvage Officer.	
		21st	Received relief from C.R.E. today. About ½ Coy on to be employed on clearing the German trenches. B.Coy. will start as an eye witness approached where the last enemy thrust of Road just below Ypres. at a point near MORTELDGE
			Examiner to HURST PARK funnels & glider guns. C. Coy. will make a concealed track from our front line forward through Sanctuary Wood to KLEIN WOOD.
			B Coy will be in bivouac at Archimedes Camp.
		22nd	Capt Morgan M.O. & Capt. Fraser returned from leave today.
		23rd	Operation Orders for the offensive now issued today. A Coy's attacked, addressed about our own billets & the Canal Bank today, falling two joints our Thursday from Base. Have been drawing a lot of gas shells over here the Canal Bank C2C's making things very unpleasant for troops billeted there. We have lost no known cases of gassing however
		24th	D Coy marched to Canal Bank today, relieving B Coy. 1st C.coy. out to Rem Camp.
		25th	Received heavy art. fire today. At 4 a.m. report that the phone lines but in Salique or that account hitherto has first been resumed that movements into battle position will be preferred under further orders.	

WAR DIARY or INTELLIGENCE SUMMARY

Army Form C. 2118.

Place	Date	Hour	Summary of Events and Information	Remarks and references to Appendices
RAMP A25a 1.9.	July 26th		Weather has improved. The ground is drying up before of Ephraits. Life on the Canal Bank is pleasant. There are a lot of fine shells coming over every night. The enemy sent aeros over to Field Ambulance suffering from the effect of gas but have Jellie Cours & received 2 Lt Falconer sent on 6 days leave today. Lt P.S. Dunn returns from leave.	
	27th		Received intimation to move into new positions for the period on Aug 21st to 29th/30th? The divisional Z day will be the 31st. Good weather continues.	
	28th		B Coy moved up to L'Ealu. Camp today & joined Coy.	
	29th		Today BTC Coy move into Canal Bank & D Coy move from Canal State Camp. Other Bn's & horse to precede for the Push. Headquarters 1st Co Coy & Tmo moved to Canal Bank this evening. C Coy had bad luck today with landing B & Sgt Mackay, Pom BREEN & White Corpls amongst a pass'y kittens & wounding 24 others. Shell hit Lom Shell in the Coy, but hit heavy.	
	30th		Weather & tempy clear, but not entirely promising. ZERO hour is 3-50 am Tomorrow.	
	31st		Our artillery opened great before Zero this morning. Retaliation of the enemy was very slight on Canal Bank. At 4.30 am a Cavalry Officer reported at Bn HQ's. An officer & 50 O.R.y B.A.C. reported.	

WAR DIARY or INTELLIGENCE SUMMARY. (7)

Army Form C. 2118.

Place	Date	Hour	Summary of Events and Information	Remarks and references to Appendices
CAMP AZBA 1.9	July 3/19	Cont.	6 a.m. at 5 a.m. Glen-faj'a h.k. went C.O.Z. with two scouts, 2 Lt Bennet Jolley Captain Cain to Recce the area of inland track as far as KUBERT Wood. The Cavalry flanks his forces with him to find out of cavalry can go through. Two platoons of C. Coy of B Coy have gone out to look at 6:30 am. If they report went forward the other half Coys ccc & D will. We have just heard that the BLACK Line has been taken without much trouble. At 7 am the Remainy Bn half Coy went out as it seemed four of Coys 13 Coy got shielded attack on BOUNDRY ROAD & their way to wait reinforcements. Casualties have been Gerry killed & 7 wounded. M.G. also were shelled in their way to start. had a few casualties, amongst it D.A.O. page. also was with them. M. Barid is also Keeping men down for which he will not run the fire for what force hindering but did not greatly hinder the work.	
		9:30 a.m.	Word has just come in that 2 Lt Bennet J'arf has been forward as far as KUBERT WOOD I has said that the Wire Marked on the track to that front.	
		10:30 a.m.	Word just came that on he has found their front J'arden, Prisoners are coming h.k. fair number. Casualties in own Bn. from all account less so than 2 B. heavy. So has the cavalry has gone through along the track as or as material.	

WAR DIARY or INTELLIGENCE SUMMARY

Army Form C. 2118.

Place	Date	Hour	Summary of Events and Information	Remarks and references to Appendices
Camp A25 a.1.9	July	contd.		
		3½	C Coy. Men got 2/10 Lifts. attacked & then fire went on hard. a B Coy. him 100 Lifts. 27¾ lost for work on road.	
		11.30 a.m.	Major Tait him. p.out, believed ref. not that work on the road to presently, but that the front of the. 2nd Runway though the. Her. front line. together to gradient difficulties, & that it will take a lot of work to make it passable for guns.	
		2.30 p.m.	The Co. y Coy. went out round the work of 6/17 B. F. Coys. There was considerable shelling & that neighbors with work renewals, but good progress had been made.	
		5.30 p.m.	It was war. passable for field guns as far as a Kempton Park. 7 line. track had been carried forward 6 within 150 yards of Belim Farm.	
		6 p.m.	O.R.E. 1a. ordered forms of D Coy. from reserve Coy. to Comp. near Murat Farm. will there than pitched Comp. near Murat Farm.	
		6.15 p.m.	B. Coy. relieved & returned to billets at 6.15 p.m. B. Coy. suffered casualties on the way back 1 man heavy, killed & 6 wounded. O. Coy. had 3 men slightly wounded.	
		7 p.m.	D Coy. have gone out to continue work on track & g. road. each melinite to. make the road passable for field guns as far as Hurst Park. The weather during the day has been good.	

Capt. L. C. Coy
R. Royal Eng. Forces

WAR DIARY
or
INTELLIGENCE SUMMARY

Army Form C. 2118.

Place	Date	Hour	Summary of Events and Information	Remarks and references to Appendices
			Casualties during July 1917:—	

Officers:—   Other Ranks:—

2/Lieut. W.M.Wilson — to Hosp (Wounded) 1.7.17.   Killed . 8.

Lieut. W.T.N.Todd — to Hosp (Sick) 3.7.17.   Died of Wounds . 8.

Lieut. T.E.Steele — to Hosp (Sick) 12.7.17.   Wounded to Hosp 62.

Lieut. W.L. Stewart — to Hosp (Sick) 13.7.17.   Sick (to Hosp) 39

Capt. W.A.R.M. McRae — ordered to attend   Wounded (at duty) 8
Med. Board while on leave in Eng.   To Base L.T. 1
1 month off strength.   To Class P.2. 2

Reinforcements:—
O.Ranks Draft (14.7.17) 11   Strength at 31.7.17 = 54 Officers
Officers Nil   991 Other Ranks

                                                        Lieut.
                         Adjt. 18th Bn. The Royal Scots (Pioneers)

S E C R E T.   Copy No. 14

1/8th. Bn. The Royal Scots (Pioneers).

OPERATION ORDER NO. 4.

By Lieut.-Colonel W. GEMMILL, D.S.O., Commanding.

23rd. July, 1917.

1. The 51st. Division in conjunction with other Divisions right and left will attack the enemy's positions on a day and hour to be notified later.

2. The 51st. Division will attack with

    152nd. Inf. Brigade on Right.
    153rd.   "   "   Left.
    154th.   "   "   in Reserve.

3. The 51st. Division Front extends from MORTALDJE ESTAMINET on right to 5 Chemins Estaminet on Left.

4. The 1/8th. Royal Scots (Pioneers) will be employed in making a road and a cross-country track for guns and ammunition. Separate instructions regarding the work have been issued.

5. On the night 29th/30th. July, "B" and "C" Companies will move into dugouts in the Canal Bank, and "D" Company and Headquarters to Intermediate Camp. Separate instructions for this move have been issued, which should be completed by 9 p.m. on 29th. instant.

6. O.C. Divisional Tramways will hand over to an officer of Tramway Company on or before the 29th. and will return with his men to the Transport Lines. 30th.

7. Headquarters will be at Intermediate Camp with Advanced Headquarters at Dugout No. 135 Canal Bank. from 9 p.m. on 29th. instant.

8. Acknowledge.

                                                  A. Jones, Lieut.,

Issued at 4.15 p.m.   Adjt., 1/8th. Bn. The Royal Scots (Pioneers).

Copy No. 1 - Adjt. for O.C.   Copy No. 8 - Transport Officer.
     2 - Major J.A. Todd.   9 - Quartermaster.
     3 - O.C. "A" Company.   10 - Regtl. Sergt. Major.
     4 - O.C. "B" Company.   11 - N.C.O. i/c Lewis Guns
     5 - O.C. "C" Company.   12 - Tramways Officer.
     6 - O.C. "D" Company.   13 - War Diary.
     7 - Medical Officer.   14 - File.

SECRET. Copy No. 14

1/8th. Bn. THE ROYAL SCOTS (Pioneers).

Instructions for Work on "Z" and following Days.

By Lieut.-Colonel W. GEMMELL, D.S.O., Commanding.

23rd. July, 1917.

1. The Work of the Battalion is to be on a road and on a cross-country track from our own front line forward, to enable artillery to get forward as soon as possible.

2. The routes to be followed have already been pointed out to all officers and N.C.Os. taking part in operations on the model trenches. Maps showing routes have been issued to Companies.

3. "B" Company will repair the road.
   "C" Company will make the cross-country track.
   "D" Company will be in Reserve.

   In addition to the above work, 2/Lieut. W.G.Young and 1 N.C.O. and 10 Men of "D" Company will be employed putting up sign-boards in and behind the German Lines.

4. The following tools will be carried by each Company :-

   1 shovel will be carried by every man.
   1 pick   - by every 10th. man ("B" Coy. every 5th. man.)
   2 Folding saws- by each platoon.
   8 prs. wire-cutters-   do.
   2 light crowbars-   do.
   8 pairs gloves.-   do.

5. The track ("C" Company) is to be a 'two-way' track and is of first importance. 200 men from Trench Mortar Batt. will be attached to O.C. "C" Company at "Zero + 1 hour to help with this work. In addition, O.C. "C" Company can call upon the Infantry holding the BLUE LINE to supply 200 men if required.
   OC. "C" Company will have a special party(strength about half a platoon) to push forward along the line of the track to remove wire from the track to enable cavalry to push through. A Cavalry liason officer will be attached to "C" Company on "Z" day to go with the party and see the route of track.
   The Track is simply to consist of a way with shell holes filled in and trenches filled in. Notice boards will be put up (ED) - one every hundred yards. Track

   The road requires to be done in a more permanent way than the track, but the first consideration is to make it passable for guns.

   An R.E. Officer is attached to Forward Brigade Headquarters who is responsible for sending word to Report Centre, Canal Bank, when he considers it is possible for parties to work.
   "B" and "C" Companies will each send a runner to Report Centre by "Zero Hour" who will convey messages from Report Centre to Coys. and return. An officer will also remain at Report Centre to see that orderlies from 8th. Royal Scots, 400th. and 401st. Field Coys. R.E. are available and get their messages. This officer will be detailed later by O.C. "B" Company.

   (7. Finally, officers

   See amendment No 1.

S E C R E T.   Copy No.. 14

1/8th. Bn. THE ROYAL SCOTS (Pioneers).

ADMINISTRATIVE INSTRUCTIONS FOR ACTIVE OPERATIONS.

By Lieut.-Colonel W. GEMMILL, D.S.O., Commanding.

Reference Maps -   23rd. July, 1917.
Belgium & Part of France
   Sheets 27 & 28.

1. **DRESS.** - Fighting Order. Packs and greatcoats will be stored at Transport Lines by Companies. Waterproof sheets and blankets will be taken to Intermediate Camp and the Canal Bank.
    Iron rations will be carried and water-bottles filled.

2. **DUMPS.**   R.E. Stores :-
         ESSEX FARM
         MARENGO HOUSE
         LA BELLE ALLIANCE Farm.
    Divl. Ration Dump :-
         MARENGO HOUSE.

3. **RATIONS.** Every man will carry his iron rations. Rations for "Z" and "Z + 1" days will be stored by the 25th. instant at the Canal Bank and Intermediate Camp.

4. **MEDICAL.** Regimental Aid Posts at - C.20.b.9.7.
                                          - C.14.c.0.4
    Collecting Post.   - C.20.a.8.8.
    Advanced Dressing Station - ESSEX FARM.
    Walking Wounded - H.3.d.5.8 (on road between Intermediate Camp and VLAMERTINGHE).

5. **BADGES.**
    Men carrying folding saws will wear a piece of green cloth on left shoulder.
    Men carrying wire-cutters will wear white on right shoulder.

6. **ECHELON "B".** All surplus officers and Other Ranks will remain at Transport Lines - the whole under the charge of Major Todd.

Acknowledge.

            A.D. JONES,   Lieut.,
Issued at 4.15 p.m.   Adjt., 1/8th. Bn. The Royal Scots (Pioneers).

Copies to   all recipients of Operation Order No. 4.

Army Form C. 2118.

WAR DIARY
or
INTELLIGENCE SUMMARY.
(Erase heading not required.)

Vol 30

27 Ps

Confidential

WAR DIARY
of
1/8th "THE ROYAL SCOTS"
FROM
1st AUGUST to 31st AUGUST 1917
VOLUME N° 34.

WAR DIARY
or
INTELLIGENCE SUMMARY.

(Erase heading not required.)

Army Form C. 2118.

Place	Date	Hour	Summary of Events and Information	Remarks and references to Appendices
REAR CAMP A.27.a.1.9 FORWARD CAMP CANAL BANK	August 1st		Heavy rain storm at 1.30am this morning, & continued throughout the day. As the ground is almost impassable, Coys were nearly kept employed collecting material. 5/15 (Sheffield) 7 in cleaning of Dugout Road. "D" Coy had 3 men wounded during the morning.	
	2nd		The same state continued. "B" Coy are employed carrying up planks etc for duckboards on the Road, "C" the same. "A" in open to Atwick Cott.	
	3rd		The weather is still very bad with chances of better wheel prospect. The road keeping up. Mr Mackay went on leave today.	
	4th		The weather has improved considerably. Both Coys are being moved on the work. As Coy constructed on the sector front from our own front line to past beyond Hampton Post.	
	5th		Better weather today. Good progress has been made on the work.	
	6th		2 Lt Spence went on leave today. Instructions have reached us to the effect that our work & billets in Canal Bank have to be handed over on the 7th inst to the 5 & 6 York Pioneers & the II C Bn. We on the other hand take over the work of the 5 Yorks from the roads & also their billets at GHENT FARM from BRIELEN. 6th 7th & York have been working for the Kings Corps. So we will be under Corps rather from the 8th inst.	

WAR DIARY
or
INTELLIGENCE SUMMARY. (2)

(Erase heading not required.)

Army Form C. 2118.

Place	Date	Hour	Summary of Events and Information	Remarks and references to Appendices
REAR CAMP A.27.a.1.9 FORWARD CAMP B.22.d.6.0.95	Aug 1917	7g	Weather rather unsettled with occasional showers but on the whole fine day. The road to Hooge order for istaded hopp from MORTELDJE EST to HURST PARK, but has still to be widened & cleared. The evening the Coys took over the billets of the 8th Yorks at FRONT COTT. The 8th Yorks moved in to pre billets in CANAL BANK from 10 AM tomorrow we come under the orders of the 9TH DE XVIII Corps & take over the work of the 8 Yorks. Our work is to be the BOUNDRY ROAD from HAMMONDS CORNER to MORTELDJE ESTAMINET. This road has to be widened & a double clothboard track is to start. The Coy will be employed laying a double clothboard track from PILCHEM ROAD along to track to BELOW FM. The C.O. went to Rear Camp this evening, he & Lieutenant going on 10 days leave to England tomorrow. 7th The weather is very bad I am afraid. We have received permission to send in Coy Cooks & 2nd Camp to be refilled & bathed. The Coys are now working as follows:- A Coy. under A.D.L.R. 2nd Army. B & C Coy are working on BOUNDRY RD & RD Front. B Coy have gone back to Rear Camp today for 4 days rest. 9th The C.O. & 2/Lt W.T Gray left for England today on leave Major To. Todd in Command 10th The Bn has been allotted three pipers for Parades, Leave & has been given to 2 Lt Brandon & 2 Lt Reid. They leave tomorrow.	

Army Form C. 2118.

WAR DIARY
or
INTELLIGENCE SUMMARY. (3)
(Erase heading not required.)

Place	Date	Hour	Summary of Events and Information	Remarks and references to Appendices
G28a1.9 1322 a3905	August 11th		(2/Lt) Young returned to the Bn. today. The Officer has been attached to Divis'n for instruction at Camp Commandant to WINDMILL CAMP & 2/Lt Fenwick returned today from the XIIIth Corps Lewis Gun Course. Four Lewis Guns have been posted at Battery positions near MORTELDJE EST to protect the batteries against hostile aircraft.	
	12th		B Coy relieved A Coy today at GHENT CAMP taking over A Coys work on the BUNDARY Rd.	
	13th		Meg have finished the checkerboard track & are now working along with B Coy on BUNDARY Rd.	
	14th		2/Lt Fenwick went on leave today & 2/Lt Mackay returned from leave.	
	15th		We are having of tended weather now & good progress being made with the roads.	
	16th		C Coy relieved D Coy today & took over their work. The forward Road have again been extended & ready for infantry transport. RE Coy Pioneers. Our 1st Reinforcement drafts now in the section from MORTELDJE EST & the WILLOWS & the section from KEMPTON PARK BANER to the CRONIER Fm to CANE AVENUE. B Coy are working on the CRONIER Fm to the WILLOWS. The Road has to be widened to 18/1 & drained.	[signature]

WAR DIARY or INTELLIGENCE SUMMARY

Army Form C. 2118.

(Erase heading not required.)

Place	Date	Hour	Summary of Events and Information	Remarks and references to Appendices
J28c1.9 & B22d60.05	August 17th		27th Divn. went on leave today. The 112th Brigade pushed in our front yesterday & were successful in gaining their objective. On front line to how over the STEENBEEK & to the LANGEMARCK LINE. Who are on our left were also successful, taking the town of LANGEMARCK. On the night the final task was not attempted but preparations made.	
	18th		A new allotment of leave has been granted the Bn, it is 38 p/ rank per week plus one adnl. of 3 officers & 33 ORs going on leave per week.	
	19th		The weather & splendid. Held a front there was OC. today my Corps. [illegible] Lectures & we have had a Mens Canteen operation open. Their operates seems to be PIPERINGHE & its Surroundings. They heavily came over between 9.30 PM & 11.30 PM.	
			HRE: 49 W: him. That then Bad. Air Craft given were successful in giving down two of the Squadron & this enemy.	
	20th		Day silence. 3 Coy today. [illegible] is now getting some of the light for a few hours. Each AE Coy now fitting trench walking & strengers up & the Lgt Infantry to MORTEL DYC ECH school in front ready for our work.	
	21st		The weather continues to be fine with good taking temps that kept the air clear. There is great activity among ea. the Aerops. & many exciting encounters with enemy	

Army Form C. 2118.

WAR DIARY
or
INTELLIGENCE SUMMARY. (3)
(Erase heading not required.)

Instructions regarding War Diaries and Intelligence Summaries are contained in F. S. Regs., Part II. and the Staff Manual respectively. Title pages will be prepared in manuscript.

Place	Date	Hour	Summary of Events and Information	Remarks and references to Appendices
A 28 a 1.9. & B12 a 60 0.5	1918 August 21st		Enemy planes have been bothersome & the enemy has approached in most threatening & dangerous numbers several enemy planes in the evening, during the last few days. The enemy put down a very heavy barrage on BOURRY R? this morning at 10 a.m. but our C.By. were working & kept it up until horses. C.By. fortunes were withdrawn without casualties. Our transport whilst was working on the road got cut off by the barrage but managed to get through without hurt. 2/Lt Peyton who was in charge of our transport was much responsible for this. Then A.P.S. showed Pond Cartoun? Sanuary, 1st Bombr Trans.	
	22nd		Lt. CO returned from leave today. Yesterdays shelling has damaged C.By. Road considerably. It will take a day or two to get on the change. Our guns have been very active today, several batch of prisoners have been seen coming in. Capt Young & Lt. Magurisse? left on 10 days leave.	
	23rd		7th P.O. came forward & advanced Camp today & returned Major T.A. Todd who returned to rear Camp.	
	24th		B.By. relieved C.By. today. Not much main work.	
	25th		2/Lt Spence returned from leave today. The following newsmen of the B. have been awarded the military medal by the Field Marshal Commanding in Chief under authority by his Majesty	

2353 Wt. W2544/1454. 700,000. 5/15. D. D. & L.   A.D.S.S./Forms/C. 2118.

WAR DIARY
or
INTELLIGENCE SUMMARY.

Army Form C. 2118.

Place	Date	Hour	Summary of Events and Information	Remarks and references to Appendices
Q28a19 & B22d60.55	August 23rd		Contd. Majesty the King, Major A. Blyth, Sgt G. Dixon, L/Cpl. O. Lamb & Pte. P. Gammon.	
	"	10.15	Bn. prepared to move and light baggage sent to HENT COTTAGES dumps.	
	24th		Heather showing strong wind from East with heavy rain showers. Battn. got 2nd Lt. Spours relieved from leave. 2nd Lt. Stevens relieved in the morning. Lieutenant Wilson and Rifleman Evans wounded from leave. This afternoon Bn. troops rested in my left sector, between WIELTIE & SIEGFRIED SAINT JEAN & attacked further infantry on the left in the afternoon from dumps.	
	28th		Battn. still holding C Coy advance to Coy. L. Cpl. Pyffrin & support. The Battalion shelled & the Fourteenth Lancers advancing in support arrived. Enemy by the Major G. Bn. Hqrs.	
	29th		Battn. continues on moods Inst I.T. Dismounts from the Trench.	
	30th		F.O.O. Stemmer Attacks 15th Brigade to C.p. West Pill Box Artillery.	
	31st		11.30a.m. B. Coy. works on road ROCHESTER and proceed over the STEENBECK. C Coy takes over continuation ROCHESTER & REGINA CROSS and proceed forward ROCHESTER road from junction with light endeavour ALGERIAN COTTAGE forward K STEENBECK with nothing. D Coy. works on road from RODOLPHE	M

Army Form C. 2118.

WAR DIARY
or
INTELLIGENCE SUMMARY. (7)

(Erase heading not required.)

Instructions regarding War Diaries and Intelligence Summaries are contained in F. S. Regs., Part II. and the Staff Manual respectively. Title pages will be prepared in manuscript.

Place	Date	Hour	Summary of Events and Information	Remarks and references to Appendices
A28 a 19 R22 d 60.05	August 30		FARM L CHIEN FARM — CHIEN FARM — CHIEN FARM L MILITARY ROAD along REGINA CROSS — CHIEN FARM ROAD and MILITARY ROAD down STEENBEECK. 8 days move F GHENT COTTAGES CAMP	
		91.	Improvement in weather. 2nd Lt. Munro returns from leave.	

Wt. Minshintoph
to adjt. R Royal Arts
(Pioneers).

WAR DIARY

INTELLIGENCE SUMMARY.

(Erase heading not required.)

Army Form C. 2118.

Summary of Events and Information

Casualties during August, 1917

Officers: Nil
Other Ranks:- Killed   1
              Wounded   29
              Died of Wds 2
              Wounded (at duty) 4
              Hospital, Sick 43
              ___
              79

Strength at 31.8.17 = 51 Offs., 1013 ORs.

Reinforcements:-
Officers – 2/Lt. TRIMSH, C.S.O. from Base 15.8.17
O. Ranks –
Draft. (8.8.17)   28
"   (15.8.17)   22
"   (19.8.17)   22
"   (23.8.17)   3
"   (24.8.17)   13 NCOs
"   (28.8.17)   6
                   ___
                   94

Mgfarlan
Captain
for Adjt. 1/Inniskilling (Royals)

Place	Date	Hour

Remarks and references to Appendices

Army Form C. 2118.

WAR DIARY
or
INTELLIGENCE SUMMARY.
(Erase heading not required.)

Vol 31

Confidential

War Diary
of
1st The Royal Scots
From
1st September to 30th September 1917
Volume No 35

Army Form C. 2118.

WAR DIARY
or
INTELLIGENCE SUMMARY.
(Erase heading not required.)

Place	Date	Hour	Summary of Events and Information	Remarks and references to Appendices
A 28 a 19 B 22 d 30.05	Sept.	1.	Arty continues intermittent fire. To day is having slight burst nuisance from junction of light railway near ALGERIAN COTTAGE onward to STEENBECK. B and D Coys are in woods in the Pioneer area. At present they are making their personal air shelters happy. This is rather a big job as there are large numbers White kobe full guard which require the cleared out before the real spelling in can begin. They are working on BOUNDARY ROAD, BARN + FARM ROAD and FERDINAND FARM ROAD. Early this morning afternoon purchase count down thanx Hdqs. The Pioneer sergeant and tools came in recoinnoitring after. Later in the day he was confirmed.	
		2.	Weather good. Much booming straight.	
		3.	Weather continues good. Work is interrupted by shellfire but no casualties	
		4"	2nd Lts. Young, Blackwood and Davidson go on leave. Work again hindered by shelling At 11pm 2 bombs were dropped on Mr. Napper lines. Pte Irvine killed in when Pte and wounded 3 men. 2.4 horses were killed outright in a casualty wounded that they had to destroyed and 12 were wounded also the park horses which the R.O. hit got at mobilisation were killed At midnight a bomb was dropped in the Mr line at GHENT COTTAGES but no damage was done	
		5.	Weather continues fine onshore frequence at night enemy aeroplanes but no neighbourhood opens	M.

WAR DIARY
or
INTELLIGENCE SUMMARY.

Army Form C. 2118.

Place	Date	Hour	Summary of Events and Information	Remarks and references to Appendices
Area 19 B2d 60.05	Sept.	5	Wire, but no damage to wire.	
		6	Gen. D. Mash goes on leave. Enft. spraying of aeroplane activities from dawn. Hostile batteries quiet, work but intermittent. Instructions received for Gen. Ritchie's report & 2nd Harcastle for 2nd. MIK & he pointed 6PCAM.	
		7	Howitzer fire rather continuous satisfactory. B and D Coys. are working on MILITARY ROAD and FERDINAND FARM ROAD. On the 7ths brown sent Gray and was working across the STEENBECK. He received a complimentary letter from Chief Engineer XIII Corps congratulating on the recent work done whilst working for the VIII Corps.	
		8	Work continues. G.M. Ritchie leaves no to report & 9rd Harcastle Regiment to Duty on Sun.	
		9	3 Coy. Kept Repairs to our lines by shell fire – no casualties. Enemy considerable attn. especially at night in area between Canal Bend and our lines.	
		10	Work continues. 2nd & 4 Steele 13 murder 93 on leave. Gen. Ritchie returns K.B. as 2nd Harcastle Field Coy. home & Sun.	
		11	Work continues. 3coys held up by gas in May R. work, and working parties dispersed by shell fire to avoid occasions. No casualties. At 10.30 am. 5 German aeroplanes at a considerable height flew over this area of our lines, 2 hours have helped our gunners landed on either side of the road at 3 Coy Office lines billet, two of them landed amongst stacks of straw from shelter trip, and caused a number of casualties. Instant work. From 1pm. to 6pm	M.

Army Form C. 2118.

WAR DIARY
or
INTELLIGENCE SUMMARY. (3)
(Erase heading not required.)

Instructions regarding War Diaries and Intelligence Summaries are contained in F. S. Regs., Part II. and the Staff Manual respectively. Title pages will be prepared in manuscript.

Place	Date	Hour	Summary of Events and Information	Remarks and references to Appendices
A28 a 19 B 2nd 10.55	Sept.	11	The enemy intermittently shelled the neighbourhood of the camp with H.V. shells. Several shells landed in the bivis but caused no damage.	
	"	12½	The enemy continued shelling the country J. of the camp. During the early hours of the morning, Pn. 1 of the shells landed at the entrance of a shelter occupied by the 6th Platoon of "D" Coy wounding three men. Sgt. Elia shot at Field Ambulance took in it by the other 4/6 men Sgt. Bes Canonier S. Young. The enemy also sent over a large number of J.P.A. shells during the night but these not do much effect in the trench being to our front. A.G.'s all. Capt returned from camp today. He is relieved Lieutenant S.C. Gore. During the day various Huns dove no enemy shelling.	
		13½	Weather very fine but tooth like haze. The work of preparing well of the travel tramway being laid by "A" Coy is now at the N. N$EN B$EK & the junction is complete. Work 100 yards beyond that. "A" & "B" Coys open the NEEN BEEK & MOOKLEEN & every tramway. "B" & "D" Coys have now got the MILITARY Road in order for wheeled traffic on the N$EN B$EK to a point at U.29.c.3.6. No enemy to our front today. There have been little shelling near our camp.	
		14¾	Weather. A brighter morning & still hot and a strong W.wind blowing.	
		18	2nd Lieut Y. young returned from leave today. E.A. again suffered intermittent on camp but no important damage. [signature]	

WAR DIARY or INTELLIGENCE SUMMARY

Army Form C. 2118.

(Erase heading not required.)

Instructions regarding War Diaries and Intelligence Summaries are contained in F. S. Regs., Part II. and the Staff Manual respectively. Title pages will be prepared in manuscript.

Place	Date	Hour	Summary of Events and Information	Remarks and references to Appendices
GHENT COTTAGES B22d 60,05		9AM 11A	Capt. R.E. Allen, 2nd Lt. Dawson & T. Blackwood returned from Corps today. 2nd Lt. A Augustus came over to Bn. HQ at 11:30 A.M. today & confirmed reports to the effect of G attached office to the vicinity of our Camp. First phases & being carried on the work. Both the Tramway & MILITARY ROAD being completed up to & across the V.T.R.Y & R.E. 	
		17½	Information received from Bn. today. Received order No.2192. About Sept 2nd the XVIII Corps will take over Frontage. Situation & Composition will be V Corps on Right & XIV Corps on Left. 6th Corp Bn. will relieve 13th & 15th Bns. The XIX Corps on Right of the 29 & 3 Bus on their Left. The attack will commence on the 13th and 15th. 585 Bn. or their reps at Rn. 29 3 Bus on their Left. The attack will commence on the 13th and 15th. 585 Bn. will send down parties to be killed in forward area as reserve at 6 p.m. the 18th Bdy. Bde. The Bn. will move forward to forward area as officers at Bn. HQ at the HINDENBURG FM. Bdy will children the Miny Rouse D coy into dugout relief, arrangements are at Coat km HINDENBURG FM. Bdy will occur to be a screen in field to POELL GAEN. Work on ZERO DAY will be 'A' coy Cr km Tramway as guides and forward supplies. 'B' coy will be occup engrave Winnipeg – Langemarck Road + Lengemarck Rd + Lep km to reform. 'B' coy will Iron Cross rifle – Winnipeg - Langemarck Road from junction with MILITARY ROAD at 029 6 00.15 - Cross Winnipeg on Army by tramways. Bn. operation order on attack. (Gaz. Grennay & 2/2 Ambulance) also and progress & army roads with the work, weather any blue building.	
		19½	B. Coy D coy. moved forward into positions at Canal Bank, Minty House & beyond the V.T.R.Y. in the evening. 49th Brance formed part of the position at BRITANNIA FARM at 7.37 P.M.	

WAR DIARY
or
INTELLIGENCE SUMMARY.

Army Form C. 2118.

(Erase heading not required.)

Instructions regarding War Diaries and Intelligence Summaries are contained in F. S. Regs., Part II. and the Staff Manual respectively. Title pages will be prepared in manuscript.

Place	Date	Hour	Summary of Events and Information	Remarks and references to Appendices
GHENT COTTAGES B2d Co. 05	Sept.	20?	The attack commenced at 5.40 a.m. & the heavy rain & bad visibility did not permit of a heavy assault of rain falling, but it cleared up and on the forenoon. In advanced two platoons of "D" Coy, left behind at 6.30 a.m. forward on the LANGEMARCK-WINNIPEG Road. 'B' Coy having their second try found the enemy had a heavy barrage on the LANGEMARCK Road making advancement of the new front establish. The art. & M.G. STEENBEEK held him on the ebbing lands. About 11.30 a.m. the shelling having slackened the platoons were put on the move to clearing the road of fallen trees & the coy & getting rid of sheltering. Most men had had 6 to 7 Days to laws of the Coy platoon in reserve & being machine gunners, very little work could be done however on account of practically continuous shelling. The enemy put down of heavy barrage on the Road at 1.30 P.M. & the Platoon were ordered to the entrenchments, which was a piece for forty. M.G. teams were in charge, the trenches taken dig were so scarce. Further orders were impossible. C Coy left behind at 6.30 a.m. for work on the Tramway. Either caught all day & spending without any great interruption. Rails laid in the afternoon. Very good progress was made. The main being laid beyond Mon de RASTA for 50 yards beyond Pt. STEENBEEK. Three platoons were employed laying rails & making the formation. The other two being to material gained from ADMP 243 Road	Q

2353 Wt. W2544/1454 700,000 5/15 D. D. & L. A.D.S.S./Forms/C. 2118.

Army Form C. 2118.

WAR DIARY
or
INTELLIGENCE SUMMARY. (6)
(Erase heading not required.)

Instructions regarding War Diaries and Intelligence Summaries are contained in F. S. Regs., Part II. and the Staff Manual respectively. Title pages will be prepared in manuscript.

Place	Date	Hour	Summary of Events and Information	Remarks and references to Appendices
GHENT COTTAGES B22.60.05	Apr		*Continued*	
		10.00	"C" Coy had from Canadians clearing the Coy area of stand loose gear. B Coy in Reserve. Not called upon. The attack has been a success all objectives having been gained.	
		21.00	B Coy went out early & continued work on the LANDEMARCK Rd. Four Prisoners were marched about 100 other ranks had to be accommodated and [illegible] wheeling. C Coy had a good time & made good progress. They have been on 20 any body lying [illegible] of ground which has been a lot of [illegible] before the [illegible] can be made to [illegible] it is nothing more than shell craters. B Coy Relieved "D" Coy [illegible] the Bn. 6-day from the Railway Bank. They were of great [illegible] to working with the Bn. H.Q. relieved to GHENT COTTAGES today.	
		22.00	"A" Coy relieved "B" Coy today taking over their billets at MINTY HOUSE. "B" Coy proceeded to Billets at GHENT COTTAGES. In addition to the works on the LANGEMARCK Rd & Tramway Tramway has been laid from the LANGEMARCK Rd to [illegible] loop near the POELCAPELLE Rd. A Coy is on the Tramway Construction. B Coy on duck board tracks & D Coy on the Roads. All work has been carried out by similar 250 yards. That Rifle Ammunition has been [illegible]	
		23.00	Prisoner and Dismounted today in accordance. The Personnel & supervised for Battery at 11am. The B3 will be separated by Officer from [illegible] to this instructions have been received today that the Bn. will be relieved on the 14/13/20/5 by the 11th Division. The Bn. & Brown with G. BAPAUME AREA	28

Instructions regarding War Diaries and Intelligence Summaries are contained in F. S. Regs., Part II. and the Staff Manual respectively. Title pages will be prepared in manuscript.

WAR DIARY
or
INTELLIGENCE SUMMARY. (7)

(Erase heading not required.)

Army Form C. 2118.

Place	Date	Hour	Summary of Events and Information	Remarks and references to Appendices
GHENT COTTAGES B22 d 60, 05	Sept. 23rd contd		1 NCO & 3 men of D Coy were wounded by a shell which landed close to a dugout in their forward billets, 2 of the men are rather seriously wounded. The enemy are sending over bombing squadrons practically every day & bombing the vicinity of this Camp, so far we have had no casualties from this.	
	24th		EA dropped bombs in A Coy lines Camp at 11 a.m. today killing one man & severely wounding another. The man was buried at the Cemetery near 51st CCS today. We have been instructed to hand over our work & billets to the 6th East Yorks Pioneers for the 11th Div tomorrow. The Bn is to go into Camp tomorrow near ERPERINGHE (BROWNE CAMP). We understand the Division less Artillery is to be withdrawn from the XVIII Corps & will proceed to the VI Corps Reserve Area near BAPAUME in the course of the next few days.	
	25th		The forward Coys [illegible] A, B & D Coys moved into GHENT COTT Camp this morning. The Bn moved into BROWNE CAMP after dinner today. Operation Order for the move is attached.	
	26th		Capt Pringle rejoined the Bn today from his duties as Area Commandant of the XVIII Corps Area of the Canal Bank. The Bn was employed today in [illegible] cleaning & physical training. The Bn was bathed & given clean underclothing.	
	27th		The Bn was employed during the day at Physical Training, Close order drill. The CO inspected A & B Coys during the forenoon.	[illegible]

2353 Wt. W2544/1454 700,000 5/15 D. D. & L. A.D.S.S./Forms/C. 2118.

WAR DIARY
or
INTELLIGENCE SUMMARY.

Army Form C. 2118.

(Erase heading not required.)

Place	Date	Hour	Summary of Events and Information	Remarks and references to Appendices
BROWNS CAMP	Aug 30.1		[illegible handwritten entries]	

WAR DIARY
or
INTELLIGENCE SUMMARY.
(Erase heading not required.)

Army Form C. 2118.

Place	Date	Hour	Summary of Events and Information	Remarks and references to Appendices
			Casualties during month:-	
			Officers:- Lieut. J.C. MURRAY wounded 25/9/17. Died 23.9.17.	
			2/Lt. Mackay A. - to Hosp.(S) 10.9.19.	
			Capt. Alison C.E. - do - 23.9.19.	
			O. Ranks:- Wounded 24.	
			Wounded aided 10.	
			Died of wounds 3.	
			Killed in Action 1	
			Reinforcements:- 2/Lieut. E JEFFREY - from 56th Labour Coy	
			O. Ranks:- Draft 9 o.r. joined 8.9.17	
			" 7 o.r. " 9.9.17	
			" 8 o.r. " 13.9.17	
			" 6 o.r. " 15.9.17	
			" 2 o.r. " 23.9.17	
			" 4 o.r. " 26.9.17	
			Strength at 30.9.17 = 51 off. 1010 other ranks	
			2/10/17	
			Signed Cahan	
			A/Lt/Col R_____ (Pioneer)	

SECRET.   Copy No. 10

1/8th. Bn. The Royal Scots (Pioneers).

OPERATION ORDER No.5

By Lieut.-Colonel W. GEMMILL, D.S.O., Commanding.

19th. Sept., 1917.

1. On or about 20th. September, the Division in conjunction with the Divisions on right and left will resume the offensive.

2. The 154th. Inf. Brigade will attack with two Battalions of the 152nd. Inf. Brigade attached.

3. The work of the Pioneer Battalion will be :-

   (1) To continue Trench Tramway as far as possible to LANGEMARCK - WINNIPEG ROAD.
   (2) To repair Military Road to its junction with LANGEMARCK ROAD and then clear LANGEMARCK-WINNIPEG Road to its junction with POELCAPELLE ROAD.

4. "C" Company will continue the tramway.
   "D" Company will work on the road.
   "B" Company will be in Reserve.

5. On 19th. instant, "D" and "C" Companies will move forward as arranged with Officers Commanding Coys., and "B" Company will move to CANAL BANK. These moves to be completed by 7-30 p.m. Headquarters will move to Dugout No. 63 (immediately behind MULLER COTTAGE) at same hour.

6. Administrative Instructions are attached.

7. Acknowledge.

                                                     Captain,

                             Adjt., 1/8th. Bn. The Royal Scots (Pioneers).

COPY No. 1 - Adjt. for C.O.   6 - Medical Officer.
         2 - Major Tait.   7 - Quartermaster.
         3 - O.C. "B" Company.   8 - Regt. Sergt. Major.
         4 - O.C. "C" Company.   9 - Transport Officer.
         5 - O.C. "D" Company.   10 - War Diary.

SECRET.   Copy No. 10

1/8th. Bn. The Royal Scots (Pioneers).

ADMINISTRATIVE INSTRUCTIONS TO OPERATION ORDER No.5.

19th. September, 1917.

Reference Maps :- PILCKEM
                  POELCAPELLE.

1. **DRESS.** Fighting Order. Greatcoats will be carried, wrapped up in waterproof sheets. Iron rations will be carried and water-bottles filled.

2. **RATIONS.** Water, cooking utensils, Bivouac sheets, and tools will be sent up by G.S.Wagons. "D" Coy.'s will be sent to the end of ID Track on PILCKEM ROAD. O.C. "D" Coy. will arrange to send 1 N.C.O. and 2 men to accompany this wagon and unload same, and later to provide a carrying party to take stores forward from this point.
"C" Company's will be taken to a point near MINTY FARM. O.C. "C" Company will arrange an unloading and carrying party from this point.

3. Packs and blankets will be left in Reserve Billets with a guard over them.

4. **TRANSPORT.**
The Transport Officer will arrange to have rations forward to GHENT COTTAGES as soon after 3p.m. on the 19th. as possible.
1 G.S.Wagon each for "C" and "D" Coy. will report at GHENT COTTAGE CAMP at 2 p.m. to take forward, sheets, cooking utensils and tools.

5. **MEDICAL.**
Regtl. Aid Posts are at — C.5.a.7.1 MONT DO ROSTA.
                           C.5.a.1.9.

   Divl. Collect. Posts.   RUDOLPH FARM.
                           MINTY FARM.

6. **ECHELON "B"**
All surplus officers and other ranks will remain at GHENT COTTAGE CAMP - the whole under the charge of Major Tait.

                                              CAPTAIN.
                    Adjt., 1/8th. Bn. The Royal Scots (Pioneers).

ISSUED AT 7 a.m.

Copies to all recipients of O.O.No. 5.

SECRET.   Copy. No. 12

1/8th. Bn. The Royal Scots (Pioneers).

OPERATION ORDER NO.5.

By Lieut.-Colonel W. GEMMILL, D.S.O, Commanding.

Reference Map,   24th. September, 1917.
　　BELGIUM, Sheet 28 N.W.

1. The Battalion will move to BROWNE CAMP, A.23.b.9.1, on the 25th. September, 1917. Transport Lines will remain in present position.

2. **Detail for 25th. September;-**

　　　Reveille　6-30 a.m.　　　　　　　　Breakfast 7-0 a.m.
　　　Dinner　　12-30 p.m.　　　　　　　 Tea on arrival at Browne Camp.

3. **PARADE.**
　　　The Battalion will parade as follows :-
"B" Company will parade ready to march at　　2 p.m.
"C" Company　　　　　　　　do.　　　　　　　2-15 p.m.
"D" Company　　　　　　　　do.　　　　　　　2-30 p.m.
"A" Company will march from their Camp at　　2-50 p.m.
"H.Q. Staff" will move in rear of "A" Company under the R.S.M.
Companies will move by platoons at 100 yards distance.
There must be a distance of not less than 200 yards between Coys.
Cookers will go with Companies.

4. **DRESS.**
　　　Dress will be "full marching order." Tam o'Shanters will be worn. Steel helmets will be attached to the pack by the pack straps.

5. **ADVANCE PARTIES.**

(a) Officers Commanding Companies will detail 1 N.C.O. and 4 men per Company to report at the Battalion Orderly Room at 1 p.m. on the 25th. instant. This party will proceed to BROWNE CAMP and take over billets allotted to the Battalion. Captain J. Richardson will be in charge of the party.

(b) An advance party consisting of 1 N.C.O. and 19 men under Captain J. Richardson will proceed by train on the morning of the 26th. instant to the VIth. Corps Southern Reserve Division Training Area. The train to carry the party to ACHIET-LE-GRAND will leave POPERINGHE at 7-0 a.m. on the 26th. instant, and the party will report to the R.T.O. at POPERINGHE STATION by 6 a.m. on that date.
　　　Rations for consumption on 26th. and 27th. instant will be carried. Rations for consumption on 28th. and until arrival of the Battalion will be drawn from the Town Major in the new Area.

(c) This party will be detailed as follows :-
　　　Companies will detail 1 man per platoon.
　　　Transport Officer　will detail　1 man.
　　　Quartermaster　　　　"　　　　　1　"
　　　Headquarters　　　　　"　　　　　1　"
　　　O.C. "B" Coy.　　　　 "　　　　　1 N.C.O.

6. **DETAILS AT TRANSPORT.**

　　　The Battalion Pipe Band, Lewis Gunners, and all details other than those attached to Transport and Q.M.Stores for duty will rejoin their Companies &c. at BROWNE CAMP at 5 p.m. on the 25th. instant.
　　　The Battalion Pipe Band will report at Battalion Headquarters there. The Transport Officer will make all arrangements for this.

7. **ACKNOWLEDGE.**

　　　　　　　　　　　　　　　　　　　　　　　　　　　　Captain,
　　　　　　Adjt., 1/8th. Bn. The Royal Scots (Pioneers).
Issued at 6-30 p.m.

SECRET.   Copy No...12..
                  1/8th. Bn. The Royal Scots (Pioneers).

              TRANSPORT ARRANGEMENTS FOR OPARTION ORDER NO.6.

                                                  24th. September, 1917.

1.   The Battalion will move into BROWNE CAMP, A.23.b.2.1, on 25th.
     September, 1917.   Transport Lines will remain in present position.

2.   The following Transport will report at Battalion Headquarters
     at 11 a.m. on 25th. instant, and will be distributed as follows :-

          2 Tool Wagons per Company.   These wagons, in addition to
            Coy. Tools will carry Officers' Kits and Mess Boxes.
          1 Baggage Wagons for "B" and "C" Company, to carry blankets.
          1   "   "   "A" and "D" Company,   do.   do.
          1 Limbered Wagon for Details' Blankets.
          1 Medical Cart.
          1 Limbered Wagon for Lewis Guns, Shoemakers & Tailors, Armourer
            Sergeant,
          1 Limbered Wagon for Orderly Room, Pioneers, and Signals.
          1 Limber for H.Q. Officers.
          1 Mess Cart for Headquarters.

          Horses will also be sent forward for Company Cookers.
          The water-cart at present at GHENT COTTAGES WILL proceed to
          BROWNE CAMP at 2 p.m. filling en route.
          Companies will detail one brakesman to accompany each wagon.
          The Medical Officer will detail one brakesman for Medical Cart.
          The Regtl. Sergt.Major will detail one brakesman for
          each of the following limbers :-

                    Shoe.& Tail.& Lewis Gun Limber.
                    Orderly Room Limber
                    Headquarters Limber.
                    Blankets Limber. (H.Q)

3.   BIVOUAC SHEETS AND TENTS.
          Companies will arrange to have all Bivouac Sheets and Tents
     under their charge brought to a point near the Battalion Canteen
     and handed over to the Reg. Sergt. Major before 10 a.m.

4.   BLANKETS.
          Blankets will be tightly rolled in bundles of 10, and securely
     tied.   All bundles will be labelled.

5.   UNLOADING PARTIES.

          Officers Commanding Companies will each detail one man (
     surplus to the brakesman) to accompany the G.S.Wagons allotted to
     them to BROWNE CAMP, where they will unload the wagons, and stand
     guard over the baggage, etc. until the Coy. arrives.
          Company Tools will not be unloaded. They will be taken
     to Transport Lines.

                                                Captain,
                           Adjt., 1/8th. Bn. The Royal Scots (Pioneers).
Issued at 6-30 p.m.

Copy No. 1 - Adjt. for C.O.   Copy No. 8 - Transport Officer.
         2 - O.C. "A" Coy.   9 - Quartermaster.
         3 - O.C. "B" Coy.   10 - Regtl. Sergt.Major.
         4 - O.C. "C" Coy.   11 - N.C.O.i/c L.Guns.
         5 - O.C. "D" Coy.   12 - War Diary.
         6 - Captain Richardson.   13.- File.
         7 - Medical Officer.

SECRET.   Copy No. 12

1/8th. Bn. The Royal Scots (Pioneers).

OPERATION ORDER No. 7

By LIEUT.-COLONEL W. GEMMILL, D.S.O., Commanding,

28th. September, 1917.

Reference Maps :-
    Hazebrouck. 1:100,000
    Lens. 11   1:100,000
    Sheet 27 and 28. 1:40,000

1. The Battalion will move on the night of the 29th./30th. to COURCELLES in accordance with the following arrangements :-

    Entraining Station - PROVEN.   DETraining Station - BAPAUME WEST.

2. "A" Company (less 2 platoons), "C" Company and "D" Company will parade in the following order, ready to move off at 9-30 a.m. on the 29th.   All details, with the exception of Signals and Cyclists and Band will rejoin their Companies for the move.

            Signals and Cyclists. Band
            "A" Coy. (less 2 platoons)
            "C" Company.
            "D" Company.

(b) Companies will march with connecting files at 200 yards distance.
(c) "B" Company with Cooker and O.C. Coy's horse, will parade ready to march at 1-45 a.m. on 30th. instant.   Separate instructions for this move will be issued to O.C. "B" Company.

3. ENTRAINING.
    (1) Two platoons of "A" Company will act as entraining party at PROVEN Station.   Their duty will be the loading of all vehicles on railway wagons.   Captain Mitchell will act as entraining officer and will report to the R.T.O., PROVEN at 10 p.m. on 29th. instant.
    (2) The Transport Officer will be responsible for the entraining of the horses.

4. DRESS.
        Full Marching Order.   Rations for the 30th. instant will be carried by the men.   These will be issued to Companies by 29th. September.

5. Transport arrangements will be issued separately.

6. Acknowledge

                                        C. Jones
                                                Captain,

            Adjt., 1/8th. Bn. The Royal Scots (Pioneers).
Issued at   a.m. on 29th. September.

    Copy No. 1 - Adjt. for C.O.   Copy. No. 8 - Transport Officer.
         2 - O.C. "A" Company.   9 - Quartermaster.
         3 - O.C. "B" Company.   10 - Regtl. Sergt. Major.
         4 - O.C. "C" Company.   11 - N.C.O. i/c Lewis Guns.
         5 - O.C. "D" Company.   12 - War Diary.
         6 - Captain Mitchell.   13 - File.
         7 - Medical Officer.

-2-

9. The Transport Officer will arrange to take breast ropes for horse trucks with him.

10. The Entraining Platoons under Captain Mitchell will parade ready to march off at 7-30 p.m.   A Marching-Out State in duplicate will be given to Captain Mitchell.

11. The Transport Officer will arrange direct with O.C. "B" Company about taking over the horses for "B" Company Cooker.

12. O.C. "B" Company will detail 2 officers' servants to look after Officers' Kits and mess- Boxes on arrival of the Battalion at COURCELLES.   These servants will be attached to "A" Companyv for the Move.

                                                                     Captain,

                            Adjt., 1/8th. Bn. The Royal Scots (Pioneers).

Issued at 11-30 a.m. on 29th. Sept.

Copies to all recipients of Operation Order No. 7.

SECRET.   Copy. No. 12

1/8th. Bn. THE ROYAL SCOTS (Pioneers).

TRANSPORT ARRANGEMENTS FOR OPERATION ORDER No. 7

1. The Battalion will move on the night of the 29th./30th. to COURCELLES.

    Entraining Station:- PROVEN.   Detraining Station - BAPAUME WEST.

2. Transport (less "B" Coy. and O.C. "B" Coy's horse will parade at Transport Lines ready to march to PROVEN Station at 8 p.m. to-night.

3. Transport for the move will be distributed as under :-

    2 Tool wagons per company. These wagons, in addition to Coy. Tools will take officers' kits and mess boxes.
    1 Baggage wagons for "A" and "B" Coy. Blankets.
    1   do.   for "C" and "D" Coy. Blankets.
    1 Medical Cart for medical stores.
    1 Limbered wagon for Lewis Guns.
    1   do   for Orderly Room and Signals.
    1   do.   for Armourer Sergt., Shoemakers & Tailors and Pioneer Sergt.
    1   do.   for Headquarters.
    1   do   for Transport Officer.
    1   do.   for Quartermaster.
    1 Mess Cart for Headquarters. The mess cart will also take a mess-basket from each Company. These mess-boxes will be off-loaded at PROVEN Station and taken into the Railway carriage.
    Pack ponies will carry spare S.A.A.

    In addition to the above 1 motor-lorry will report to the Quartermaster at 6 p.m. and will be at his disposal to shift the Q.M. Stores to PROVEN STATION.

4. LOADING OF WAGONS &c.

    The tool-wagons, Headquarters limber and Mess-cart will be loaded and ready to move to Transport Lines by 7-0 p.m.
    The baggage-wagons and G.S. Wagons Limbers will be sent to BROWN Camp by 3 p.m. and all loading finished by 4 p.m., when they will return to Transport Lines.

    The Water-carts will be filled and ready to march with Transport at 8-0 p.m.

    Horses for "A", "C" and "D" Company Cookers will be sent to BROWN Camp at 7 p.m.

    Blankets will be rolled in bundles of 10, and will be securely tied and labelled. The Blankets of Headquarters Details will be dumped at the R.S.M.'s Tent by 3-0 p.m. this afternoon.

    Coys. will detail 1 brakesman for each Tool Cart.
    "A" Coy. do   1   do.   for "A" and "B" baggage wagon.
    "C" Coy. do   1   do.   for "C" and "D" baggage wagon.
    M.O.   do   1   do   for Medical Cart.
    R.S.M.   do   1   do   for each of following limbers, Lewis Guns Orderly Room, Shoemakers & Tails., H.Q.

                                              / The T.O. will arrange.

Army Form C. 2118.

WAR DIARY
or
INTELLIGENCE SUMMARY.
(Erase heading not required.)

Vol B 32

29 R.

Confidential

WAR DIARY

of

1/5th Bn. The Royal Scots

From

1st October 1917 to 31st October 1917

Volume No 36

Army Form C. 2118.

WAR DIARY
or
INTELLIGENCE SUMMARY.
(Erase heading not required.)

Instructions regarding War Diaries and Intelligence Summaries are contained in F. S. Regs., Part II. and the Staff Manual respectively. Title pages will be prepared in manuscript.

Place	Date	Hour	Summary of Events and Information	Remarks and references to Appendices
DRAVEN To BAPAUME	March 1st		Entraining and Employment of the Troop. About 2.30 am the Troop entrained and we arrived about 1 am at [illegible]	
			1. When I left [illegible] the BA HOPPE of found The Bar Parked of from The Bar Left of Cassel	
			8.30 am. Ming we arrived at Lock L HAZEBROUCK from there made for [illegible] Cassel	
			ETAPLES arriving at 10.30 about 12 midnight. The day was fine [illegible] ever good and [illegible]	
			about 1 [illegible] [illegible] met the [illegible] [illegible] The [illegible] [illegible]	
	2nd		We arrived at BAPAUME [illegible] and marched to billets at AVESNES LE COMTE arriving there at 7.30 am. The Transport left at 7.30 am. [illegible]	
			accommodation for the Bn. was found quite ample & [illegible] excepting the Officers v Sergt. [illegible] [illegible]	
			[illegible] the Bn. had been [illegible]. A draft of 45 OR's or RE's joined the Bn. A new [illegible] & Lieut.	
	3rd		The Bn. was employed during the day on Physical Training, Close order drill, [illegible] [illegible] [illegible]	
			[illegible] they do marched [illegible] parade [illegible] at an daybreak. [illegible] hour [illegible] [illegible]	
			to take over the trench in relief of the 7th Bn. B 21 Division on the 5th inst. The [illegible]	
			[illegible] [illegible] [illegible] on as [illegible] [illegible] [illegible] 22.9.11 [illegible] [illegible] [illegible]	
	4th		Parade up to yesterday PE by special man, [illegible] [illegible] being used from [illegible] [illegible]	
			to [illegible] [illegible] [illegible] [illegible] [illegible] [illegible] [illegible] [illegible] [illegible] [illegible]	
	5th		[illegible] the [illegible] [illegible] [illegible] [illegible] [illegible] [illegible] [illegible]	

Instructions regarding War Diaries and Intelligence Summaries are contained in F. S. Regs., Part II. and the Staff Manual respectively. Title pages will be prepared in manuscript.

WAR DIARY
or
INTELLIGENCE SUMMARY. (2)
(*Erase heading not required.*)

Army Form C. 2118.

Place	Date	Hour	Summary of Events and Information	Remarks and references to Appendices
COURCELLES le COMTE	[illegible]	5th	Cold. [illegible] by [illegible] of the Bn. [illegible] the [illegible] commenced. [illegible]	
			were:- Cpl McDonald B Coy, L/C Green B Coy, [illegible] A Coy, [illegible] McNab [illegible]	
			L/Cpl [illegible] D Coy, Sgt Blythe C Coy, L/Cpl [illegible] D Coy, Sgt [illegible] B Coy, Pte [illegible] A Coy, L/C	
			Pepper C Coy (Transport), Sgt Coutts C Coy, Sgt [illegible] B Coy, Sgt [illegible] D Coy, [illegible]	
			C Coy, Cpl Fraser D Coy. The [illegible] received the Medaille Militaire. Sgt [illegible]	
			also [illegible]. The Bn [illegible]	
			billets [illegible]. Another draft of 91 ORs ex RE joined Bn today.	
		6th	The Bn in accordance with Bn Orders went into the line today taking over from the 6th DLI.	
			Pioneers H.Qrs, A & B Coys being in billets near HENIN sur COJEUL with C & D Coys at	
			NEUVILLE VITASSE. There is about 2 miles between the half companies. Transport lines	
			& QM Stores are near BOIRY BECQUERELLE. 66 ORs have been sent to the 9th Bn Royal Scots	
			& a further 70 ORs have to be sent to the 5/6th Royal Scots. The 136 ORs Ex R.E. recently	
			joined are to take the place of the men sent to the 9th R Scots & the 5/6th Royal Scots.	
		7th	The Bn has settled down in their new billets & find them fairly comfortable. The billets	
			are shelters built against the banks of sunken roads. Considerable amount of work will	
			be necessary before they are made comfortable enough for winter quarters.	[initials]

D. D. & L., London, E.C.
(A7883) Wt. W809/M1672 350,000 4/17 Sch. 52a Forms/C/2118/14

Army Form C. 2118.

WAR DIARY
or
INTELLIGENCE SUMMARY. (3)

(Erase heading not required.)

Place	Date	Hour	Summary of Events and Information	Remarks and references to Appendices
HENIN SUR COJEUL	Oct 1917			
	7th		The Coy went out to work today on Communication Trenches. A copy of the Organization of the present scheme of work & a Tracing showing the work allotted to each Coy. The work & Scheme of manhandling the trenches, Widening & deepening or resurfacing the O.T.L. Trenches, Rivet Conrods, & the work in Particular in follows: Coldron Coy: Pann Alley & Forli Avenue. B Coy: 1st Avenue. C Coy: Church Trench & Chatham Trench. D Coy: Southern Avenue.	
	8th		The weather has changed to cold with high winds & occasional heavy showers. There was no aerial of the enemy a very quiet & work finished without any interruption from the enemy.	
NEUVILLE VITASSE	9th		Major Tarte, Capt. Walton & Capt. Young left the Bn today to proceed to England for 6 months duty at home. Mr Maxwell has taken over command of B Coy & 2nd Lt H.F. Jones command of D Coy. Capt. Runge has taken over the duties of Capt Young II Corps Commandant of the HINDENBERG LINE. Good progress is being made with the work by all the Coys.	
	10th		The weather is still unsettled. Build down been employed on the Rd is now very complete.	
			Settled down.	
	11th		Good progress is being made on the work. Weather now settled.	
	12th		Arrange Commendations being made for the Brit. takeing part in the III Corps attack. Brig. Major Todd	

Army Form C. 2118.

WAR DIARY
or
INTELLIGENCE SUMMARY. (4)
(Erase heading not required.)

Instructions regarding War Diaries and Intelligence Summaries are contained in F. S. Regs., Part II. and the Staff Manual respectively. Title pages will be prepared in manuscript.

Place	Date	Hour	Summary of Events and Information	Remarks and references to Appendices
HENIN & NEUVILLE VITASSE	Octbr	contd		
		12th	Major Todd & 2nd in Command of Coys from the Main Command. That Coy, has formed a Chursh Committee for the different social & sports & it is now Commdts. the Bn will endeavour to enter for all events. The events are as follows: Cross Country Running, Boxing, Fencing, Football, Cinderellas, Rapid Firing, Rev. Sleeve Shooting, Football, Bayonet Fighting, Tug of War, Lewis Gun, Lessor Pack, Wiring & certain events for the Artillery.	
		13th	Weather is still very bad. Work progressing well.	
		14th	As per proceeding.	
		15th	6 & S. R. from the Bn were sent to the S.L. R. Engrs dash [?] to alter altums with the Windsor from SAG. 3rd Echelon. An Italian S/O Coy has been attached to our ADRIAN Huts at ARGYLE Camp. Lyd NPT [?] has taken the present plan. Bn. on the 4th inst. has been strengthened. 6th 7th 9th Bn. Royal Scots Scotsy.	
		16th	A & B Coys having practically camps & the New CT. nor work commences on the Reserve Line. Widening & further slopping down & making cutting site for the garages of the front A. Coy. will work on CONCRETE RES. & B. Coy on CUCKOO RES. C. Coy being a party under Lt. Bennett Working at part of the 15th Coy. Bde front Strength. Very little was in future. 4 yr 200 yd 7 WOS	

WAR DIARY
or
INTELLIGENCE SUMMARY. (G)

(Erase heading not required.)

Army Form C. 2118.

Instructions regarding War Diaries and Intelligence Summaries are contained in F. S. Regs., Part II. and the Staff Manual respectively. Title pages will be prepared in manuscript.

Place	Date	Hour	Summary of Events and Information	Remarks and references to Appendices
HENIN	October 14th		Coy completed the wiring of the 134 thy Bde Front. Coy travelling 350 yards 3 wires.	
NEUVILLE VITASSE			C "B" Coys have started on the wiring cover to the Rt Brigade of the Reserve Coy Line through EMBRETTS & CUCKOO PASSAGE. The weather is still mild and clear.	
	15th		Work continues as before. Weather much the same.	
	17th		Coy has finished work on HAWK & SWAMP & Coys Sectors & also the Reserve line from HAWK SWAMP with a SOUTHERN AVE. widening of the line to front of CUCKOO PASSAGE. B Coy continues work on SOUTHERN AVE.	
	20th		A party under Lt Munro drove from Aunet to MONT LE PREUX to erect Nissen shelters at ... Gun emplacement and huts. Also 16 7½ pent officers & 12 OR shelter at ARGYLL CAMP, erecting ADRIAN HUTS for a Brigade Camp. Both work carrying on satisfactorily.	
	26th		The weather seems yesterday has set in wet & cold.	
	27th		Lt Ruthven & Lt Wilkinson & 2Lt C. Eden 2nd Lieut relieved from Canw Entry Capt Rollasford returned the Bn from duty with the War Dept. Salvage Coy has been in duty. Churcey in attachment Capt Rolwnsken proceeds today from Camw.	
	28th		Inter Coy Football was played the Bn MC Company & the 1st Bomb of the Division Football Tournament. C Coy & Lt ... Cpl Keen & Cpl Gray & Lieut...	

WAR DIARY or INTELLIGENCE SUMMARY

Army Form C. 2118.

Place	Date	Hour	Summary of Events and Information	Remarks and references to Appendices
HENIN	October			
&				
NEVILLE VITASSE	24th		24th. The Brigade to the line have front [covering] stations to [have] Bde. There [chiefly work] is [dugouts] to the support & Reserve Lines. The Rgt. Bde. are [chiefly] to dugouts the Left Bde. Ldugouts	
			The Bn. has been instructed to [send] [officers] [for] staff [to supervise] the work	
			Also an officer [from] each Brigade [reports] to [supervise] the making of [new] [dugouts] at H.Q 458	
			[An] [enemy] [sniper] [or] [gun]	
			25th. The Bn. has [relieved] the "[Ratty Ldn]" & all [reports] to the [accumulation] of the [enemy] [guns]	
			in the [reserve] trenches & the Bn. is [ordered] [instructions] to [make] [dugouts] the [following]	
			trenches Lane & CONCRETE to hold two platoons [Tredcap] an [enemy] [dugout] to hold one platoon	
			The [DUGEOND of SHAWK] to hold one platoon, the 21.59 & [Reinforce] to hold one platoon	
			& the 21.58 & BRETTEN or to hold one platoon. [The above are in the Rgt. of Reserve line]	
			In the Left Brigade sector the [trenches] have to be made so BAKE TRENCH to [hold] one platoon	
			each & that [trench] line to have four [bays] that it [will have] [nets] in all. The above work is	
			[urgent] & [was started] to day	
			The work [progress] [well]. The [weather] [be] [relieved] [mostly] [fine] [throughout]	
			26th [Instruction] has [been received] that the division is to be [relieved] [this] [Bde.] [The Field] [On]	
			[Rgt] [on] [to] [be] [attached] to the [Western] [Div] [were] [moved] to the [new] line on the 30?	

Army Form C. 2118.

WAR DIARY
or
INTELLIGENCE SUMMARY
(Erase heading not required.)

Instructions regarding War Diaries and Intelligence Summaries are contained in F. S. Regs., Part II. and the Staff Manual respectively. Title pages will be prepared in manuscript.

Place	Date	Hour	Summary of Events and Information	Remarks and references to Appendices
HENIN	October			
"	29th		Work of the Bn. finished at 5 P.m. Bn.gl. Pols [orderly] proceeded from HENIN with the Advance Party	
NEUVILLE VITASSE	29th		The Remainder of the Bn. then Relieved in Brigade (17th Division) in the Front Line. Representations from the Brigade party who were working at AREYUX Dump went to BEAURAINCOURT by day to our attendance from B.Y. Orders.	
	30th		The Bn. Reported today & all work also handed over to them. The Gas Gas parties were	
HENIN to	30th		Who were Serving J Kingston shoulder Orders left tonight in the men to attached.	
BEAURAINCOURT	30/31st		The Bn. marched to BEAURAINCOURT today as per arrangements to 20 N.Y. machine Guns at 5 P.m. the Bn. accommodated in NISSEN HUTS. 2 Minutes this far from the Bn.	
	31st		From ADMIN LE PETZ at BEAURAINCOURT today	
	31st		the Bn. details were published as to when relief & proceed to Camp near YPRES tomorrow. Operation Orders for the Move is attached	

3/10/17

[signatures]

WAR DIARY
INTELLIGENCE SUMMARY.
(Erase heading not required.)

Army Form C. 2118.

Place	Date	Hour	Summary of Events and Information	Remarks and references to Appendices
Reinforcements			Casualties during month of October 1919 :-	
			Officers :- Capt. M.P. Thorborn. Officers :- Capt M.P. Thorburn to 9th Devons	
			Joined 1/10/19. 15-10-19	
			O.Ranks :- 1-10-19. 4SOR O.Ranks :- Wounded 1	
			7-10-19 5 Wounded at duty 1	
			4-10-19 91 Sick. 45	
			15-10-19 6 —	
			19-10-19 8 47	
			24-10-19 6	
			29-10-19 5	
			166	
			Strength at 31st Oct, 1919 = 46 off 1008 O.R	

Capt.
Adjt 1/8th Bn. The Royal Scots
(Ronin)

War Diary

SECRET.   Copy No. 12

1/8th. Bn. The Royal Scots (Pioneers).
ADDENDUM No.1 to OPERATION ORDER No. 8.

8th. October, 1917.

2- PARADES.

After sub-para (b) add :-

" (c) All details other than the Band, Signallers and Cyclists, and Police will march in rear of "B" Company under an N.C.O. to be detailed by the Regtl. Sergt. Major."

                                                    Captain,

                Adjt., 1/8th. Bn. The Royal Scots (Pioneers).

Issued at 7 p.m. to recipients of O.O.No. 8.

SECRET.   W.O.   Copy No. 12.

1/8th. Bn. The Royal Scots (Pioneers).

OPERATION ORDER No. 8

By Lieut.-Colonel W. GEMMILL, D.S.O., Commanding.

5th. October, 1917.

REFERENCE MAPS :-
  LENS 11. 1:100000
  Sheet 51 B.S.W. 1:20,000

1. The Battalion will move at 2 p.m. on 6th. October, 1917, in accord-ance with the following instructions :-

   Headquarters, "A" and "B" Coys. move to shelters in T.3.a.
   "C" and "D" Coys. to shelters in N.20.b.
   Transport and Q.M.Store to Transport Lines in T.1.d.2.3.

2. PARADE.
   (a) Companies will parade in the following order ready to march at 2 p.m.
               Signals & Cyclists.
               Band.
               "A" Company.
               "B" Company.
               "C" Company.
               "D" Company.
               R.E. Draft of 91 O.R.
               Reg. Police.
   Transport will march in rear of the Battalion.
   Companies will parade in column of route. The head of the column will be at cross-roads in the village facing the HAMLINCOURT Road, and the companies formed up in the above order along the BOCQUOY - COURCELLES Road. Company cookers will march in rear of Coys.
   (b) Transport will be drwn up on the HAMLINCOURT ROAD between COURCELLES and COURCELLES Station by 1-30 p.m.

3. ROUTES.
   Headquarters, "A" and "B" Companies by road via HAMLINCOURT to main ARRAS- BAPAUME Road, BOYELLES, BOIRY BECQUERELLE, HENIN-sur-COJEUL. (If dry, the overland track will be taken from from BOYELLES to billets.)
   "C" and "D" Companies - by road via HAMLINCOURT to main ARRAS - BAPAUME Road, BOYELLES, MERCATEL, NEUVILLE VITASSE.
   Transport will proceed by the same route as "A" and "B" Coys to new Transport Lines just beyond BOIRY BECQUERELLE.

4. DRESS. Full marching order. Tam o' Shanters will be worn.

5. O.C. "D" Company will detail Lieut. Munro to take charge of the draft of 91 Other Ranks for the move and until further orders. The draft will be accommodated in Nissen Huts at Transport Lines at T.1.d.2.3, and will break off from the column on reaching that point.

6. ADVANCE PARTIES.

   Officers Commanding Companies will detail an advance party consisting of 1 N.C.O. and 4 men per Coy. to proceed in advance of the Companies to take over the billets to be vacated by the 7th. D.L.I. (Pioneers), and to act as guides on the arrival of the Coys.
   O.C. "A" Coy. will detail an officer to take charge of "A" and "B" advance parties.
   O.C. "C" Company will detail an officer to take charge of "C" and "D" Advance parties.
   Advance parties will move at 10 a.m. on 6th. instant.

7. Transport arrangements will be issued separately.

                                            Captain,
                                   Adjt., 1/8th. Bn. The Royal Scots (Pioneers).

Issued at 5.30 p.m.

SECRET.   Copy. No. 12

TRANSPORT ARRANGEMENTS FOR OPERATION ORDER No.8
1/8th. Bn. The Royal Scots (Pioneers).

War Diary

5th. October, 1917.

1. The Battalion will move at 2 p.m. on 6th. October, 1917 to new billets as detailed in Operation Order No. 8.

2. Transport for the move will be distributed as under :-

   2 F--- Tools wagons per Coy. These wagons, in addition to Company Tools will take officers' kits and mess boxes.
   1 Baggage Wagon for "A" and "B" Coy. Blankets.
   1   do.   for "C" and "D" Coy. Blankets.
   1 Medical Cart for medical Stores.
   1 Limbered wagon for Lewis Guns.
   1   do.   for O.Room and Signals.
   1   do.   for Armourer Sergt., Shoemakers & Tailors, and Pioneer Sergt.
   1   do.   Headquarters.
   1   do.   Transport Officer.
   1   do.   Blankets of Headquarters Details.
   1 Mess Cart for Headquarters.
   Pack ponies will carry spare S.A.A.

   In addition to the above 1 motor lorry will report to the Quartermaster at 7 a.m. and will be at his disposal to shift Quarter-master's Stores to new Transport Lines. The Quartermaster and personnel of Q.M.Stores will proceed with this lorry. The lorry will return and take the blankets of the draft (91 O.R.) and other stores to new Transport Lines.

3. The Transport will move direct to new Transport Lines: The T.O. will be notified later at what hour he will send forward wagons etc. to Company billets.

4. **LOADING OF TRANSPORT.**

   The Transport Officer will have all baggage wagons, G.S.wagons, limbered wagons etc. at Battalion Headquarters, and Coy. Headquarters as detailed above by 11 a.m. on the 6th. instant. All wagons etc. will be loaded ready to pull out by 12-30 p.m.
   Horses for Coy. Cookers will be at Coy. H.Q. by 1-30 p.m.

5. **BLANKETS.**

   Blankets will be rolled in bundles of 10, and will be securely tied and labelled. The blankets of Headquarters details will be dumped at Battalion Headquarters by 11 a.m. ready to load.

6. **BRAKESMEN.**

   Coys. will detail 1 brakesman for each tool wagon.
   "A" Coy.   do.   1   "   for "A" and "B" Baggage wagon.
   "C" Coy.   do.   1   "   for "C" and "D"   do.
   M.O.   do.   1   "   for Medical Cart.
   R.S.M.   do.   1   "   for each of the following wagons :-
                                       L.Gun Limber, Shoe.& Tail.Limber,
                                       O.Room Limber, H.Q.Limber, and H.Q.
                                       Blanket Limber.

7. **WATERCARTS.**

   The Transport will detail the watercarts as follows :-

   1 to "A" and "B" Coy. for regular service.
   1 to "C" and "D" Coys. for regular service.
   these water-carts will be ready to march with the Coys to which they are attached at 2 p.m.

S. acknowledge.

                                                    Captain,
                                  Adjt., 1/8th. Bn. The Royal Scots (Pioneers).
Issued at p.m. to recipients of Operation Order No. 8.

The following will be the organisation of work in the present Sector of Line :-

The Battalion is responsible for :-

(1) Revetting and maintaining Communication Trenches up to the Support Line.

(2) Certain Roads.

The Support Line runs along BROWN SUPPORT – CURTAIN TRENCH – BULLFINCH – L.18 – ROE.
The Reserve Line runs along CONGREVE RES.– CUCKOO RES.– MALLARD RES.– GANNET TRENCH – BISON TRENCH – a gap in Cojeul Valley – then BART TRENCH.

1. Communication trenches to be kept up.

RIGHT Sector.
{ AVENUE TRENCH.
{ PIONEER ALLEY.
{ FOSTER AVENUE.
{ SHAWK AVE. from MALLARD Res. to BULLFINCH Support.

LEFT Sector.
{ SHIKAR AVE.
{ SOUTHERN AVE.
{ DURHAM AVE.

2. Road from WANCOURT to DUMMAPPE and thence to ARRAS – CAMBRAI Road.

As the work on (1) is most urgent (2) will not be started in the meantime.

The above work consists of (1) Maintaining trenches in their present condition and repairing and renewing duck-boards. (2) Where trenches are not revetted (a) To cut away the sides of the trenches to a slope of at least 3/1 (b) clear a berm of 2 feet (taking care not to leave the parapet too steep) and (c) continuing the revetment.

In addition to the above work the G.O.C. wishes "stops" where the C.Ts. cross the Support and Reserve Lines. Separate instructions will be given to O.C., Coys. regarding these.

The above work is allotted to Coys. as follows :-

AVENUE TRENCH   – "B" Coy.
Pioneer Alley)
FOSTER AVENUE)   – "A" Coy.
SHAWK AVENUE)
SHIKAR AVENUE)   – "C" Coy.
SOUTHERN AVE)   – "D" Coy.

It is important that this work should be completed before the weather gets too bad, and all available men will be employed. The work will be carefully organised to get the best and quickest results.

All officers and N.C.Os. i/c parties are to be in possession of written instructions, and, if possible, a sketch of the work they are to do.

A Jones Captain,
12/10/17.   Adjt., 1/8th. Bn. The Royal Scots(Pioneers)

S E C R E T.   1/8th. Bn. The Royal Scots (Pioneers).   Copy. No. 12

OPERATION ORDER No.9,

By Lieut.-Colonel W. GEMMILL, D.S.O. Commanding

29th. October, 1917.

Reference Map - LENS 11
    Scale - 1:100,000

1. The Battalion will move on 30th. October, 1917 to BEAULENCOURT in accordance with the following instructions :-

2.   Reveille 6-0 a.m.   Breakfast :- "A" and "B" Coys 7-30 a.m
                                                             "C" and "D" Coys 7-0 a.m.
    Dinner - on the march.   Tea - On arrival.

3.- PARADE.
        Companies will parade ready to march as follows :-

            Signals and Cyclists
            Band
            "B" Company.
            "A" Company.
            Regimental Police.

The above will be ready to march at 9-0 a.m. The head of the Column will be opposite the DURHAM SHELTERS Sign Post.

"C" and "D" Companies will parade at their Company Billets ready to march at 8-30 a.m. Company Cookers will march in rear of Companies. One watercart will march in rear of "A" Company, and one in rear of "D" Company Water-carts will be filled before starting. Transport will march in rear of the Battalion.

4. ROUTE.
        The Battalion, less "C" and "D" Coys., will march via HENIN to main ARRAS - BAPAUME ROAD - Bapaume - BEAULENCOURT.

"C" and "D" Companies will march by road via MERCATEL and main ARRAS- BAPAUME ROAD to junction of HENIN and BAPAUME-ARRAS Road wher they will join the Battalion.

Companies will march with 50 yards distance between platoons as far as main ARRAS - BAPAUME Road. From thence the Battalion/with 100 yards distance between Companies and sections of Transport.

5. DRESS.
        Dress will be Full Marching Order. Tam o' Shanters will be worn Leather jerkins will be worn under the equipment. One blanket per man will be carried in the pack. Transport will be provided for the remaining blankets, water-proof sheets and great-coats.

Blankets will be rolled in bundles of ten, with water-proof sheets outside. All bundles will be securely tied and labelled and stacked at Company Headquarters in time for loading.

6. The 1 N.C.O. and 12 Other Ranks of "D" Company at present at HENIN R.E.Dump will be attached to "A" Company for the move. The R.S.M. will arrange to have the blankets, greatcoats, and waterproof sheets of these men at "A" Company Headquarters in time for laoding. This party will hand their days rations over to "A" Company cooks.

7. All details other than Dandm Signallers, Cyclists, and Police will march in rear of "A" Company under an N.C.O. to be detailed by the Reg. Sergt.Major.

7. Transport arrangements will be notified later.

9. Acknowledge.

                                                                                   Captain,

Issued at   p.m.   Adjt., 1/8th. Bn. The Royal Scots (Pioneers).

SECRET.   Copy.No. 12

1/8th. Bn. The Royal Scots (Pioneers).

TRANSPORT ARRANGEMENTS FOR OPERATION ORDER No.9

1. The Battalion will move on the 30th. October, 1917 to BEAULENCOURT as detailed in Operation Order No.9.
   Transport for the move will be distributed as under :-

   2 Tool Wagons per Company. These wagons in addition to Coy. tools will take officers kits and mess-boxes.
   2 Baggage wagons for "A" Coy. Blanket, Greatcoats & Waterproof Sheet
   1 Motor Lorry   "B" Coy.   do.   do.
   1   do   "C" Coy.   do.   do.
   1   do.   "D" Coy.   do.   do.
   1   do.   Q.M.   do.(to make 2 journeys, if
   1 Medical Cart for Medical Stores.   (necesary.
   1 G.S.Limber for Lewis Guns.
   1 G.S.Limber for Orderly Room and Signals.
   1 G.S.Limber for Armourer Sgt, Shoe.&Tails., Pioneer Sergt.
   1 G.S.Limber for Headquarters
   1 G.S.Limber for Transport Officer.
   1 G.S.Limber for Blankets &c.of H.Q.Details.
   1 G.S.Limber =half for T.O. and Half for H.Q.Details.
   1 Mess Cart for Headquarters
   1 Civilian Cart for Canteen Stores.
   Pack Ponies will carry spare S.A.A.

2. The motor lorries will report as follows :-

        2 at "C" & "D" Coys.billets at 7-0 a.m.
        2 at "A" & "B" Coys.Billets at 8-0 a.m.
   O.C.Coys. concerned and the Q.M. will be on the look-out for the arrival of the lorries.

3. LOADING OF TRANSPORT.

   The T.O. will arrange to have all the necessary transport sent to Company and Battalion Headquarters in sufficient time to allow Coys &c. to have them loaded before the following hours :-
        H.Q., "A" and "B" Coys.   8-30 a.m.
        "C" and "D" Coys.   8-0 a.m.

4. BRAKESMEN.
   Coys. will detail one brakesman for each tool wagon.
   "A" Company will detail 1 brakesman for each Baggage Wagon.
   M.O.   ''   ''   Medical Cart.
   R.S.M. will detail 1 brakesman for each of the following :-
        L.Gun Limber, O.Room Limber, Shoe.&Tails Limber, H.Q. Limber, H.Q.Details Limber.
   The T.O. will detail 1 brakesman for each of the 2 remaining limbers.

5. Horses for Coy. Cookers and water-carts will be at Coy. H.Q. at 8a.m.

6. Transport will march in rear of the Battalion from junction of HENIN ROAD with main ARRAS - BAPAUME ROAD.

7. Acknowledge.

   Issued at   p.m.
                                                                Captain,
                       Adjt., 1/8th. Bn. The Royal Scots (Pioneers).
   Copy No.1 - Adjt. for C.O.   No. 7 - Transport Officer.
        2 - O.C. "A" Company.   8 - Quartermaster.
        3 - O.C. "B" Company.   9 - Regtl. Sergt. Major.
        4 - O.C. "C" Company.   10 - N.C.O. i/c Lewis Guns.
        5 - O.C. "D" Company.   11 - War Diary.
        6 - Medical Officer   12 - File.

WAR DIARY
or
INTELLIGENCE SUMMARY

Army Form C. 2118.

WAR DIARY
of
1/9 Bn. THE ROYAL SCOTS

FROM
1st November 1917 to 30th November 1917

VOLUME No 37

Confidential

WAR DIARY or INTELLIGENCE SUMMARY.

Army Form C. 2118.

(Erase heading not required.)

Instructions regarding War Diaries and Intelligence Summaries are contained in F. S. Regs., Part II. and the Staff Manual respectively. Title pages will be prepared in manuscript.

Place	Date	Hour	Summary of Events and Information	Remarks and references to Appendices
BEAULENCOURT	September 1st		The Bn. moved to day to accordance with arrangements to Ynodin Railway & Tendon Station in Aulnois Railway Camp LEGHELLE at 12 non. The Bn. is billeted in Nissen huts.	
Railway Camp LEGHELLE	2nd		The men went to R.E. making accommodation in METZ EN COUTURE for their billeting. CS boys went to METZ today to arrange the work. The village is in ruins with no very few houses standing. The work will however consist of cleaning & clearing from the ruined houses & erecting shelters or marquees for those who cannot inhabit the houses & must live with occasional sleep. Other necessary work.	
	3rd		Coys. proceeded to work at 8.30 am & proceeded to METZ & billetting of the men. Rations were sent forward with dinners. Arrangements are being made to bring the Coys one day until each Coy is they have accommodation themselves in the village. Material is being sent forward by R.E. & Railway.	
	4th		A & B Coys proceeded to work at 7.30 am returned to billets at 5 pm & progress is being made but owing to shortage of supplies and many difficulties material arriving.	

Army Form C. 2118.

WAR DIARY
or
INTELLIGENCE SUMMARY.
(Erase heading not required.)

Place	Date	Hour	Summary of Events and Information	Remarks and references to Appendices
RAILWAY CAMP LECHELLE	5th		Coys paraded for work at 7.15 am parade. Coys. parties. Wagons have been prepared. Disposal is "C" Coy to "D" Coy. Work the Rail. material from Ry. Pumps, METZ to "E" Coy on sinking accommodation for Ens. Coys Empl. Br. Deps. from hut METZ Rainey Quarry workshops. The men are alKesker.	
	6th		Br. D. Coys moved into METZ & Coy.	
	7th		Accommodation for another Coy in Empl. H.Q. & Br. Coy. moved into METZ Garage.	
	8th		A. Coy. moved into METZ & Coy. H.Q. & Coy. Room at Railway Camp.	
	9th		Good progress is being made with the work. Weather is now plentiful & bitter cold.	
	10th		B. Coy. moved into Belch in METZ today. H.Q. & Transport remain at Railway Camp. Weather still shows with snow, but mild.	
	11th		E. Coy. have started to clear ground in METZ. Other Cases are about getting things away from every for accommodation tin. trips.	
	12th		Accommodation for Coys has been Empl.tel.	
	13th		2nd Lt. Robbie & 2nd Lt. Perkins joined the Bn. from the 4th Res. Bn. on the 5th inst.	
	14th		The Bn. football team got into the 3rd Round of the G.C. Tournament by beating the 5th Div. Team 3-0.	

WAR DIARY or INTELLIGENCE SUMMARY

Army Form C. 2118.

Place	Date	Hour	Summary of Events and Information	Remarks and references to Appendices
HQ: Railway C&MP Transport	Nov 13th		HQ: Transport moved to LITTLEWOOD CAMP near YPRES today. Aerodrome for 4070 has been completed at METZ.	
Cap METZ.			Bn. HQ. Transport & 2 in other moved to NEUVILLE today. The weather is still very rainy but not very pleasant.	
Bn. HQ NEUVILLE			17th Different accommodation has been made at METZ & the Bn is allotted to the Baggage & Gun Poisson who start to move to 13 Bn 183 O.S. Bren 17 Bty & relieving a relieving officer to METZ then Bn. will remain to METZ during the forenoon shooting early. By Transport of 17 Bn will be at NEUVILLE the burden have been received from 32 Ladder Army to send 120 I.B., J.L. & 12 R.E. depot to 32 which formed the Bn. during the 1st week of Octbr. 34 & 12 R.E. depots to 32 arrangements have been made to send this chaps away on the 19th inst.	
			8th Operation orders for the coming offensive have been received from the Bn. below.	
		19.30	No 5 Pln on the Staff are dispatched to ROVENBERG ready for the move to Pl.inner at METZ the evening. Bn Specials order & Administration Instructions who instructions to work of the Bn for today are attached.	
			20th Other officers started the morning about 6.00 am. Then started from Station House & Sand Clone C	

Army Form C. 2118.

Army Form C. 2118.

WAR DIARY
or
INTELLIGENCE SUMMARY. (4)

(Erase heading not required.)

Instructions regarding War Diaries and Intelligence Summaries are contained in F. S. Regs., Part II. and the Staff Manual respectively. Title pages will be prepared in manuscript.

Place	Date	Hour	Summary of Events and Information	Remarks and references to Appendices
HQ 3rd Bays METZ REAR H.Q.	Nov	20th	to be going with B & C Coys went out in the first ship at 7.30 am to work on the road from TRESCAULT towards RIBECOURT. The Bn was with A. Coy in Billets near TRESCAULT had reached the work at 9.45 am the shelling having gradually ceased, the front line found to be further forward than the line the B Echs Horses were drawing was moved to the Nine Hundred Line back from the noise in the shelling in which the noise of Guns & horses of the attack had been a source from all sounds of the attack I/E Coys returned about 4.30 pm Bn L & M Coys which were not yet in the outskirts of the GRAND RAVINE which were relieved that evening and returned to their billets at TRESCAULT in the Sunken Rd - at 7.30 pm B/L Coy returned R & S Coys 8 2/2 Pm. the attack had been a source from all sounds of the attack I/E Coys returned about 4.30 pm Sunken Road near TRESCAULT from 11 am onwards enemy shelling very spasmodically at the Rd suffered no casualties during the day the Horse B Cord Coys were also worked on the road	
Transport VIENVILLE		21st	today all received instructions to work on the road running from K.36.C.0.1 to K.30.a.7.2. B & C Coys went out on the morning shift at 9.15 am B & C Coy Do the afternoon shift. The weather was made favourable for Bandsmen Latches & Whistlers with their rates most used by Battery. the Bn suffered no casualties during the day enemy shelling spasmodically throughout	B

WAR DIARY or INTELLIGENCE SUMMARY (5)

Army Form C. 2118.

(Erase heading not required.)

Place	Date	Hour	Summary of Events and Information	Remarks and references to Appendices
H.Q.rs Coys METZ				
Rear H.Q.rs & Transport NEUVILLE	22nd		Today Coys were employed chearing ways to the vicinity of the trench previously worked on by the Bn. & making additional tracks leading to the FLESQUIÈRES RIDGE just East of great many trenches had to be filled in to safeguard the exchange transport from H.Q.rs Coys to METZ Coy.	
	23rd		A & D Coys were moved to which is situated in the old Hun Line in K30 c&d. C Coy was employed the same work as yesterday. The enemy is still very quiet. The back Area being very quiet indeed	
	24th		A & D Coys were sent to work today on the road running from FLESQUIÈRES to FLESQUIÈRES. I was relieved in the afternoon by O.R.B Coys who had moved into Heyencourt near Dr Coys. H.Q.rs & Transport moved into billets near TRESCAULT at Q.3.d central. The Guard Div. Returned our Div. East right.	
	25th		The Bn. was again employed on the road they were on yesterday. Orders were just from received that the Bn. along with the 284th H Field Coy are to be attached to the Tk Corps for work & are to be under the CRE A.T. Coy. Coys gave orders for moves tomorrow into dugouts in the old Hun Line in K.27 & 21.	
	26th		The Coys moved into dugouts in K.27 & 21. Today were successful in finding accommodation.	
	27th		H.Q.rs Transport & Personnel at Q.3.d central. The Coys were employed today as follows C Coy making a ramp into Canal at K.26.c.5	

WAR DIARY or INTELLIGENCE SUMMARY

Army Form C. 2118.

Place	Date	Hour	Summary of Events and Information	Remarks and references to Appendices
H.Q. "Transport" at D3d Central Map reference M.27-21.	Nov. 27"		**Corbie** Online L No.1 & No.2 Coy was employed repairing the road running from J.30.b towards J.36 Central. C & D Coys were employed clearing the bottom of the Somme from H.9.a to H.32.a. The Road A.6. is used as a Roadway being dry.	
	28"		A & B Coy were employed in spreading so also was D Coy. C Coy are now empty coys in Machinery. A Corduroy Road from K.15.a.2.6.6. K.16.a.7.4.	
	29"		Coys were all employed in spreading but C Platoon J.C. Coy were sent to high C Coy on. New Road which is important very urgently required for Traffic.	
	30"		Coys were employed as far yesterday with the exception of C Coy who have forwarded work on the Ramp & are now employed with Coys on the Road. Transports sent H.Q to be shifted tonight to RAPAUL COURT from TRESCAULT as there was a breakthrough by the Huns through COUZEAUCOURT (which METZ which threatened to cut us off) From the trench leading to the back areas the "Tunnel" by the enemy was successfully checked however as although at one time the situation was very critical.	

Arthur Clifton Lieut.
78 Royal West Surrey

30/11/17

Army Form C. 2118.

WAR DIARY
or
INTELLIGENCE SUMMARY.
(Erase heading not required.)

Place	Date	Hour	Summary of Events and Information	Remarks and references to Appendices
			Casualties during Month of November 1917:-	
			Reinforcements - Officers :- 2nd Lt. J.H. Rothen & Officers & RMO McGuire NNI	
			2 Lt. D. James 3 Joined 17.11.17.	
			To R & 6 Magazines 23.11.17	
			Other Ranks :- 3-11-17 - 4 O.Rs	
			5-11-17 - 151 O.Rs Other Ranks :- 21.	
			20-11-17 - 4 O.Rs 21 O.Rs	
			23 O.Rs	
			Strength at 30 November 1917 - 47 Off. 909 O.Rs	

R. Jones
Major
Adjt. 1/5 Bn The Royal [ ]

S E C R E T.   Copy No. 11

1/8th. Bn. The Royal Scots (Pioneers).

OPERATION ORDER No. 11

By Lieut.-Colonel W. GEMMILL, D.S.O., Commanding.

19th. November, 1917.

Reference Maps :- BEAUCAMP. 1:10000
DEMICOURT 1:10000
GOUZEAUCOURT 1:20000
57 c. 1:40000

1. On a date and hour to be notified later, the Third Army will attack the enemy's lines from CANAL DU NORD (just West of HAVRIN-COURT) to the South on a two Corps front.

2. The main attack of the IVth. Corps will be carried out by the 51st.(Highland) Division on the right with the 62nd. Division on the left.

3. The 51st. Division will attack with :-

152nd. Inf. Brigade on the RIGHT.
153rd. Inf. Brigade on the LEFT.
154th. Inf. Brigade in RESERVE.

4. There will be no preliminary bombardment.

5. The Battalion will be employed :-
   (a) On repair of road Q.4.a.2.1 to K.29 central and forward. Six sections Field Coys. R.E. with 150 attached Infantry will also be employed on this road. The work of the R.E. is to bridge trenches and craters where necessary, and the work of this Battalion is to clear and repair the road. Twenty G.S. Wagons are expected to be available to assist.
   This work, details of which will be issued later, is to be pushed forward rapidly as soon after ZERO as possible.

   (b) A small party under a N.C.O. to put up Notice Boards.

   (c) The men presently employed at R.E. Dumps will remain there.

6. A R.E. Officer will act as Liason Officer in the Forward Area and will send word to Adv. Div. Report Centre (Q.14.a.8.2) when he considers the situation will permit work to commence. A runner from the Battalion will be posted at Report Centre to bring information to Bn. H.Q., but Companies ordered out first to work will also make their own reconnaisances in order to take advantage of any chance of working.

7. Administrative Instructions are issued separately.

8. Battalion Headquarters will be at Q.19.c.60.70.

9. Acknowledge.

Captain,

Adjt., 1/8th. Bn. The Royal Scots (Pioneers).

Issued at 10-30 a.m.
Copy No. 1 - Adjt. for O.C.
    2 - Major Todd.
    3 - O.C. "A" Company.
    4 - O.C. "B" Company.
    5 - O.C. "C" Company.

No. 6 - O.C. "D" Company.
    7 - Medical Officer.
    8 - Transport Officer.
    9 - Quartermaster.
    10 - Regtl. Sergt. Major.
    11 - War Diary. ✓

War Diary SECRET.

O.C. "A" Company.
O.C. "B" Company.
O.C. "C" Company.
O.C. "D" Company.
Transport Officers.

INSTRUCTIONS FOR WORK ON Z DAY.

The Battalion will work in 3 shifts of 4 hours each. (This may be altered so that the 2nd. & 3rd. shifts go out together,) with the exception of the following parties :-

(1) 1 Officer, 1 N.C.O. and 10 men of "C" Company putting up notice boards, instructions will be given verbally to the officer detailed by O.C. "C" Company.

(2) 1 Platoon of "A" Company clearing a road through TRESCAULT for guns. This road will be shown on Map to O.C. "A" Company tomorrow morning.

1st. relief for road consists of 3 platoons of "A" Company 2 platoons of "B" Company, 1 Limber for tools and Lewis Gun and 6 G.S. Wagon-loads with road metal.

2nd. relief:- 2 platoons of "B" Company, 3 platoons of "C" company, 1 limber with tools and 6 G.S.Wagons with road metal.

3rd. relief:- 1 platoon of "C" Company and "D" Company with 1 limber for tools.

Limbers will be used for carting material on the work if required and will return with the party with which they went out.

6 G.S.Wagons will take up metal with first relief and will be kept on the work to cart bricks or other material if required returning to METZ after 6 hours work.

6 G.S.Wagons with 2nd. relief will be employed in the same way returning to METZ after 6 hours work.

1st. relief will be ready to move at 8a.m.

Battalion transport will provide the 3 limbers required.

1st.Limber to be at BN. H.Qrs. METZ at 7-30 a.m.
2nd. " " " " " at 11-30 a.m.
3rd. " " " " " at 3-30 p.m.

D.A.C. will provide the G.S.Wagons.

Work on the road must be continuous i.e. No party will cease work until arrival of the relieving party. The senior officer of each party will hand over the work to the relieving party.

It is impossible to give instructions about the work in the meantime, the great thing is to get a road fit for wheeled traffic as soon as possible.

A. Jones, Captain,

Adjt., 1/8th. Bn. The Royal Scots (Pioneers).

19/11/17.

S E C R E T.　　　　　　　　　　　　　　　　　　　　　　Copy. No. 11

1/8th. Bn. The Royal Scots (Pioneers).

ADMINISTRATIVE INSTRUCTIONS. to OPERATION ORDER No.11

19th. November, 1917.

1. Surplus Kits will be stored at the Quartermaster's Stores at NEUVILLE and in METZ (place to be selected later). On "Z" day officers and men will pack their kits and leave them in their billets — blankets rolled up in bundles of 10 and labelled.

2. Dress. Fighting kit will be worn over leather jerkins (which must be taken off when men are at work). Steel helmets, Box Respirators, and P.H.Helmets will be worn. Iron rations will be carried, also 50 rounds S.A.A. per N.C.O. and man.

3. RATIONS. A special breakfast ration will be issued.

4. TOOLS. Each man will carry a shovel or a pick in the proportion of 1 pick to 4 shovels. In addition, a number of crow-bars, wire-cutters, wiring-gloves and folding-saws will be carried by each Company. Two Limbers will accompany each party and will be available to take up tools.

5. LEWIS GUNS. One Lewis Gun will accompany the Working party. The Lewis Gun Sergeant will arrange that this goes up in one of the limbers with a team of 1 N.C.O. and 3 men, and that a similar party as relief goes up with the second working relief. This Lewis Gun will be mounted to protect men working from hostile aircraft.

6. DUMPS.
　　R.E. Dumps　—　TRESCAULT and METZ.
　　Rations — at　Q.15.c.2.9 (for consumption on "Z + 1" day)
　　　　　　　　　　　　　　　　　　　　　　if required
　　S.A.A.　—　Q.11.a.8.9
　　　　　　　　Q.11.b.9.7
　　　　　　　　Q.5.d.2.5.
　　Grenades —　Q.15.c.2.9
　　Water　　—　TRESCAULT.
　　Petrol Tins at Div. Grenade Dump.

7. MEDICAL.
　　Right Brigade　R.Aid Post —　Q.10.b.9.5
　　Left Brigade　R.Aid Post —　Q.10.a. 5.7
　　Adv. Dress. Stn.　　　　—　Q.14.d.3.8
　　Walking Wounded　　　　—　P.18.d.

8. The following will be the positions of Headquarters at ZERO :-

　　51st.(H) Division.　　—　LITTLE WOOD (YTRES).
　　152nd. Inf. Brigade.　—　Q.10.c.9.7
　　153rd. Inf. Brigade　 —　Q.10.a.4.4.
　　154th. Inf. Brigade　 —　METZ.

9. SIGNAL OFFICE.
　　　Advanced Div. Exchange — Q.14.a.8.2.

10.　Acknowledge.

　　　　　　　　　　　　　　　　A. Jones
　　　　　　　　　　　　　　　　　　　　Captain,
　　　　　　Adjt., 1/8th. Bn. The Royal Scots (Pioneers).

Issued at 10-30 a.m.

　　Copies to all recipients of Operation Order No. 11.

On His Majesty's Service.

Army Form C. 2118.

WAR DIARY
or
INTELLIGENCE SUMMARY.
(Erase heading not required.)

Confidential

WAR DIARY.
of
1/5 Bn THE ROYAL SCOTS
FROM
1st December 1917 to 31st December 1917
VOLUME No 38.

WAR DIARY or INTELLIGENCE SUMMARY

Army Form C. 2118.

Place	Date	Hour	Summary of Events and Information	Remarks and references to Appendices
REAR HQ & TRANSPORT at ROYAULCOURT Adv HQ & 3 Coys at K.12.c.7.2	December 1st		Work for the Coys as follows. A & C Coys on bogged road from Capos at A.15.a.4.3.6 to HAVERINCOURT ROAD at K.13.d.4.2. D Coy cleaning bottom of the Canal of debris & broken timbers along from K.19.a.4.5. to J.33.central. B Coy repairing the road from Cambrai at J.33.a.6.1. to HERMIES. The weather is good & temperate for the line of year.	
	2nd		Work as for yesterday. Two new C.B.Coy huts erected on the works today. The training are whitening the back areas any possible &	
	3rd		Weather still continuing good. The work is as for yesterday.	
	4th		We got work to begin the Divi today. The Divi has been brought back from rest & to in the line in front of MOEUVRES. The Coys moved independently to Camp just outside LEBUCQUIERE. A.C. & D.Coys to link B.Coy who were back. Rear HQ & Transport moved to Camp near FREMICOURT Coords. 47D. Joining them there. The move was completed by 6.P.M.	
	5th		The work for today was wiring & that was our front line before the Advance. All the Coys were out. A & B Coys erected in afternoon from the Cambrai road near D.29.central to the left of C & D Coys worked from the Cambrai road & the Bapt to about 1200 yds. if was out but offer. The Coys worked under particularly trying conditions being	

Army Form C. 2118.

WAR DIARY
or
INTELLIGENCE SUMMARY. (2.)
(Erase heading not required.)

Place	Date	Hour	Summary of Events and Information	Remarks and references to Appendices
H.Q. FREMICOURT Coys near LEBECQUIERE	Dec. 3rd		Enemy shelled two or three times during the night. A considerable amount of our shell came over & at times the men had to work in their gas masks. 2nd Lt Taylor of C/Coy was killed, also Pte Gunner of A/Coy. 2nd Lts Webb of A/Coy & Meering T.S. Thew wounded. B Coy was employed enlarging bivouacs & completing wire to left of Lindon Road. A Coy was employed widening & deepening RAT ALLEY. Parties have been sent to the R.E. Dump at BEUGNY & LOUVERVAL. A Platoon of C Coy is repairing hidden huts. 7th D Coy completed Officer funk on right of Lindon Road today. C Coy is working at RAT ALLEY & making my Rifle post to the support of same. RAT ALLEY. Then Coy is also erecting screens at J.2.a central to screen the road. The weather has been wet, making it very uncomfortable for the men in tents. Accommodation is being made by the Bn: near BEUGNY into which the Coys will move as soon as they are ready. 8th Coys worked today on new C.T. running from J.3.a.6. from RABBIT ALLEY at D.29.c. The tracks L.h to be 7ft wide at top & 6ft deep. The tunnel can only be worked on at night as it is under observation from the enemy. The Ength of the tunnel will be about 1800x. D Coy moved into billets at BEUGNY today. 9th Coys were again employed on new C.T. C Coy moved into new billets here BEUGNY today.	

WAR DIARY
or
INTELLIGENCE SUMMARY. (3)
(Erase heading not required.)

Army Form C. 2118.

Place	Date	Hour	Summary of Events and Information	Remarks and references to Appendices
Hqrs of FREMICOURT	Dec. 9th 1917		The C.O. left for one month's leave today. Major S.T.C. Todd h.n. command of Bn. during his absence	
	10th		Work continued on new C.T. The weather is still very unsettled rain.	
	11th		B. continued work on new C.T. Night quiet. 4 troops move in. Three new billets at BEUGNY	
	12th		Work continued on C.T. Night again quiet and good work done. Sept. N.C.O. Jones Adjutant	
			goes on leave. Capt L/C Jessanth Macaro returns from leave. B. troop move into new billets at	
			BEUGNY	
	13th		Work continued on C.T. Night very quiet. Lt. Chant reports for duty from hospital.	
	14th		Work continued. Party alibids push by day. Lt. Parr firstly returns to duty & A. troop mobile	
			Also two billets on 4th mt. from front from trenches	
	15th		Still working on C.T. Large party working by day. 2nd Lt. Lollender from 3rd Royal Scots	
			and 2nd Lt. Lunic from 1st (Reg.) Royal Scots reports for duty. They are posted to B. and C.	
			Coys respectively. 2nd Lt. Kennedy of C. Coy. listed whilst working by night to C.T.	
	16th		Work on C.T. continued	
	17th		Digging of C.T. finished. Laying of duckboards & drainage started	
	18th		Bn. is now working by day at the front slopes of trenches. Mining & support line started	

Army Form C. 2118.

WAR DIARY
or
INTELLIGENCE SUMMARY. (4)
(Erase heading not required.)

Instructions regarding War Diaries and Intelligence Summaries are contained in F. S. Regs., Part II. and the Staff Manual respectively. Title pages will be prepared in manuscript.

Place	Date	Hour	Summary of Events and Information	Remarks and references to Appendices
H.qrs at FREMICOURT	Nov 18 Cont.		Gd. dawn to dusk. Lt. Col. Gemmell returns from leave.	
	19		Work continues on C.T. Another say party busy of parapet line continued	
	20		Work continues. Post at Kill Wood. Party of parapet line continued	
	21		Work continues. Party continued. Lt. Wilcocks returns from leave.	
	22		Front & Kill continues. Work is difficult but satisfactory progress made. Dugs in new All posts & battles at REUGNY Nissen huts now & erection have been started	
	23		Work continues. Two sapping schemes started along number of German landscapes came from front BEUGNY and FREMICOURT. Spread work took new BC Hdqs and Bttn Intro drainage two communication trench. These are numerous of casualties in both tHeagts. 2 m Multi advance from leave 2/ Chapt goes to leave	
	24		Bn started a new C.T. from STURGEON SUPPORT to near DOIGNIES - DEMICOURT. All new Hqs not yet & accepted post inspect took satisfactorily. Rather fair	
	25		Xmas day. Parade. Men have great day. Bands play throughout the day.	
	26		Work continues on C.T. Weather again wet. 2/ Young goes to leave.	
	27		Work continues satisfactorily. Ground very hard owing to frost. L/ Burrough returns from leave.	
	28		Work continues. Fine uneventful day.	M

D. D. & L., London, E.C.
(A7883) Wt. W609/M1672 350,000 4/17 Sch. 52a. Forms/C/2118/44

Army Form C. 2118.

WAR DIARY
or
INTELLIGENCE SUMMARY. (S)
(Erase heading not required.)

Instructions regarding War Diaries and Intelligence Summaries are contained in F. S. Regs., Part II. and the Staff Manual respectively. Title pages will be prepared in manuscript.

Place	Date	Hour	Summary of Events and Information	Remarks and references to Appendices
Halys nr FREMICOURT	1917 Dec	28.	Work continues n.C.T. There was practically all days. D Coy about the gaols in MARSH SUPPORT. B Coy was support line. 2nd Lt Armstrong reports from 4th (Res) Royal Scots for duty and goes to E D Coy staff. A.B. Jones Lieutenant returns from leave	
		29.	First shift hilts, work continues, gun proposes Enemy quiet	
		30.	Coy Bodwin with a STORES on AVENUE & MARSH SUPPORT	
		31.	Relief. B.n. has been given a billet on the nights of the 31st inst. for general breakfast. Heavens film have been provided & any casualties cannot for the be.	
			We held in the lines that BELONG the enemy.	

WAR DIARY
or
INTELLIGENCE SUMMARY.
(Erase heading not required.)

Army Form C. 2118.

Place	Date	Hour	Summary of Events and Information	Remarks and references to Appendices
	December 1919		Casualties during month:	
			Killed in action - 2/Lieut J.C. TAYLOR - 4.12.19	
			Other ranks: Killed in action = 3	
			Wounded = 9	
			(minor) Sick = 2	
			Officer: 2/Lieut WALMSLEY - 2nd Base (unfit) 16.12.19	
			Other ranks: 2/R of (Sick) = 135	
			Reinforcements:—	Off. O.R.
			3-12-19	— 8
			15-12-19	— 0
			29-12-19	— 12
			31-12-19	— 10
				30
			Officers: 2/Lieut GLOVER J.H. } 15-12-19
			" LAURIE R.D. }
			" NEALE J. — 29-12-19

Numerical Strength 19 = 25 Off.
                            892 O.R.

A Dore Capt.
O/C 1/4 Monts and (France)

S E C R E T.   1/8th. Bn. The Royal Scots (Pioneers).   Copy No. 11

OPERATION ORDER No.10

By Lieut.-Colonel W. GEMMILL, D.S.O., Commanding.

Reference Map - LENS 11.   31st. December, 1917

1. The Battalion will move on the 1st. November, 1917, to RAILWAY CAMP, LECHELLE in accordance with the following instructions :-

2.   Reveille   6-30 a.m.   Breakfast   7-30 a.m.
     Dinner - on arrival.   Tea   4-30 p.m.

3. PARADE.   The Battalion will parade in column of route formation, ready to march at 9-30 a.m., on the main BAPAUME-PERONNE Road. The head of the column will be 500 yards from the entrance of the Camp along the BAPAUME-PERONNE Road towards LE TRANSLOY.

                Signals & Cyclists.
                Band.
                "D" Company.
                "C" Company.
                "B" Company.
                "A" Company.
                Regimental Police.

All details other than the Band, Signals, Cyclists, and Police will march in rear of "A" Company under an N.C.O. to be detailed by the Reg. Sergt. Major.
    Transport will march in rear of the Battalion. Cookers and water-carts will march in rear of Companies as per last Move.

4. ROUTE.   The Battalion will march via LE TRANSLOY, ROCQUIGNY, LECHELLE.

5. DRESS.
    Dress will be full marching order. Tam o'Shanters will be worn Leather Jerkins will be worn under the equipment. One blanket per man will be carried in the pack. Transport will be provided for the remaining blankets, water-proof sheets, and great-coats.
    Blankets will be rolled in bundles of 10, with water-proof sheets outside. All bundles will be securely tied and labelled and stacked at Coy. Headquarters in time for loading.

6. TRANSPORT.   Distribution of Transport will be as per O.O.No.9. The Transport Officer will arrange to have the necessary transport forward to Bn. H.Q., and Coy. H.Q. in sufficient time to allow Coys. &c. to have them loaded by 9-0 a.m. Horses for Coy. Cookers and water-carts will be sent to Coy. Headquarters at 9-0 a.m.
    Motor lorries for the move will report at this Camp at 8-0 a.m. The Quartermaster and O.C., Coys. concerned will be on the look-out for the arrival of the lorries.

7. Acknowledge.

                                                Captain,
                                Adjt., 1/8th. Bn. The Royal Scots (Pioneers).
Issued at 3-30 p.m.

        Copies to recipients of Operation Order No. 9.

Army Form C. 2118.

WAR DIARY
or
INTELLIGENCE SUMMARY.
(Erase heading not required.)

WA 35

Confidential

War Diary

of

1st Bn. The Royal Scots.

From

1st January to 31st January 1915.

Volume No 39

WAR DIARY or INTELLIGENCE SUMMARY.

Army Form C. 2118.

(Erase heading not required.)

Place	Date	Hour	Summary of Events and Information	Remarks and references to Appendices
H.Q.N. TRANSPORT. FREMICOURT.	1915			
Boys at Bullecourt	January		Mess Day held a.c Victory Day at Bullecourt was marked by major General	
			E.M. Hacker C.B. D.S.O the G.O.C. of the Division & Lieutl Colonels the Co's of the	
Bevmetz			the Division between 12 noon & 1 P.m. the G.O.C. saw the men at their dinners & expressed	
			his approval of the way the men behaved that.	
	2nd		Work was continued to day.	
	3rd		Work the new C.T. MAISON AVET was continued today. The first visit with railway was opened.	
	4th		A new C.T. No. known ROACH AVENUE was started today. The hurdles from the	
			MOUND through DENICOURT village & thence down the Sunken road.	
	5th		Very severe frost & continuous work on trench. By 6 employed trenching the	
			double apron fence in front of the new supporting with some slaver lines	
			the entrance to the dugout & MAISON SUPPORT are now completed the tunneling	
			party commenced	
			Ee this morning the frost was extreme. Severe till 3 p.m. there was sign of a change	
			by 5 p.m. so we had to leave & heavily. The following Warrant/NCOs Form from	
			received by the following Officers NCOs & men of the Bn.	
			Unmedals to Corporator E.P. MEEN. MILITARY CROSS L/Cpl. W. Ring. R.K. KKKERS & F.C.T. CROSS.	
			MILITARY MEDALS	

Army Form C. 2118.

WAR DIARY
or
INTELLIGENCE SUMMARY.
(Erase heading not required.)

Instructions regarding War Diaries and Intelligence Summaries are contained in F.S. Regs., Part II. and the Staff Manual respectively. Title pages will be prepared in manuscript.

Place	Date	Hour	Summary of Events and Information	Remarks and references to Appendices
FREMICOURT	1915			
BULECOURT	Jany 6th Batt: Xmas Honours List. Major J.A. TODD Mentioned in Despatches			
			Capt: J. WATSON "	
BEUGNATZ			Lt: F.R. BURNET "	
			Lt: F.J.S. SUTHERLAND "	
			Br: Major R.D. THOMPSON Military Cross	
			Sgt: Major R. DARROCH D.C.M.	
			Coy QMSgt: T. WELCH Mentioned in Despatches	
			Sgt: B. GRAY "	
	7th		Weather has changed again to frost. Work has turned to Roads, Water Supply etc.	
			The Divisor. of the Support Line.	
	7th		Work as for yesterday. Good pss? are being made.	
	9th		Very front little of the Barrage connecting the entrances to dugouts were finished	
	10th		Work as before. Erte Coys mucoled that & their work on Roads today. The weather is now very clear & visibility good, so the enemy must know them at work	
			Ste. Coys managed to withdraw without casualties	
	11th		Artly Main Line taken off RONEL 1 sector ordinary Rabbit Alley to Point 26	19

D. D. & L., London, E.C. (A5883) Wt. W869/M1672 350,000 4/17 Sch. 42a Forms/C/2118/14

Army Form C. 2118.

WAR DIARY
or
INTELLIGENCE SUMMARY.
(Erase heading not required.)

Instructions regarding War Diaries and Intelligence Summaries are contained in F. S. Regs., Part II. and the Staff Manual respectively. Title pages will be prepared in manuscript.

Place	Date	Hour	Summary of Events and Information	Remarks and references to Appendices
FRENICOURT	1915.			
BULGNY	Jany 12th		Major To Todd left today to meet the B.E. Crown & instruction at REUEN. Capt Fleming	
BEUMETZ			& 2000 OR are at present at the Course. Major Todd will be 30 days	
	13th		Today shows signs of a thaw, but the frost has still a good hold of the ground.	
	14th		A Bn of Northumberland Fusiliers 9.90 OR from the 21st Div. Joined at DOUL ENS and	
			turned today. All the men and horses clean B1.	
	15th		RABBIT ALLEY was complete by Feb 1st. 26 today. Room & jockey having every week	
			on trenches difficult.	
	16th		Instructions have been received that the Bn is to be relieved by the 6th Division	
			the relief will commence on the 19th and should be complete to the 21st ...	
			the Division will move and Corps Area will be relieved near DOULLENS-PERNES	
			the Bn will be relieved on the 20th instant by the 11th Brigade Regt Person	
			to the 6th Div	
	17th		Work as usual. Frost slowly thawing.	
	18th		Two Coys for out and one Coy in morning, by ... took the new Instructors of Lines	
	19th		Work on the Instructor's Lines had to be discontinued on account of hostile	
			shelling. All work on Cabinet ... being kept nearly always enemy snipers	

Army Form C. 2118.

WAR DIARY
or
INTELLIGENCE SUMMARY.
(Erase heading not required.)

Instructions regarding War Diaries and Intelligence Summaries are contained in F. S. Regs., Part II. and the Staff Manual respectively. Title pages will be prepared in manuscript.

Place	Date	Hour	Summary of Events and Information	Remarks and references to Appendices
GREVICOURT BUCQUOY	1918 January 20th		Advance parties of the 11th Bn. Lancs. Regt. arrived today & took over the work. Junction orders for the move to ACHIET LE GRAND are attached.	
BEUMETZ	21st		The Bn. moved to RITZ Camp, ACHIET LE GRAND today in accordance with Orders attached. Rain fell during the morning & long afternoon and held off while the Bn. was on the move. The Bn. is accommodated in NISSEN Huts & fairly comfortable though crowded	
ACHIET LE GRAND RITZ CAMP	22nd		Today the Bn. was employed cleaning up & having Kit inspection. The weather is frost but cold.	
	23rd		Today the Bn. along with the R.E. Coys are employed building NISSEN HUTS & enlarging RITZ Camp to hold a Brigade. Pioneer Bn. Field Ambulance T.M. Battery 1 Field Coy & Brigade H.Q'rs. We expect that we will take over a eight day to hold this.	
	24th		Work as per yesterday. R.E Coys are erecting a Camp for the Bn. near the Sunken road. Corner of LOG EAST WOOD	
	25th		Work as per yesterday. Weather fine but cold.	
	26th		Work as per yesterday. Good progress being made.	
	27th		Lt Hon. R.B. Winton joined the Bn today. Bn. moved into Pioneer Camp this evening	AL

Army Form C. 2118.

WAR DIARY
or
INTELLIGENCE SUMMARY.
(Erase heading not required.)

Instructions regarding War Diaries and Intelligence Summaries are contained in F. S. Regs., Part II. and the Staff Manual respectively. Title pages will be prepared in manuscript.

Place	Date	Hour	Summary of Events and Information	Remarks and references to Appendices
PIONEER CAMP	Jany 28th	1916	A.C. & D. Coys also HQrs moved into Pioneer Camp today, the Camp is almost completed.	
			The Well sketched. RITZ Camp is now completed & two Coys are working at LOG EAST CAMP & completing Stuck. Training will be started.	
			29th Work as per yesterday. The weather is good.	
			30th Two Coys are employed on LOGGAS' CAMP & two at BUCKINGHAM CAMP.	
			31st Work as per yesterday. It is expected that all work on Camps will be completed tomorrow.	

Lieut Col & OC 6/Pioneers
5th Rifle Brigade Pioneers
3/1/16

WAR DIARY
or
INTELLIGENCE SUMMARY.
(Erase heading not required.)

Army Form C. 2118.

Place	Date	Hour	Summary of Events and Information	Remarks and references to Appendices
			Casualties during Month:-	
			Wounded 2. O.R.	
			Accidents Wounded 2. O.R.	
			20 Deaths (Sick):- Lieut. C.H. Sucer 1.1.18	
			2/Lieut. W. Stark 29.1.18	
			O.R. 25.	
			Base (Invalid) 2.	
			25th 2.1.18 ot	
			Reinforcements:-	
			Lieut. Hon. R.B. Watson 29.1.18	
			Chaplain W.B. Cowan C.F. 18.1.18	
			Other Ranks:-	
			29.1.18 01	
			14.1.18 23	
			13.1.18 91	
			11.1.18 2	
			8.1.18 2	
			10	
			128	
			Strength at 31.1.18 - 41 off	
			999 o.r.	
			[signature] Lt Col	
			O.C. 1/8 Royal Scots (Pioneers)	

S E C R E T.   Copy No. 11

1/8th. Bn. The Royal Scots (Pioneers)

OPERATION ORDER No.12

By Lieut.-Colonel W. GEMMILL, D.S.O., Commanding.

19th. Jan. 1918.

Refer. Maps - LENS 11 (Scale 1:100000)
            - Sheet 57c   do.; 40.000

---

1. The Battalion will move on January 21st., 1918 to ACHIET-LE-PETIT in accordance with the following arrangements.

2.   Reveille 6-0 a.m.   Breakfast 7-30 a.m.
      Dinner   11-30 a.m.   Tea on arrival.

3. PARADE.
    a. Companies will parade ready to march as soon as the relieving Unit arrives. Companies must be prepared to move off at 12-30 p.m.
    The Battalion will parade in column of route in the following order :-

                Cyclists.
                Band.
                "A" Company.
                "D" Company.
                "B" Company.
                "C" Company.
                Rear Party.

"A" and "D" Companies will parade on the road running from "A" Company billets to the R.E.Dump. The Head of the Column will be at the crucifix. "B" and "C" Companies will parade on the road running from DELSAUX FARM to R.E.Dump. Head of column to be where the Light Railway crosses the road.
    Companies will march with an interval of 100 yds. between Coys.
    Cookers will march in rear of Companies.
    One water-cart will march in rear of "D" Company.
    One   do.   do.   "C" Company.

(b) Transport and Headquarters Details (less Cookers and Water Carts)(Cyclists and Band) will parade ready to move off at 8-30 a.m. and must be West of the ALBERT-BAPAUME Road by 10-30 a.m.
    The Transport Officer will be in charge of this party.

(c) The Band and Cyclists will parade with "C" Company at 11-30 a.m. for dinner. The Quartermaster will arrange to send dinner and tea ration for the 21st. to "C" Company for Cyclists and Band.

4- DRESS.
    Dress will be full marching order. Tam o' Shanters will be worn. Leather jerkins will be worn under equipment. One blanket per man will be carried in the pack. Transport will be provided for the remaining blankets, waterproof sheets and greatcoats.

5- ROUTE.
    The Battalion (less Transport and Hq.Details) will march via main CAMBRAI - BAPAUME ROAD to BAPAUME, thence via AVESNES-LES-BAPAUME -BIHUCOURT-ACHIET-LE-GRAND to approximately G.15.a.6.0. Transport and Details will take the same route.

                                            /6 - MARCH DISCIPLINE.

6- MARCH DISCIPLINE.

Strict march discipline will be observed on the march by both Battalion and Transport. The incoming Units of the relieving Division will be passed on the road.

O.C. "A" Company will detail one officer to report at Battalion Headquarters at 8-0 a.m. on the 21st. This Officer will be in charge of the Details marching with Transport.

O.C. "C" Company will detail one officer and 6 other ranks to act as rear guard. This party will march in rear of the Battalion and pick up stragglers.

7- Transport arrangements are being issued separately.

8- ACKNOWLEDGE.

Jones Captain,

Adjt., 1/8th. Bn. The Royal Scots (Pioneers)

Issued at 10.30 a.m.

Copy No. 1 - Adjt. for Commanding Officer.
2 - Captain Mitchell.
3 - O.C. "A" Company.
4 - O.C. "B" Company.
5 - O.C. "C" Company.
6 - O.C. "D" Company.
7 - Medical Officer.
8 - Transport Officer.
9 - Quartermaster.
10 - Regtl. Sergt. Major.
11 - War Diary.
12 - File.

SECRET.   Copy No. 11

                1/8th. Bn. The Royal Scots (Pioneers).

                AMENDMENT No.1 to OPERATION ORDER No.12

                                                    19th. January, 1918.

1. Para.3, sub-para.(a) of Operation Order No.12 will be amended to read :-

    " Companies will parade ready to march as soon as the relieving Unit arrives. Companies must be prepared to move at 12-30 p.m.
        The Battalion will parade in column of route in the following order :-
                Cyclists.
                Band.
                "A" Company.
                "B" Company.
                "C" Company.
                "D" Company.
                Rear Party.

    "A" Company will parade on the road running from "A"Company billets to the R.E.Dump. The head of the Column will be at the crucifix. "B" and "C" Companies will parade on the road running from DELSAUX FARM to the R.E.Dump. The Head of the column will be where the light railway crosses the road.
        "D" Company will fall in in rear of of the Battalion when the Column reaches FREMICOURT.
        Companies will march with an interval of 100 yards between each Company.
        Cookers will march in rear of Companies.
        One water-cart will march in rear of "B"Company.
        One water-cart will march in rear of the rear Company."

2. Acknowledge.

                                            Captain,
                    Adjt., 1/8th. Bn. The Royal Scots (Pioneers).

Issued at 6-30 p.m.

                Copies to recipients of Operation Order No. 12.

SECRET.   Copy No 11

1/8th. Bn. The Royal Scots (Pioneers)

TRANSPORT ARRANGEMENTS FOR 20th. JANUARY, 1918.

1.   An advance party will march to the Camp near ACHIET-LE-PETIT at present occupied by the 11th. Bn. Leicester Regt.(Pioneers) on the 20th. instant.
   Stores, Tools &c. will also be sent forward on that date in accordance with the following arrangements.

2- ADVANCE PARTY.
            The party will consist of :-

   2/Lieut. White. A.M. to be detailed by O.C."B"Coy.
   2 Other Ranks per Company to be detailed by O.C., Coys.
   2   "   from Bn.Transport   - detailed by T.O.
   1   "   Q.M.Stores   - detailed by Q.M.
   1   "   Bn. Headquarters   - detailed by R.S.M.

   The advance-party will move with the Transport and on arrival at destination, the officer in charge will report at the Orderly Room of the 11th. Bn. Leicester Regt.when he will be instructed where to dump the Tools, Stores etc.   The Transport will then return to the Battalion Transport Lines.
   The Officer i/c Advance Party will take over billets Transport Lines etc. and will put his men in charge of same when the relieving unit moves out on the 21st. instant. until the Battalion arrives.
   Rations and billets will be provided by the 11th.Bn. Leicester Regt.(Pioneers).

3- TOOLS, STORES etc. to be sent forward.

   Companies   - Company Tools and Surplus Mess Kit.
   Quartermaster - Stores.
   T.O.   - Blacksmith's Tools, Saddlers Tools. &c.
   Shoemakers and Tailors Material and Tools.
   Armourer Sergt.'s Tools.
   Pioneer Sergt's Tools.

4- ALLOTMENT OF TRANSPORT.
         The T.O. will arrange to have the following transport at Coy. H.Q. and Q.M Stores at 7-30 a.m. on 20th. instant :-

   2 Tool Wagons per Coy.
   2 Baggage Wagons.for Q.M.
   1 Limber for T.O.
   1   do. for Tailors, Shoemakers, Armourer Sergt. and Pioneer Sergt.

   All wagons will be loaded by 8-0 a.m. and will move off at that hour, along with the Advance Party.   The 2 Baggage wagons and the 2 limbers will join the Company Wagons in FREMICOURT.   The Officer i/c Advance Party will provide brakesmen for all vehicles.

5- The approx. situation of the 11th. Bn. Leicester Regt. Camp is G.15.a.6.0.   The route will be the same as laid down in O.O.No.12.

6. Transport arrangements for 21st.instant will be issued later.

7. ACKNOWLEDGE.   Captain,
                                   Adjt., 1/8th. Bn. The Royal Scots (Pioneers).
   Issued at   a.m.
            Copies to recipients of O.O.No.12.

Army Form C. 2118.

WAR DIARY
or
INTELLIGENCE SUMMARY.
(Erase heading not required.)

Instructions regarding War Diaries and Intelligence Summaries are contained in F. S. Regs., Part II. and the Staff Manual respectively. Title pages will be prepared in manuscript.

JR 36

Confidential

WAR DIARY

OF

8th Bn. THE ROYAL SCOTS

FROM

1st FEBRUARY TO 29th FEBRUARY 1915

VOLUME No 40

WAR DIARY
or
INTELLIGENCE SUMMARY.
(Erase heading not required.)

Army Form C. 2118.

Place	Date	Hour	Summary of Events and Information	Remarks and references to Appendices
PIONEER CAMP. "Sheet 57 E G.28.b.3."	February 1918 1st		Bn. went to MUSEN HUTS. Men comf[orta]bl[e] today. The weather is excellent being cold & dry & on the whole frosty.	
	2nd		Bn. Coys were in Infantry training today, being pioneers, close attention will have to be given to this in order to put the Bn into proper Pte.	
	3rd		Training continued as for yesterday. The weather keyed it [is?] continuing without a thaw, the 133rd I.B. Bde. Infantry training continued. The troops are keen on the dismal Bn ----- to being of Bayonet in the trenches ----	
	4th		The 6th met a wheat day the Bde. York see the Lewis Gun Band & enable the Bdery. Infantry Training continued today, the Cross Country Run in the 13th York was keen off.	
	5th		The Bn. got rid of there 2 but 7 to overmay the fleet 10 to forward. Training before me continued & keeping to switch the Platoon & Company drill & range shooting. The weather still continues excellent.	
	6th		132nd Inf. Bde. offices were held today, there be seen strength not of 15 expect, During the evening a Bn. Concert was held in the Y.M.C.A. Hut ASNIET LE GRAND. The Concert was a great success ---- enjoyed by all ranks.	
	7th		Coys Rained today are entered the training General II J Guard of Station of my Lewis ----- front Throwing of bayonet training. The weather still continues good.	
	8th		Inf. Training during the forenoon. The Bn. G.O.C. inspected the Bn. at 2:30 pm today, Infinite difficulty being heavy some should be face at 2:30 & the inspection had to be out-drilled.	

WAR DIARY or INTELLIGENCE SUMMARY

Army Form C. 2118.

Place	Date	Hour	Summary of Events and Information	Remarks and references to Appendices
ROMERIL CAMP.	Feb 1915 1st		GOC informed himself west of Canal with the Bn.	
	2nd		The Bn. takes over the Camp from the 6th. Bn. taking over began & then completed by 12.15pm	
		4.45	New Bn. taken over from the 11th Bn. Lancashire Regt. in the usual manner. Battery Relieved.	
		10.0	Bn. church parade at the YMCA Hut. Relieved by Guard at 9.30am	
	11th		The operation orders for the move Romeril Camp attached. The Reserve exhibited	
			Bivd. at FRERICOURT BUSGY + BEUGRTZ.	
	12th		The Bn. moved today in accordance with Operation Orders No 13 attached + arrived in billets at 4.15pm	
HQ: FRERICOURT A B C Coy BUSGY D Coy BEAMETZ	13th		The CO has gone home on leave & Major F.R. Tickell is in Command of the Bn. Capt F.S. Roker Reft. the Bn. today for Groveth Corp at Photo. The Adjt of the 9/R.B. Tour from Base for two days to the 9/R Regd Bn. The 9 & 7 R of R. Ben & 182 men of the present New Bn. in for the 14" Army	
		9.15	were sent to like the places of the men just sent to the 9th R.B. the following were sent to allotted Companies B Coy will work on the Maury Trenches clearing bottom of Trench. Communication trick clearing, beam Sandbag parapet. ROACH AVE, STURGEON AVE & RABBIT ALLEY. C Coy will work on the INTERMEDIATE line from HERCULES L- DOIGNIES clearing beam making of both wearing channel. D Coy will work on WALSH SUPPORT	89

Army Form C. 2118.

WAR DIARY
or
INTELLIGENCE SUMMARY.

(Erase heading not required.)

Instructions regarding War Diaries and Intelligence Summaries are contained in F. S. Regs., Part II. and the Staff Manual respectively. Title pages will be prepared in manuscript.

Place	Date	Hour	Summary of Events and Information	Remarks and references to Appendices
	1915		Cont'd	
	Sept 13th		Support. Making dugout to left of PM127 digging out dump for 3 Flammers. Track roadway	
			For position. Wiring in front of the work also making Telephone Lightbox and for the	
			Flammers. It has been arranged that the Coy will be out working all the time, B Coy and	
			The rest for 3 days when it will relieve B Coy. D Coy will relieve C Coy after being out	
			3 days. Then A Coy will relieve C Coy.	
	14th		Weather flood. Wind is chill, but showery.	
	15th		Good progress is being made with the work till Coys are able to work during the day	
			the weather being still & comfortable for.	
	16th		Every front arm to another chasm. Pte Bowes of B Coy was killed outright by shrapnel	
			from the shell working on CASSIN SUPPORT. He was buried at FRONCOURT CEMETERY	
			today.	
	17th		Weather fine. Good steady little progress to being made with the work.	
			As yesterday.	
	19th		B Coy relieved D Coy today. Relieving our three billets in BEAUMETZ. B Coy now ready	
			B Coy billets in BAVRE.	
	20th		Today we played the 256 & 7th Bde RFA in the Bde Football Tournament winning by 1-0. There was	

D.D. & L., London, E.C.
(A783) Wt. W809/M1672 350,000 4/17 Sch. 50a.   Forms/C/2118/14

Army Form C. 2118.

WAR DIARY
or
INTELLIGENCE SUMMARY.
(Erase heading not required.)

Place	Date	Hour	Summary of Events and Information	Remarks and references to Appendices
PREMICOURT	1918 Feby		Contd	
	20th		Horse transport to be the same for each to attack the 7th Black Watch to be kept to relay the 25th Bde RE. There were before discovery the front line given orders it is shown that the relief was very hard & fast & given.	
	21st		West ordinance to before River Ancre & arms finished & B Coy were working on RABBIT & STRUGGLE.	
	22nd		Enemy have resumed submission their forces Rive & to relieved to 3 Coy Lewis the Coy being taken from each Bn. & from Hors morning Bn. & the two battalions is to have their reliefs out.	
	23rd		The above order by enemy German Bns has been cancelled that German Bns will be reconstituted as a 3 Coy basis the Coy being absorbed by the other three Coys. Instruction have been received that when there were in favorite, Coy Commdrs. entire in fact but that the front line staffing up Myr Ta Tett & info. of Lt. Lafourcade & Review.	
	24th		B Coy began to BEAUCOURT today. B Coy returning to BOISRY. Rgt.l Michell + h Command J. th. Bn.	
	25th		A draft of 9 N.C.O from 7/8 R.Scot. joined the Bn today. Who Bn. h. Beauval will relieve home. Three have taken sent to a Mess Coy today. Bg. has been allocated amongst the other three Coys.	

(signed) C.M.P.

Army Form C. 2118.

WAR DIARY
or
INTELLIGENCE SUMMARY.
(Erase heading not required.)

Instructions regarding War Diaries and Intelligence Summaries are contained in F. S. Regs., Part II. and the Staff Manual respectively. Title pages will be prepared in manuscript.

Place	Date	Hour	Summary of Events and Information	Remarks and references to Appendices
FREMICOURT	1915 Feb 26th		Weather continues fine.	
	27th		Good progress being made with work to render the Hindenburg line INTERMEDIATE line & now almost completed. We stayed the 7th Black Watch today in the line in front of the 20th Division. Found a hand & very keen games cooked up a chain	
	28th		Weather very cold, snow fell	

Signed Capt? & Adjt
2/5 Bn The Royal Welsh
Fusiliers
28/2/18

Army Form C. 2118.

WAR DIARY
or
INTELLIGENCE SUMMARY.
(Erase heading not required.)

Instructions regarding War Diaries and Intelligence Summaries are contained in F.S. Regs., Part II. and the Staff Manual respectively. Title pages will be prepared in manuscript.

Place	Date	Hour	Summary of Events and Information	Remarks and references to Appendices
			Casualties during February 1918:	
			O. O.R. Reinforcements	
			Killed in Action 1 — 9.2.18 8 0.01	
			Wounded 3 — 20.2.18 10 19	
			2º Arm. Sch. 19 — 23.2.18 1	
			2º Eng Sick (Hurst & Bain) — 25.2.18 91 10.5	
			1 23	
			Posted 6 O.R. R.Dive — 90.01	
			Strength at 28/2/18 = 42 O.N.R. 97 0.R.	
			[signature] Capt.	
			Adjt. 18ᵗʰ Royal Scots (Pioneers)	
		2/3/18		

SECRET.   Copy. No. 12

1/8th. Bn. The Royal Scots (Pioneers).

Transport Arrangements for Operation Order No.13.

11th. February, 1918.

1. The Battalion will move on the 12th. February to FREMICOURT and BEUGNY as detailed in Operation Order No. 13.
   Transport for the Move will be distributed as follows :-

2 Tool Wagons per Coy.- to take one blanket per man, greatcoats and waterproof sheets.
1 Baggage wagon for "A" and "B" Coys. to take officers' valises and Mess Boxes.
1 Baggage wagon for "C" and "D" Coys. to take officers' valises and Mess Stores. ("D" Coy. to load first).
1 Medical Cart for Medical Stores.
1 Spring Cart for Canteen Stores.
1 Mess Cart for light stores from H.Q. and Coy. Messes.
1 Limber for Q.M. Stores.
1   do.   O. Room and Signals.
1   do.   H.Q. details and Band. (Blankets etc.)
1   do.   Half for T.O. and Half for H.Q. details.
2   do.   Headquarters.
1 Motor Lorry for H.Q. and Q.M. Stores.
1   do.   "A", "B", "C" and "D" Coys.

2- Loading of Transport.
        The T.O. will arrange to have all necessary transport at Bn.H.Q., Coy.H.Q., and Q.M.Stores at 10 a.m. on 12th. instant - horses to return to Transport Lines.
All vehicles will be loaded and ready to move at 12-30 p.m. The Transport Officer will draw out vehicles at 12-45 p.m.

3-Blankets and Greatcoats.
        Blankets will be rolled in bundles of 10 with W.P. Sheets outside
        Greatcoats will be rolled in bundles of 5.
        All bundles will be securely tied and labelled and stacked at Coy. H.Q. and Bn.H.Q. by 10 a.m. on 12th. ready for loading.

4-Brakesmen.
        Coys. will detail one brakesman for each Tool wagon.
        O.C. "B" Coy.   do   do   for "A" and "B" baggage wagon.
        O.C. "D" Coy.   do   do   for "C" and "D" do.
        Medical Officer do   do   for Medical Cart.
        Reg.Sgt.Major   do.   do   for each of the following :-
        2 limbers H.W., 1 Limber O.Room & Signals, 1 H.Q. details.
        Q.M. will detail one brakesman for Q.M.Stores Limber.
        T.O.   do   do   for Remaining Limber.

5-Motor Lorries.
        Two motor lorries will arrive at this Camp at 8-30 a.m. on 12th.inst. and are allotted as per para.(1). All stores will be ready stacked for loading at that time. Coys. H.Q., and Q.M.Stores will each send an orderly with these lorries to unload and look after the stores at destination.

6.Mess Boxes.
        The Mess Cart will go round H.Q. and Coy.Messes between 12-30 p.m. and 1 p.m. Mess boxes will be stacked ready for loading by 12-30 p.m. on 12th inst.

7. The following Transport will go forward to Coy. H.Q., unload, and return to Trans.Lines in FREMICOURT :- 2 Tool wagons per Coy., Baggage wagons, Mess cart, Coy.Cookers (horses to return to Trans.Lines), Water Carts (refill at Fremicourt waterpoint, supply coys. afterwhich horses will return to Trans.Lines.)
The remainder of the Transport will go direct to Transport Lines at FREMICOURT.

                                                    Captain,
        Adjt., 1/8th. Bn. The Royal Scots (Pioneers).

Issued at 2-0 p.m.

S E C R E T. Copy No.

1/8th. Bn. The Royal Scots (Pioneers).

OPERATION ORDER No.13

By Lieut.-Colonel W. GEMMILL, D.S.O, Commanding.

17th. February, 1918.

Reference Maps :- LENS 11.(1:100,000)
Sheet 57c.(1:40,000)

1. The Battalion will move to FREMICOURT and BEUGNY on February, 12th., 1918, in accordance with the following arrangements.

2. Reveille 6-30 a.m.　　　　　Breakfast 7-0 a.m.
　Dinner 12 noon.　　　　　　 Tea on arrival.

3. Parade,
　　　　The Battalion will march at 1-0 p.m.
　　　　The Battalion will parade in mass on the old Football Ground near the Camp in the following order :-
　　　　　"D" Company - Right Company.
　　　　　"C"　do.
　　　　　"B"　do.
　　　　　"A"　do. - Left Company.
　　　　　H.Q.Details.
　　　　　Rear Party.
　Cyclists and Band will draw up on the right side of "D" Coy.
　Right Markers from Companies will report to the R.S.M. at 12-45 p.m. on the parade ground.
　Rear Transport will be drawn up on the ACHIET-LE-GRAND road - the of the Transport to be clear of the parade ground.
　Companies will march with a distance of 100 yards between each Company. Transport will march 100 yards in rear of the rear Company. Cookers will march in rear of Companies.
　　　　One water-cart in rear of "C" Company.
　　　　One water-cart in rear of "A" Company.
　H.Q.Details, including Police and prisoners will march in rear of "A" Company without an interval.

4- Dress,
　　　　Dress will be full marching order. Tam o' Shanters will be worn. Leather jerkins will be worn under the equipment. One blanket per man will be carried in the pack. Transport will be provided for the extra blanket, water-proof sheet, and great-coats.

5. The Battalion will march via ACHIET-LE-GRAND, BIHUCOURT, BAPAUME, and main CAMBRAI-BAPAUME Road. H.Q, H.Q.Details, and Transport (less Cookers and water-carts) will break off at FREMICOURT. "A", "B", "C", Companies will proceed to BEUGNY and occupy their old billets there. "D" Company's destination will be notified later.

6- March Discipline,
　　　　Strict march discipline will be observed on the march by both Battalion and Transport.
　O.C. "A" Company will detail 1 officer and 6 O.R. to act as rear-guard. This party will march in rear of "A" Company and pick up stragglers.

/7-Advance Parties.

-2-

7- Advance parties.

The Advance parties will consist of :-

      1 officer per Company.
      1 Q.M.Sgt. do.
      1 O.R.   per platoon.

"A", "B" and "C" Coys. advance parties to BEUGNY.
"D" Company advance party to BEAUMETZ.
All to report to the opposite numbers by 2-0 p.m. on 12th.inst.
An advance party from H.Q. consisting of 1 off.& 4 O.R. will report to H.Q. 11th. Leicester Regt. at 10-30 a.m. on 12th.inst.

8- Transport arrangements will be issued separately.

                                                              Captain,

Adjt., 1/8th. Bn. The Royal Scots (Pioneers).

Issued at 11-30 a.m.

Copy No. 1 - Adjt. for C.O.	Copy No.7 - Transport Officer.
2 - Major Todd.	8 - Quartermaster.
3 - O.C. "A" Company.	9 - Medical Officer.
4 - O.C. "B" Company.	10 - Regtl. Sergt.Major.
5 - O.C. "C" Company.	11 - Lewis Gun Sergt.
6 - O.C. "D" Company.	12 - War Diary.

SECRET.   Copy No.

1/8th. Bn. The Royal Scots (Pioneers).

TRANSPORT ARRANGEMENTS FOR THE 11th. February, 1918.

1. Stores, Tools etc. will be sent forward to FREMICOURT and BEUGNY on the 11th. instant in accordance with the following arrangements :-

2. **Stores, Tools etc. to be sent forward.**

   Companies   - Company Tools.
   Q.M.   - Stores.
   T.O.   - Blacksmith's and Saddler's Tools, etc.
   Shoemakers & Tailors' Material & Tools.
   Armourer Sergeant's Tools.
   Pioneer Sergeant's Tools.

3. **Allotment of Transport.**

   The Transport Officer will arrange to have the following transport at Company Headquarters and Q.M.Stores at 2-30 p.m. on the 10th. instant for loading:-
   1 Tool Wagon per Company.
   2 G.S.wagons for Q.M.
   1 Limber for Tailors, Shoemakers, Armourer Sgt., Pioneer Sgt.
   1 Limber for T.O. (to join above Transport en route on 11th.)
   All vehicles to be loaded by 8-30 a.m. on 11th. instant.

4. The above Transport will move off at 8-30 a.m. on the 11th. inst. to the following destinations :-

   Q.M.Store Wagons   )
   "D" Coy. Wagon   )   H.Q., 11th.Bn. Leicester Regt.
   T.O. Limber   )   at FREMICOURT.
   Pion.Sgt.&c.Limber   )

   "A" Coy.Tool Wagon   )
   "B" Coy.Tool Wagon   )   Company H.Q. at BEUGNY.
   "C" Coy.Tool Wagon   )

   Company Storemen and Quartermaster's Storeman will accompany the wagons and act as brakesmen. These storemen will stay and look after tools and stores until the Battalion arrives on 12th. instant. They will take rations for consumption on 12th. with them.
   The T.O. will send one man to unload his limber and hand over the tools to the Quartermaster's storeman at FREMICOURT who will be responsible for them.
   The R.S.M. will detail 1 man from H.Q. to proceed with Pioneer Sgt. &c. limber for this purpose.
   All vehicles will return to Transport Lines when off loaded.

5. **LEWIS Guns.**
   Eight Lewis Guns and teams will proceed to the H.Q. of the 11th.Bn. Leicester Regt. on the afternoon of 11th. inst. leaving this Camp at 1-30 p.m. The party, as detailed separately, will be under Sergeant Souness and will carry with them rations for 12th.instant.
   Accommodation for the night 11/12th. will be found for the party at the H.Q. of the 11th.Bn. Leicester Regt. Sergeant Souness will on arrival report to the Adjt. of that Battalion, who will instruct him regarding the posting of his guns on 12th. instant.
   The T.O. will arrange to have the Lewis Gun limber forward for loading early to-morrow. Rations for 12th. will be sent for driver and team. The limber will return to Transport Lines at FREMICOURT after the guns have been posted on the 12th. instant.

6. One officer per Company will report at the H.Q. of 11th. Bn. Leicester Regt. at 10-30 a.m. on 11th. inst. as arranged direct with O.C., Coys. Horses will be at Bn. H.Q. at 9-0 a.m. on that date.

Issued at 6 p.m.
11/2/18.   R. Jones Captain,
                     Adjt., 1/8th. Bn. The Royal Scots (Pioneers).

51st Divisional Troops

WAR DIARY

1/8th BATTALION

THE ROYAL SCOTS

Pioneers

MARCH 1 9 1 8

Army Form C. 2118.

WAR DIARY
or
INTELLIGENCE SUMMARY.
(Erase heading not required.)

Confidential

WAR DIARY

OF

1/8 Bn THE ROYAL SCOTS

FROM

1st March 1918 to 31st March 1918

VOLUME Nº 41

WAR DIARY
or
INTELLIGENCE SUMMARY.

Army Form C. 2118.

Instructions regarding War Diaries and Intelligence Summaries are contained in F. S. Regs., Part II. and the Staff Manual respectively. Title pages will be prepared in manuscript.

(Erase heading not required.)

Place	Date	Hour	Summary of Events and Information	Remarks and references to Appendices
HQ. FREMICOURT	1918			
2 Coys BUGNY	MARCH 1st		Work is as follows:- A Coy in working on a BLOCK in RABBIT ALLEY. Forming up	
1 Coy BEAUMETZ			POSTS between LSEVIER Rd and DOWNES ALLEY & C.T. Working in a Shelter at T.21.c.	
			both garrison of the Ripa Line and the sectors. Making a SAP from DOWNES	
			ALLEY. Has an exp. Shelter at S. Paul to INTERMEDIATE a Shelter between HERMIES & DEMICOURT.	
			2 Wired Post Sectors are now employed on the Wire between S Paul & 6th Ave connection	
			Revetting & Wire making. Posts extending & disposed of for garrison. D. Coy are completing	
			the Wired shelter to WELSH SUPPORT & wiring the 13th Supp the Sucrie Line.	
			All the working Coys are Repairing and work being done during the day also	
			In case of a, of sunny showers Comn.	
		2nd	Coy shift of 3 OR's drummed to hosp. the weather was disagreeably wet & snowy	
		3rd	Coy shift of 1 OR's left the Bn. on his furlough. to the 55th Div'l Arm. Camp B. good	
			army forward.	
		4th	Took a bath. Weather finer than last nite.	
		5th	Nothing of interest. Weather finer.	
		6th	Weather improved. Mild & Sunny. Played the 1st Leinsters, 7 - the 1st Btn of 38th rail 2-1	
		7th	Mr R Magor is left for a tour to the home depot today.	

WAR DIARY
or
INTELLIGENCE SUMMARY.

Army Form C. 2118.

(Erase heading not required.)

Place	Date	Hour	Summary of Events and Information	Remarks and references to Appendices
	1918			
FREMICOURT	MARCH 8th		Weather continues fine. Nothing of special interest to report. Capt. Mitchell proceeds on leave.	
	9th		Work as before. Weather continues fine.	
	10th		Depot in Work completed except trucking. O.A.H. withdrawn from line.	
	11th		B Coy working on DOIGNIES – DEMICOURT – road. Drove pass on leave.	
	12th		Work continues satisfactorily. DEMICOURT – DOIGNIES road heavily shelled. Major Todd proc on leave.	
	13th		Work continues. Uneventful day.	
	14th		Work continues satisfactorily.	
	15th		Work as before. Weather good. Lt Jeffery returns from leave.	
	16th		Report in TROUT commenced. 2nd Lt Young proc on leave.	
	17th		Nothing special to report. Work continues satisfactorily.	
	18th		DEMICOURT – DOIGNIES road badly shelled during previous 24 hours necessitating a lot of extra work for B Coy.	
	19th		Lt Falconer proc on leave. 2nd Lt Roberts returns from leave. Quiet day.	H.C.
	20th		Work continues. Quiet day. Nothing to report.	

Army Form C. 2118.

WAR DIARY
INTELLIGENCE SUMMARY.
(Erase heading not required.)

(3)

Place	Date	Hour	Summary of Events and Information	Remarks and references to Appendices
	1918			
	MARCH 21st		At 5 a.m. an intense bombardment opens on the whole front. Instructions are received to move A & C Coys from BEUGNY to assembly positions at SAPPER CAMP	
	LEBUCQUIERE		At 6 a.m. Coys and Bn. H.Q. move there. Capt Richardson is sent to Division to act as Liaison officer. The Batt. takes up a position in sunken road behind SAPPER CAMP and whilst there suffer casualties from shell fire. Capt. Morgan R.A.M.C. and 2nd Lt Rennie were wounded. A & C Coys were then ordered to a still more position in rear of sunken road and there await orders. At 12.30 p.m. orders are received for the Bn. for B Coy to proceed to support the 153rd Infy Bde. behind the MORCHIES - BEAUMETZ line on left of CAMBRAI Rd. Two Coys + Bn. H.Q. Coy in sunken road behind this line well in line to deliver and immediate counter - attack should the enemy force a footing on the brow. During the day B Coy had been under the orders of the 152nd Infy Bde. They were heavily shelled in the morning in their billets in BEAUMETZ and at 6 a.m. took up a position in sunken road east of the village. At 11 a.m. orders were received to dig in, in front of sunken road, and they spent the rest of the day their being troubled only by a little intermittent shelling. Transport moved from FREMICOURT to near BANCOURT in the afternoon	O.G.G.

WAR DIARY
or
INTELLIGENCE SUMMARY.

Army Form C. 2118.

(Erase heading not required.)

Place	Date	Hour	Summary of Events and Information	Remarks and references to Appendices
CAMBRAI FRONT.	1918 MARCH 22nd		Position. Bn. H.Q. in MORCHIES - BEAUMETZ sunken road. A Coy. two platoons in sunken road and two platoons dug in 300 yds. behind sunken road. C Coy. in front dug that morning N.W. of CHAUFOURS WOOD. B. Coy. in their trench in front of sunken road east of BEAUMETZ. About 8 A.m. C Coy were heavily shelled and as this post had been taken over by a Coy. of Cheshires, they consolidated a shell hole position in the rear. At 2 P.m. A Coy were heavily shelled and under cover of this the enemy approached close to the left of their trench. Accordingly they entrenched their line to the left behind MORCHIES and held on to this position till 6 P.m. keeping back overwhelming numbers of the enemy by their fire. The platoons on the right under 2/Lt W.G Young and 2nd. O. B. Goodwin having extricated post back, "D" Coy were then forced to retire across the sunken road, just as the enemy entered it on the right, and they took up a position in the rear of MORCHIES on the left of "C" Coy. This latter Coy. during the afternoon had been heavily shelled and ordered to H.Q. first, but under the leadership of Col. Gemmell advanced through this line and took up a position 200 yds. in rear of MORCHIES. Later the Coy. went forward to this night and "A" Coy which to its entire with them, probably were in close touch of the enemy. About 9 P.m. during which time patrols were in close touch of the enemy.	9C

WAR DIARY
or
INTELLIGENCE SUMMARY.
(Erase heading not required.)

Army Form C. 2118

Place	Date	Hour	Summary of Events and Information	Remarks and references to Appendices
Bn. H.Q. & Coys. CAMBRAI FRONT. TRANSPORT 1m. W. of GREVILLERS.	1918 MARCH 22nd (contd)		At 2 p.m. they were ordered to retire back after a half an hour's rest to FREHICOURT. During the morning and afternoon 'B' Coy. had been heavily shelled and the O.C. Coy. Act. Capt. H.E.R. James wounded in the enemy's advance. In the enemy's advance N. of the CAMBRAI Rd. one platoon under 2nd Lt. J. Rabbe went to left the Leybertha farm a defensive flank to the North of BEAUMETZ than they had put on attack by enemy's troops capturing our prisoners. At midnight the Coy. less one platoon were ordered to withdraw to FREHICOURT where they rejoined the Bn.	
	23rd		Bn. billets in FREHICOURT were heavily shelled in the morning, so the Bn. withdrew to a location W. of the village facing the CAMBRAI Rd. Capt. Ag. A.D. James was wounded at this time and 2nd Lt. W. G. Cabins appointed Act Adjt. At 11:30 a.m. orders were received to consolidate a trench known as the RED LINE running from E. of BANCOURT to the CAMBRAI Rd. Position of Coys. from L to R. 'A', 'B', & 'C'. The rest of the day was spent in strengthening the position. Bn. H.Q. in sunken road running N.W. from BANCOURT. 4 officers & 80 O.R.'s. returned from leave & Echelon B reinforced the Bn. in the afternoon. At dusk one platoon of 'B' Coy. under 2nd Lt. Groves went with drawn to form a reserve and dug a post in front of Bn. H.Q.	U.G.C.

WAR DIARY
or
INTELLIGENCE SUMMARY.
(Erase heading not required.)

Army Form C. 2118.

Instructions regarding War Diaries and Intelligence Summaries are contained in F.S. Regs., Part II. and the Staff Manual respectively. Title pages will be prepared in manuscript.

Place	Date	Hour	Summary of Events and Information	Remarks and references to Appendices
Nr BAPAUME	1918 MARCH 24th		During the morning the strengthening of the RED LINE was continued — working was resumed to turn all huts in front of the line and this was done. In the afternoon, in accordance with Bde orders patrols were sent forward towards MILL CROSS & BERGNY. They reported the GREEN LINE in front of FREMICOURT still held but that the 19th Div were preparing to evacuate it, which they did and under orders passed through the RED LINE at this time 2.30 p.m. There was a heavy bombardment of the line and of enemy movement beyond and during this Lt Jeffrey of 'B' Coy was killed and other casualties suffered. At 4 p.m. a first as the attack was developing orders were received to remove Bn HQ to the red Bde HQ on the BANCOUR – BAPAUME Rd. At 4.30 p.m. word was received that the Yorkshires on the right/immediate left 153rd Bde were retiring and that the right flank of C Coy under 2nd Lt SCOTT had firmed a defensive flank. The whole Bn then without a shot being fired Col Greenwell went forward and led it back into the line. During the night flank was made on the Bn on the right by platoons from the right. The enemy suffered severe casualties from the inflict fire of our Lewis Guns as he advanced on BANCOURT. This what was ultimately cut. In the first 4th platoon of B coy under 2nd Lt Lewis was annihilated when was sent out for the Bn to occupy at the crossroads BAPAUME – ALBERT GREVILLERS – TILLOY	

WGC

WAR DIARY
INTELLIGENCE SUMMARY

(Erase heading not required.)

Instructions regarding War Diaries and Intelligence Summaries are contained in F. S. Regs., Part II. and the Staff Manual respectively. Title pages will be prepared in manuscript.

Place	Date	Hour	Summary of Events and Information	Remarks and references to Appendices
	1918			
	MARCH 24th (contd)		b. it where LOUPART WOOD. where it arrived about 9 p.m. from where it marched to the new position allotted to it which LOUPART WOOD. The Battalion moved during the day from GREVILLERS to a field 1 mile N.N.E. of MIRAUMONT.	
Bn. H.Q. & A, B, C Coys at Loupart Wood	25th		The Platoon of 'B' Coy. who were 2nd C. of J. Ridge has been attached with Lafoële for two days rejoined the Bn. which they did at 10 a.m. proceeded to dig a line 80 yds in front + rear of the wood. The Platoon of 'B' Coy. were entrenched as outposts 130 yds in front. The enemy attacked this line about 11:30 a.m. from the direction of GREVILLERS being apparently close up to our line on the right — where there was dead ground but on the left could be seen about 3000 yds away marching in dense columns — when they came within range they were scattered by our Lewis Gun fire. About 1:30 p.m. the right flank was left in the air by the retiral of troops on the right and a platoon of 'C' Coy under 2nd C/H MacKenzie swung round into the wood to form a defensive flank and held on there till 2.15 p.m. C.C. Gemmill was killed by a shell about 2 p.m. in S.E. corner of the wood others wounded being 2nd Lt ___ and rather it. Kim and Capt Kenny who took over Command at 2.30 p.m. when the Bn. retired to the road on the south. 'C' Coy Bn. which ___ as the enemy went round behind the line on the road on the trench. D.C.L.I	

WAR DIARY
INTELLIGENCE SUMMARY. (8)
(Erase heading not required.)

Place	Date	Hour	Summary of Events and Information	Remarks and references to Appendices
	1918			
	MARCH 25th (Contd)		Quiet followed by "B" Coy and then "A" Coy. The retreat was conducted in orderly fashion in spite of the heavy M.G. fire. One platoon of A Coy holding on long enough to cover the retreat of the rest of the Bn. by their fire. The majority of the Bn. re-assembled on the ridge at the S.E. of ACHIET-LE-PETIT, but Lt. Muir A'Coy with 2nd Lts White "A'Coy & Mackay "B' Coy with some 50 men refused to read TREES where although carefully unauthorised they took up a commanding position and held it for some time inflicting heavy losses on the enemy who were advancing in mass formation on TREES. The rest of the Bn. now numbering only 12 officers and 120 O.Rs dug in on the forward slope in front of ACHIET-LE-PETIT., when they soon came under intense M.G. fire from the opposite ridge at a range of about 200yds. Permission was then obtained to withdraw the Bn. on account of its exhausted condition to take up the ridge of the 62nd Div. having taken over the forward position. At midnight orders were received to march to HEBUTERNE via PUISIEUX-AU-MONT. On the 25th the Transport moved Quiet to the MAILLY—MAILLET—FORCEVILLE Rd. and then to the FONQUEVILLERS— SOUASTRE Rd.	
	26th		The Bn. arrived at HEBUTERNE about 3 a.m. faced again at 6.45 a.m. and marched to FONQUEVILLERS where they joined the Transport & thro' and then marched Bn. proceeded to SOUASTRE	1N.A.C

WAR DIARY
or
INTELLIGENCE SUMMARY.
(Erase heading not required.)

Army Form C. 2118.

Place	Date	Hour	Summary of Events and Information	Remarks and references to Appendices
	1918			
	MARCH 26th (Contd)		arriving that about 9 a.m. About 10.30 a.m. an alarm was given that the enemy were approaching and the Battalion under C.R.E.'s orders dug in, in three lines to the north of SOUASTRE, and Eng that R.E. 5 p.m. when orders were received to march to PAS and the night was spent there.	
	27th		The Battalion paraded at Pas at 10.30 a.m. and marched via LUCHEUX to CANTELEUX. Capt Patchell returning from leave, arrived there before the Bn and took over command. For the previous seven days the weather had remained warm and bright.	
CANTELEUX	28th		Uneventful day. The Bn rested after weeks fighting and marching. Some rain in the evening.	
	29th		The Transport moved off at 9 a.m. under orders of the 152nd Inf Bde. The Bn. paraded at 2.45 p.m. and marched to PREVENT where they entrained at 8 p.m. While waiting for the train the King passed through the Town and personally congratulated the Bn. and Division on the fight they had put up.	
BAS RIEUX	30th		Bn detrained at 2.30 a.m. at Rilleres and marched to BAS RIEUX. Uneventful day – rain in afternoon. Transport arrived by road at 3 p.m. Major Yeld returned from leave in the evening but took command.	O.C.C.
	31st		Quiet day. Weather showery. Bn. overhauling and preparing equipment etc.	O.C.C.

WAR DIARY or INTELLIGENCE SUMMARY

(Erase heading not required.)

Place	Date	Hour	Summary of Events and Information	Remarks and references to Appendices
			Casualties during March 1918:-	
			Officers: Lt Col Cameron W DSO Killed in Action 23/3/18 Lieut Clark M20 from 5th 2/3/18	
			Lieut Sthey E " 23/3/18	
			Lieut Lamb RD " 21/3/18 Lieut Jones 4 M.C. from 2nd 2/3/18	
			2nd Lt May Wounded 22/3/18	
			2nd Lt Jones GD " 23/3/18	
			Captain Jones n/34 MC " 21/3/18	
			Morgan Jn McRae a/c 01	
		O.Ranks	Killed in Action 23	
			Wounded 132	Reinforcements 30 2·3·18
			Wounded & Missing 11	2 4·3·18
			Missing 34	2 8· "·18
			Accidental Injury 1	31 " · "
			Other Sick 35	16
			Casualties at 31·3·18 = 3x off 1/35 or	
				W+Q Colour 2/Lieut
				W+Q B... 2 Lt 4/5

CASUALTIES.

OFFICERS.

KILLED:-
- Lieut. R. F. Simpson.   21.3.18.
- 2/Lieut. W. H. Kay   23.3.18.

WOUNDED:-
- Lt.Col. J. G. Thom, D.S.O., M.C.   23.3.18.
- Captain I. Cumming   21.3.18.
- " Sir J. H. Seton, Bart.   24.3.18.
- " J. Archibald   25.3.18.
- 2/Lieut. C. H. Sadleir
- " A. C. Cairns   24.3.18.
- Captain K. Mackay   21.3.18.
- 2/Lieut. C. McLean   24.3.18.
- " B. Carre   21.3.18.
- " A. A. Hagger
- " J. Davidson

UNACCOUNTED FOR:-
- Major C. E. Cornwall   25.3.18.
  (South African Defence Corps)
            (attached)

- 2/Lieut. G. Rutherford, M.C.   21.3.18.

- Lieut. de More, (American Army)
            (attached).

OTHER RANKS.

KILLED	35
WOUNDED	158
UNACCOUNTED FOR	74
DIED OF WOUNDS	6

AGGREGATE   16 Officers   273 Other Ranks.

Probably 6th Gordon Highlanders and see 152nd Bde report.

152nd Bde.

CASUALTIES.

OFFICERS.

KILLED:-

Lieut. R. W. Simpson.   21.3.18.
2/Lieut. W. H. Kay   23.3.18.

WOUNDED:-

Lt.Col. J. G. Thom, D.S.O., M.C.   23.3.18.
Captain I. Cumming   21.3.18.
Sir J. H. Seton, Bart.   24.3.18.
   „ J. Archibald   25.3.18.
2/Lieut. C. H. Sadlair   "
   A. C. Cstrus   24.3.18.
Captain K. McCrae   21.3.18.
2/Lieut. C. Moreau   24.3.18.
   W. Catto   21.3.18.
   A. A. Esser   "
   J. Davidson   "

UNACCOUNTED FOR:-

Major C. E. Cornwall   25.3.18.
(South African Defence Corps)
(attached)

2/Lieut. G. Rutherford, M.C.   21.3.18.

Lieut. de More, (American Army)
(attached).

OTHER RANKS.

KILLED.   35

WOUNDED.   154

UNACCOUNTED FOR.   74

DIED OF WOUNDS.   0

AGGREGATE   10 Officers   273 Other Ranks.

51st Divisional Troops.

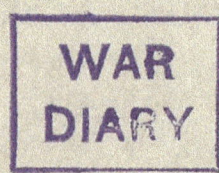

1/8th BATTALION

THE ROYAL SCOTS

Pioneers

APRIL 1918

Appendix - Account of Operations 9th-13th

Army Form C. 2118.

WAR DIARY
or
INTELLIGENCE SUMMARY.
(Erase heading not required.)

WO 38

Confidential

WAR DIARY
OF
1/8 Bn. THE ROYAL SCOTS
FROM
1st April 1918 to 30th April 1918
VOLUME Nº 42

Army Form C. 2118.

WAR DIARY
or
INTELLIGENCE SUMMARY.
(Erase heading not required.)

Place	Date	Hour	Summary of Events and Information	Remarks and references to Appendices
BAS RIEUX	1918 APRIL 1st		The Bn. started reorganisation and training. Weather bright and warm. Both parades at LILLERS.	
	2nd		Training continued – particularly squad & gas-drill. Same train in the evening.	
	3rd		Weather showery. Two drafts joined the Bn. – one 25 O.Rs. the other 43 O.Rs.	
	4th		The Training of new bombing section for Platoon started & also Apprentice Bn. Bombing Officer. Draft of 50 O.Rs. joined the Bn.	
	5th		Very wet in morning, so training cancelled on in billets. Major H.J. HUMPHRYS D.S.O. M.C. 7th Black Watch arrived to temporarily command the Bn. Draft of 83 O.Rs. joined and Capt & Adj. A.D. JONES rejoined from France.	
	6th		Lt. Young W.G. & Davidson S. with 50 O.Rs. joined Bn.	
	7th		Eight officers were called for by Division to be temp attached to H.Q. Gordon H. 2/Lts. Dick W., Mowie A., White A.M., MacKenzie H., Lamb C.S.O., Robbie J.H., Innes W., and Callaway A.H. were sent. "C" Coy had rifle practise on range at ALLOAGNE in afternoon at which shooting was poor. A draft of 41 O.Rs. joined the Battn.	M.G.C.

Army Form C. 2118.

WAR DIARY
INTELLIGENCE SUMMARY.
(Erase heading not required.)

Place	Date	Hour	Summary of Events and Information	Remarks and references to Appendices
BAS RIEUX	1918 APRIL 8th		A & B Coys to ALLOUAGNE RANGE for Musketry. The shooting was good up to standard. C Coy continued Training as per programme.	
		9ᵃ	Training continued in morning. At 2.30 p.m. his Officers were asked for Lipo Cont. on 'G' Staff Div. and Lt. Falconer A.B. and 2Lt. Calder C & G were sent. At 3h.m the Bn were ordered to move in fighting order to MONT BERNENCHON where to night was spent. There was some shelling but no real casualties were caused.	
		10ᵃ	The morning passed quietly but at midday a gas bombt was given by Lt. Col Carey...	
ON PACAUT FRONT			PACAUT. Coon after midday there was a to be carried out by Lt. RB's Coy except Lewis gnrs. B Coy & Capt Clark B by t Col Rumsfield ... recent events by a forward in front of PARADIS then advance by HQre ... Ultimately the Bn to support the front line ... of D.C. H & Comm Highlanders.	
		11ᵃ	At 1 a.m Lt Col Hawkshaw ... Lt. Col Hawkshaw allocated ... 300 yds E of church M.E. corner of PARADIS Church being made to the Canal of the Liner. At 8 a.m. ... of Hawkshaw being wounded Capt Pirie with ... most casualties among the officers. Capt Pirie ... Col Leger Bas Rieux. ... Bn Crewas R.B. commanding A.M. Capt Leger Bas Rieux.	

Army Form C. 2118.

WAR DIARY
or
INTELLIGENCE SUMMARY.

(Erase heading not required.)

Instructions regarding War Diaries and Intelligence Summaries are contained in F. S. Regs., Part II. and the Staff Manual respectively. Title pages will be prepared in manuscript.

Place	Date	Hour	Summary of Events and Information	Remarks and references to Appendices
ON PAGANT FRONT.	APRIL 1918 11 (Contd)		[illegible handwritten entries]	C.S.M.

Army Form C. 2118.

WAR DIARY
or
INTELLIGENCE SUMMARY.
(Erase heading not required.)

Instructions regarding War Diaries and Intelligence Summaries are contained in F. S. Regs., Part II. and the Staff Manual respectively. Title pages will be prepared in manuscript.

Place	Date	Hour	Summary of Events and Information	Remarks and references to Appendices
ON THE PACAUT FRONT	1918 APRIL 12th		About 2 a.m. the enemy delivered a heavy attack and broke through on the left. B Coy were engaged all day in severe fighting shewing great courage and carried on until told night fall. Ultimately the Coy retired behind the canal. At C Coy H.Q. there were practically no officers on duty — the Coy Comdr Capt H.W. Bell being wounded. The enemy was opposed by the HQ men from which however all escaped except the O.C. and Lieut A.L. Neveu who was taken Pris. of War. Wire rations + A Coy Hqrs also retired with other troops across the canal. In the front Lieut BERNENDS rallied the remainder of C Coy in about 20 men the other ranks could with others & 152 A.B. of R.82 under orders of Lieut THADDEN. They were soon joined by C Coy in which Capt SKIM, the Coys Comdr was quite hurt. The night without but they found a shelter and cover inside the woods. Company with all other troops in the vicinity of BUSNES was shortly split up amongst French & British units to incur whose company they formed part.	
BUSNES	13th	About 7.30 p.m. all men of the Btn in Bussinet area had orders to march to BUSNES where W.O. Cleary will pay £40	
BUSNES			Btn formed two battalions	

WAR DIARY
or
INTELLIGENCE SUMMARY.

(Erase heading not required.)

Army Form C. 2118.

Instructions regarding War Diaries and Intelligence Summaries are contained in F. S. Regs., Part II. and the Staff Manual respectively. Title pages will be prepared in manuscript.

Place	Date	Hour	Summary of Events and Information	Remarks and references to Appendices
HOLLANDERIE Nr BUSNES	1915 April 13th (Contd)		Staff and one section C.H. Coys at HOLLANDERIE. Capt Grant H.E.R. reported sick	
REAR HQ & TRANSPORT at FONTES.			Mess and four B Coys in afternoon Capt Mitchell and took command of both parties who were not now even slightly in touch. Confirmed Brev. Lt Col Green as Comdg the Royal Scots by wire.	
	14th		The 153rd Inf Bde Confirmed Brev. Lt Col Green K Coy at HOLLANDERIE. Quiet day. No fire. at Viery Lines	
	15th		Information received that B Bn will not come covered the situation however to Royal Scots to meet him	
			Orders received to be ready to move at 7.300 PM. Regt arr. The Bn horses under the cars of 153rd Inf Bde and marched via HAZEBROUCK to ST HILAIRE where Billets	
ST HILAIRE.	16th		Transport and Echelon B joined Bn in the am	
			Quiet day spent in re-organising R Coys and reducing extras Ech Depot f 30 carrials and 60 re-inforcements arrived	
	17th		Training commenced from Divn Came miles at Strength A.H.B. Cameron bar at officers joined. Return New Uniforms came up on S.S. Thursday & missing and the party was sent post	D.S.C.
	18th		Heavy rain in morning all inspection also carried on in billets B.H.Q.Y.Com	

WAR DIARY
or
INTELLIGENCE SUMMARY.
(Erase heading not required.)

Army Form C. 2118.

Place	Date	Hour	Summary of Events and Information	Remarks and references to Appendices
ST HILAIRE	1918 APRIL 18th	(Cont'd)	Came from 2/R.S. Kit arrived. Capt Pateril came as R.M.O. Capt Yates E.O. R.A.M.C. attached for duty with Cdn Bn.	
	19th	12 noon	Received a Cdn draft of 9 officers & 140 men. Cold day with snow and hail storms at intervals. A Coy on duty all morning, sending up H.O. & O.R's 32 O.R's per pltn & morning.	
	20th		The Coy Comdrs & Pltn Comdrs went up to the line in morning. B Coy on duty. Officers went to shoot Coy in morning.	
	21st		C Coy left in the early morning to go to the 1st Army Musketry Camp at MATRINGHEM. B Coy did the march and fired in the morning and went to the MON CLEMENCEAU – the Lunch [illegible] for the Bn. A Coy was on fatigue in the morning. B Coy in the afternoon.	
	22nd		The Bn. (less C Coy) [illegible] been shot about orders of the C.R.E. (58th Div.) Left at 8 am [illegible] of [illegible] to FIEFIUS, halted St VERANT. Rd to H.Q. marched to BERGUETTE. Rear B H.Q. Bn Lunched to LILLETTE CHATEAU and H.Q. went on at B12 and 3 [illegible] Clocks and 6 km Rendezvous at the [illegible] Cdr Coys at 1pm 4pm. Before H.K Bn. arrived at 8 clocks and 6 km Rendezvous at the [illegible]. There was wounded Bay 1st C of B. 8.10 am. [illegible] on [illegible].	

WAR DIARY or INTELLIGENCE SUMMARY.

Army Form C. 2118.

Place	Date	Hour	Summary of Events and Information	Remarks and references to Appendices
Adv. HQ. BERGUETTE REAR HQ. LILLETTE	APRIL 23rd 1918		The Commanding Officer and Engineers visited the front in the morning. Work begun on new camp. Further instructions awaited.	
Adv B Coy St VENANT C Coy MATRINGHEM			N. Coy ST VENANT. A Coy & Hd Qrs work on the camp. Hd Qrs of C Coy at Matringhem.	O. C. B Coy Helena Ed.
	24th		A & B Coy are working on two shifts on the breastworks to front and westwing N.W. ST VENANT. B Coy are out in the morning and A in the afternoon. Work very satisfactory.	
			Being made three posts have been finished and this new line extended over 200 yds from river for about 150 yds distance ao so to make good field of fire. Relief to found with LIBBIS or LA GORGUE at FONTES. C Coy are supplying two officers at MATRINGHEM. Had attack not let them make good instruction.	
	25th		Two officers and 11 ORs recruits recruits reported. Capts Hart & Young I required after sick wards duty at home both returned fit & well. Work at ST VENANT indent now H.Q. moved forward to FAUQUEMBERGUES	
	26th		Weather chill and misty - work for the two officers Capt Young attended Div. H.Q.	
	27th		C and B Coys Changed over this morning. B Coy under Capt H.E.R. Young took to misstation Camp at HATRINGHEM. Work continued at ST VENANT, every day and night	

Army Form C. 2118.

WAR DIARY
or
INTELLIGENCE SUMMARY.
(Erase heading not required.)

(8)

Place	Date	Hour	Summary of Events and Information	Remarks and references to Appendices
Adv.H.Q. FAUQUEGLON	1918 APRIL 28th		Heavy rain during the night. In the afternoon A Coy billets in front of FAUQUISLON	
A + C Coys.	"		were heavily shelled so that they had to move back. There C Coy are Billeted in the	
Rear H.Q. LILETTE CHATEAU			fields. Very heavy gunfire in the evening.	
B Coy. MATRINGHEM		29th	C. Coy. echelon B joined Coy in the morning. Work near 2nd/LIEUT continuing very	
			satisfactorily. Two more posts have now been finished and much wiring and	
			clearing has done.	
		30th	Very wet out all day. Going to enemy billet at 1 Bn H.Q (Rear) has to cross about	191 C
			a thousand yards heavy clay so as to be off the main road.	

(Erase heading not required.)

Summary of Events and Information

Place	Date	Hour	Summary of Events and Information	Remarks and references to Appendices

Casualties during October 1916

Reinforcements

Lieut Col Hinchcliffe To me Assumed Command
Capt. Dennis W.J. ?? 15
" Cato C.P. G/M/C Joined Unit 19
Lieut Class I M.C.
" " "
Lieut Aert 92 Died Disease Capt Woo J M.C 17 Promoted to Capt
" Brinton G. C/B Returned
" Rettie FP
2/Lieut Calloway J.M. Lieut Young J.D 8.10.16

Major Bell F.B Wounded 2/10/16 Jones A.M 12.10.16
Capt+Adj Jones A.O " 12/10/16 Capt. Churchill D Rejoined
Lieut Ross Sm M.C (RAMC) " 13/10/16 Brewster C.P
" Burdett F.A. Wounded+Missing 10/10/16 Scollo JR 20.11.16
" Ross G. Missing 10/10/16 Bent 27.11.16
" Reid G. " " Arrived ex M.O 15.11.16
2/Lieut Kerr C.E Killed " Little 19.11.16
" Summers 17 "
Lieut Weekes J.D (MC) 2/Lieut Pratt R Sykes C 2/Lieut 27.11.16
Andrews O. "
Killed in Action 20 Oliver "
Wounded 94 Campbell J "
Missing 51 Capt Smith G OC time to C Capt Forsyth
Cert of wounds 1 Lieut Young J
Shellshock missing 4
20 hospital Sick 89 Other Ranks Church Services 100

M.R.Falconer Lieut
Capt P Forsyth O. C

152nd Infantry Brigade.
153rd Infantry Brigade.
154th Infantry Brigade.
C.R.A.
C.R.E.
1/8th Royal Scots.
Div. M. G. Bn.
A.D.M.S.
Signals.
"Q"

Units will forward their accounts of the Operations beginning on April 9th 1918 to the "G" Office as soon as possible.

Brigades should enclose a copy of the accounts furnished by their Battalions.

F.W. Bewsher Major

Colonel,
General Staff,
51st (Highland) Division.

24th April 1918.

Headquarters,
    51st. (High) Division.

Herewith.

Lieut.-Colonel,
Commanding 1/8th. Royal Scots (Pioneers).

25/4/18.

1/8th. Bn. The Royal Scots (Pioneers).

REPORT ON OPERATIONS Commencing APRIL, 9th 1918.

April,

9th. At 5-0 p.m. the Battalion moved from BAS RIEUX to MONT BERNENCHON and spent the night there.

10th. At midday orders were received to advance to PACAUT and this was immediately done. About 10 p.m. orders were received from 153rd.Inf. Bde. that one Company was to report to H.Qrs. 1/7th. Gordons for the purpose of forming blocks on roads running East from L'EPINETTE - CIX MARMUSE Road. "B" Company therefore moved off and Col. HUMPHRYS, who followed, sited these posts in conjunction with O.C., Coy. on an average 300 yards East of road. Each block consisted of a trench to hold 25 men with a support trench to hold 20 men 500 yards behind. Four Vickers Guns were at the disposal of the Coy. in the various posts.

11th. At 5 a.m. orderlies reported that the enemy had broken through and were close to Bn. H.Q. at R.13.d.5.3 Col.Humphries then returned to join the other two Coys. who were in Divl. Reserve at PACAUT and PARADIS. "C" Company was then ordered to move East of PARADIS Church to road bend at R.19.c.4.8 and later took up a position running N.and S. from R.19.a.6.2 to R.19.c.6.0. One platoon was in reserve at Bn.H.Q. at Q.24.d.6.8. This Company was not in touch with anyone on Right or Left. A M.G.Officer with 4 Vickers Guns reported, and 3 of these were placed in the line, one being held in reserve. Patrols sent along roads running N.E. and E. on flanks of position came in touch with the enemy. The line was maintained until well after 9a.m. and casualties were inflicted on the enemy at ranges well under 300 yards.
  The remaining Company (A Coy.) had dug in one line running N.and S. 500 yds. West of PARADIS Church. All the officers in "C" Coy. except one had now been wounded and shortly afterwards Col.Humphries was himself hit when taking out a Lewis Gun to engage the enemy who were massing on North of Bn. H.Q. The right flank of "C" Coy. was swung round and in this operation the last officer was wounded. Captain Mitchell then took Command of the Battalion.
  In the meantime "B" Company had been forced to retire northwards with the other troops in front and for the rest of the day fought a rear-guard action under the Command of O.C. 1/7th. Black Watch.
  At midday "C" coy. was attacked by the enemy who were driven off. Shortly afterwards, however, an officer from the right reported that all troops on that flank had retired, so the Coy. retired a short way under orders of Major Todd who had come up to take command, and again established connection on their flanks.

12th. During the early hours, when still dark, the enemy delivered a heavy attack on the left and all the troops on that flank retired. "B" Company were engaged in very mixed fighting and later were forced back across the Canal.
  "A" and "C" Companies were in the meantime heavily engaged with their flanks in the air and fought until practically surrounded when they retired. The Bn.H.Q. at Q.23.c.7.8 was surrounded by the enemy and Major Todd and the Adjutant failed to escape.

/ "A" Coy. less 1 platoon

1/8th. Bn. The Royal Scots (Pioneers).

REPORT ON OPERATIONS Commencing 9th. April, 1918. (contd)

12th.   "A" Company, less one platoon, retired across the Canal in front of Mont Bernenchon - the remaining platoon having retired South with elements of 152nd. Inf. Bde.
    "C" Company on retiral from PARADIS position established touch on the left with some R.Es. and formed a line through PACAUT WOOD, where they held up a strong enemy attack about 5 p.m. The troops on their right, however, again retired and a defensive flank was therefore formed on that flank. After dusk all the troops in this neighbourhood withdrew across the Canal, and men of this Battalion received orders to march to BUSNES.

13th.   By 3-0 a.m. all men of the Battalion had reached the neighbourhood of BUSNES and though lying in reserve as ROYAL SCOTsCompany of 153rd. Inf. Bde. Composite Battalion took no further part in the fighting.

Casualties for period 9th. - 13th. April, inclusive:-

Officers - WOUNDED :-

Lt.Col.	Humphrys. H.J. D.S.O., M.C.	11-4-18
Captain	Fleming. W.A.	do.
	Richardson. J.	do.
Lieut.	Watson. Hon.R.B.	do.
	Burnet. F.A.	do.
	Anderson. A.F.B.	do.
	Dods. J.B. (Since Died of W.)	do.
	Brunton. G. do.	do.
2/Lieut.	Robbie. J.H.	do.
	Callander. A.H.	do.

        MISSING :-

Major	Todd. J.A.	12-4-18
Capt.& Adjt.	Jones. A.D.	do.
Capt.	Ross. M.C., R.A.M.C.att.	do.
Lieut.	Munro. A.	do.
2/Lt.	White. A.M.	do.
Lieut.	Reid. G.	do.

Other Ranks :-

Killed in Action	20
Wounded	88
Wounded & Missing	4
Died of Wounds	1
Missing	67

Lieut.-Colonel,
Commanding 1/8th. Bn. The Royal Scots (Pioneers).

24th. April, 1918.

Army Form C. 2118.

WAR DIARY
or
INTELLIGENCE SUMMARY.
(Erase heading not required.)

VC 3a

CONFIDENTIAL

WAR DIARY
OF
1/8th Bn. THE ROYAL SCOTS (PIONEERS)
FROM
1st MAY 1918 to 31st MAY 1918

VOLUME No 43

36 Pp.

Army Form C. 2118.

WAR DIARY
or
INTELLIGENCE SUMMARY.
(Erase heading not required.)

Instructions regarding War Diaries and Intelligence Summaries are contained in F. S. Regs., Part II, and the Staff Manual respectively. Title pages will be prepared in manuscript.

Place	Date	Hour	Summary of Events and Information	Remarks and references to Appendices
ST VENANT.	1918 May 1st		Nothing special to report. Companies proceeding with routine front of ST VENANT.	
	"	2nd	Weather changed for better - was fairly wet again. After the afternoon Coy. Officers had finished with Orders, A & C boys returned to LISETTE CHAT at 5 p.m. Objectives during the 24hrs 4hy shell on the works, all the morning was fixation and took conditions and method to every. All the same	
	"	3rd	"A" and "C" Coys. had 5th instructors visits to the officers a body from the "Balmorals" gave arrival on electic generator. "B" Coy. advanced from MATRINGHEM (First Army Musketry Camp) in the afternoon and were trained in LISETTE Captain G. A. BALLANTYNE in the evening	
	"	4th	Transport left by road for new rest sectors at 8 a.m. The Coy. inspected Coys at different hours throughout the day. During the evening of the day all were training. Anything	
	"	5th	Our 10th advance party left by motor lorry at 8 a.m. Majors.A. and the Batt. paraded at H Rue and marched from LISETTE to 2118. No further news. The train was late on arriving. So there was a want of in morning again.	

D. D. & L., London, E.C.
(A7883) Wt. W809/M1672 350,000 4/17 Sch. 50a Forms/C/2118/14

WAR DIARY "D"
or
INTELLIGENCE SUMMARY.

(Erase heading not required.)

Army Form C. 2118.

Instructions regarding War Diaries and Intelligence Summaries are contained in F. S. Regs., Part II. and the Staff Manual respectively. Title pages will be prepared in manuscript.

Place	Date	Hour	Summary of Events and Information	Remarks and references to Appendices
	May			
	5th (Cont?)		Very steady ammunition was prepared for the men.	
	6th		Bn. arrived at HQ about 9am & marched through COMBES to BRAY where I am billeted in huts. In afternoon "B" & "C" Coys left to take over from Canadian Pioneers the manning of two posts in the western system. Out to work from here. The work is to clear out what was trenches & old dugouts in front of posts. Coys quite comfortable with billeting of dug out accommodation in huts.	
	7th		Very wet day in morning, but cleared up later. Punns were laid in huts at finish but late in the show. All materials - less Gunner Lewellen asst Brokers & Scouts paraded for special instruction under Specialist Officers. A Coy was hey with Infantry & Pioneers manning "B" & "C" Coys commenced work on BROWN LINE last night but were obliged to stop at 10.45 pm on account of heavy rain.	
	8th		Quiet on our front. Fine bright warm day. "A" Coy & relieve "B" & "C" continues training. - "A" Coy having most of the men was Coach. "B" & "C" Coys continued their work of clearing & extending the Camp.	

WAR DIARY "3"
or
INTELLIGENCE SUMMARY.

Army Form C. 2118.

Place	Date	Hour	Summary of Events and Information	Remarks and references to Appendices
May	8th (cont.)		Mr FARBUS - VIMY - GIVIN Line in front of their pos's and in rebuxing their pos's.	
	9th		Another good day. "B" + "C" Coys no longer responsible for holding pos's. Work of maintaining H.G.T.'s carried on. These Coys engaged in raining & cleaning. "A" Coy and specialists continue training at BRAY Camp. detaching GUNN LINE. 7th Coy and specialists continue training at his various duties. Lieut. T.R.C. Shiner proceeded to Eng to day to resume his various duties. Lt Lockland returned to duty after a prolonged absence. O Ranks on strength incees of 900 sent to the to Infantry School (Camp).	
	10th		Quiet in morning but ceases later. "B" + "C" Coys subjected to slight gas shelling. A notice S 22 M sent to D Coy ordering Battalion to 700. Capt Christie attached for Traffic Control Officer. "A" Coy + specialists trained. "B" + "C" Coys doing good work.	
	11th		Another good day. "B" Coy. started working on MISSOURI TRN raising "C" Coy on AEROPLANE TR and continuing other work. "B" shelled at work in trenches.	

Army Form C. 2118.

WAR DIARY
or
INTELLIGENCE SUMMARY.
(Erase heading not required.)

"A"

Instructions regarding War Diaries and Intelligence Summaries are contained in F. S. Regs., Part II. and the Staff Manual respectively. Title pages will be prepared in manuscript.

Place	Date	Hour	Summary of Events and Information	Remarks and references to Appendices
	May 12th		Dull morning but clear later. Church Parade as formed at BRAY CAMP. "B" Coy making good progress & running. "C" Coy carrying on with Romanel	
	13th		Schick, Knapp and Scales went to Divl. Schools of Instruction. Nothing of special interest. Coy doing useful work on BROWN LINE and C.T's	
	14th		Beautiful day. "A" Coy relieved "C" Coy at RIDGE POST. Coys making good progress on trenches & wiring	
	15th		Nothing of special interest	
	16th		"B" Coy completed 325x of NEW CUT in MISSOURI & reclaim lots of BRAY LINE. Wire work progressing. Very warm to-day	
	17th		Considerable amount of drilling around A & B Coy held but in no wiring.	
	18th		"C" Coy at Rouge parade. "A" Coy went up on wire. Progress with trench work. "B" Coy continue on MISSOURI. Weather still very warm.	
	19th		Church Parade at BRAY CAMP. Inoculation "Scabies" inspection. "A" "B" continue work.	

Army Form C. 2118.

WAR DIARY or INTELLIGENCE SUMMARY

Army Form C. 2118.

"5"

Place	Date	Hour	Summary of Events and Information	Remarks and references to Appendices
May	20th		"A" Coy heavily shelled during morning in billets. Considerable number of shells hit. 2nd Lieut W Gillispie slightly wounded. Bring & reclaiming trenches proceeding. "C" Coy complete 3 Rifling Point Sheds & engaged dismantling huts. Draft of 5 ORs arrived from Base. Lts Grens Jones get acting rank of Captain.	
	21st		"C" Coy + HQ detail at Botha. "B" Coy cut 8 new Firesteps in MISSOURI. "A" Coy contour work.	
	22nd		"C" Coy relieved "B" Coy at RAILWAY Post. "A" Coy begin new work on REDLINE wiring + reclaiming. "C" Coy improving MISSOURI. 2nd Lieut Mackay goes to course at LE TOUQUET	
	23rd		"B" Coy bathed. 50 men inoculated. "A" Coy continue wiring + improving RED LINE - complete Dug-out in RIDGE Post. "C" Coy wire + Chevaux MISSOURI. Corps shelled at work. Very high wind + cloudy. Wretched day. "A" + "C" Coys dig new trench 2'6" deep between FOLLY + TONY - distance 280x. "B" Coy interrupted in training by rain.	
	24th		2nd Lieut Calder goes to First Army Musketry Course.	

Army Form C. 2118.

WAR DIARY
or
INTELLIGENCE SUMMARY.
(Erase heading not required.)

"6"

Place	Date	Hour	Summary of Events and Information	Remarks and references to Appendices
May	25th		"A" + "C" Coys. completed new CuT between FOLLY + TONY. "A" Coy erected 200x of PlateX wire in front of REDLINE. Capt. J.S. Pringle returned from leave after only having 3 months tour of duty.	
	26th		Enemy heavy barrage on front systems + put over two shells. Coys interrupted on work, but escape without casualties. Quiet during remainder of its day. Enemy attack British -French troops on 40 kilo front between Soissons + RHEIMS. "B" + H.Q. Coys at Church Parade with Div. School at ECOIVRES.	
	27th		"A" Coy cut tie firebays in MISSOURI. Wire improved REDLINE. "C" Coy began new dug-out in REDLINE + continue other work. "B" Coy training at BRAY. Enemy continue attack South + also begin in the NORTH	
	28th		"A" + "C" Coys shelled at work, but managed to do some wiring + Clay kneeled second NewCut of MISSOURI. Lt. Davidson, 2nd Lieuts. Dives + Jenkinson Go to Div. School	
	29th		"B" Coy + H.Q. Coy at Baths. "B" Coy carried out Musketry Practice at Range. "A" + "C" Coys continue work	

WAR DIARY
or
INTELLIGENCE SUMMARY.
(Erase heading not required.)

Army Form C. 2118.

Place	Date	Hour	Summary of Events and Information	Remarks and references to Appendices
May	30th		"C" Coy put up 250x of Plate I wire. Cut through CAYRELLE ROAD + duck walk part of NEW MISSOURI. "B" Coy relieved "A" Coy at RIDGE POST. weather continues good.	
	31st		"A" Coy had a day of company inspections + talks. Sentences on Pte. ANDERSON & BOUGHTON promulgated. "C" Coy continued new cut on SOUTH SIDE of CAYRELLE ROAD, erect 200x of wire in front of TOWN, and "B" Coy widened + deepens over 150xd RED LINE.	

Jos Thorpe
Lt Col.
Comdg. 1/8 Bn. THE ROYAL SCOTS
(PIONEERS)

Casualties during May 1918.

Officers:-
2/Lieut Jamieson R.C. To Home 11th to Reserve 26/5/18
 "   Shires I.K.G. Joint to remove Medical Board 9/5/18
 "   Reid   "   Joint (Cambridge) for R.A.F. 26.5.18
Lieut Bell   "   Joint (Cambridge) for R.A.F. 24/5/18
2/Lieut   To Leave
                   Wounded (at Duty)   20.5.18

Reinforcements
Capt E.W. Ballantyne Joined 8/5/18
Capt O.J. Anyle   "   24/5/18
Lieut J.S. Sutherland to R.E. School
                                      8.5.18
                                      2.5.18
                   Other Ranks   12 O.R   2.5.18
                                     9   "   3.5.18
                                     6   " 13.5.18
                                    43   " 17.5.18
                                    35's   26.5.18
                                    20 "   30.5.18 ?

Wounded - 11 Other Ranks
To Hospital (Sick) 135 -"-

Strength at 31.5.18 = 29 Offrs. 882 O.R.

1st June 1918.
                                W. Anderson Lieut-Col.
                                Comdg 11th Bn. The Royal Scots

Army Form C. 2118.

WAR DIARY
or
INTELLIGENCE SUMMARY.

(Erase heading not required.)

WO 40

CONFIDENTIAL

WAR DIARY
OF
1/8th Bn. The Royal Scots (Pioneers)
FROM
1st June 1918 to 30th June 1918.
VOLUME No. 44.

37 R.S.

WAR DIARY
or
INTELLIGENCE SUMMARY.

(Erase heading not required.)

Army Form C. 2118.

Place	Date	Hour	Summary of Events and Information	Remarks and references to Appendices
BRAY CAMP	1918 June 1st		Nothing of special interest.	
	2nd		"C" & "B" Companies gas shelled during early morning but good progress made with "Transport" Competition held and proved great success. Transport & Q.M. work.	
	3rd		Wires moved from MAROEUIL to BRAY. "B" & "C" Companies put up a considerable amount of wire and did good work in POST LINE.	
	4th		Nothing of special Interest. "B" & "C" Companies continue work and "A" Coy Training	
	5th		Lieutenants J.T. Richinson and J.O. Chisholm joined the Battalion from home – Strength of 10 O.Rs received.	
	6th		"C" Coy completed wiring of SWITCH LINE at POINT du JOUR and relaying of MISSOURI trench. "B" & "C" Companies began work on OPPY sector of POST LINE. "A" Coy. continues training. Enemy appears to be held up by French in the South.	
	7th		"A" Coy relieved "C" Coy as RAILWAY CUTTING. "B" Coy completes revetting of mine from BAILLEUL. 16 "R" Tracks. distance over 1,000 yards.	
	8th		Work continued by "B" and "C" Coys. Some shelling and gas. "C" Coy have a few casualties act.	

Army Form C. 2118.

WAR DIARY
or
INTELLIGENCE SUMMARY.
(Erase heading not required.)

"2"

Place	Date	Hour	Summary of Events and Information	Remarks and references to Appendices
BRAY CAMP	June 8th (Contd)		Lieutenant W.E.G LAWRIE and draft of 3 other ranks join Battalion from Base.	
		9th	Beautiful day. During 1st Divisional Gas Attack work restricted to day work.	
		10th	"A" and "B" Companies make good progress with work on POST LINE and with wiring. "C" Coy. and Headquarters Coy. engaged making slits under huts for protection against bombing.	
		11th	Companies continue work and "C" Coy. have an entertainment at the Balmoral.	
			Draft of 2 other Ranks from Base.	
		12th	"C" Coy. gives demonstration in wiring to Officers of Divisions behind. "B" Coy. completes nearly 600 yards of POST LINE and "A" Coy. and continue work on the line.	
		13th	Position on French front appears more settled and they make hopefully counter attack putting of Battalion interior to report.	
		14th	N.C.Os. and men of Battalion present red with ribbons by Both Commanders. Division have a Chinese Gas Beam attack on the OPPY sector and this work comparatively uninterrupted but "B" and "A" managed to complete work on POST LINE trench.	
		15th	"C" Coy. retires to "RIDGE POST". draft of 10 other ranks arrived from Base, and 39 men at Divisional Wing return to the Battalion. During the enemies Gas Beam attack by 15th Division.	

Army Form C. 2118.

WAR DIARY
or
INTELLIGENCE SUMMARY.
(Erase heading not required.)

"3"

Instructions regarding War Diaries and Intelligence Summaries are contained in F. S. Regs., Part II. and the Staff Manual respectively. Title pages will be prepared in manuscript.

Place	Date	Hour	Summary of Events and Information	Remarks and references to Appendices
	Jun 15th (cont)		on the right. Companies send out wiring parties at POINT DU JOUR, as arranged on to new work.	
	16th		Congenial weather continues. "A" & "C" Companies begin new switch line at POINT DU JOUR. 2/Lt CALDER returns from Musketry Course.	
	17th		Capt. W.E. THORBURN arrived of along with an appointment to Corps position, and LIEUT R.A.D. RITCHIE returns to Battalion after over a year absence with 2nd Corps. 2/LT CALDER and 3 Sergeants go to 153rd Brigade as Wiring Instructors. Staff of 11 other ranks from Bn. - CAPT OVENS returns from Army Special School. Work on Trenches and Wiring continues.	
	18th		Capt. J.S. PRINGLE and R.SM. DICKMAN, D.C.M. go to 1st Army Musketry School. Companies continue on new trench but interrupted by shelling. "B" Coy up at ROCKLINCOURT making new billets.	
	19th		"B" Coy. march up to new billets in ROCKLINCOURT and finish making their billets. B.Q. gives lecture to Divisional School. "A" and "C" Companies continue work. CAPT. JONES goes to Rentices. Fine weather broken - very heavy showers.	
	20th		Headquarters bombed at 1 a.m. Work continues.	
	21st		Headquarters move from BRAY to ROCKLINCOURT. Right Division have very successful raid. Operations	

WAR DIARY
or
INTELLIGENCE SUMMARY.
(Erase heading not required.)

Army Form C. 2118.

Instructions regarding War Diaries and Intelligence Summaries are contained in F. S. Regs., Part II. and the Staff Manual respectively. Title pages will be prepared in manuscript.

Place	Date	Hour	Summary of Events and Information	Remarks and references to Appendices
June	21st contd	Night	Nothing else of interest.	
	22nd		"B" and "C" Companies complete whole of second track or new trench or POINT du JOUR.	
	23rd		"B" Coy begin new exit from MISSISSIPPI Trench to GAVRELLE ROAD. "A" and "C" companies continue work on Switch Trench and wiring. Headquarters Company, Transport and R.M. Stores move from BRAY to new billets near MAROEUIL - NEUVILLE ST. VAAST ROAD. Staff of 13 O.Rs arriving from Base.	
	24th		"B" Coy begin two new dug out shafts and "A" Coy on BROWN LINE. Other work proceeding.	
	25th		"C" Coy completes excellent belt of wire in front of BAILLEUL and "B and C" Companies finish work on POINT du JOUR Switch LINE - Good bit of work.	
	26th		MAJOR MITCHELL goes on leave to DINARD and CAPT TAIT takes over. 2ND LIEUT BOYD and OLIVER return from Courses and 2ND LIEUT. BLACKWOOD is struck off strength. Companies continue work on Trench etc.	
	27th		"A" Coy relieved "C" Coy at RIDGE POST. LIEUT. SUTHERLAND goes home on leave.	
	28th		The three Companies do excellent work on BROWN TRENCH. LIEUTs COUTTS and GORDON, and 2ND LIEUT. FRASER and 10 O.Rs joined from Base.	

Army Form C. 2118.

WAR DIARY
or
INTELLIGENCE SUMMARY.
(Erase heading not required.)

Instructions regarding War Diaries and Intelligence Summaries are contained in F. S. Regs., Part II. and the Staff Manual respectively. Title pages will be prepared in manuscript.

5

Place	Date	Hour	Summary of Events and Information	Remarks and references to Appendices
	June 29th		LIEUT. DAVIDSON and 2ND LIEUTS HOWIE and SYNE go to Courcelette Road on divisional Xmas intermpts work.	
	30th		2ND LIEUT. TAINSH appointed divisional Camouflage officer. Companies continue work in BROWN TRENCH. "B" Coy now filled in new Cable trench to GAY RELLE ROAD, over 1000 yards.	

W Thalven
Lieut. Colonel.
Comdg 1/on Batt. The Royal Scots
(Pioneers)

Army Form C. 2118.

WAR DIARY
or
INTELLIGENCE SUMMARY.
(Erase heading not required.)

Instructions regarding War Diaries and Intelligence Summaries are contained in F. S. Regs., Part II. and the Staff Manual respectively. Title pages will be prepared in manuscript.

Place	Date	Hour	Summary of Events and Information	Remarks and references to Appendices

Casualties during June 1918
Officers.

O.C.in W.E.R. Major No. Morgan C.B. 19.6.18
Lieut. 2/Lt. Hicks   16.6.18
"   "   Boyd   "
"   "   Willis   28.6.18
"   "   Graham   "
                          30.6.18
N.T. Blackman & Offr. disch. to U.S. Dist European Exp. return
                          " Klingel

Confirmation
Lieut. Whitbread to Capt. 5/4/18
"   Laurie   " "   2.6.18
"   Smith   " "   28.6.18
"   Eyston   " "   "
2/Lt Fraser   " Lieut 28.6.18

Other Ranks.
Joined   4 other Ranks
To Hosp.(sick)   138
                    —

Other Ranks.
                    16 O.R.   5.6.18   26/4/6
                    2 "   11/6/18   26/4/5
                    "   22/6/18   26/6/5
                    13   29/6/18   27/6/18

Strength at 30.6.18 = Offr 43
                      O.R. 868.

                                      10
1st July 1918   W Shurs
                                      Lieut. Col.
                                      Comdg 13th Bn. The Royal Scots (Reg.)

51st (Highland) Div. Troops.

1/8th THE ROYAL SCOTS (PIONEERS)

J U L Y, 1 9 1 8.

Army Form C. 2118.

WAR DIARY
or
INTELLIGENCE SUMMARY.
(Erase heading not required.)

CONFIDENTIAL

WAR DIARY

of

1/8th Bn. THE ROYAL SCOTS (PIONEERS)

FROM

1st JULY 1918 TO 31st JULY 1918.

VOLUME No. 45.

Army Form C. 2118.

WAR DIARY
or
INTELLIGENCE SUMMARY.
(Erase heading not required.)

Instructions regarding War Diaries and Intelligence Summaries are contained in F.S. Regs., Part II. and the Staff Manual respectively. Title pages will be prepared in manuscript.

Place	Date	Hour	Summary of Events and Information	Remarks and references to Appendices
ROCLINCOURT	1918 July 1st		Relatively hot day. Work on BROWN TRENCH and wiring continued. "A" Coy. built covered trench along BAILLEUL ROAD from OUSE ALLEY to SUGAR FACTORY to give covered approach to M.G. Emplacement.	
	2nd		Weather warm continuing. Companies continued work on BROWN TRENCH and wiring. Nothing of interest to report.	
	3rd		Weather dull and cooler with strong breeze. "A" Coy. completed belt of wire to wire North of BAILLEUL ROAD to OUSE ALLEY. Companies continued work on improvement of BROWN TRENCH. "C" Coy. relieved "B" Coy. in RAILWAY CUTTING. "B" Coy. billeted.	
	4th		Wiring and improvement of BROWN TRENCH continued. "A" + "C" Coys. dug New Cut at BOUNDARY ALLEY to A.A. "B" Coy. continued 100' 1st Bank of BOUNDARY ALLEY southwards from New Cut.	
	5th		Nothing of importance to report. Work on lining of BROWN TRENCH also wiring	

Army Form C. 2118.

WAR DIARY
or
INTELLIGENCE SUMMARY.
(Erase heading not required.)

Instructions regarding War Diaries and Intelligence Summaries are contained in F.S. Regs., Part II. and the Staff Manual respectively. Title pages will be prepared in manuscript.

Place	Date	Hour	Summary of Events and Information	Remarks and references to Appendices
	1918 July	6th	Capt. TAIT left for DISTRICT COURS ROUEN. Work on BROWN TRENCH continues also wiring. "C" Coy attn working along road linking up RAILWAY C.T. railway road. 13 O.R. rejoined Battalion from hospital.	
		7th	"A" Coy. Will. went through BAILLEUL ROAD into BROWN TRENCH carrying out and placing bridges to position - also continue formation of LIGHT RAILWAY also to this position. wiring continues.	
		8th	Capt. & Regt. A.B. FALCONER left for Third Army Rest Camp. "A" Coy. daily very good work in wiring. New cut linking up RAILWAY C.T. along road begun. MAJOR MITCHELL returned from leave from DINARD.	
		9th	"C" Coy. completed new cut from SWITCH on POINT on JOUR to EFFIE TRENCH. Work on BROWN TRENCH and new cut linking up RAILWAY C.T. completed. Weather cloudy, rain in afternoon & evening.	
		10th	Work taken over by 10th & 11th CANADIAN ENGINEER BATTALION, and "A" and "C" Coys. withdrawn from RIDGE and RAILWAY POSTS to ROCKLINCOURT ZINES. Strong wind but weather fine.	
		11th	Head Quarters move from ROCKLINCOURT to transport lines in anticipation of move tomorrow.	

Army Form C. 2118.

WAR DIARY
or
INTELLIGENCE SUMMARY.
(Erase heading not required.)

Instructions regarding War Diaries and Intelligence Summaries are contained in F. S. Regs., Part II. and the Staff Manual respectively. Title pages will be prepared in manuscript.

Place	Date	Hour	Summary of Events and Information	Remarks and references to Appendices
	1918			
	July 11th	6 p.m.	Men accommodated in shelters in trench and under cover very wet - weather very wet.	
	12th		As Air Raid Orders received Battalion marched to CHAU de la HAIE and entrained on Light Railway. Battalion detrained about one mile north of BAILLEUL and marched to BUNEVILLE a distance of 4 miles where it was billeted for the night. Divisional Salvage Coy under Capt. L. YOUNG attached to the Battalion during the move for accommodation and rations.	
	13th		Battalion moved according to Orders received to AVERDOINGT where it rested. Billets - 3 Coy being billeted in Ig PLANQUETTE one mile away.	
	14th		At AVERDOINGT. Marching Orders received to entrain by 2 p.m. tomorrow. "C" Coy proceed to TINQUES to act as Loading Party No 153rd Infantry Brigade to which Brigade Battalion attached during move.	
	15th		According to Orders Battalion resumed Battalion marched to TINQUES where it entrained Transport headed Battalion - Whilst Transport, experiencing another one by "C" Coy and Train left in two. "X" Coy followed by a half train.	
	16		In train from about 7 a.m. to 12 hours at a point where half mile from rails was the breakfasts & journey resumed through lovely country. Weather very warm. Detrained at FAMBUIS	

D. D. & L., London, E.C.
(A5853) Wt. W809/M1672 350,000 4/17 **Sch. 52a** Forms/C/2118/14

Army Form C. 2118.

WAR DIARY
or
INTELLIGENCE SUMMARY.
(Erase heading not required.)

Instructions regarding War Diaries and Intelligence Summaries are contained in F. S. Regs., Part II. and the Staff Manual respectively. Title pages will be prepared in manuscript.

Place	Date	Hour	Summary of Events and Information	Remarks and references to Appendices
	1916			
	July 16th	Cont.	train went on to ROMILLY arriving there at 9 p.m. Battalion detrained and received instructions to march to CHANTEMARLE during the march Battalion bivouacked at the roadside for the time	
	17th		Battalion arrived at CHANTEMARLE at 7 a.m. when it went billeted.	
	18th		There was a commanding officers inspection of the Battalion at 8 a.m. following this orders were received during the morning Battalion paraded at 11 a.m. and marched a distance of 18 Kilometres to ½ mile SOUTH of SOIZY aux BOIS when rations were received for two days and Battalion bivouacked for the night.	
	19th		Following up and orders received at 3 a.m. for the Battalion to be at Cross Roads one mile SOUTH of BRUGNY, a distance of 23 Kilometres from the 12.30 p.m. the Battalion reached its march at 7 a.m. Weather very hot. Men exhausted carrying packs + extra ammunition. It was found that the Cross mentioned could not be reached at the time stated and LIEUT W.G. YOUNG Acting adjutant was sent on ahead but found no one with orders for the Battalion, so when the Battalion arrived at 3 p.m. it bivouaced in adjacent woods	
	20th		Following march orders received during the night the Battalion paraded at 4 a.m. and marched to one mile NORTH of BELLEVUE passing through EPERNAY en route	

Army Form C. 2118.

WAR DIARY
or
INTELLIGENCE SUMMARY.
(Erase heading not required.)

Place	Date	Hour	Summary of Events and Information	Remarks and references to Appendices
1918				
	July 20 M Coyler		distance about 20 Kilometres – men very exhausted on arrival at destination on account of	
			heat & extra ammunition carried. Socks were dumped at later hr. "C" Company of	
			the Battalion with its destination at BELLEVUE the Division worth the 62nd division on	
			the right and the 9th French division on its left attacked the enemy on a Battalion	
			front and at the time observed had taken practically all its objectives. "C" Coy was	
			out repairing a road under the R.E.'s but had to withdraw on account of shell fire	
			They had six men wounded.	
			Rest of "C" Company's movements were intimately at TINQUES.	
	July 17th		Entrained at HERMES and were motored in French buses to AVIZE, from the town of	
			Divisions there + were informed that 133rd Infantry Brigade were at CHIVILLY + marched	
			that place in the evening. Learnt that 1/32th Brigade were at CHOVILLY + that the 153rd	
			Brigade at PIERRY Billeted in CHOVILLY to the right.	
	July 18th		Marched to PIERRY and billeted. Company was there by 2nd Lieut. W.G. CALDER who	
			had joined Coy over night. He had been informed there their Battalion was at MANCHY and	
			Coy continued its march to that place, their Battalion had not there having extended it	
			+ coming short day billeted in MANCHY.	

WAR DIARY or INTELLIGENCE SUMMARY

Army Form C. 2118.

Record of "C" Company's movements Cont'd

Date	Hour	Summary of Events and Information
July 19th		Preparing to Order received Company moved to DIZY MAGENTA where men were billeted in MARNE canal. Orders received for Company to join up with Field Coy R.E. in vicinity of BELLEVUE which was reached in the afternoon.
July 20th		Company ordered to assist Field Coy R.E. through FOREST de REIMS along with R.E. Work intimated with heavy shelling. Coy repairing Battery.
July 21st		According to Orders Company marched at 4 a.m. Battery was shelled & the camp and marched a distance of about 5 kilometers and bivouacked in position in BOIS de SABRUG just west of NANTEUIL. Shelling was experienced on the way. "C" Coy had 1 man killed and 4 wounded. Details Mess Storez come up by transport whilst there were several casualties amongst the following amongst the following amongst the following casualties by shellfire in "C" Coy. 2nd LIEUT R.A. JAMIESON killed. 2nd LIEUT A. McK GORDON severely wounded, 2 O.R. killed & wounded. "B" Coy 1 man killed 2 wounded. Transport 1 man killed & 2 wounded. Bad day for the Battalion. French have had a great advance between SOISSONS and REIMS, enemy driven back over the MARNE. Division on Divisional front refused any safety a try.

WAR DIARY or INTELLIGENCE SUMMARY

Army Form C. 2118.

Place	Date	Hour	Summary of Events and Information	Remarks and references to Appendices
	July 22nd		Very noisy night with artillery fire constantly recurring. Thanks of XXII Corps Commander and French Commander, shewing the division for the 50th work. Had above during the last two days. "B" Coy under Capt PRINGLE sent to the 154th Brigade as an apporting troops. Lieut. MACKAY went to BOIS DU SOUTRON according to bring in wounded. Battalion went into the line, relieved the 6th GORDONS. "B" Coy attacked to the 7th A & S. HIGHLANDERS, and assisted REGT in cutting path in woods. This continued till midnight, when they received orders to take positions in a trench south of the 154th Infantry Brigade near — morning at 6 am.	
	23rd		Battalion holding line. Heavily artillery heavily shelled from 6am till 8am & evening afterwards. shared. "B" Coy under CAPT. PRINGLE attacked on a 250 yards front with 7th A & S. HIGHLANDERS on their right and 4th GORDONS on their left. We had contemplation of the Coy who carried on hastily and lost heavily. The Platoon in the right under 2nd LIEUT. R.F. FRASER and the Platoon on the left under 2nd LIEUT. J.F. CRAWFORD got through but did not return. "D" Coy reached their objective destroyed two enemy machine guns and captured 28 prisoners. As the troops on the flanks failed to make any advance they had to withdraw as they were in danger of being cut off. The company had 80 casualties. LIEUT. J.C. CHISHOLM	

Army Form C. 2118.

WAR DIARY
or
INTELLIGENCE SUMMARY.
(Erase heading not required.)

Instructions regarding War Diaries and Intelligence Summaries are contained in F. S. Regs., Part II. and the Staff Manual respectively. Title pages will be prepared in manuscript.

8.

Place	Date	Hour	Summary of Events and Information	Remarks and references to Appendices
	July 23rd Cont.		was severely wounded & subsequently died of wounds. 2nd LIEUT. J. DEIVER was also wounded.	
	24th		Battalion in line. The 133rd Infantry Brigade relieved by the 35th French Infantry Brigade.	
			Tonight our Battalion marched back to old quarters in wood about 1 mile NORTH of BELLEVUE. A great amount of gas shell fire had to be endured when approaching	
			through the woods but the relief was completed without any casualties. 2nd LIEUT. W.D. ARMSTRONG and 2nd LIEUT. R.A.F. LIDDLE left to be instructors R.A.F. transfer.	
	25th		Battalion rested in Bivouacs in Wood. CAPT. & ADJT. A.B. FALCONER returned from 1st Army Rest Camp. LIEUT. G.R. FENWICK from leave and 2nd LIEUT. G. SYME returned from XVII CORPS. Lewis Guns School. 23 O.R's rejoined Battalion from base details &c.	
	26th		A & B Coys were going to bed in the afternoon when sudden orders received for Battalion to relieve 2/8th WEST YORKS tonight in the line Battalion gun Coys & B marched out of camp at 4 p.m. in a downpour of rain. Some shelling of roads, but relief completed without mishap. Battalion in reserve and holding spur of FORET de la MONTAGNE de REIMS, which French had held successfully for 3 days although fairly isolated. Night quiet, but very wet.	
	27th		Quiet at dawn - Sunrise an operation with 62nd Division and French attacked at 6 a.m., but found enemy had withdrawn. Battalion kept in reserve but not used.	

(A7283) Wt. W869/M1672 350,000 4/17 Sch. 52a. Forms/C/2118/4

D. D. & L., London, E.C.

WAR DIARY or INTELLIGENCE SUMMARY

Army Form C. 2118.

Place	Date	Hour	Summary of Events and Information	Remarks and references to Appendices
1918				
	July 28th		Battalion attached under C.R.E. "C" Coy. working on road at NANTEUIL. Other Companies making quarters habitable. Good progress made to-day by "C" and ourselves. Enemy back's not even beyond their old line. Neither unsettled & considerable amount of rain. Echelon "B" and transport moved forward to NANTEUIL.	
	29th		Beautiful morning. "A" & "B" Companies engaged repairing track from BOIS de L'AVENAY to CHAUMUZY. "C" Coy. worked on road between CHAUMUZY to NAPPES.	
	30		"B" Coy. on railway. Machine guns and "C" across with lorries. River Coy Allies still making good progress. 2nd Lieut's P.A.F. LIDDLE and W.D. ARMSTRONG return from interview with R.A.F. officers.	
	31st		Battalion moves back to transport lines in BOIS de SARBRUGE, NANTEUIL.	

WAR DIARY or INTELLIGENCE SUMMARY

Army Form C. 2118.

Casualties during July 1918.

Officers:-

Killed in Action — 21.7.18
Lieut Jameson R.S.
Lieut Chisholm "   — 23.7.18
Lieut Gibson "   — 31.7.18

Died from wounds
received in action

Lieut Fairweather R.S. — 23.7.18
Lieut Lindsay 2/Lt   — 2.7.18 — Rec'd 6:1.7.18
1 — 19/7/18   — 2.7.18 — " 14.7.18
2/Lt Markay R.   — 2.7.18   " 14.7.16
2/Lt — 31.7.18   — 3.7.16
      "Rec'd Area"

Other Ranks:- Killed — 18
              Wounded — 63
              Missing — 3
              Died from wounds — 3
              2 shock cases — 6

Reinforcements
                    O/Ranks
Officers   1st
Nil.   27.7.18   14
                    4.7.18   4
                    5.7.18   25
                    11.7.18   14
                    25.7.18   14
                    Total   74

Strength at 31.7.18:- Officers — 38
                     Other Ranks — 791

1st August 1918.

W. Thorburn .... Colonel,
Comndg. 2/8 Bn. The Royal Scots. (Pioneers)

Confidential   TROOPS   1/8 BATTALION,
                                  ROYAL SCOTS
                                  (PIONEERS).

1/8th.Bn. The Royal Scots (Pioneers).

No. 656
7/8/18

Report on Operations commencing July, 21st.1918.

1918.
July,20th.   Battalion bivouaced in Wood one mile North of BELLEVUE, in the FORET de REIMS, due North of EPERNAY.

July,21st.   Orders were received at 4 a.m. for Battalion to move forward and take up a position in Woods just West of NANTEUIL. This was carried out in good time. The Battalion bivouaced in the BOIS de SARBRUGE, half a mile West of the Village of NANTEUIL. There were several casualties by shell fire on the march and also while Tool Wagons were being unloaded on the road which passes through BOIS de SARBRUGE, 2/Lieut.R.A.JAMESON being Killed and Lieut. A.McR.GORDON severely wounded.

July,22nd.   Orders having been received to send one company to the 154th. Inf.Brigade as supporting troops. "B"Company under Captain J.S.PRINGLE was sent in the morning and were attached to the 7th. Argyle & Sutherland Highlanders. First of all they were detailed to assist the R.Es, in cutting a path in the wood. This continued until mid-night when they received orders that they were to take part in an attack with the 154th. Infantry Brigade at 8 a.m. next morning. Remainder of the Battalion according to orders received, relieved the 6th.Gordon Highrs. in the line in the evening, in a position between two roads running through the BOIS de COURTON about 2,000 metres S.E. of ESPILLY.

July,23rd.   From Zero hour at 8 a.m. to 8 a.m. during the attack by the 154th.Brigade on right the enemy barrage came down on Battalion Headquarters. Battalion Headquarters withdrew further back in the course of the afternoon.
"B"Company with the 7th. A. & S.H. on their right and the 4th. Gordon Highrs. on their left attacked in a N.N.W. direction on a front of 250 yards. The objective was a Sunken Road 250 yards due South of ESPILLY a distance of about 500 yards from the jump off point.
The Company was subjected to an intense barrage and the two centre platoons were practically wiped out. The platoon on the right under 2/Lieut.R.P.FRASER and the one on the left under 2/Lieut.J.F.McD.CRAWFORD, however managed to push forward and ultimately the Company Commander Captain J.S.PRINGLE managed to get forward in the centre with a few stragglers. The platoons obtained their objective, captured two Machine Guns killed their crews, inflicted considerable losses on the enemy and captured 33 prisoners.
The troops on the right and left failed to advance and the position becoming untenable owing to sniping from the rear the survivors were forced to fight their way back.
Lieut. J.O.CHISHOLM was severely wounded and has since died.
2/Lieut. OLIVER was also severely wounded.

July,24th.   The remainder of the Battalion continued to hold that part of the line they had taken over.
The 153rd. Inf. Brigade, to which the Battalion was attached was relieved by the 35th.(French)Infantry Brigade. The Battalion withdrew to the wood just North of BELLEVUE and was then joined by "B"Company. Heavy Gassing, shelling and some Bombing of the woods, roads etc. took place during the relief.

July,25th.///

(2)

July, 25th.   Battalion rested in Bivouacs.

July, 26th.   The Battalion relieved the 2/8th. West Yorks.
               During the relief the roads were heavily shelled and the
               tracks through the woods gassed but the relief was carried
               out in good time.
               The Battalion was in reserve and held the spur of BOIS de
               COURTON to the East of POURCY.

July, 27th.   The Battalion was not required in this mornings successful
               attack by the Division.

July, 28th.   The Battalion was placed under orders the C.R.E. and
               "C" Company repaired the road North of NANTEUIL.

July, 29th.   Two companies cleared and made passable the side road from
               POURCY to CHAUMUSSY, bridging the swamp in the BOIS de
               L'AULNAY, this considerably relieving the traffic on the
               main road, which was constantly shelled. The third company
               under Captain G.H. BALLANTYNE repaired the road between
               NAPPES and CHANMUSSY giving immediate passage to the French
               Artillery.

July, 30th.   Battalion searched the woods for trophies and succeeded in
               salving a considerable number of enemy and our own Machine
               Guns.

July, 31st.   Battalion was relieved and returned to NANTEUIL.

    Casualties for Period July, 21st. to 31st. 1918.

    Officers - Killed in Action.
         2/Lieut. R.A. JAMESON.   21/7/18.

         Died from Wounds.
         Lieut. J.C. CHISHOLM.   23/7/18.

         Wounded.
         Lieut. A.McK. GORDON.   21/7/18.
         2/Lieut. J. OLIVER.   23/7/18.
    Other Ranks.

         Killed in Action.   =   21
         Died from Wounds   =   3
         Wounded.   =   82

                                              Lieut.-Colonel,
         Commanding 1/8th. Bn. The Royal Scots (Pioneers).

7th. August, 1918.

Army Form C. 2118.

WAR DIARY
or
INTELLIGENCE SUMMARY.
(Erase heading not required.)

Vol 4

39 R

CONFIDENTIAL

WAR DIARY

OF

1/8TH BN. THE ROYAL SCOTS. (PIONEERS).

FROM

1ST AUGUST 1918 to 31ST AUGUST 1918.

VOLUME No. 46.

Army Form C. 2118.

WAR DIARY
or
INTELLIGENCE SUMMARY.
(Erase heading not required.)

Instructions regarding War Diaries and Intelligence Summaries are contained in F. S. Regs., Part II. and the Staff Manual respectively. Title pages will be prepared in manuscript.

Place	Date	Hour	Summary of Events and Information	Remarks and references to Appendices
	1918			
NANTEUIL	August 1st		Division being relieved Battalion marched by way of HAUTVILLERS and EPERNAY to PIERRY where they billeted for the night. Weather tropical, but men marched well.	
	2nd		Battalion continued march through CUIS, CRAMANT, AVIZE to MESNIL le OGER. Weather cooler and showery. Everyone in good spirits.	
	3rd		Battalion marched back to AVIZE and entrained for new area. Left at 8 p.m. and travelled by way of ZEZANNE and PARIS which was passed about midnight.	
	4th		Journey continued by way of NOYELLES, TREPORT, and ST. POL to PERNES, where Battalion detrained shortly before midnight.	
	5th		Waiting buses conveyed Battalion to BILLETS at ESTRÉE CAUCHIE which was reached at 4 a.m. After late reveille remainder of day devoted to cleaning up and inspections. 2/Lieut. GILLESPIE gave to Machine Gun Corps as transport officer.	
	6th		Battalion re-organising and commenced training. Billets good and men comfortable. Lieuts. RICHARDSON and DAVIDSON returned from courses, and Lieut. RITCHIE proceeded on course at ROUEN. Divisional General called informally & expressed gratification with Battalion in recent operations.	
	7th		Training of Battalion continues much anticipating rumours. Beautiful day.	

Army Form C. 2118.

WAR DIARY
or
INTELLIGENCE SUMMARY.
(Erase heading not required.)

Place	Date	Hour	Summary of Events and Information	Remarks and references to Appendices
	1918 August 8th		His Majesty the King passed through ESTREE CAUCHIE. Battalion lined road.	
	9th		CAPT. A.C. HARRISON, 2ND LIEUT. G.E. YOUNG, M.C., and a draft of 58 joined Batt. Training proceeding.	
			CAPT. TAIT, and 2ND LIEUT. HOWIE reported from Cambrai, and 2ND LIEUT. A. MACKAY from leave. Draft of 45 arrived. Shrivel made of unsuccessful advance party 2ND D.L.S.R. Battalion training.	
	10th		Training continues. 2ND LIEUT. GRAHAM returned from hospital.	
	11th		Beautiful day. Church Parade. 12 reinforcements joined Battalion.	
	12th		C.O. attends all day lecture by Inspector General of Training. Battalion training.	
	13th		Word received of projected move to forward area. Orders for further orders. Drawing clothing. Buried (mother of after holding them in) on 2nd Front (Western).	
	14th		Bath for Company were arranged as has to be postponed owing to light moving orders. Having prevented arrival. Continue training.	
	15th		Beautiful day. Battalion sports were held in the afternoon. Much interest was shown which were very successful. Large numbers of	

Army Form C. 2118.

WAR DIARY
or
INTELLIGENCE SUMMARY.
(Erase heading not required.)

Instructions regarding War Diaries and Intelligence Summaries are contained in F. S. Regs., Part II. and the Staff Manual respectively. Title pages will be prepared in manuscript.

Place	Date	Hour	Summary of Events and Information	Remarks and references to Appendices
	1918 August 15th		Battalion in rest camp. Coys carrying on ordinary training.	
			N.E. huge raid for three days seen from rear of the Salient wide front 5	
			miles pushing from the shores of the First Sweep to the south of Ypres	
	16		Bn. moved to Bokeck camp. Relieved a platoon 8th Q & Shks.	
			Divl. Hqrs transport offrs. arrived at Camp. The 6 Bgd. have left	
			Bn. Cookhouse to the rear. Bn. cookhouse relieved by	
			transport to Elpinghand at that MISSORBOY y 6th Bgde arrived	
	17		10 Bn. Royal Irish Rgt. at HAZEBROT Bn. arrived by bus & marched	
			Battalion marched into camp & commenced training	
			ESTREE CAUCHIE. ECURIE SIDING were reached about down. Bn. then	
			detrained & marched to billets in FLANDERS Gds. division on Riencourt	
	18th		B Coy of four sections to BLANG POST & A Coy for y to 25 Bgd on	
			CHEMIN CREUX Roadway	
	19th		B Coy & gun work takes over A 16 on Railway	

Army Form C. 2118.

WAR DIARY
or
INTELLIGENCE SUMMARY.
(Erase heading not required.)

Instructions regarding War Diaries and Intelligence
Summaries are contained in F. S. Regs., Part II.
and the Staff Manual respectively. Title pages
will be prepared in manuscript.

Place	Date	Hour	Summary of Events and Information	Remarks and references to Appendices
	1918 August 20		Battalion moved to Rutherford Camp where Lieut Col b [illegible] and Regimental staff were billetted for the night. A Coy Sherwood Regiment was [illegible]	
ST CATHERINE				
	21		View Rifle to day. County officers went and [illegible] to Coy. [illegible] A gun with 2 N.C.O.s and Bren Gun team [illegible] came to [illegible] for [illegible] [illegible] formed relief of O/R. Brigade D/N. [illegible] + E/Pm Battn	
	22		Draft of 10 O.R. arrived. Strike of troops [illegible]	
	23		[illegible] billeted by G.O. Commanding. John's Post. Court [illegible] no interest	
	24		2 coys relieved B & C Brigade Post. A Coy took over [illegible] left and a [illegible] on right the line. Life [illegible] the [illegible] exchanges on a day to day basis.	
	25		Enemy Action from our side cutting to B. there were gun fire on Cantonment or inf C.O. took over Camp issued in Orders to dispose of a platoon [illegible] issued. O. & D. Coy worn by [illegible] more 11 struck to Km.	
	26		Division standard [illegible] to [illegible] mountain [illegible]	

Army Form C. 2118.

WAR DIARY
or
INTELLIGENCE SUMMARY.
(Erase heading not required.)

Instructions regarding War Diaries and Intelligence Summaries are contained in F.S. Regs., Part II. and the Staff Manual respectively. Title pages will be prepared in manuscript.

Place	Date	Hour	Summary of Events and Information	Remarks and references to Appendices
	1918			
	August 26		Went out shortly after ZERO & two runners were sent from "A" HQtrs & B platoon	
			with the of TAMPOUX. B Coy. sent out at night a fighting patrol	
			with "B" in Signature trench moved up to WASHING WORKS. Did not reach	
	27		"C Company" in general area of TAMPOUX near E. Canadian Coy HQrs. our patrols reached	
			RAILWAY LINE & OSIER dump — unoccupied.	
			GREENLAND HILL. B Company moved from P.25.d to ROEUX - TRENCH	
			Good news from front lines.	
	28		Two Platoons of "B" Coy. oppose BORDER LANE. 2 Platoons of "A" Coy had	
			tracts to POINT DU JOUR. 2 C Coy. TAMPOUX – FRESNES Road for a distance	
			of 2 kilometres – a good day's work.	
	29		Good news of continued success NORTH and SOUTH of BAPAUME &	
			on our own front. B Company stair while of NORTHUMBERLAND LANE	
			up to GAVRELLE. "A" & "B" Coys went forward just after ZERO hour made	
			strong points in WINDMILL & COOPER trenches. Casualties – 2 men wounded	
			enemy barrage was fairly heavy but erratic.	

Army Form C. 2118.

WAR DIARY
or
INTELLIGENCE SUMMARY.
(Erase heading not required.)

Place	Date	Hour	Summary of Events and Information	Remarks and references to Appendices
	August 30th		During night 29/30 2 Platoons "A" Coy. went up to wire strong point at COPPER locality. The other two Platoons continued advance Bye on No 8 L.O. "C" Company engaged in hand and rest track from ARRAS-LENS Railway Cratevate. B: No Que moved to ORANGE POST. "B" Coy to position just south of POINT DU JOUR.	
	31		"C" Coy. Curting sup for 30/31 st. Continuous construction of wiring point at WINDMILL COPSE. Two Platoons of "A" Coy. wire COPPER Strong Point. During day of 31 st. "B" Coy thrust on road through CHEMICAL WORKS and rail track.	

Army Form C. 2118.

WAR DIARY
or
INTELLIGENCE SUMMARY.
(Erase heading not required.)

Casualties during August 1918.

Officers - Nil
Other Ranks :
Killed in Action = 1
Wounded in Action = 7

On leave - Front Lyne
2nd Lieut Hodgson E. 27/8/18   7/Lt Mackay A. 27/1/18
Lieut Young M.G.M.S. 3/8/18
2nd Lieut White J. 16.8.18
2nd Lieut White G. 16.8.18

To Hospital - Sick - 7/Lt R.P. Grant 17.8.18
To Hospital - Gas - 80 Other Ranks

Reinforcements

	Officers		Other Ranks	
	Major Longmore N.H.S. 0.80	27/8/18	79	9/8/18
	Capt. Harrison a.t.	3/8/18	11	19/8/18
	2nd Lieut Young R.S.A.C	8/8/18	29	11/8/18
			14	21/8/18
			3	
			134	

Strength at 31.8.18   Officers = 38
                      Other Ranks = 845

1st September 1918.

[signature]
MAJOR
Commdg 1/5th Bn The Royal Scots (Pioneers)

Army Form C. 2118.

WAR DIARY
OF
INTELLIGENCE SUMMARY.
(Erase heading not required.)

F/51. 9/11 43

CONFIDENTIAL.

WAR DIARY
OF
1/8TH BN. THE ROYAL SCOTS (PIONEERS)
FROM
1ST SEPTEMBER 1918 TO 30TH SEPTEMBER 1918.

VOLUME No 4.

Place	Date	Hour	Summary of Events and Information	Remarks and references to Appendices

Army Form C. 2118.

WAR DIARY
or
INTELLIGENCE SUMMARY.
(Erase heading not required.)

Place	Date	Hour	Summary of Events and Information	Remarks and references to Appendices
FAMPOUX	1918 Sept 1st		Battalion continues work of pushing forward roads and begins writing Line of Resistance	
		2nd	"A" Coy continues making of strong point at WINDMILL COPSE. "C" Coy push forward FAMPOUX – FRESNES road as far as INN CROSS ROADS, and "B" Coy continue making of track for the gunners and roads. 1 N.C.O. killed and 2 men wounded.	
		3rd	Companies continue work on Line of Resistance. Working parties on roads.	
		4th	" "	Considerable amount of shelling of a.m.
		5th	"A" Coy busy digging new position for Line of Resistance South of PLOUVAIN road and in front of HAUSA WOOD. "B" Coy complete repair of road from ROEUX to CHEMICAL WORKS. "C" Coy engaged wiring. LIEUT. RITCHIE returns from course at ROUEN.	
		6th	Companies continue work. C.O. returns from Leave. 2/LIEUT. Hon. R.B. WATSON returned from leave.	
		7th	CAPT. A.C. HARRISON goes to join 4th ROYAL SCOTS. Companies experience considerable amount of shelling and gassing at work, otherwise things continuing as usual.	
		8th	Nothing of special interest.	
		9th	"D" Coy complete fairweather track from RAILWAY BRIDGE on ARRAS – LENS railway to INN CROSS ROADS beyond FAMPOUX. "C" Coy continue wiring and "A" Coy digging new trench in front of HAUSA WOOD	

Place	Date	Hour	Summary of Events and Information	Remarks and references to Appendices
	1918 Sept	10th	Bad weather interrupted work somewhat. Nothing of special interest.	
	"	11th	Word received that Division is being relieved by 49th (W.R.) Division on 13th inst. Companies continue work as usual.	
	"	12th	Captain J.W. Watson reports Bath. from leave after nearly a year's absence. Draft of 13 O.R. comes from Base. Companies finish working on this area.	
		13th	Bath. marches by road via Mont St Eloi and Chamblain l'Abbé to CAMBLIGNEUL where they bivouac in fairly comfortable quarters. News of great American success in the St Michel Salient.	
		14th	Bath. re-organizing billing & cleaning up. Lieut W.E. Young D.S.O went to Military Course Kent Contr. recruits from there.	
		15th	Bath. marches via CAUCOURT & SAVOIN LE-GALE. Bivouac nr. Bruit a little around ten a pleasant village.	
		16th	Bath. regains training. NCO's class formed.	
		17/8	Training continues	
			do	
		19	do	

WAR DIARY
or
INTELLIGENCE SUMMARY.
(Erase heading not required.)

Army Form C. 2118.

Place	Date	Hour	Summary of Events and Information	Remarks and references to Appendices
	1918 Sept.			
		20	Batt marches via ESTREE CAUCHIE and MAISNIL BOUCHE to CHATEAU de LA HAIE. Billets in Nissen Huts at CANADA CAMP. Baggage down next Base.	
	"	21	Batt walked intercept training. Draft of 10 Officers joined from Base.	
		22	Sunday. Church Parade. Boxing tournament during afternoon.	
		23	Batt marches over VILLERS au BOIS, MONT ST ELOY, ECURIE, ROCLINCOURT to area in the nearer immediately North of SCARPE, leaving 19th (Western) Division (49th Division) Batt bivouacs without incident	
	"	24	Coys upon work. 1 Coy. working on Railway between FARBUS & ROEUX. Remainder B Coy on ROEUX BROWN ROAD and widening a coy. Rack. Draft of 15 OR joined from Base. Went various kit. 2nd Brit. Crusade of PALESTINE reported.	
		25	11 OR moved to kick in Tour J ATHIES. All 3 Companies working between road and railway. No officer of interest.	
		26	New RADOPhue joined up to 20 Coy on Reiss affair.	
		27	Working of above in read.	
		28	Lieut (act Capt) W.E.G Lawn promoted N Coy Infantry & Chara.	

WAR DIARY
or
INTELLIGENCE SUMMARY

Army Form C. 2118.

Place	Date	Hour	Summary of Events and Information	Remarks and references to Appendices
	Sept. 28		News of our success in Palestine heard of. "C" Company further work on trench & dugouts on ROEUX - PLOUVAIN Road. "B" continues work on PLOUVAIN Road. "A" at work on the railway.	
	29		Success on all fronts continues. No Batt. news of General interest.	
	30		Bulgaria surrenders unconditionally. Fine advances east of YPRES & on the right between CAMBRAI and ST. QUENTIN. A wonderful month of progress ends.	

Army Form C. 2118.

WAR DIARY
or
INTELLIGENCE SUMMARY.
(Erase heading not required.)

Instructions regarding War Diaries and Intelligence Summaries are contained in F. S. Regs., Part II. and the Staff Manual respectively. Title pages will be prepared in manuscript.

Place	Date	Hour	Summary of Events and Information	Remarks and references to Appendices
			[Illegible handwritten entries — faded pencil]	

[Signature] W. Thorburn
Commanding 16th Bn. The Royal Scots (Pioneers)

Appendix IX   Diary.

S E C R E T

51st Divisional Artillery OPERATION ORDER No:152.

Map Reference:-   27th August-1918.
   51B, N.W., 1/20,000.

1. The 154th Infantry Brigade will carry out an operation to-morrow the 29th instant to capture the line of CLOD TRENCH to I.15.a.3.6, thence to I.9.c.15.15, and thence along WALK and WILLOW Trenches to WHISPER Trench.

2. This attack will be covered by the 255th, 256th, 177th and 180th Brigades R.F.A., and the 2nd Canadian Brigade R.G.A.

3. The attached tracing shows the mean point of impact of the 18-pdr barrage and the times of lifting off. The tracing shows the 1st and 2nd objectives by GREEN CROSSES. The protective barrages are the lines C.1 - C. and F.

4. On final protective barrage 255th Brigade R.F.A. will take the Northern portion from I.8.b.8.9 to the North, 256th Bde R.F.A. from last-named place to the railway; RIGHT GROUP from the railway southwards to I.20.b.6.4.

5. The 4.5" hows. will fire as follows, in all cases keeping 200 yards ahead of the 18-pdr barrage.

D/255 will cover the lane of the 180th Brigade R.F.A. until Zero plus 20, when they will resume their place in the barrage on their lane.

D/180, with 4 hows., will fire on the railway cutting at I.14.b. 50.85 till Zero plus 10, when they will lift on to the two small copses and MILL on the railway at I.14.b.6.9, I.8.d.7.0 and I.8.a. 80.05 till Zero plus 20, after which it will concentrate on trenches and trench junctions in its own lane beyond the line E. - E. until Zero plus 70, when it will lift on to all approaches east of the final protective barrage in its own lane.

D/177, with 4 hows., will take part in the barrage in its own lane, lifting for the final protective barrage on to all approaches from the east including the western exits from PLOUVAIN.

The remaining two hows. of D/180 and D/177 will enfilade the railway cutting, beginning at I.14.b.50.85 eastwards, remaining on this task till the end of the barrage.

D/256, from Zero to conclusion of protective barrage, will put down a smoke screen along the ROEUX - PLOUVAIN Road from I.20.b.5.9 to I.15.b.3.2.

6. The 2nd Canadian Brigade R.G.A. have been asked to carry out the following tasks.

Bombard HAUSA and DELBAR Woods, the low ground and approaches to the south and east of them, the western exits from PLOUVAIN, the railway from I.9.d.9.4 eastwards to the FRESNES line, and the FRESNES line on whole Divisional front.

P.T.O.-

7. Rates of Fire will be
Zero to Zero plus 15   RAPID.
Zero plus 15 to Zero plus 25   NORMAL.
Zero plus 25 to Zero plus 30   RAPID.
Zero plus 30 to Zero plus 40   NORMAL.
Zero plus 40 to Zero plus 70   SLOW.
Zero plus 70 to Zero plus 80   NORMAL.
Zero plus 80 onwards   SLOW.

8. The 18-pdr barrage will be A, except when crossing organized trench systems, when it will be 50 per cent. AX-106, and on protective barrage, when it will be all AX-106.

A corrector will be chosen calculated to give one burst in three on graze.

Hows., less D/256, HX-106.   D/256, BS.

9. Right Group will ensure that the inner flanks of the two Brigades overlap sufficiently to ensure the railway being enfiladed during the whole operation.

10. As the Infantry on either flank of the barrage zone have been withdrawn to 200 yards north and south of it respectively, the greatest care will be taken that all fire is put down within the flank limits of the barrage zone as shown in the tracing.

11. All Brigades will send forward F.O.Os. Liaison and O.Ps will be as usual.

12. Synchronization by telephone.
13. Zero Hour will be 6.30 a.m.
14. ACKNOWLEDGE BY WIRE.

James C. Duffus
Major R.F.A.
A/ Brigade Major, 51st Divisional Arty.

Copies to— 255 Bde RFA   (5)   51 Div.G. (1)
           256 "   "   "   152 Inf Bde (2)
           177 "   "   "   154 "   " (15)
           180 "   "   "   Can.Corps R.A. (1)
               2 Can.Bde.RGA (4) Office (1)
                                 Diary (2)

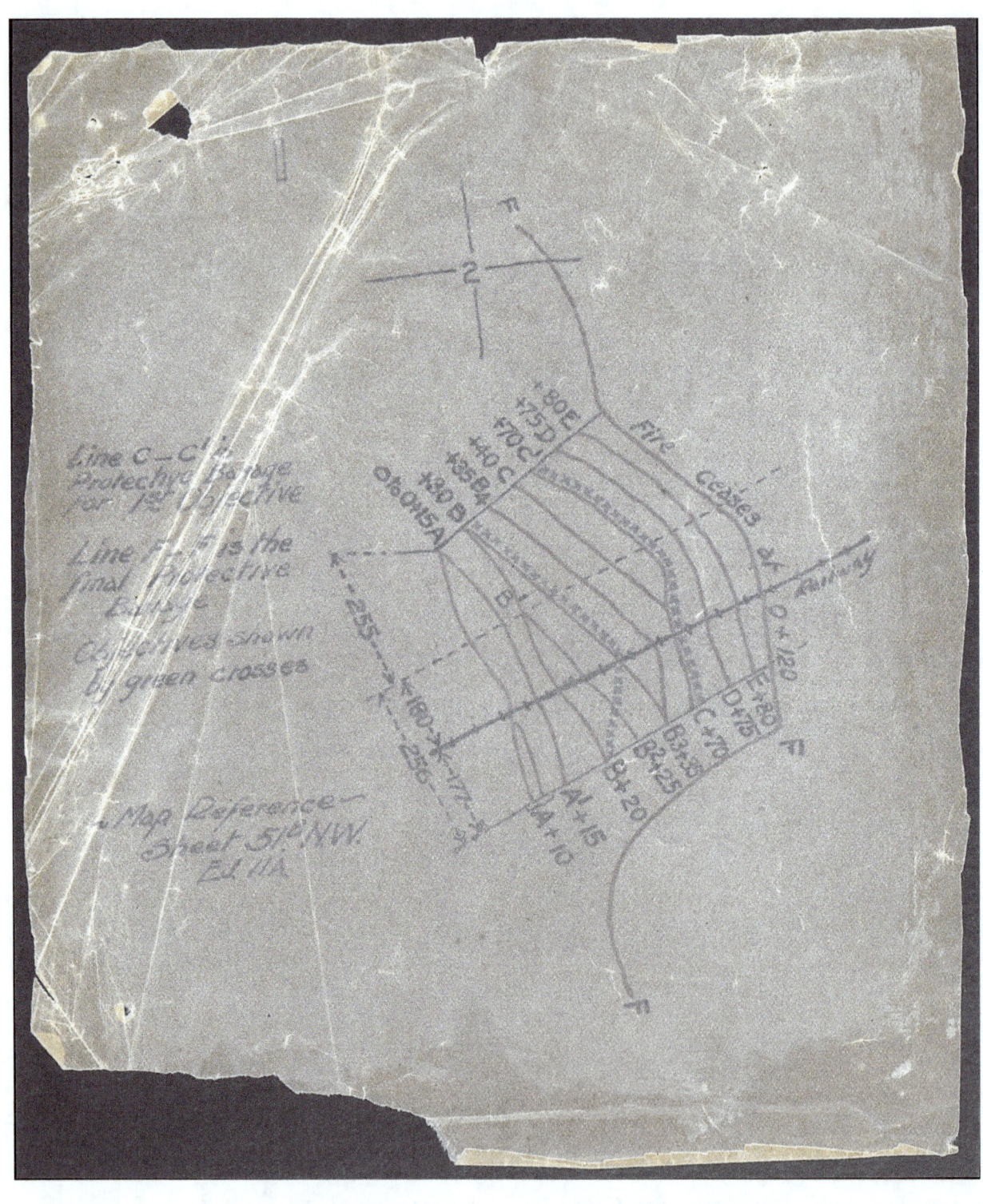

On His Majesty's Service.

War Diary —
8th Royal Scots
October 1918

Army Form C. 2118.

WWI 44

WAR DIARY
or
INTELLIGENCE SUMMARY.

(Erase heading not required.)

CONFIDENTIAL

WAR DIARY
of
1/8th Bn. THE ROYAL SCOTS (PIONEERS)
from
1st OCTOBER 1918 to 31st OCTOBER 1918

VOLUME No. 48

Army Form C. 2118.

WAR DIARY
or
INTELLIGENCE SUMMARY.
(Erase heading not required.)

Place	Date	Hour	Summary of Events and Information	Remarks and references to Appendices
Inch	Oct 1st	1918	Work proceeds that Divisional Training reviews by the 8th Divisional Draft of 1st R.I. joined Battalion from Base. Capt. J. Young resigned the appointment of District Salvage Officer and rejoined Battalion. 2nd Lieutenant Cotter was now acting as Divl Salvage Officer.	
	2nd		Nothing of special interest. Training is most	
	3rd		Battalion moved by roads to CELLAR CAMP NEUVILLE ST VAAST. Billets in Nets. Rails comfortable. Lieut Roomes with "C" Coy with the Young R.S.M.C. Pte O.S. and Rev. J.O. Little Q.S.T. Coy to Coy left to join 1/4th & Royal Scots Battalion School Brigade Scoot last 30.9.18 Nothing into Capt Lyle to goes to sir	
	4th		Conference re organizing Companies. Divisional Baden Powell Team Kent Coy officials useful	
	5th		3rd Dist D.A.C. Coys to Goods to sir	
	6th		Church Parade. Capt. Barclay rejoins Bn after course at 1st Army Infantry School. Battalion Football Leaf Kent 30 K.R.R. Nges No 2 Coys to sir. Bn proceeds the Division moves to CAMBRAI sector.	

WAR DIARY
or
INTELLIGENCE SUMMARY.

Army Form C. 2118.

Place	Date	Hour	Summary of Events and Information	Remarks and references to Appendices
In the Field	Oct 1918 7th		Orders for most. On right our two front Battalions Consols over ten as whole across from 2nd/3rd Northants hips considerably.	
	8th		Chasing rear of Continual enemy all along the line. Battalion enbussed at NEUVILLE ST VAAST (after a 2 hours) went returners by way of ARRAS Cambrai Road BUSSY to area just north of PRONVILLE where some pickets about 22 hours but everything until 5 in early - Battalion quietly until dawn on this Bourne shite.	
	9th		CAMBRAI invaded - taken by Canadian XVII Corps without Casualties. Battalion hips for night bivouac. Headquarters of Battalion entrained in part of the DURANT trench of the HINDENBURG LINE.	
	10th		Battalion left at 13 hours onwards via INCHY-en-ARTOIS & MOEUVRES to trained autobm. this turns out to be an old ground about 2 kilometre West of BOURLON VILLAGE, but thanks to the Compy. Officers taking the Battalion a short cut, it arrived in time to make itself normally comfortable and Barricas Shelb the night passed without incident	

Army Form C. 2118.

WAR DIARY
or
INTELLIGENCE SUMMARY.
(Erase heading not required.)

Place	Date	Hour	Summary of Events and Information	Remarks and references to Appendices
June	Nov 1918			
	11th		Orders received from Division that Batt. moves forward this afternoon. Moves off at 15 hours but progress through BOURLON VILLAGE was slow owing to traffic. Darkness came upon before CANTAING was reached. The traffic at junction of ARRAS and BAPAUME Roads caused a Blockade without control. After strenuous effort by the County Officer in regulating the traffic the Battalion eventually got through again up hours of strenuous waiting. Eventually the night was quiet & the Batt. reached its appointed point in Battalion bivouacs in the open about a kilometre south of the DOIGNT Road.	
	12th		Morning broke fine with quite a number of enemy people moving about. Battalion had more moves off at 5.30 hours to ESCAUDOEUVRES on North East out-skirt of CAMBRAI where 2/Lieut M.A. Armstrong and party moved & billets in houses. "C" Coy went out in the afternoon & repair road from ESCAUDOEUVRES to IWUY. Battalion again moves this morning to vicinity of THUN ST.MARTIN.	
	13th		Guards those however too enemy to comply so comp. officer went Battalion	

Army Form C. 2118.

WAR DIARY
or
INTELLIGENCE SUMMARY.
(Erase heading not required.)

Instructions regarding War Diaries and Intelligence Summaries are contained in F. S. Regs., Part II. and the Staff Manual respectively. Title pages will be prepared in manuscript.

Place	Date	Hour	Summary of Events and Information	Remarks and references to Appendices
Bures	Oct 1918 13th		Is a switched front about 1 kilometre South West of Iwuy at	
			Iwuy. Half the men were used in repairing front line as a temporary trench.	
	14th		"B" Coy. moved into billets Iwuy–Rieux Road. Arrivals - 4 other ranks are still ungummedly debate. 5 of the officers and 2nd Lt. Bagatt who return to Battalion.	
	15th		Companies continue with Battn. H.Q. moved to a Railway Siding	
	16th		Very wet night. Companies are a bit uncomfortable in this "immense quarters" or concealment. Companies continue work. "B" Company are filled short of Map references owing to recent engagements of "C" Coy.	
	17th		Allied Air Force aeroplane activity & great successes in Flanders. Coy on as usual.	
	18th		Bugler appeared. Further progress in the battle zone sound of Q UENTIN. The thing of great Batt. arrived.	
	19th		Companies continue routine exposure "C" Coy. moved up to AVENSNES-SEC.	

Army Form C. 2118.

WAR DIARY
or
INTELLIGENCE SUMMARY.
(Erase heading not required.)

Instructions regarding War Diaries and Intelligence Summaries are contained in F. S. Regs., Part II. and the Staff Manual respectively. Title pages will be prepared in manuscript.

Place	Date	Hour	Summary of Events and Information	Remarks and references to Appendices
	Aug 1918 19th		[illegible] in the morning and alarms known through the billets	
	20th		Battn moves up to AVESNES-LE-SEC. "B" Battery not at AVESNES ROAD.	
			"B" Company under 2/Lt I. WAY - AVESNES LE-SEC. Rear of "C" Coy 16 men. Manual the wings. Game progress made for the [illegible] by 3 wiring on our left.	
	21st		"B" Coy to [illegible] out in [illegible] - VALENCIENNES Road to [illegible] at DOUCHY	
			VAULCHIN [illegible] "C" Coy attack [illegible] on VAULCHIN Road and [illegible] DOUCHY in the morning "B" Coy moved to POVG ON [illegible] [illegible] [illegible] "A" & "C" Coys joined "B" Coy at DOUCHY. Wiring parties continue work on [illegible] in rest of "B" in company HQ built up and [illegible] to HQ Bn. Capt G T HARVEY joined B.	
	22nd		"C" Coy began work on Causeway Railway Bridge and tonight "B" Coy made on to Road "A" Coy repairing Culvert B 58m/4[illegible] Bridge at DOUCHY.	
	23rd		Division attacks this morning in cooperation with IV Division on right continued "C" Coy continue on Bridge. "A" Coy take over	
			MPING Culvert. "E" Coy	

Army Form C. 2118.

WAR DIARY
or
INTELLIGENCE SUMMARY.
(Erase heading not required.)

Instructions regarding War Diaries and Intelligence Summaries are contained in F.S. Regs., Part II. and the Staff Manual respectively. Title pages will be prepared in manuscript.

Place	Date	Hour	Summary of Events and Information	Remarks and references to Appendices
THIANT	Oct. 1918			
	26th		In the afternoon, Major R.F. Grant M.C. 9th D.L.I. took over command. Out-post precautions on order being commenced.	
	27th		Divisional attack against this morning. Division carried with all Our morning. Cpl. Irving a Lewis Sgt. Medcalf. Mr. R. McIntyre 2 Lt. Hopkins - Coy. S.M. was from Durance S/B Lieut. A.E.D. Redward joined Battalion from 2nd Corps Sch. & 8 O.R. return to & n.e. men. 2nd Lts. M—— & H. from Reserve Bn. at the motor transport driving ration's Transport being sent to THIANT. "B" Coy working on roads from THIANT to HONNOR roads THIANT.	
			Work continued on Railway bridge roads.	
	28		Roads more Railway near THIANT cleared to get into THIANT. "D" Coy moved to from THIANT through RAIMS to ——, bringing France. Great comfort afforded to Troops during the Weather during that time. "C" Coy working on Road MAING & Divisional Laundry transport WORKING	
	29		Divisional relieved by Canadian Division moving to	

WAR DIARY
or
INTELLIGENCE SUMMARY.
(Erase heading not required.)

Army Form C. 2118.

Place	Date	Hour	Summary of Events and Information	Remarks and references to Appendices
Bois de...	28		Centre arm. inspected by C.O. Under gunfire.	
		3 pm	A Company working on road LA PYRAMID to DEGOUTIN to THIANT and B Company on road THIANT to MONCHAUX. "C" Coy. working by two platoons in strong points. Railway bridge at QUERENAING - THIANT Road B.W.	
			nightly continues.	
	31st		Companies working on cliffs under R.E. during Ranger Railway Bridge on QUERENAING - THIANT Road. Divisional troops work on Truly road. Weather bad weather. Rest of Austr in training from reserve.	

1st November 1918

Army Form C. 2118.

WAR DIARY
or
INTELLIGENCE SUMMARY.
(Erase heading not required.)

Instructions regarding War Diaries and Intelligence Summaries are contained in F. S. Regs., Part II. and the Staff Manual respectively. Title pages will be prepared in manuscript.

Place	Date	Hour	Summary of Events and Information	Remarks and references to Appendices

SECRET

1/8th. Bn. The Royal Scots (Pioneers).

REPORT ON OPERATIONS Commencing 11/12th October 1918.

October 11th. On the night of the 10th. the Battalion had bivouaced 2 Kilometres West of BOURLON WOOD. On the 11th. orders were received to move forward to the western outskirts of CAMBRAI, a distance of about 9 Kilometres. The Battalion moved off at 15.00 hours but owing to congestion of traffic, progress was very slow and destination was not reached until 22.00 hours. The Battalion bivouaced in the open in the neighbourhood of NEUVILLE St.REMI.

" 12th. Battalion moved to ESCAUDOEUVRES at 08.00 hours and went into billets in Northern end of Village. One Company cleared and repaired ESCAUDOEUVRES - IWUY Road.

" 13th. Battalion moved to THUN ST.MARTIN but as there was no accomodation in the village, the day was spent making shelters in T.10.d. Two Companies were employed on IWUY-AVESNES-le-SEC and IWUY-LIEU ST.AMAND Roads.

" 14th. Battalion remained in Bivouacs - Southwest of IWUY and
19th. continued work on forward roads. The AVESNES-le-SEC Road was made fit for Motor traffic up to within ¼ a mile of the village. A destroyed bridge at T.6.c.2.0. on IWUY-RIEUX Road was cleared and road opened for Motor traffic in three days. Continuous shifts were worked and the C.E. Corps complimented the Battalion on the rapidity with which the work had been completed.

" 19th. On the evening of the 19th. one Company was ordered to move
20th. to AVESNES-le-SEC and make good roads through the village. Roads were ready for Motor traffic by dawn the 20th.

" 20th. The Battalion moved to AVESNES-le-SEC and commenced work on PAVE-de-VALENCIENNES - DOUCHY and AVESNES-NOYELLES-DOUCHY Roads. Main roads generally found in fair condition, but a considerable amount of heavy work on craters at X roads.

" 22nd. On the 22nd. Battalion moved to DOUCHY and cleared roads
1st.Nov. forward up to the R. ESCAILLON. All roads through THIANT leading to bridges were cleared and open for traffic on the 24th. The obstruction caused by collapsed bridge at J.15.c.0.5. involved a great deal of work. Continuous shifts of two Platoons were worked and by the 28th. it was open for two way Motor traffic.

On the 24th. roads east of the River were reconnoitred and on subsequent days were repaired between THIANT & MAING, MONCHAUX & MAING, MAING & QUEREMAING.

" 29th. On the 29th. the Division was relieved and work was handed over to 49th. Division, the Battalion, however, was detailed for work under Corps, and parties of 2 Platoons were provided on continuous shifts to assist 401 Coy. R.E. to clear destroy-ed bridge at K.20.d.9.1. This work was taken over by 50th. Division on the 1st. November and on the 2nd. the Battalion moved back to ESTRUN.

During the period work was frequently interfered with by shell fire, more especially gas shelling, but parties were generally able to "switch" and continue work beyond zones.

Casualties for period 11/12th to 28/29th. October 1918.

Officers :- NIL
Other Ranks :-
Died from Injuries.

W.Thorburn
Lieut.-Colonel,
Comdg., 1/8th. Bn. The Royal Scots (Pioneers).

5/11/18

Army Form C. 2118.

WAR DIARY
or
INTELLIGENCE SUMMARY.
(Erase heading not required.)

Vol 45

42 RS

CONFIDENTIAL

WAR DIARY

OF

1/8th Bn THE ROYAL SCOTS (PIONEERS)

From

1st November 1918 to 30th November 1918

VOLUME 49

WAR DIARY or INTELLIGENCE SUMMARY.

Army Form C. 2118.

(Erase heading not required.)

Instructions regarding War Diaries and Intelligence Summaries are contained in F. S. Regs., Part II, and the Staff Manual respectively. Title pages will be prepared in manuscript.

Place	Date	Hour	Summary of Events and Information	Remarks and references to Appendices
	November 1918			
	1st		Battalion employed off work on roads and on Railway Bridge across	
AVESNES-LE-TOMARS Road			Events were made by Civilians and refugees on our front.	
	2nd		Battalion moved at 0800 hours to ESTRUN by cross country roads the Rly &	
			Bridge of H.Q.6 St HERAND being still out of it. Though bridging in	
			the village badly damaged men were very probably able to cross on	
			foot men in front Column having built bridges for Battalion on to	
			arrived at 10 o'clock. Much trouble was had in finding	
			Billets.	
	3rd		Battalion further employed in improving of billets. Service sent.	
	4th		Battalion warned for a forced day. With no billets arrived [?]	
			accommodation front in village no short notice for Bn and Stores	
			of 3rd Cavalry Brigade who crossed at the same [?]	
			rumour.	
	5th		Battalion marched to PAILLENCOURT, they arriving at about 18.15	
			where billets were found by Divisional Staff Officers Accommodation	

Instructions regarding War Diaries and Intelligence Summaries are contained in F. S. Regs., Part II. and the Staff Manual respectively. Title pages will be prepared in manuscript.

WAR DIARY
or
INTELLIGENCE SUMMARY.
(Erase heading not required.)

Army Form C. 2118.

Place	Date	Hour	Summary of Events and Information	Remarks and references to Appendices
	November 5th cont'd		visited the village and expressed great satisfaction with work that was being done in billets. Official confirmation received of signing Armistice with Austria.	
	6th		Companies engaged in preparing billets in village and hall in village cleaned out [illegible] accommodation for 500 persons made. Companies do 1 hours close order drill before proceeding to work. Lieut J.J.C. Henderson joined Battalion from Base. Very wet day.	
	7th		Companies continued work on billets and A Company commenced work on two footbridges across canal. A party of 10 [illegible] [illegible] from the Battalion formed part of the detachment (Divisional) attending a ceremonial parade in PLACE DAME VALENCIENNES [illegible] when the MAIRE and municipal council thanked the British Army for the liberation of the town. The Divisional Band played selections at the football match this afternoon.	
	8th		Improvement of billets in village continues but weather very wet	

D. D. & L., London, E.C.
(A7883) Wt. W509/M1672 350,000 4/17 Sch. 52a Forms C/2118/14

WAR DIARY
or
INTELLIGENCE SUMMARY

Army Form C. 2118.

Place	Date	Hour	Summary of Events and Information	Remarks and references to Appendices
	November 1918			
			[illegible handwritten entries, largely faded]	
			Disquiet amongst German Army noticed from R.E.3 sources...	
			...Base...	
			Aircraft spirit set...	
			Gloriously fine day. R.T.C. companies working on bookings...	
			...short empl. as use B. or fields entered into from...	
			Ground 1st Army infantry school Kay R.M. meeting in a room at...	
			X'mas Divisional	
	10th		Much time spent in interviews for the Commanding Officer.	
			Gave a lecture on the Present State and how circumstances...	
			Austria + Hungary, ... Britain	
			... ... when the British Fleet left a year or...	
			Draft Lectures Reports by ... Col. ...	
	11th		Telegram received that Armistice with Germany agreed and hostilities would cease at 1100 hours. Has guns and was given out to the Brigadier and a Holiday proclaimed.	

Army Form C. 2118.

WAR DIARY
or
INTELLIGENCE SUMMARY.
(Erase heading not required.)

Instructions regarding War Diaries and Intelligence Summaries are contained in F. S. Regs., Part II. and the Staff Manual respectively. Title pages will be prepared in manuscript.

Place	Date	Hour	Summary of Events and Information	Remarks and references to Appendices
November 1918	12th		Conference during the morning of the morning Lyns Bruening Scott arrived in the afternoon. C Coy conference that afternoon was cancelled.	
	13th		Instruction parade in the morning him a Divisional Cross Country Race took place in the afternoon. Bn won by t. Brown Fusiliers	
	14th		Genl. Hughes came from the DHQ, sent by t. Genl. to the Cops. Coland D.S.O. referred Battalion from Hospital Brigadier Paton in the morning the coy officers were on parade and went into the Battalion & the reminders came out & arrived much noted by Arriving on the Salute. The Divisional Commander made the ninety immediately thereafter the orator was reading but very anxiety had to be a anxious to see the Battalion and went thru their & inspected them for their opinion wont done in the past.	
	15		Guns on billets at HORDAIN Lyns Scag Ramo referred a Bruen today on relief. Capt Yates training on leave. A Rugby football match	

D.D. & L., London, E.C. (A583) Wt. W60/M1672 350,000 4/17 Sch. 52a Forms/C/2118/14

WAR DIARY
or
INTELLIGENCE SUMMARY.
(Erase heading not required.)

Army Form C. 2118.

Place	Date	Hour	Summary of Events and Information	Remarks and references to Appendices
November 1918	15th (Cont)		Took place at INVY to-day between a team from the Battalion and a team from ye Black Watch. The result was a win for ye Battalion by 11 points to Nil.	
	16th		Battalion Parade followed by Battalion Drill then troops continuing billets in village continued. During morning a verbal warning order was received that Battalion would be going forward to work under O.C. XXII Corps.	
	17		Battalion standing by for orders to move but no orders received. Companies under Company Commanders fine training and cross country running.	
	18		No movement orders yet received. Battalion Parade. Then Companies Sprint Cross Country running. The Comdg Officer has inspect planning ground for Divisional Sports.	
	19		Information received that Battalion will not now move forward.	
	20th		Battalion Parade Training for Sports [illegible] & Winners in W.O. games Battalion from [illegible]	

Army Form C. 2118.

WAR DIARY
or
INTELLIGENCE SUMMARY.
(Erase heading not required.)

Instructions regarding War Diaries and Intelligence Summaries are contained in F. S. Regs., Part II. and the Staff Manual respectively. Title pages will be prepared in manuscript.

Place	Date	Hour	Summary of Events and Information	Remarks and references to Appendices
November 1918	21st		Companies employed making Divisional Sports Ground during morning. Battalion trials for sports held in the afternoon. Weather fine but cold.	
	22nd		Battalion bathed at ENUY. Football team played a team from 49th Div'n Tr'n'g Cyl R.E. at PAILENCOURT in afternoon and won by 1 goal to Nil.	
			Lieut Clark joins the Battalion from Base.	
	23rd		Battalion Sports Day held during morning. W.P.O. Coy "winning" Musketry Competition. A Football match between 1 Platoon and 9.15 "C" Coy.	
	24th		Church Parade – teams in a.m. by the Rev. Gallwey C.F. The Batt'n Officers entertained at Company Recds. Boxing competition in afternoon.	
	25th		Battalion Parade. After the Parade "A" Coy carried out a Musketry Competition on	
			"spoon" camps. "B" Coy with "D" Division shoots Lewis L. Gun match and a Tug of War. The Divisional General Officers visited the Battalion during the afternoon.	
	26th		Battalion Parade. B Coy carried out Musketry Competition. A C of E Service was held on Parade. The afternoon lecture – "From Mons to Cambrai" by Rev'd Wm Gallway.	
			Battalion Concert given in the afternoon.	
			Major R. Gibbons joins the Battalion from Base.	

Army Form C. 2118.

WAR DIARY
or
INTELLIGENCE SUMMARY.
(Erase heading not required.)

Instructions regarding War Diaries and Intelligence Summaries are contained in F. S. Regs., Part II. and the Staff Manual respectively. Title pages will be prepared in manuscript.

Place	Date	Hour	Summary of Events and Information	Remarks and references to Appendices
November 1918	27th		[illegible handwritten entries]	
		2pm		
		3pm		
	30			
	1/12/18			

Army Form C. 2118.

WAR DIARY
or
INTELLIGENCE SUMMARY.
(Erase heading not required.)

Instructions regarding War Diaries and Intelligence Summaries are contained in F. S. Regs., Part II. and the Staff Manual respectively. Title pages will be prepared in manuscript.

Place	Date	Hour	Summary of Events and Information	Remarks and references to Appendices
			Casualties during November 1918	
Strength at			Officers –	
30. 11. 18 =			Captain [illegible] D.S.O.: Joined from Hospital 13.11.18	
Offrs.	O.Ranks.		[illegible] To Hospital – Sick – 18.11.18	
49	859		Other Ranks	
			Wounded (Acc.) (at duty) 2	
			To Hosp. Sick – 17	
			Officers to & from Leave	
			Capt. & Adjt. [illegible] 1 – 28/11/18 · 2/Lt. [illegible] 14/8-11-18 · Lt. [illegible] 20/11/18	
			Capt. [illegible] 17 – 30/11/18 · [illegible] 14/30-11-18 · [illegible] 23/11/18	
			" Ballantyne [illegible] 1 – 13/11/18	
			" Young [illegible] 1 – 11/11/18 · Reinforcements	
			" Pringle [illegible] 1 – 13/11/18 · Officers · Other Ranks	
			2/Lt. Sutherland [illegible] 19 – 30/11/18 · [illegible] 20/11/18 · 11 [illegible] 7/11/18	
			" [illegible] 13 – 27/11/18 · [illegible] J.C. 6/11/18 · 1 [illegible]	
			" Coutts [illegible] 1 – 13/11/18 · Wilson [illegible] 27.11.18 · 6 [illegible]	
			" [illegible] 6 – 5/11/18 · Scott C.C. 22/11/18 · 2 [illegible] 15/11/18	
			" [illegible] 29 – 30/11/18 · 2/Lt. [illegible] [illegible] · 3 [illegible] 17/11/18	
			2/Lt. [illegible] 1 – 7/11/18 · [illegible] 27/11/18 · 1 [illegible] 19/11/18	
			" McKay [illegible] 29 – 30/11/18 · 2 [illegible] 19/11/18	
			" Graham [illegible] 1 – 11/11/18 · 2 [illegible]	
			" Armstrong [illegible] 1 – 6/11/18 · 5 [illegible] 23/11/18	
			" [illegible] 7 – 23/11/18 · 2 [illegible] 27/11/18	
			" [illegible] 1 – 11/11/18	
			" Crawford [illegible] 8 – 23/11/18	

[illegible] Lieut. Col.,
Commdg 1/8th Bn. The Royal Scots (Pioneers)

Army Form C. 2118.

WAR DIARY
or
INTELLIGENCE SUMMARY.
(Erase heading not required.)

1/8 46

43 RS.

CONFIDENTIAL

WAR DIARY
OF
1/8th B. THE ROYAL SCOTS (ROVERS)
FROM
1ST DECEMBER 1918 TO 31ST DECEMBER 1918

VOLUME 50

Army Form C. 2118.

WAR DIARY
or
INTELLIGENCE SUMMARY.
(Erase heading not required.)

Instructions regarding War Diaries and Intelligence Summaries are contained in F. S. Regs., Part II. and the Staff Manual respectively. Title pages will be prepared in manuscript.

Place	Date	Hour	Summary of Events and Information	Remarks and references to Appendices
Glasgow 1918	1st		Church Parade	
	2nd		Battalion returned to INVERGORDON from furlough	
	3rd		Battalion employed in Company training. 25 Yards Range Shoot. Brass fuse caps & heads for Bombs in the Live Bombing Ground Canvas decoys for aeroplanes	
	4th		Ditto	
	5th		Musketry & Morning Parade 9.16 a.m. in afternoon drill	
	6th		Recreation employed during manoeuvres.	
	7th		Nothing of special interest. Battalion continues last post by Order Lieutenant High-ty-3 Gone to N.C.O.	
	8th		Beautiful day. Church Parade Comdg. Officer gave all leave to Divine Service in Glasgow 1930	
	9th		Lectures on "BURNS". Instruction class 72 Minors	
	10th		to the drawing Board	

WAR DIARY or INTELLIGENCE SUMMARY

Army Form C. 2118.

Place	Date	Hour	Summary of Events and Information	Remarks and references to Appendices
Quarouble 1918	11th		Army work out Route March exercise &c	
	12th		Nothing of Special Interest	
	13th		Do.	
	14th		Do.	
	15th		Do.	
	16th		Do.	
	17th		101 Miners proceed home for demobilization. Colours handed back to Battalion at Haulchin 10th	
	18th		Commanding officer returns from Paris leave	
	19th		Battalion association team beat 5th Seaforth Highlanders by 2 goals to 1	
	20th		Colours arrive from home	
	21st		Nothing of Special Interest	
	22nd		30 Miners leave Battalion to proceed home for demobilization. Instructions received that officers & men on leave do not require to return to former employment open for them.	
	23rd		59 Miners & 1 Pivotal & 1 Long Service man go home for demobilization. LIEUT MACDONALD and 2ND LIEUT R.D. LAWRIE conducting officer. Battalion team beat 5½ M.G. Battalion by 3 goals to 1.	
	24th			

Army Form C. 2118.

WAR DIARY
or
INTELLIGENCE SUMMARY.
(Erase heading not required.)

Instructions regarding War Diaries and Intelligence Summaries are contained in F.S. Regs., Part II. and the Staff Manual respectively. Title pages will be prepared in manuscript.

Place	Date	Hour	Summary of Events and Information	Remarks and references to Appendices
1918				
	Dec. 24th		Successful Battalion Officers dinner	
	25th		Beautiful Christmas Day. Xmas cith + Tug of War competition during the forenoon and Officers against N.C.O. match in the afternoon.	
	26th		12 Miners from home for demobilization. "B" Coy's Christmas dinner	
	27th		H.Q. Coy's Christmas dinner.	
	28th		"C" Coy " Very wet + uncertain weather.	
	29th		Battalion Rugby XV. beat 32nd R.F.A. Brigade by 35 points to 3 in first round of Divisional championship.	
	30th		Battalion Association team beat Royal Engineers by 2 goals to 1 in first round of Divisional championship.	
	31st		Holiday.	

Army Form C. 2118.

WAR DIARY
or
INTELLIGENCE SUMMARY.
(Erase heading not required.)

Place	Date	Hour	Summary of Events and Information	Remarks and references to Appendices
Strazeele	31-12-18		Casualties during December 1918.	
			Officers:-	
			2/Lt. N.L. Anderson Joined from hospital 14.12.18. 2/Lt. Macauley joined from 6 Coy. G. Army. 6.12.18 the Royalists 6.12.18.	
		6 pm	To hospital - Sick. 13. To U.K. for demobilisation (Miners) 20½ " " " (Aero Crews)	
			Officers in Temperatures	
			Captain J. Fair B. 5.18. 1- 6/12/18.	
			Captain 2/Lt. Carkeronal 1- 3/12/18.	
			Captain 2/Lt. Horsey 1/12/18	
			2/Lt. S. Maskelyne 1/12/18	1/12/18
			Lieut. G.K. Zemmick 1- 3/12/18	2/ 1/18
			2/Lieut. R. Macaulay 1- 13/12/18	3/ 6/18
			" W. Horsburton 2- 14/12/18	5/12/18
			" G.J. Scott 26- 31/12/18	1- 12- 8
			27- 31/12/18	3- 7- 8
			Lieut. Young W.K.R.C. 3 U.K. for systems 11- 12- 2/18	12- 12- 8
			Lieut. Sharpe J.	23- 12- 8
				29- 12- 8
			Lieut. Robson Hon. R.B. To U.K. Demobbing Offr 14/12/18	
			2/ " Kidd L.V. Do.	22-12-18
			" Macaulay J. Do.	23-12-18
			Lieut. McDonald J.D. Do.	23-12-18
			2/ " Lawrie Do.	
			Lieut. Lawrie H. To Own Regt. New Draftees December 2/12/18	

J. Smith
Lt. Col.
Comdg 9th (S) Royal Scots (T)

Confidential.

Headquarters, "A"
    51st.(Highland) Division.

    Herewith copy of War Diary for the Month of
January, 1919.

                            Lieut.-Col.,
    Commanding 1/8th. Bn. The Royal Scots (Pioneers).

1/2/19.

Army Form C. 2118.

WAR DIARY
or
INTELLIGENCE SUMMARY.

(Erase heading not required.)

WAR DIARY
of
1/8th Bn. The Royal Scots (Pioneers)

From 1st January 1919 to 31st January '919.

VOLUME No. 51

Army Form C. 2118.

WAR DIARY
or
INTELLIGENCE SUMMARY.
(Erase heading not required.)

Instructions regarding War Diaries and Intelligence Summaries are contained in F. S. Regs., Part II. and the Staff Manual respectively. Title pages will be prepared in manuscript.

Place	Date	Hour	Summary of Events and Information	Remarks and references to Appendices
	1919			
	10th		Nothing of Special Interest.	
	11th		Do	
	12th		Transport leave to proceed by Road to BRACQUEGNIES.	
	13th		Battalion move by Buses to Bracquegnies passing through VALENCIENNES and MONS en Route.	
	14th		Battalion somewhat scattered but all Ranks comfortable. Companies putting things in Order and Civilians very interested.	
	15th		Nothing of Special Interest.	
	16th		Battalion Association team were beaten fourteen nil by beating R.A.S.C. by 3 goals to Nil.	
	17th		Nothing of Special Interest.	
	18th		Do	
	19th		"A" XV at Rugby team beat "A" XV at 14th Black Watch by 6 Two to Nil	
	20th		Nothing of Interest.	

WAR DIARY
or
INTELLIGENCE SUMMARY.
(Erase heading not required.)

Army Form C. 2118.

Place	Date	Hour	Summary of Events and Information	Remarks and references to Appendices
	1919			
	1st		New Year's Day kept as a holiday and all succeeded in celebrating the occasion in some way or another.	
	2nd		Nothing of special interest.	
	3rd		Do	
	4th		Do	
	5th		Move of Battalion to new area, which was to take place on Tuesday postponed.	
	6th		Battalion Rugby team was selected. M.G. Bn. by one try to Nil.	
	7th		Commanding Officer goes on leave. Battalion represented team beat Divisional Headquarters on Soccer round of Divisional Competition.	
	8th		General change in weather. Monteneros go for route march.	
	9th		Instructions received that after 12th next, Officers and men on leave will not to be Ambulance. Another wretched day.	

Army Form C. 2118.

WAR DIARY
or
INTELLIGENCE SUMMARY.
(Erase heading not required.)

Instructions regarding War Diaries and Intelligence Summaries are contained in F. S. Regs., Part II and the Staff Manual respectively. Title pages will be prepared in manuscript.

Place	Date	Hour	Summary of Events and Information	Remarks and references to Appendices
	1919 21st		Nothing of interest.	
	22nd		Lieutenant W. B. Harrison died at Pietro.	
	23rd		Battalion Rugby team beat 6/A. Gordon Highrs by 18 points to Nil in 3rd round of Champion tie.	
	24th		Bn Association team defeated by 4/A. & I. Highrs in League Match. "B" Company gave a successful Dance.	
	25th		Wintry weather and first fall of snow this Winter.	
	26th		Nothing of interest. Demobilisation during week has been brisker.	
	27th		Battalion gave Military Funeral to 2 Belgian Soldiers – interesting ceremony.	
	28th		Major Mitchel and Captain Tait go to both Balls at Brussels. Lieut. G.H. Ballantyne is in London and of Battalion.	
	29th		Commanding Officer returns from leave.	
	30th		Nothing official – still intensely cold.	
	31st			

WAR DIARY
or
INTELLIGENCE SUMMARY.
(Erase heading not required.)

Army Form C. 2118.

Place	Date	Hour	Summary of Events and Information	Remarks and references to Appendices
			Casualties for January 1919.	
			Officers :- Capt. J.L. Pringle to 6.03 horses Aldershot 31/1/19. Other Ranks :-	
			Capt. G.W. Watson To leave 2/1/19.	
			Lieut. H. Bowen To leave 8/1/19. To Hospital sick 10	
			Lieut. H.W. Wilson do 9/1/19.	
			W.J. Young M.D. do 12/1/19. To UK for Demobilization 43	
			2/Lt. W.S. Gibbs do 27/1/19.	
			Capt. J. Young To UK for Demobilization 25/1/19. Total. 53	
			Lieut. J. McKay do 25/1/19.	
			" H. Smith do 26/1/19.	
			2/Lt. J. Harrison To Hospital 3/1/19.	
			2/Lt. J.G. Crawford do 23/1/19.	
			Reinforcements :-	
			Officers :- N i l.	
			Lieut Col. H. Thorburn From leave 28/1/19. Other Ranks :-	
			2/Lt. W.H. McDonald Rtd from hospital 4/1/19. - 2	
			" J. Lawrie Shadwick Officer 16/1/19. 6/1/19. 3	
			2/Lt. A.J. Yea do 13/1/19. 15/1/19. 4	
			2/L. A.J. Coutts From Portugal 6/1/19. 22/1/19. 2	
			" J. White From leave 12/1/19. 26/1/19. 3	
			L.Qmr. 30/1/19. 1	
			Total. 14	
			Strength as 31.1.1.19 :- Officers O.Ranks	
			46 583	

W. Thorburn Lieut. Colonel
Commdg. 1/5th Bn. The Royal Scots
(Tenures.)

Army Form C. 2118.

WAR DIARY
or
INTELLIGENCE SUMMARY.
(Erase heading not required.)

WAR DIARY
of
18th Bn THE ROYAL SCOTS (Pioneers)

From 1st January 1919 to 28th January 1919

VOLUME No 52

Place	Date	Hour	Summary of Events and Information	Remarks and references to Appendices
BROUGNIES	1919 February 1	1-28pm	Battalion office settled at BROUGNIES. Demobilization proceeds rapidly and Battalion reduced to "CADRE" strength. 150 men who enlisted after 1st January 1916 are here to serve in Army of Occupation. Captain E.B. Ballantyne and C.R.Keith, the Adjt Mr G Graham MC Armstrong & of Cmdts & 2 Orderlies volunteer for the Army of Occupation. Companies find leaves to civilian suit and in no hurry to enjoy the relaxation of a pleasant month.	

WAR DIARY
or
INTELLIGENCE SUMMARY.
(Erase heading not required.)

Army Form C. 2118.

Place	Date	Hour	Summary of Events and Information	Remarks and references to Appendices
Officers			Remarks for February 1919	
			Other Ranks	
			2n/R for Demobilization	
			Capt S.J. Fair 7/2/16	To Hospital Sick 10
			" J.A.S. Butterfield 12/2/19	Sick (Demobilization) 82
			Lt B. Morris 13/2/19	And from England 43
			" R.T. Fannie 13/2/19	note C /73
			" R.B. Summers 13/2/19	
			" J.C. Rem 3/2/19	
			" A.J.A. Young 19/2/19	Reinforcement
				Other Ranks
			2n/R - Leave -	
			Lieu C.C. Scott 26/2/19 - 12/3/19	
			" A.J. Graham 26/2/19 - 7/3/19	
			" A.J. Curtis 10/2/19 - 24/2/19	
			2n/R - Regt Adjutant -	
			Major Mitchie F.B. me 7/2/19	
			Lt Cuthberts RFB 27/2/19	
			" Boivin CdA 2/2/19	
				Officers Other Ranks
			Strength at 28/2/19 33 79	

Commdg 16th/17th Bn Royal Scots (Kennedy)

Army Form C. 2118.

WAR DIARY
or
INTELLIGENCE SUMMARY.
(Erase heading not required.)

B5 M 49

46R.

WAR DIARY
OF
11th Bn THE ROYAL SCOTS (PIONEERS)

From 1st March 1919 to 31st March 1919

VOLUME 53

Army Form C. 2118.

WAR DIARY
or
INTELLIGENCE SUMMARY.
(Erase heading not required.)

Instructions regarding War Diaries and Intelligence Summaries are contained in F. S. Regs., Part II. and the Staff Manual respectively. Title pages will be prepared in manuscript.

Place	Date	Hour	Summary of Events and Information	Remarks and references to Appendices
March 1919	12th	11a	Parades continue as per Saturday. Service by Church. Drive through camp ... for sample officers and ...	
			Lines.	
	13th		Kirby Officer proceed home for Demobilization	
	13th		Notify of ... special interest.	
	14th	9a	Draft of 6 Officers and ... 29 ... ranks home to ... Kinsale ...	
			Said Farewell ... at ... forms part of the army of ...	
			Occupation on the Rhine.	
	15th		Major ER Wilkie MC of the ... and Command.	
	16th		Return ... to MONAGE and open conference the ...	
			Divisions Schools & Conferences at ... the ...	
			...	
	17 and		Nothing of special interest.	
	18th		Private instruction as usual. Remainder of Officers and ... sent home	
			for Demobilization. First ... in Motors and off.	
	17-31		Rising Return. first Batch ... and any Trophies ... 29 ? ...	

www.ingramcontent.com/pod-product-compliance
Lightning Source LLC
Chambersburg PA
CBHW081433300426
44108CB00016BA/2360